Tradition and the Talents of Women

TRADITION
and the
TALENTS
of
WOMEN

EDITED BY
Florence Howe

UNIVERSITY OF ILLINOIS PRESS
Urbana and Chicago

"Laughing at Leviticus: *Nightwood* as Woman's Circus Epic"
© 1991 by Jane Marcus. "Feminism on the Border: From
Gender Politics to Geopolitics" © 1991 by Sonia Saldivar-Hull.
"Miranda and Cassandra: The Discourse of the Feminist
Intellectual" © 1991 by Elaine Showalter. "The Cypher:
Disclosure and Reticence in *Villette*," by Karen Lawrence,
© 1988 by the Regents of the University of California.
Reprinted from *Nineteenth-Century Literature* 42, no. 4 (March
1988), 448–66, by permission.

This book is printed on acid-free paper.

Library of Congress Cataloging-in-Publication Data

Tradition and the talents of women / edited by Florence Howe.
    p.   cm.
    ISBN 0-252-01685-8 (cloth : alk. paper). — ISBN 0-252-06106-3
(paper : alk. paper).
    1. American literature—Women authors—History and criticism.
    2. English literature—Women authors—History and criticism.
    3. Influence (Literary, artistic, etc.)   4. Women and literature.
    I. Howe, Florence.
    PS147.T74   1991
    810.9'9287—dc20   90-10835
                                                          CIP

To Mary Anne Ferguson,
mother, teacher, scholar, colleague, friend,
and inspiration for this collection

CONTENTS

PART THREE

"The Centrality of Marginality"

PART FOUR

The Tradition of Socially Engaged Literature

PART FIVE

Reprise: The Tradition Re-Visioned

PREFACE

This book is dedicated to Mary Anne Ferguson in honor of her ground-breaking scholarship, her teaching, and her professional service. As part of a "pioneer" generation of feminist scholar-teachers who attempted to win equal academic opportunity for women, Ferguson's history dramatizes some of the problems women have faced in the past, as well as some of their future possibilities. The major themes of this volume—"tradition" and women's "talents"—are epitomized in her life and work. Her own talents as a scholar have helped restore a buried tradition of women writers and have also helped readers come to a critical understanding of the images of women presented in the Western tradition of writings by men. Her life, which has at once exemplified and questioned traditional patterns of female behavior, reminds us of the tenacity of women outside and inside the academy, especially women not granted the privileges of men. Through her work and her example—the work of her life—she has contributed to opening the U.S. academy's door somewhat more generously to women.

In her article "The Female Novel of Development and the Myth of Psyche," Ferguson characteristically interprets the emergence of a nontraditional pattern for female stories of development by finding in the new stories told by American women writers of the 1970s traces of an old one—the myth of Psyche—which she sees being transformed to meet new historical conditions.[1] After contrasting the traditional comic and "spiral" pattern of the male bildungsroman, as exemplified in the twin journeys of father and son in the *Odyssey*, with the more tragic and "circular" pattern typical of literary representations of women's development in works by both men and women, she calls attention to a group of recent novels (by such writers as Eudora Welty, Lisa Alther, and Erica Jong) that use the myth of Psyche as a "rich paradigm for representing the adventures of a sexually mature female who profits from her often painful encounters with reality to become a self-confident adult in control of her own destiny" (p. 229). By departing from "a view of women as passive" that has been "integral to the male novel of development," and by departing as well from earlier women writers' tendency to show female characters "either as finding satisfaction within their limited development in the domestic sphere or as expressing their dissatisfaction through various self-destructive means" (p. 229), the new "Psyche" novels Ferguson discusses provide a literary analogue for the tragicomic story of her own career, with its multiple journeys confounding any attempt to fit it neatly into either a "spiraling" or "circling" pattern.

Born in Charleston, South Carolina, during the great postwar influenza epidemic of 1918 and encouraged to attend college at Duke by an Episcopal minister (women from her kind of southern family very seldom went to college), she graduated Phi Beta Kappa in 1938, having held during some semesters no fewer than six jobs to help finance her education. Because it was wartime and young men were scarce, she became a fellow and teaching assistant in Duke's English department during the next two years, as she earned a master's degree with a thesis on Shelley. Following her first husband to navy bases in Oklahoma and Texas, she worked at a variety of nonacademic jobs that required verbal and other administrative skills—the skills of an expert secretary that she would later put to good use (though she had no idea of doing so then) as chair of an English department. After working briefly in academic jobs at the University of North Carolina, Queens College, and the University of Connecticut, teaching English to classes composed largely of veterans, she went through a relatively amicable and not atypical postwar divorce after her husband had completed a Ph.D. with her help. In 1948 she remarried, and she spent the next twenty years—again in a pattern not atypical of many intellectual women of her generation—working continually in part-time academic jobs but not pursuing a "career." Instead, she was rearing three children with her husband's help, and helping him in his career as a professor of English. In 1962, however, she took the then unusual step of returning to graduate school for a doctorate in medieval literature (a field she chose partly because it was as far as could be from her husband's field of nineteenth-century American literature). With his psychological and material support, she completed her degree quickly (by 1965) and began a phase of her development that was dramatically nontraditional but also tragicomically typical of many relatively privileged women who attempted, with the help of the women's movement of the 1960s, to reshape their lives in middle age.

She tells the story of her literal and metaphysical journeys in an essay ironically called "A Success Story." The journeys began when she sought employment after receiving her Ph.D. and found—to her and her husband's dismay—that university antinepotism rules hindered their efforts to teach in the same institution or even in the same geographical area. When she was fifty-one, and in the midst of an odyssey that eventually involved two moves back and forth between Columbus, Ohio, and Boston for both husband and wife, the story took a turn for the better:

> The year was 1969; fortunately for my mental health, the women's movement had reached academe and my professional organization, the Modern Language Association, had formed a Commission on the Status of Women. I wrote urging the commission's consideration of antinepotism rules as de facto discrimination against women; at the University of Massachusetts in Boston, as well as my husband's original institution, I was as well qualified for my job as he was for his, but no one had entertained the idea that he should be the one to lose status. I was invited to join the commission and for three years worked to fight discrimination against women in academe.[2]

Partly through the efforts of the MLA commission, institutions of higher learning, including the University of Massachusetts at Boston, did begin to revise their rules for and attitudes toward female employees. In 1970, after a year of unemployment during which she completed a bibliography of *English Translations from Medieval Sources* and began major work on the first edition of her anthology *Images of Women in Literature,* Ferguson won a full-time position as associate professor of English at the University of Massachusetts. Tenure and a promotion to professor swiftly followed, and in 1972, so did her husband. He had resigned his position at that university so his wife could teach there full time; in 1972, he was rehired. Finally "at home" in the same house, after years of weekly commuting between Ohio and Massachusetts, the couple also finally enjoyed jobs commensurate with their credentials.

Mary Anne Ferguson's journeys were not really over, however, for in 1974 Alfred Ferguson died. She contemplated moving again so she could teach in her main scholarly fields of Old English and medieval studies, but she decided instead to redefine herself as a scholar of nineteenth- and twentieth-century literature, especially literature by women. During her years in the English department at the University of Massachusetts, she worked continuously with the women's studies program, serving as coordinator from 1970 to 1972 and as project director of an NEH planning grant for women's studies from 1973 to 1975. Having committed herself to feminist scholarship, teaching, and nurturing several generations of faculty and students at her university, she also served for three years—from 1982 until her retirement in 1985—as chair of the English department.

On the occasion of her retirement, the women's studies program honored Mary Anne Ferguson as their "pioneer woman," citing her scholarship, her development of new courses, her mentoring of young faculty, and her feminist advocacy on behalf of both women's studies and the

English department. The citation read by her colleague Jean Humez, one of the contributors to this volume, describes her as "a demanding, creative, and . . . loving teacher"; and junior faculty testify to her mentoring skills and her general contribution to the intellectual growth of the English department. She advised young feminist scholars to finish their books before devoting significant time to university service, and she advised young mothers trying to divide their time between finishing dissertations and caring for small children to keep a "toehold" in academe. She worked to assure part-time women faculty of opportunities for tenure-track positions and guided them through the tenure process, even through negative decisions on to appeals. In short, she never forgot her own complex journeys in, and on the margins of, academe. She has "no regrets," she tells us, "about the road not taken" when in 1948 she chose marriage and family. "But," she adds, "if I were to start over again, I would try to spend less time in the holding pattern. Today the academy may be less rigid than in 1965, but it is still hostile to women's life cycle" ("A Success Story," p. 18). The final sentence of her autobiographical essay modestly challenges those of us still in or about to enter academe: "Women who have achieved some measure of success within the academy can try to make it a more hospitable environment" (p. 18). As a teacher, colleague, and administrator, she has sought to do just that, for women and for men.

As a scholar she has also sought to make academe more hospitable to women, most notably through her efforts to change the ways in which the Western literary tradition is defined, understood, and reproduced when it becomes "canonized" through specific historical practices in the classroom and in academic publishing. Through articles on such writers as Sherwood Anderson, Alice Walker, Eudora Welty, and Lisa Alther,[3] and especially through the four editions (there will soon be a fifth) of her influential anthology *Images of Women in Literature*, she has attempted to critique negative stereotypes of women, stereotypes that acquire psychic force partly because they reach students with an authority ascribed to "tradition." As she remarks in the introduction to the third edition, "Authors—both male and female—expose the wastefulness of stereotypical thinking and its cost to individuals and society through irony and satire, through description of women's self-perception, through overt expression of anger. Some works reveal the mythic base that reinforces the stereotype; others use stark realism to explode the myth. But cumulatively the selections document the tenacity of the stereotypes in spite of a variety of perspectives." "The effect of reading these works," she adds, "especially for women, is likely to be anger and depression."[4]

In an effort to counter this negative effect on readers, who have repeatedly written to her about their responses to the anthology, she has
continually revised both the selections and the critical presentation of
the "images" they illustrate. Most dramatically, she adds in the fourth
edition (1986) an entirely new section called "Self-Images," which contains letters and material from diaries and autobiographies by such
women as Käthe Kollwitz, Anaïs Nin, Zora Neale Hurston, and a
nineteenth-century diarist from Vermont named Arozina Perkins. The
selections reflect the growing importance, in feminist criticism, of such
"fragmentary" genres; they also show, as Ferguson notes, "how some
women in the past and some doubly caught by race and economic class
as well as by gender have perceived themselves" (4th ed., p. ix). She also
notes the significance of the diarists' stress "on their spiritual and moral
development, topics seldom treated in other literature with the immedi-
acy of these self revelations." As the addition of the "Self-Images" section suggests, she has worked to counter the depressing effects of
traditional literary representations of women by anthologizing "lost" literature by women of the past as well as recent works by contemporary
women writers who articulate new feminist perspectives. Printing works
both by well-known authors and by some just beginning their writing
careers, or just beginning to reach a general audience (sometimes
through their appearance in *Images*), Ferguson observes that during the
1970s and '80s, "some women—and some men—writers are creating a
body of literature that may be labeled feminist. This new literature
shows fully human women characters who . . . assume responsibility for
their own acts and are thus capable of heroism and of tragedy"; moreover, the selections from this new body of literature "explore the dynamics of mother-daughter relationships, of friendship among women . . . of
sexual unions between women . . . [of] links with women of the past
and women of different classes and races; they invite women to find, by
developing a sense of community with other women, ways of evaluating
themselves positively" (3rd. ed., pp. 16–17).

The successive editions of her anthology serve not only to expose for
critical discussion a certain textual history of women but also, as Mary
Louise Briscoe observes in a review, "to document significant changes in
our study of women in literature."[5] Examining the four editions as a
history of recent feminist theory, and of developments in Ferguson's
own knowledge and critical perspective, we can point, for example, to
the new account of feminist interdisciplinary scholarship since the early
1970s that she adds to the introduction of her third edition (1981). The
revised introductions, which also include a description of recent work in
the field of feminist literary criticism, are accompanied by an expanding

list of "Suggestions for Further Reading" in both the third and fourth editions. Along with changes in the introductions come revisions in the selections and the section headings categorizing the different "images." Two sections illustrating the "submissive" and the "dominating" wife are combined, in the third edition, under the heading of "Wife," and the selections for this section include, in the fourth edition, stories about battered women and an interracial couple. In an even more dramatic instance of culturally significant revision, the section entitled "The Old Maid" in the first edition (1973), which includes texts by W. H. Auden, Katherine Mansfield, and Mary Wilkins Freeman, becomes "Women Alone" in the second and third editions, with eight rather than three selections (always complete works, rather than excerpts); retitled "Women without Men," in the fourth edition this section expands to fourteen texts, including a poem by May Sarton dedicated to, and about, another woman (Camille Mayran). The negative stereotype of the old maid has thus clearly been complicated and indeed transformed in the process of revising the anthology. Similarly, a small section in the first and second editions called "The Liberated Woman: What Price Freedom?" is progressively expanded, in the third and fourth editions, under the title "Women Becoming." Instead of the challenging question that suggests largely unpleasant costs of liberation or freedom for women, the revised title and selections show "women in the process of changing, of breaking out of the old rigid patterns." And, Ferguson adds, "readers recognize themselves in the new images" (3rd ed., p. 11). Such recognition gives courage and hope to women students searching for ways to live in a world still not ideally hospitable to them. It also gives information to men who would live companionably with women.

The revisions in the successive editions of her anthology testify generally to Ferguson's possession of what Tillie Olsen calls the acumen of the "true reader"; whether they illustrate traditional or nontraditional images of women, the works in the anthology testify to the editor's taste, judgment, and abiding concern for literary quality. The revisions also remind us of her continuing labor of self-education; they reveal wide reading not only in several national literatures but also in recent feminist scholarship in many fields. The new literature by women that she has helped to make visible, through her anthology, her critical essays, and her service on the board of directors of The Feminist Press, dramatizes her belief that acts of feminist imagination are closely tied to "psychologists', historians', and anthropologists' current research into and theories about women's real lives" (*Images,* 4th ed., p. ix). This remark provides a fitting close to an account of her achievement, for she never forgets that literature has something essential to say to us as we try to lead human lives.

NOTES

1. Mary Anne Ferguson, "The Female Novel of Development and the Myth of Psyche," in *The Voyage In: Fictions of Female Development,* ed. Elizabeth Abel, Marianne Hirsch, and Elizabeth Langland (Hanover, N.H.: University Press of New England, 1983), pp. 228–47.

2. Mary Anne Ferguson, "A Success Story[?]" in *The Road Retaken: Women Reenter the Academy,* ed. Irene Thompson and Audrey Roberts (New York: Modern Language Association, 1985), pp. 14–18. This quotation is from p. 17; subsequent references will be given in parentheses in the text. Mary Anne Ferguson wanted a question mark following the title, but it was omitted in the published version.

3. See Ferguson's articles "Sherwood Anderson's *Death in the Woods:* From Mythopoesis to a New Realism," *MidAmerica* 7 (1980), 73–95; "No More Squeezing into One" (on Walker), in *Face to Face: Fathers, Mothers, Masters, Monsters—Essays for a Nonsexist Future,* ed. Meg McGavran Murray (Westport, Conn.: Greenwood Press, 1983), pp. 257–71; *"Losing Battles* as a Comic Epic in Prose," in *Eudora Welty: Critical Articles,* ed. P. Prenshaw (Hattiesburg: University Press of Mississippi, 1979), pp. 305–24; and "Lisa Alther: The Irony of Return?" *Southern Literary Quarterly* 21 (Spring 1983), 103–16.

4. Ferguson, *Images of Women in Literature* (Boston: Houghton Mifflin, 1981), p. 11. This quotation is from the third edition; the first was published in 1973, the second in 1977, the fourth in 1986. A fifth edition is forthcoming in 1991. Subsequent citations will give edition and page reference.

5. Mary Louise Briscoe, "Realities of Women's Lives: The Continuing Search," *College English* 50 (Nov. 1988), 802–11; the quotation is from p. 803.

ACKNOWLEDGMENTS

The volume began when members of Mary Anne Ferguson's English department at the University of Massachusetts/Boston decided a volume of scholarly essays would be an appropriate commemoration of her major contributions both to the literary history and criticism of women writers and to the development of a literary curriculum that included women. In addition to these substantial achievements, Ferguson's work as chair of the English department had also contributed significantly to the hiring, retention, and promotion of black and white women and members of minority groups of both sexes, and, through these faculty members and her own teaching, to the lives of thousands of students. As scholar, teacher, administrator, and practicing feminist, Mary Anne Ferguson deserved high honors.

Members of Ferguson's department—Lois Rudnick and Jean Humez, in particular—turned to her colleagues in the Modern Language Association, where she had served as one of the first members of the Commission on the Status and Education of Women in the Profession. I was honored to be invited to edit the volume. Members of the commission, from its earliest years to more recent ones, agreed to contribute essays. These members include Elaine Showalter, Elaine Hedges, Nellie McKay, Nancy Hoffman, and Deborah Silverton Rosenfelt. Nancy Hoffman is also a colleague at the University of Massachusetts. Two of Mary Anne Ferguson's three daughters are themselves professors; Margaret Ferguson and Jean Ferguson Carr are contributors to this volume. Other contributors are colleagues in that wider universe of feminist scholarship, conscious that their essays honor Mary Anne Ferguson. Like other contributors already mentioned, this group—Jane Marcus, Blanche Gelfant, Karen Lawrence, Nancy Porter, Sonia Saldivar-Hull, Charlotte Goodman—includes both professors and holders of special chairs and at least one new doctoral recipient just beginning her first assistant professorship. Thus assembled, the group of feminist scholar-critics includes both real and symbolic daughters, appropriate especially to honor one of the significant mothers of this current wave of feminist scholar/activists.

Many people contributed to the making of this volume. Without Lois Rudnick's early persistence and continued labors, there would not have been a beginning. I am especially grateful to Jean Ferguson Carr,

Margaret Ferguson, Elaine Hedges, and Jane Marcus for criticism and encouragement. For helping me get through difficult days, and for many different kinds of labor on versions of this manuscript, I want to acknowledge my assistant, Julie Malnig. For their commitment to this volume, I thank the University of Illinois Press, Carole S. Appel and Ann Lowry, and especially their anonymous second reader. For their patience and their generosity I am very grateful to all the contributors to this volume. They have, as a group, agreed to contribute the volume's royalties to The Feminist Press at The City University of New York, where the funds will be earmarked as matching monies for the applied-for Challenge Grant of the National Endowment for the Humanities.

Tradition and the Talents of Women

FLORENCE HOWE

Introduction:
T. S. Eliot, Virginia Woolf,
and the Future of "Tradition"

> For masterpieces are not single and solitary births; they are the
> outcome of many years of thinking in common, of thinking by the
> body of the people, so that the experience of the mass is behind the
> single voice.
>
> —Virginia Woolf, *A Room of One's Own*

The title of this volume invokes T. S. Eliot's "Tradition and the Individual Talent" to recall not only the long shadow of his poetry and criticism on the experience of literary women of my generation, but also the
longer patriarchal British and American history into which Eliot placed
himself.[1] For half a literary life of those feminist activist literary critics
now in their fifties and sixties, the "tradition" was as Eliot saw it: a
singular series of male "monuments." Bound into an anthology, these
represented the "curriculum" to be studied and then taught to students.
But as we all know, two decades ago, toward the end of the 1960s, a shift
of consciousness occurred in academe more singular, more presumptu-
ous than Eliot's. For the first time in history, academic women acting in
unison, with and without organizations, noted the maleness of "the" tradition, its lack of historicity, its potential and actual damaging impact on
women students, artists, and others, and they called for the reconstruction of a "lost" female history and culture. Not surprisingly, the cultural
archeology restored to view many female voices that Eliot and his male
contemporaries must have heard quite clearly, as well as others both
known and unknown in their own time. Among Eliot's contemporaries,
perhaps most prominent among them, internationally as well as for U.S.
and British feminists, is Virginia Woolf, whose *A Room of One's Own* is
probably the single most important feminist critical text read today.[2]

In this Introduction, I will use Eliot and Woolf to mark the shift that occurred twenty years ago and that will, perhaps in another twenty years, produce a reconstituted "tradition." At this moment, twenty years into the work of restoration and redefinition, of recovering "lost" texts, of rereading or "overreading"[3] the contexts of familiar ones, I can see emerging not "the" female tradition but many different strands, still separated often by race, class, sexual preference, and certainly by nation. I can see also an effort, in the direction suggested by Virginia Woolf, to stretch definitions both of the writer and of literary genres.

Later in this introduction, I will trace the emergence of several strands of a female literary tradition that have thus far served to allow the rewriting of literary history; the revision—toward expansion—of the traditional literary canon; and the practice of a literary criticism anchored in history and conceiving of a "theory" of "difference." All the essays in this volume directly or indirectly serve these purposes.

> Though we see the same world, we see it through different eyes.
> —Virginia Woolf, *Three Guineas*

Virginia Woolf and T. S. Eliot were contemporaries, more than acquaintances, if less than friends. They were both consummate artists; they were both critics. Their lives and their literary achievements illuminate the history of this century's significant shift from a narrow Western literary tradition to the visible richness of at least two "different," gendered literary traditions, refusing now to melt into any one pot, refusing to "squeeze into one."[4] As critics, Eliot and Woolf wrote essays that revised the literary canon for generations that followed them. Eliot's achievement was not a minor one. Assuming the primacy of the text and the power of the (male) critic, and ignoring the problem of "reception," and even reputation, Eliot added Donne and other metaphysical poets to the literary canon, and provided new appreciation as well for varieties of Jacobean poetic drama.[5] Most critical for this volume, Eliot assumed that the literary history of the West was a male heritage, while Woolf knew that there was more to the past than his or other patriarchal views.

It was "useless," she wrote in *A Room of One's Own*, "to go to the great men writers for help, however much we may go to them for pleasure."[6] For "a woman writing thinks back through her mothers." Further, she continued, "if one is a woman one is often surprised by a *sudden splitting off of consciousness,* say in walking down Whitehall, when from being the natural inheritor of that civilisation, she becomes, on the contrary, outside of it, *alien and critical.*"[7] In other words, the concept of tradition for women writers is complicated by the place of women inside a society in which they are considered the "other," in which they feel "alien and critical," and in which they are perceived as oddities if they wish to pursue what are presumed to be male activities and prerogatives. A significant body of feminist theory and feminist literary criticism, knowingly or not, follows from Woolf's experience of "a sudden splitting off of consciousness."[8] Beyond even the cause of this volume, and beyond even the study of literature, one can see Eliot and Woolf as cultural icons, he of the past, she of the present and future.

When I read T. S. Eliot in 1949, I was a student at Hunter College, and "Tradition and the Individual Talent" had been in print for thirty years. I read it and Eliot's other literary essays, then and in the years that followed at graduate school and in my first teaching jobs, as though they were gospel. The poet—as Wordsworth, Coleridge, and Arnold had maintained before him—was seer, his work sacred knowledge. For my generation—women and men born in the late 1920s and the '30s— Eliot was the star in both the literary and critical firmaments. His poems were to be deciphered and memorized; his criticism was to be emulated. He was the twentieth century's major poet/critic. He was even also a dramatist. And of course he fit the mold (or was it constructed around him?) of the New Criticism, to practice which one needed only the poem—and the memory of all other poems in the male, white, Western tradition of poetry.

At Hunter, Virginia Woolf's name appeared only on a list recommending that we read, were there time, *To the Lighthouse*.[9] In the early 1950s, at the University of Wisconsin, I read *Mrs. Dalloway* because it was one of the contemporary novels in Ricardo Quintana's sophomore literature course, for which I was a teaching assistant. But in my graduate courses Woolf's name was absent as writer or critic. And I did not read *A Room of One's Own* until the early sixties, when I had decided to write a dissertation on *Mrs. Dalloway* as "an unpremeditated novel," and to read all Woolf's then extant criticism.

Woolf was and still is one of the most prolific and underrated critics of the century. Since her death, more than a dozen volumes of her criticism have appeared, and there are other essays uncollected still. She began writing criticism for the *Times Literary Supplement* as early as 1904, when she was twenty-two, and when Eliot was still a day student at Smith Academy, two years from his matriculation at Harvard. It is instructive to compare her reticence about her long history of reviewing with Eliot's brag to his mother in 1919, when he had been living in England for five years, "There is a small and select public which regards me as the best living critic, as well as the best living poet, in England."[10] Certainly Eliot must have known of Woolf's critical essays long before

1922, since her reviews appeared as often as, or more often, than his own. Yet, writing to Ezra Pound of his hopes for *The Criterion*, Eliot says, "there are only half a dozen men of letters (and no women) worth printing. . . . "[11] Several years earlier, writing to his father of his editorial work for the *Egoist*, Eliot makes his bias as plain: "I struggle to keep the writing as much as possible in Male hands, as I distrust the Feminine in literature, and also, once a woman has had anything printed in your paper, it is very difficult to make her see why you should not print everything she sends in."[12]

Eliot was canonized not only as author, but, perhaps more important, as critic. He was canonized even while he was alive—he was invited by academics to speak on criticism. He was still alive when academics began to write important books about his literary criticism. Why did that happen? And why did it not happen to Virginia Woolf, his contemporary and his senior by six years, who was writing criticism long before he began? Why did he not consider her a peer as critic? Why, more than half a century later, is she still not regarded as a critic and included, along with Eliot, in "mainstream" critical anthologies?

In many ways Woolf and Eliot are fascinatingly similar as gifted writers who invented new formal structures and created unforgettable images, characters, and rhythms of speech. Unlike many writers, Woolf and Eliot were also scholars, readers of the past with a purpose. Similarly also, both Eliot and Woolf were engaged professionally in the production of art by their contemporaries. They were consciously tastemakers. As creators of culture, they edited and published poetry, fiction, and criticism, for journals and as books. Woolf published Eliot, of course—both the early *Poems* (1919) and *The Waste Land* (1923), as well as a volume of criticism, *Homage to John Dryden* (1924). He, in turn, could have published her major critical essays in *The Criterion*. But he did not.[13]

As critics, Eliot and Woolf may seem to offer some initial similarities. Like most "modernists," they both disavow "emotion" or "anger" in differing degrees, searching for words and images to separate art from artist. As Eliot put it, "The more perfect the artist, the more completely separate in him will be the man who suffers and the mind which creates; the more perfectly will the mind digest and transmute the passions which are its material." His most memorable "analogy" for this process "was that of the catalyst," the poet's mind the "shred of platinum."[14] Through *A Room of One's Own*, one of Woolf's themes is anger, both the anger of women writers and the anger against women of the male professor/newspaper editor/Foreign Secretary/Judge, etc., who, "with the exception of the fog . . . seemed to control everything." "It seemed

absurd," she continues, "that a man with all this power should be angry. Or is anger, I wondered . . . the familiar, the attendant sprite on
power?"[15] Male power and male anger against women serve as subtexts
to Woolf's critical view, for example, that Lady Winchelsea's poetic
seventeenth-century mind has not, like Shakespeare's, "'consumed all
impediments and become incandescent.' "[16] For Woolf, the writing of
"literature" must be "disinterested," not ego-centered, despite the "splitting off of [feminist] consciousness."

The similarities aside, the differences between Eliot and Woolf are
most extreme. Eliot believed in individual genius, including his own.
Virginia Woolf believed that "the experience of the mass is behind the
single voice." Eliot's message to readers is "trust me"; Woolf's, "trust
your own taste." Eliot addresses the men in universities and charges
them to read Donne and the seventeenth-century metaphysicals, as well
as the Elizabethan and Jacobean dramatists. He adores the clashing of
opposing forces in drama and conceit, and, perhaps as a lesson from
Freud, he sees each generation of male writers at least partly in opposition to their writing forefathers—as he sees himself in opposition to the
Romantics. If the "individual talent" is a miracle appearing without understandable precedent, that miracle is enhanced further when it becomes part of "the tradition": "No poet, no artist of any art, has his
complete meaning alone. His significance, his appreciation is the appreciation of his relation to the dead poets and artists. . . . You must set
him, for contrast and comparison, among the dead. I mean this as a
principle of aesthetic, not merely historical, criticism." Eliot continues,
"The existing monuments form an ideal order among themselves, which
is modified by the introduction of the new (the really new) work of art
among them."[17] The miracle of the "individual talent" is, of course, a
male miracle. No women artists people Eliot's pages. The unwritten
message is plain: the best of literary art is poetry, and dramatic poetry is
as significant as lyric. Women do not write dramatic or lyric poetry.
There are no great female individual talents. There is no female tradition.

To write women out is, of course, to be profoundly anti-historical, to
eliminate not only those women living and writing around him, but all
who lived and wrote before them.[18] In an essay called "In the Hope of
Straightening Things Out," R. P. Blackmur describes his sense of the
meaning of "Tradition" for Eliot as "the weapon and resource of individual talent." Its inherent maleness comes through Blackmur's image,
and empathetically he describes the process for Eliot and other men:
"Tradition is the positive cumulus, good and bad, aside from ourselves,
and we have to find out for ourselves *all that grandmother will not tell us*

of what it is. It is the hardest work to find out what is already there. It is also, when we have it, *our means of protection against what we are not*."[19] Tradition for Eliot, as Blackmur sees it, is not only a heaping up of the monuments of the past; the accumulation fortifies as "protection" against women.

Few people have read all of Virginia Woolf's extant criticism. It is a large body of work, far beyond *A Room of One's Own* and the two volumes she collected of her own work and addressed to *The Common Reader*. Educated in libraries, rather than through a male-centered college and university literary canon, Woolf knew from reading women writers that they had also searched for literary mothers. She knew that women through the centuries had written for each other and had read other women when they could find their works in print. She writes critical essays not to rescue a single stream of dramatists or poets, but to rescue hundreds of "lost" female voices, writing often in the forms not usually honored by literary critics—the diary, journal, memoir, autobiography, and letters. She also hears the voices of those outside her class—working-class men and women. Not that she ignores the "classics," both ancient and modern; there are essays on Chaucer, on Hardy, on the Brontës, and "it is to the Greeks that we turn when we are sick of the vagueness, of the confusion, of the Christianity and its consolations, of our own age."[20] But she builds no line of monuments. Indeed, one can see her chipping away at monuments, her tools history and feminist consciousness, her interest the wide range of female experience in literature, as "outsiders" or outcasts in relation to the wider world, and as intimates, family, friends, even lovers—"Chloe liked Olivia" is her inspired phrase. In *A Room of One's Own,* she asks fundamental questions that feminist critics, social scientists, historians, and theorists are still answering: How important are the various barriers to women's achievement—marriage and the family, and the laws that control women's access to education, to employment, and to politics? What language shall women writers use? Which audience are they to write for, and under which name? And for what reason—for money, pleasure, or psychic need? Perhaps most important, "It would be ambitious beyond my daring," she says, "looking about the shelves for books that were not there, to suggest to the students of those famous colleges that they should rewrite history," modestly, as a "supplement," to be called, "of course, by some inconspicuous name so that women might figure there without impropriety."[21]

Woolf sees "talent"—female or male—as a characteristic that rises from the past "talents" of others. To state the idea in another form, the "talent" of one grows from the collective experience of many who came before. Woolf believes that the "lives of the obscure" contribute directly and indirectly to the production of culture by the "talented." She also values women and understands that, under patriarchy, the quality of their experience is of social necessity and economic circumstance vastly different from that of their brothers. Her challenge, at the close of *A Room of One's Own,* written sixty years ago, is the inheritance with which we open this volume:

> I told you in the course of this paper that Shakespeare had a sister. . . . Now my belief is that this poet who never wrote a word and was buried at the cross-roads still lives. She lives in you and in me, and in many other women who are not here to-night, for they are washing up the dishes and putting the children to bed. But she lives; for great poets do not die; they are continuing presences; they need only the opportunity to walk among us in the flesh. . . . if we face the fact, for it is a fact, that there is no arm to cling to, but that we go alone and that our relation is to the world of reality and not only to the world of men and women, then the opportunity will come and the dead poet who was Shakespeare's sister will put on the body which she has so often laid down. Drawing her life from the lives of the unknown who were her forerunners, as her brother did before her, she will be born. As for her coming without that preparation, without that effort on our part, without that determination that when she is born again she shall find it possible to live and write her poetry, that we cannot expect, for that would be impossible. But I maintain that she would come if we worked for her, and that so to work, even in poverty and obscurity, is worth while.[22]

> Tradition. Now there's a word that nags the feminist critic. A word that has so often been used to exclude or misrepresent women. . . . Why is the fugitive slave, the fiery orator, the political activist, the abolitionist always represented as a black man?
>
> —Mary Helen Washington, *Invented Lives*
>
> I think we look out of our bodies at each other.
>
> —Muriel Rukeyser

In 1969, at the invitation of Norman Rasulis and the English department of Central Michigan University, I gave a lecture called "Should Women Read Fiction?" My answer to that question, a strong "no," responded to my own rereading of the fiction I had studied in college and graduate school, and that I had been teaching to students since 1951. No, I said, for the novels admitted to the literary curriculum ended in only three possibilities for women: marriage, death, or both marriage and death.[23] This fact, along with the perception that women students, who were telling me that they read fiction "to find out what to do with [their] lives," led directly to the founding of The Feminist Press in the fall of 1970.[24] But few in 1970, besides Tillie Olsen and Elaine Hedges, could envision the existence of rich and strong bodies of literature produced by women at least during the last two centuries in the United States. My own work on American women poets began in 1970, as did Mary Anne Ferguson's research on "images of women in literature." Tillie Olsen's work on a female tradition (and other "lost" traditions) began as a talk at the Radcliffe Institute in the early '60s, and then an essay in *Harper's* in 1965, and appeared as *Silences* in 1978.[25]

In 1972, "Tillie Olsen's Reading List" began to appear in *Women's Studies Newsletter* (now *Women's Studies Quarterly*), and by 1973, when the fourth piece of this bibliography appeared, publishers and feminist critics had an extraordinary resource upon which to draw.[26] *Life in the Iron Mills* by Rebecca Harding Davis, with a biographical and literary afterword by Tillie Olsen, was issued by The Feminist Press in 1972, and Olsen's second recommendation, *Daughter of Earth* by Agnes Smedley, appeared in 1973.[27] Also in 1973, The Feminist Press published Elaine Hedges's first recommendation, *The Yellow Wallpaper* by Charlotte Perkins Gilman; in that year we also began to discuss the idea of a volume of "Black Women's Studies" and, shortly thereafter, to search for the rights to Zora Neale Hurston's work.

Through this period, from the end of the '60s to the mid-'70s, the Commission on the Status and Education of Women of the Modern Language Association began to organize programs on feminist literary criticism at the annual conventions. At the first of these in 1969, Kate Millett read from Chapter 2 of her then still unpublished *Sexual Politics*. Panelists during the '70s included Sydney Janet Kaplan, Carol Ohmann, Elaine Showalter, Tillie Olsen, Elaine Hedges, Alice Walker, Adrienne Rich, and Mary Helen Washington. By 1975 the MLA had organized itself into "divisions," the fifth-largest of which, Women's Studies in Language and Literature, also organized feminist programs. During the same period, other feminist literary sessions were being organized by the Women's Caucus for Modern Languages, by a Gay and Lesbian Caucus (and then a division as well), and by a Black Caucus (and then a division of minority literatures).

By the mid-'70s The Feminist Press and Alice Walker had found each other, as each searched for rights to republish Zora Neale Hurston. Walker, who had visited Eatonville, Florida, in 1973, published an essay called "Looking for Zora" in *Ms Magazine* in 1975. In 1975 also, Walker read an essay at the MLA annual convention called "Saving the Life That Is Your Own: The Importance of Models in the Artist's Life." Like Adrienne Rich and Tillie Olsen who followed her on this platform later in the '70s, Walker urged the importance of tradition for writers, and named as her own models Zora, Jean Toomer, Colette, Anaïs Nin, Tillie Olsen, and Virginia Woolf, thereby interestingly crossing lines of gender, class, and race.[28]

By the mid-'70s also, Lillian Robinson and Jane Marcus, among others, had begun to produce a body of socialist feminist literary criticism that emanated from Virginia Woolf's *A Room of One's Own* and *Three Guineas*. Robinson's early essays were published in 1978, but Marcus's were not collected until a decade later, when the appearance of *Art and Anger: Reading Like a Woman* made clear her early vision of Virginia Woolf as the single most important conceptual "mother" of a female literary tradition.[29]

The gates had been opened, and not only to white middle-class writers on white middle-class subjects, as The Feminist Press's books and other published anthologies of "lost" women writers indicate. In 1973, in addition to Howe and Bass's *No More Masks* and Ferguson's *Images of Women in Literature*, the following anthologies appeared: *A House of Good Proportion: Images of Women in Literature*, edited by Michele Murray; *By a Woman Writt: Literature from Six Centuries by and about Women*, edited by Joan Goulianos; and *American Voices, American Women*, edited by Lee R. Edwards and Arlyn Diamond, a collection of excerpts from nineteenth-century women writers that did, in fact, offer endings to novels quite different from those I had described four years earlier. In 1974, Louise Bernikow's *The World Split Open: Four Centuries of Women Poets in England and America, 1552–1950* was published; and in 1975, Mary Helen Washington's *Black-Eyed Susans: Classic Stories by and about Black Women*, the first of what were to be three volumes that trace a tradition of black women writers in the United States.[30]

Not surprisingly, then, just after the mid-'70s, two books announced, with confidence or reluctance, the advent of a "female tradition" in literature. Elaine Showalter, reversing John Stuart Mill's denial of the possibility that women might produce "a literature of their own," uses his phrase for the title of her book and calls her opening chapter "The Female Tradition." Showalter quotes Ellen Moers as seeing "women's literature as an international movement, 'apart from, but hardly subordinate to the mainstream: an undercurrent, rapid and powerful,'" and announces her own intention "to describe the female literary tradition in the English novel from the generation of the Brontës to the present day, and to show how the development of this tradition is similar to the development of any literary subculture."[31] For their perspective both Showalter and Moers draw from feminist historians, anthropologists, and sociologists who, by the early '70s, had begun to document the existence of a female subculture. Indeed, even before the middle '70s, when Showalter's and Moers's books were issued, challenges to the idea of a monolithic (mainly white, Western, and middle-class) female subculture were appearing from women of color and from lesbians.[32]

But of course, if one admits to the existence of female subcultures, and to the literature that such groups of women have produced, why then must one claim the need for reclamation? Where has that female tradition been? Where has it gone? Showalter, reflecting the early theorizing of feminist historians and social scientists, sees women as a "minority group" at the mercy of the "dominant society," and hence without "pattern of deliberate progress and accumulation." She sees the history of women writers as "full of holes and hiatuses, because of what Germaine Greer calls the 'phenomenon of the transience of female literary fame,'" and she quotes Greer further: "almost uninterruptedly since the Interregnum, a small group of women have enjoyed dazzling literary prestige during their own lifetimes, only to vanish without trace from the records of posterity." "Thus," Showalter concludes, "each generation of women writers has found itself, in a sense, without a history, forced to rediscover the past anew, forging again and again the consciousness of their sex." And yet, of course, Showalter presumes the existence of "the female literary tradition," which she theorizes as emerging not from biology, but "from the still-evolving relationships between women writers and their society."[33]

More reluctantly, Ellen Moers, who calls her book *Literary Women: The Great Writers,* confesses to the reader in her Preface that "once I thought that segregating major writers from the general course of literary history simply because of their sex was insulting, but several things have changed my mind." Moers's canvas ranges through British, U.S., and French literature, generally from the eighteenth century forward. The "several things" that changed her mind about the existence of a tradition of women writers included "history itself, the dramatically unfolding, living literary history of the period of my work on this book," and two significant observations emerging from that decade and a half. (She apparently began to work on this book in the early '60s.) The first of these is not surprising: "The suspicion has also grown upon me that we already practice a segregation of major women writers unknowingly, therefore insidiously," not only in literary history and criticism, but also in the anthologies prepared for the classroom. The second of Moers's observations is the special contribution of her book: "The great women writers have taught me that the literary traditions shared among them have long been an advantage to their work, rather than the reverse. They have taught me that everything special to a woman's life, from its most trivial to its grandest aspects, has been claimed for literature by writers of their sex—writers who share that quality Thackeray saw in Charlotte Brontë: 'the passionate honour of the woman.'"[34]

Moers portrays "literary traditions" in three ways: using what we may call historical sociology about the condition of women's lives; charting relationships, personal and through reading, between women writers, especially those of different generations; and summarizing key themes and imagery. Though her range is narrowly white and middle class, she is sensitive to the material differences among those women's lives, providing the reader with portraits that contrast, for example, William Wordsworth at Cambridge and Jane Austen at Bath, or Harriet Beecher Stowe writing amid cavorting children and visits from the plumber versus the "luxurious scholarly idleness" of Elizabeth Barrett Browning.[35] More significant still are other portraits of the longing for "connections" among women writers, even across the nineteenth century's unbridgeable Atlantic. Thus she describes in detail the use Emily Dickinson made of Elizabeth Barrett Browning's *Aurora Leigh;* and later, more startlingly even, the use by Gertrude Stein of George Eliot. She makes it clear that Jane Austen did not emerge as a singular and untutored genius; rather, she had read the hundreds of women novelists who preceded her. She reminds us that Willa Cather sought out and was welcomed by Sara Orne Jewett.

Like Showalter, Moers rejects the idea of a "female genius," a "female sensibility," and declares that there is "no single female style in literature."[36] Unlike Showalter, she sees women looking toward other women writers for affirmation and connection, not for difference or in competition: "their sense of encountering in another woman's voice what they believed was the sound of their own is, I think, something special to literary women—perhaps their sense of the surrounding silence, or the deaf ears, with which women spoke before there was such an echo as women's literature."[37] Yet Moers dares, in a chapter called "The Epic Age: Part of the History of Literary Women," to distinguish the themes of nineteenth-century women writers of three nationalities as bound to social causes. These include, not surprisingly, and as Showalter has also indicated, the cause of women's rights, the connections between feminism and radicalism, and the lives of women writers. But the oppression of women, social and economic, and their own recent emergence from illiteracy, Moers speculates, also makes them particularly sensitive to and interested in other causes: factory work and other aspects of lives of working-class people, including illiteracy; the theme of slavery, and the responsibility of mothers with regard to that social condition. Moers quotes from a letter written by George Eliot to Harriet

Beecher Stowe, "whom she honored as her predecessor in that great feminine enterprise of rousing the imagination 'to a vision of human claims' in races, sects, and classes different from the established norm."[38]

More skeptical and less respectful of tradition than Showalter or Moers, Mary Helen Washington, in her third and most recent volume of black women's literary history and criticism, *Invented Lives: Narratives of Black Women, 1860–1960,* maintains that "the creation of the fiction of tradition is a matter of power, not justice, and that that power has always been in the hands of men—mostly white but some black. Women are the disinherited."[39] Using Hortense Spillers's phrase, Washington sets herself the task of "piec[ing] together those 'broken and sporadic' continuities that constitute black women's literary tradition."[40] "Without exception," Washington continues, "these writers have been dismissed by Afro-American literary critics until they were rediscovered and reevaluated by feminist critics." Once this separate black women's tradition is restored at least to public view again, "the Afro-American literary tradition" will have to be read "in new ways." Washington concludes her introductory essay by underscoring the need for this revisionist history with an allusion to Anna Julia Cooper's image of a misogynist one-eyed world: "When the bandage is removed, the body is filled with light: 'it sees a circle where before it saw a segment. The darkened eye restored, every member rejoices with it.'" Thus, Washington concludes, "The making of a literary history in which black women are fully represented is a search for full vision, to create a circle where now we have but a segment."[41]

Ultimately, Washington's skepticism about the "fiction" of the male tradition—black or white—does not prevent her from envisioning a black women's tradition. Her confidence is assured not only by the contents of her anthology, but also by a decade of black feminist literary criticism, almost all of which, beginning with Barbara Smith and Barbara Christian, and continuing through Hortense Spillers, Erlene Stetson, Deborah McDowell, and others, builds on similar suppositions.[42] What are we to make of such literary theory? Briefly restated, the suppositions include the historic racism and sexism of U.S. culture, and certain thematic continuities in the literature itself, despite the "broken and sporadic" connections among black women writers. More significantly perhaps, Washington and others expect that, in time, there will be a revision of the male African-American literary tradition to include black women.[43]

Long before any of this history, in the 1950s, Barbara Grier, in the guise of Gene Damon, collected lesbian bibliography, consciously or unconsciously in preparation for future scholarship on a lesbian literary tradition. The 1981 third edition of *The Lesbian in Literature* includes some non-lesbian writers (even a handful of male writers) if their work portrays lesbians; it uses three degrees of asterisks to "grade" lesbian literature, not with regard to " 'literary' " quality, but addressing "the quality of the Lesbian material in the work," thus bypassing the question of a lesbian literary tradition "plagued," in Bonnie Zimmerman's words— and as Lillian Faderman has seen it—"with problems of definition."[44] In 1981 Zimmerman reviewed a decade of this history, noting both the question of inclusion—just who is a "lesbian"?—and of the "closet"— how dangerous has it been to write as a lesbian? She sees the tasks of lesbian critics as multiple: challenging the homophobic criticism of all, including heterosexual feminist critics; discovering "lost" texts as well as defining and decoding these and others; and "explicating the recurring themes and values of lesbian literature, and exposing the dehumanizing stereotypes of lesbians in our culture."[45] Will such work construct a lesbian feminist literary tradition? Faderman's exhaustive review, published also in 1981, does not attempt to answer that question. Rather, she divides lesbian literature into two parts: before and after the early 1970s. "It was not until the early 1970's," she notes, "with the establishment of lesbian-feminist journals and presses, that all the truth could be told without indirection and that love between women could be presented in a positive light." More interestingly still, she seems to be suggesting that only during the last twenty years has there been "a readership which demanded that its own experiences be reflected in literature." Before that, a lesbian writer could only "disguise gender ... encode messages ... hide from the censors."[46]

But what is the ultimate purpose of such tradition-making as Zimmerman, Washington, Showalter, Moers, and others project? And why, despite the evidence I offer of several female traditions in the making— as this volume indicates, for example, there is also a Chicana tradition— do I stubbornly cling to a singular "tradition" in the title of this volume? There are two major purposes: never again to allow the disappearance of women writers from history, and never again to cease insisting on their appearance inside the curriculum, the formal manner in which "tradition" becomes "canonized." Although the decades of publishing and literary history reviewed here have helped to make visible a tradition of female writers that is multiracial, lesbian as well as heterosexual, and working class as well as middle class, I am convinced that to imagine a series of separate, "monumental" traditions is only to establish (or to continue) a hierarchy among them, in which the traditional white male canon would survive dominant. Perhaps we will live in this suspended state for several decades, continuing to erode the white male

Western "tradition" piecemeal. Perhaps we will only see an "open, plural, disunified set of 'traditions.' "[47]

Perhaps we need to see literary works as part of a tradition smaller in size than monuments: mosaics, or tapestries, or quilt patterns. If these do not satisfy, perhaps Virginia Woolf's image, in "How It Strikes a Contemporary," of "writers . . . engaged upon some vast building . . . by common effort" will.[48] Or if one requires still more abstraction in the image, Jane Marcus quotes from Woolf's *Moments of Being*: "We—I mean all human beings—are connected with this: that the whole world is a work of art, that we are parts of the work of art. *Hamlet* or a Beethoven quartet is the truth about the vast mass that we call the world. But there is no Shakespeare, there is no Beethoven; certainly and emphatically there is no God; we are the words; we are the music; we are the thing itself." Marcus comments on "the rapture" the "writer feels on perception of the collective unity of art and life in history." She sees Woolf "reviv[ing] the romantic idea of literary progress while eliminating the idea of artists as a priesthood of men of genius." "While the poet is still for [Woolf] the legislator of morality," Marcus continues, "his authority is derived not from his individual talent but from his expression of collective consciousness. The 'egotistical sublime' of the patriarchy has been replaced by a democratic feminist 'collective sublime.' "[49]

However it is imaged, I am convinced that the idea of "tradition" will not vanish or dissipate, for it is an aspect of what Blanche Gelfant calls the "desire for continuity . . . elemental biology, religion, myth, and human history."[50] And Marcus, building on Woolf, offers "a real woman's poetics" as one of "commitment," not "abandonment." "Penelope's art is work," Marcus continues, "as women cook food that is eaten, weave cloth that is worn, clean houses that are dirtied. Transformation rather than permanence is at the heart of this aesthetic, as it is at the heart of most women's lives."[51] Continuity and transformation: perhaps images are, then, still to come.

Inside and outside feminist circles, most influential on the establishment of a female tradition is the teamwork of Sandra M. Gilbert and Susan Gubar, who, in *The Madwoman in the Attic*, following in the critical tradition of Showalter and Moers, read nineteenth-century women writers through the lens of their confined, repressed, maddening lives.[52] *The Norton Anthology of Literature by Women: The Tradition in English* (1985), edited by Gilbert and Gubar, established, at least for the 1980s, a canon of women writers that nevertheless cannot help failing to satisfy those who continue to mine the field of "lost" writers. At the same time, both of these volumes give those who have not been part of this two-decade work of literary reclamation a "handle" with which to begin shifting some classroom gears. Used as resources, rather than as texts, these volumes may educate some literary men and women untouched thus far by feminism, women's history, or feminist criticism.

More recent and still more ambitious is Gilbert and Gubar's projected three-volume series of criticism called *No Man's Land: The Place of the Woman Writer in the Twentieth Century,* the first volume of which, *The War of Words,* was issued in 1988. Building on their sense of a nineteenth-century "tradition" of women writers, in this first volume Gilbert and Gubar attempt a literary and social history of "modernism" that consciously sets forth to question the relationships between women and men writers. "Considering that at last it is, and has for some time been, evident," they ask, "that women do have a literary tradition, what have been the diverse effects of that tradition on both female and male talents?"[53]

One answer to that question, and one most important to this volume, appears in a chapter called "Tradition and the Female Talent." From a review of selected male misogynist fiction, including work by Max Beerbohm, Aldous Huxley, Henry James, Thomas Hardy, Somerset Maugham, Nathaniel Hawthorne, Wyndham Lewis, and D. H. Lawrence, they argue the consistency and the persistence of the fear of those whom Hawthorne first called "a damned mob of scribbling women." Further, their review of a lengthy series of misogynist statements and images wrought by male poets and critics on both sides of the Atlantic, including T. S. Eliot, allows Gilbert and Gubar to conclude that "the rise of the female imagination was a central problem for the twentieth-century male imagination." The "problem" has not diminished as the century has grown older, since "many postmodernist men of letters continued to define their artistic integrity in opposition to either the literary incompetence or the aesthetic hysteria they associated with women." Indeed, Gilbert and Gubar theorize daringly that (male) "modernism" itself can be viewed as a "reaction-formation against the rise of literary women," not only as "theme," but more significantly as "motive."[54]

The view that Gilbert and Gubar offer, of a socially constructed literary "war" between the sexes, serves several purposes. However unpleasant to those who long for reconciliation rather than conflict, it restores to the foreground the realities of male/female literary relations. (The recovery, by Bernard Benstock and Shari Benstock, of the history of literary magazines during the first half of the twentieth century may allow us eventually to see Gilbert and Gubar's view as understated.) Second, viewed from the battleground, the longing of women writers not only for respect, but for connections among themselves, becomes especially palpable. Finally, the imagery of wars serves to further separate the two traditions, and ultimately plays into the theme of "difference" so dear to feminist theorists of the '80s. Gilbert and Gubar's final chapter is called "Sexual Linguistics."

I have left for last a brief note about the third function of the establishment of a female tradition, or a variety of female traditions: the power this literary history offers to those writing literary criticism through a "theory" of gender "difference." One can understand the attractions of the idea of "difference," even of the further longing for separateness, especially when reminded, as in Gilbert and Gubar's most recent book, of the misogyny that has not, alas, retreated before the tide of feminist history and criticism.[55] And yet, this urge to theory has created a war within feminist circles more visible and perhaps more threatening even than the war waged against feminists from the outside. On the surface, the war seems to place French (or European) feminists, responsible for creating or at least promoting a "theory" of gender that begins and sometimes ends in biology and/or a revision of Freudian psychology, in conflict with British and U.S. feminists, who are alleged to be concerned "only" with placing gender within contexts of class (the British Marxists) or within history.[56]

In practice, U.S. feminist critics eschew the biological difference and urge what Showalter calls "cultural," what Marcus calls "material" difference, what Naomi Schor, Judith Kegan Gardiner, and Judith Newton call "history," and what Nancy K. Miller calls "a poetics attached to gendered bodies that may have lived in history."[57] Or as Blanche Gelfant, writing on Meridel Le Sueur in this volume, states the question of "difference" with regard to language, using a stolen language to "stool" on those who have stolen power constitutes enough difference to make a different history possible.[58] Thus, in fact, we return to the late Ellen Moers's plaintive and prescient sentence: "If ever there was a time which teaches that one must know the history of women to understand the history of literature, it is now."[59] It is still now.

> The greatness of literature is not only in the great writers, the good writers; it is also in that which explains much and tells much (the soil, too, of great literature).
>
> —Tillie Olsen (and Virginia Woolf)[60]

More than sixty years after Virginia Woolf envisioned a process of both political and literary change for women, a process to which she contributed during the rest of her life, we know that women writers have not only had a tradition of their own, but one that, at least in the past two hundred years in the West, often supported and moved on from, rather than competed with, prior generations. In subjection, sisterhood lived. The idea of competition between women writers, even today, is contained within boundaries appropriate for those who are still on the margins.[61] Women writers have not "killed" their mothers in a manner comparable to the alleged behavior of their male peers and their fathers; rather, they have been delighted to find them at last, and, as in this volume, they continue a tradition of celebrating their mothers' achievements.

Like Virginia Woolf, the contributors to this volume are interested in both the literature of women and their lives. They too are conscious that knowledge about women writers and women's history is a powerful instrument of social change. Woolf consistently remembered questions of class as she wrote about Shakespeare's sister and other women writers "lost" to us; we would add questions of color, of ethnicity, and of the women beyond the West who are discovering and recovering literary traditions of their own.[62]

Restored to view, the literature in this volume restores the multiple "talents" of women. These may be divided, for our purposes, into two major categories. First, the literature reveals the normative, everyday talents of women living in a gender-limited world, in a subculture of the patriarchy. What are these talents? Mothering and the rearing of families, sometimes in communities hostile to their survival; the passing on of the "culture" and the "tradition" by mothers and other women in the family to the children, especially but not only the daughters; enjoying the pleasures and torments of friendship and love, sometimes across racial lines in a world hostile to such relationships; the building of communities where perhaps only poverty and despair had dwelled; working as reformers or as leaders of rebellions; making the useful and the beautiful, the quilt and the pot, the garden, the kitchen, the household, the settlement house.

Second, and obviously of special importance to this volume, the essays focus on the talents of women writing in a variety of forms, finding the themes and language with which to convey the experience of living in subcultures. We now understand—as Virginia Woolf did before us—how difficult it has been, and still often is, for a woman writer to find her form and language, since readers, regardless of their gender, have grown accustomed to the works and tradition of male writers, especially to their themes. Perhaps only in our own time, and for the first time in the history of the West, is it possible for a young woman (or man) to read a significant portion of women's literature alongside men's. But the process of such reading, as this volume (and others) makes clear, is different and more complex. For though they were more numerous even than Virginia Woolf knew, woman writers were (and some would say still are) marginal and, as Amy Lowell named herself and other poets, "a queer lot." Their social position affects not only their themes, but also the manner in which they approach those themes. In this volume, and in general, literary and cultural critics are profoundly interested in decoding language and plot, not only to appreciate the artistry with which women wrote, but in order to understand the "difference" of their place in history, and that still more elusive idea, the relationship between literature and life.

The "Cypher," a sign containing both "meaning and the absence of meaning," and useful therefore as a trope signifying both women in history and the presence of women as writers, as well as the characters in that writing rescued from oblivion, appropriately opens this volume. The three essays in this first section remind us directly of the two decades of literary history we have recently witnessed. Twenty years ago, Elizabeth Cary was one of those writers said (even by Virginia Woolf) not to exist at all; no one would have written an essay on the foolish Mrs. Bennet of *Pride and Prejudice;* and *Villette* was not even accessible in paperback, much less a subject worthy of serious critical attention. The three essays also speak to the shifts in literary criticism that have accompanied the rediscovery of the lives and work of literary women. All three of these authors, to use the words of Jean Ferguson Carr, approach a text by stepping "outside" its "social world" to see the "exchanges" between it and "its formative culture."

These three literary critics employ some form of the idea of "doubling," explicitly or implicitly, even as they work within the frame of Woolf's "splitting off of consciousness" to decode what Karen Lawrence calls the "fundamental ambiguity" in the position of women as participants in a world not of their making, in which their functions are circumscribed yet subject both to consciousness and to challenge. These critics assess the dimensions of patriarchy's control of women's thinking or writing about their predicament—with or without access to publication or public performance. Was there any space that was "theirs"—even "theirs" to share with "God," and hence outside the purview of a father or a husband? Was there any way to avoid blaming the mother "for the excesses of the patriarchal culture," though she be its victim? Was there any way for the wisdom of a Charlotte Brontë—wisdom about the patriarchal control of women—to present Lucy Snowe as any trope but a "cypher," a "complex, shifting nexus of meaning and deferral of meaning that, like the sign itself, never refers to an ultimate and stable identity"? Is the consciousness of "an ultimate and stable" identity possible for women under patriarchy?

Quite appropriately, and as though to validate yet amend Virginia Woolf's imagined history of "Judith Shakespeare," Margaret Ferguson restores to view the history of Elizabeth Cary, the first English woman playwright and Shakespeare's contemporary. Cary's play could appear in print only with her initials, and only to be "erased" through time and rediscovered in this century, along with a daughter's *Life* of her mother, "passages" of which her son considered "too feminine" and so also "erased." Ferguson asks "Why the play's ideological statement [about the status and function of women as wives] is so mixed, so contradictory?" To answer the question, she teases out "the limits of Cary's choices—and her heroine's," which she sees as "complex products of a specific set of historical circumstances *and* of an individual psyche capable, to some degree, of interrogating, and even defying the 'customs' rooted in the material and ideological aspects of gender, religion, and class." Despite the demands of contemporary "customs" that assigned the ideals of "chastity, silence, obedience" to wives, Cary and the heroine of her play found some voice. Obviously, "silence" controls not only speech itself, but also the publication of speech.

Like Margaret Ferguson, Jean Ferguson Carr examines patriarchal rules that control the lives (and roles) of women, especially within the family, and the meanings of silence and the uses of speech. More directly than Ferguson, Carr focuses on the relationships between mothers and daughters, and the portrait of an ideology that held the powerless mother responsible for the future of her daughters. As Carr states the issue, Jane Austen's Mrs. Bennet "marks a lack of adult feminine power in the culture . . . and she is blamed for the excesses of the patriarchal culture." Carr "conduct[s] a double reading"—of what is there in the novel and "what is left unspoken or implicit"—to produce "a contradictory role for Mrs. Bennet" and to present evidence of Jane Austen's ambivalence about mothers. As Carr sees Austen's novel, "The treatment of the mother as comic . . . displace[s] the implicit challenge against social limitations [of gender] with a parental battle that is simpler to fight."

Karen Lawrence is also interested in questions of silence, speech, and the power of women to use language. The "fundamental ambiguity" of women's cultural position is made more complex in *Villette* when the subject of the novel is a woman writing her own story—"engag[ed] in the semiotic system," not only as "invisible" cypher, but also as a powerful "observer." Key to Lawrence's criticism is her perception that "Lucy chooses an ambiguous symbol that can suggest she is *less* significant than others (a nonentity), *secretly* significant (a code), *more* significant (a key), or significant *depending upon her relation to others,* and possessing the power to make others variously significant as well." "The 'writing' of experience on one's 'character' is painful," Lawrence tells us, not to say mysterious, a continuous process of remembering, partial, "never fully capturing any 'subject.'" And yet, Lawrence says, before the novel ends it captures the power of Lucy Snowe, who "schools the characters around her to interpret a female text different from those they have read before."

If the discovery of Elizabeth Cary amends the Judith Shakespeare legend, Jean Humez's view of women as storytellers, cultural creators, and inheritors broadens the legend beyond written literature. The second section of this volume moves west across the Atlantic to extend the concept of literature beyond poetry, drama, and fiction, to autobiography, including the tradition of oral storytelling and histories. At the same time, given the multiracial character of the United States, these essays add race to issues of gender and class. They are part of a very recent flowering of interest in the "fragmentary genres," of the recovery or rediscovery of texts—letters, diaries, memoirs, and autobiography—and of the writing of theory to account not only for the formal structure of such works but also for questions about the concept of self among women, subordinate as a gendered group, who may be further marginalized by race, class, sexual preference, and other facts of life. Before the end of the '80s, only two collections of essays on female autobiography had appeared—one edited by Estelle Jelinek in 1980, the other by Domna Stanton in 1984. Between 1987 and 1989, four volumes appeared, three of them collections, all of them considerate of women of color as well as of white women, all eager to "theorize" women's private and public lives.[63]

Nellie McKay is interested in a difficult question: How do black women survive to construct a self, even a warrior self, in a world that values neither women nor blackness? The autobiographies she chooses stretch from slavery and Harriet Jacobs through the nineteenth century and Mary Church Terrell to the civil rights movement and Anne Moody. "At the center of each of these black women's autobiographies," McKay writes, "there is a rebel with a moral cause which joins her to a tradition of women resisting and transcending the oppression of race, class, and gender."

Like McKay, Jean Humez is interested in the traditional passage from women to children of the stories of resistance and survival, especially in the black community. What kinds of stories did "ordinary" black women tell their children in order to prepare them for living in a racist world, and yet to assure that they were able to control their responses so as to survive into maturity? Humez's essay focuses ultimately on *Lemon Swamp and Other Places: A Carolina Memoir,* which restores a long history of black southern women's storytelling through the oral history of Mamie Garvin Fields.

Finally, Lois Rudnick asks a similarly provocative question: What kind of story does a strong and powerfully instrumental woman like Jane Addams construct in order to present her vision of a multicultural world in which women may make reform a necessary extension of their life's purpose? Rudnick's chief point is that Addams deliberately discards the ethic of success, the "myth of self-generation as the essential myth of the American Dream," a common theme of men's autobiographies from Benjamin Franklin's on. Instead, she reads *Twenty Years at Hull-House* as "a compelling feminist vision" that celebrates selves who are defined by and nourished by a community.

These essays view the function of autobiography as educational, political, and therapeutic, as polemic and history that create for a family and for the family of women a record of the difference that a single life might make in a world that excluded women from history and power. The plots of these autobiographies are similar: women must unite if they are to make change for themselves and others.

A phrase from Jane Marcus's essay on *Nightwood* names the third section of this volume, the "centrality of marginality." The phrase describes one characteristic of newly reclaimed "lost" literature by three women writers—Agnes Smedley, Meridel Le Sueur, and Djuna Barnes. Smedley, Le Sueur, and Barnes were journalists each of whom, for very different reasons, wrote fiction. Smedley's only novel appeared in 1929; one of Barnes's several novels, *Nightwood,* was published in 1936; and Le Sueur's only novel, rejected in 1939, was not published until 1978. While their lives and their novels are very different, they all celebrate marginality, focusing on those ordinarily invisible in literature, those whom Tillie Olsen has called "the despised."[64] Linguistically, thematically, and politically experimental, all three novels are prescient about the impending horrors of fascism. In each case, the theme of survival for women in a wretchedly impoverished world is urgent, the feminism of the writer brilliantly pioneering. Their clue to survival and even revolution is speech turned into literature, an end to their silence and invisibility.

Smedley, battling for her own life, wrote an autobiographical novel that illumines Marie Rogers's education into a brutal world, in which, as Nancy Hoffman describes it, "Love expressed in sex enslaves and humiliates women." Unlike Le Sueur's novel, and certainly very different

from Barnes's, *Daughter of Earth* portrays women's (hetero)sexuality and
the institution of marriage and the family as impossibly oppressive.
While understanding that the politics of race, class, and gender is essential to Marie's survival, "knowing" does not enable her to live within a
loving relationship. Writing, Hoffman tells us, saves Marie's (as it saved
Smedley's) life, allowing her to recommit her talents to the dispossessed.
Nancy Hoffman rounds out her essay by providing a portrait of the real
Smedley, marginalized to the end by a politics absolutely contemporary
today.

Meridel Le Sueur, born in 1900 and still alive and well in Wisconsin,
completed the published version of *The Girl* in 1977, describing it as a
"memorial to the great and heroic women of the depression" and "really
written by them." "We met every night," she continues, "to raise our
miserable circumstances to the level of sagas, poetry, cry-outs."[65] Here
where the "authority of experience" is primary, Blanche Gelfant describes the "extraordinary metamorphosis" of "a scared and silent country girl into a woman." Like Le Sueur, Gelfant continues, "Her ultimate
transformation, easily overlooked but striking, is from silent witness to
storyteller." Like others in this volume, Gelfant is interested especially in
the language of this text, a language she describes as "linguistically exciting and confused." Le Sueur attempts "an ideal of unity . . . by amalgamating discrete and incompatible discourses," the effort signifying her
feminist and socialist politics.

Djuna Barnes, who died in 1982, was, like Smedley, an expatriate in
the '20s. The marginal characters in *Nightwood* are not simply poor or
people of color; nor is the form of the novel the narrative realism of
Smedley or its language the poetic prose of Le Sueur's proletariat.
Rather, as Jane Marcus states it, the "extraordinary range of its learned
reach across the history of Western culture marks [*Nightwood*] as the
logos-loving match of *Ulysses*." "We are not accustomed," Marcus writes,
"to thinking of Djuna Barnes as a learned woman, a scholar as well as a
writer." *Nightwood* is a "great Rabelaisian comic epic," a "brilliant and
hilarious feminist critique of Freudian psychoanalysis." It is also a
"prophecy of the Holocaust, an attack on the doctors and politicians
who defined deviance and set up a world view of us and them, the normal and the abnormal, in political, racial, and sexual terms, a world
which was divided into the upright and the downcast. . . . " The "downcast" are lesbians, transvestites, blacks, Jews, circus freaks.

As we move from the '30s to the '70s and '80s, still in the United
States, the next set of essays focuses on the "tradition of socially engaged
literature" and the relationship between contemporary literature and social movements. The themes of women alone, or as "sisters," or as moth-

ers and daughters, noted by other writers in this volume, reappear here. Nancy Porter analyzes the themes of race, class, and gender as they interact with respect to female friendships in fiction set either during or immediately following the civil rights movement or in the antebellum South. She uses the trope of interracial female friendship as an indicator of the possibility of "community," an ideal realized briefly and poignantly, but as rarely in fiction as in life.

Deborah Rosenfelt surveys a large body of "feminist" and "postfeminist" fiction, searching for the "relationship between women's literature and the rise and fall" of the contemporary feminist movement. She sees especially the fiction of the late '60s and '70s as "inscribing the radical consciousness" of those years and "deliberately intervening in the ideological struggles of its time." She is interested in charting the relationships among consciousness, history, and the "texture" of fiction. Ultimately, she is optimistic about the power even of postfeminist fiction to continue to shift patriarchal consciousness.

Sonia Saldivar-Hull's essay on recent Chicana literature begins by challenging Western feminist theory and defining "border feminism," the name she gives to Chicana feminist theory. She describes the relationship between the lives of Hispanic people on the border and the literature now being produced by Chicanas, especially Gloria Anzaldua's *Borderlands,* "a mixture of autobiography, poetry, identity politics, and academic footnotes," and Helena Maria Viramontes's story "The Cariboo Cafe." Many Chicana writers consider themselves "community activists first," their concerns to produce a literature of their own and a feminism of their own defining. The context of their historical circumstances, especially the violence of a racist society that brutalizes women, shapes some of the literature; other lesbian Chicana voices "complicate" the portrait by raising into view "the new mestiza," the "mixed-race" woman, "alienated from her own, often homophobic culture."

In the final section of this volume, "Reprise," three essays recall aspects of the talents and limitations of women writers through two centuries or more, optimistic that the recovery of women's history and literature may preclude the blind repetition of the errors of the past, instead allowing for the conscious shaping of the future. Elaine Showalter examines two early British feminist polemicists in order to consider their historical and figurative relationships to contemporary feminist critics. Showalter contrasts the goals of Margaret Fuller and Florence Nightingale to develop "analyses of the cultural dilemma of the female intellectual," with their contradictory needs, to write under the eye of male mentors. "The histories of Nightingale and Fuller," Showalter says, "are important to us because they are part of that secret archive only now being explored by a new generation of feminist critics seeking our own models and our own traditions."

Charlotte Goodman celebrates the restoration to the literary canon of *Uncle Tom's Cabin,* a prime text in the tradition of socially engaged fiction, but notes "the significant omissions" in Harriet Beecher Stowe's portrait of the lives of slave women. Goodman contrasts that portrait with Margaret Walker's in *Jubilee.* "A celebration of the black female community" and "a social history of the buried life of black women under slavery," *Jubilee* restores both "verbal texts"—instructions regarding menstruation and sexuality, pregnancy and childbirth, as well as songs and sayings—and the practices of folk medicine, cooking, and sewing. Goodman, assuming the legitimacy of Stowe, urges the inclusion of *Jubilee* in the canon.

Finally, Elaine Hedges, reviewing the historical function of sewing in women's lives and its complex relationship to women's writing, transports us through two centuries of a still-living literary tradition. In Hedges's essay, as in Showalter's and Goodman's, literature becomes the text for the restoration of women's history, especially for an understanding of the relationship between the desire, even the need, of women to write literature and the limitations, including the silences, imposed on them. As Hedges writes about the "widespread reappropriation" of the metaphorical possibilities of women's textile work by contemporary women artists, who "find in it such a range of empowering creative possibilities," she also warns against an idealization of the past. "An understanding of the embattled and often adversarial relationship between sewing and writing" that existed in the nineteenth century, she says, "is essential if we are to avoid oversimplifying the historical relationship between textiles and texts."

As Hedges notes the dozens of nineteenth-century women who were forced by economic need or cultural pressure to sew when they would rather have read—or written—and as we hear of others who "camouflaged" their writing by describing it in terms of "patchwork," placing it therefore in that subordinate world of women's domestic work, we return to the beginning, to the "almost public voice" of Elizabeth Cary, and to Virginia Woolf's "lives of the obscure," to the fictive Judith Shakespeare, denied entrance into the male world of literature. We recognize also how close women writers today are to those voices, removed only a little more than a century from Stowe, Fuller, and Nightingale.

As I reread T. S. Eliot's prose this past year, I was reminded of the once seeming purity and simplicity of criticism. We were introduced to a certain pleasant mixture of philosophy and religion, supposedly free of gender, class, race, and political consciousness. For most of us, literary study and literary criticism were little more than subjects for an inquiring, discerning mind, and, in the case of Eliot, a sensitive ear attuned to the nuances of versification. The importance of literature as "thought" or as "beauty" was the point, not its function. Or so it seemed then.[66] We were not reading it deeply enough because we were not writing it; we were not seeing ourselves inside or outside its pages. And we were not aware, as we are today, of "the splitting off of consciousness," of the woman writer as outsider, "alien and critical." This awareness, the starting point of feminist criticism, breathes a social purpose directly connected to the extraordinary vision with which Virginia Woolf closed *A Room of One's Own.* She charged women to work as a community on behalf of all the women whose voices have not yet been heard. She urged women to come together to provide "the opportunity" for those silent voices "to walk among us in the flesh."

The portraits in this volume respond to that charge. Although feminist critics (as Elaine Showalter's essay reminds us) are still plagued by ambivalence, still tormented by male standards of "aggressive" criticism, they are also ready "to achieve . . . authority through both the demonstration of mastery and the admission of uncertainty." To admit that, after twenty years, we have a certain "mastery" yet that much "uncertainty" remains, to recognize that we have begun to retrieve a working outline of a long and complex history and practice of women's literature in the United States and Britain, is a challenge to those who will continue the process, not only in the West, but in every nation, not only to restore the written literature by women of the past, but to assure a place for the contemporary outpouring of women's literature, as well as the long oral traditions of storytelling and song from whence all comes. Were Virginia Woolf a witness to these decades, she too might believe that the raising of the long history she named "an eternity of dominion . . . and servility" has already begun to produce the "liberty of experience" for women to "think, invent, imagine, and create as freely as men do, and with as little fear of ridicule and condescension."[67] While Woolf was one, often alone, battling for many women named "inferior," "inadequate," or worse, we are now many, often together, battling for still more and more of us. Though we are far from declaring any major battles won, and while we see the long struggle for women's rights continuing for many, many decades more, we celebrate the contributions of women's literature, oral and written, to the long view of women's history and to gaining that shining "liberty."

NOTES

I wish to acknowledge the special sisterhood of Jane Marcus, who read and praised the first draft of this Introduction—focused on Eliot and Woolf—without reminding me that, in "Thinking Back through Our Mothers" and in other Woolf essays, she had already reached my conclusions. I am indebted also to Margaret Ferguson and Jean Ferguson Carr, and to the criticism of Elaine Hedges and an anonymous reviewer for the University of Illinois Press. Although, before writing this Introduction, I had not read the essay called "Tradition and the Female Talent," by Sandra F. Gilbert and Susan Gubar, published first in Nancy K. Miller's *The Poetics of Gender* in 1986, and then, more substantially, as a chapter in *No Man's Land: The Place of the Woman Writer in the Twentieth Century* (1988), I am pleased to acknowledge that their analysis strengthens my own.

1. Though I read Ellen Moers's *Literary Women: The Great Writers* in the very month when it was published in 1976, and wrote about it in an essay shortly afterward, I do not remember noting the title of its third chapter, "Women's Literary Tradition and the Individual Talent." Indeed, I was surprised to find that I had missed it a second time, when I had gone to my marked-up copy in search of material for this essay. Until I returned to check a quotation—and finally sighted the chapter title—I had missed seeing as well the mischievous manner in which Moers, in the epigraph to the chapter, changes Eliot's pronouns from masculine to feminine: "We dwell with satisfacion upon the poet's difference from *her* predecessors, especially *her* immediate predecessors . . . " (New York: Doubleday, 1976, p. 42; italics mine).

2. Jane Marcus writes, "*A Room of One's Own* is the first modern text of feminist criticism, the model in both theory and practice of a specifically socialist feminist criticism." Marcus lists writers and critics who have "rewritten" and "reinterpreted" *A Room of One's Own*, beginning with Sylvia Townsend Warner's "Women as Writers" and including "Mary Ellman in *Thinking about Women*, Adrienne Rich in *On Lies, Secrets and Silence*, Tillie Olsen in *Silences*, Carolyn Heilbrun in *Reinventing Womanhood*, Lillian Robinson in *Sex, Class and Culture*, Joanna Russ in *How to Suppress Women's Writing*, and Alice Walker in *In Search of Our Mothers' Gardens*." See "Still Practice, a/Wrested Alphabet: Toward a Feminist Aesthetic," in *Art and Anger: Reading Like a Woman* (Columbus: Ohio State University Press, 1988), p. 216. The essay appeared first in 1984 in *Tulsa Studies in Women's Literature*.

One could write an entire volume on the contemporary importance of Virginia Woolf to activist feminists around the globe, as well as to writers, to literary and other feminist theorists, or even to historians. A very few examples here. In 1973, the sociologist-historian Alice S. Rossi closed *The Feminist Papers: From Adams to de Beauvoir* (New York: Columbia University Press) with Virginia Woolf, Margaret Mead, and Simone de Beauvoir. "None of the selections in this collection," Rossi writes, "gave as much difficulty in the process of abridgement" as did *A Room of One's Own*. Rossi praises Woolf's analysis of the status of women, suggesting that the "painstakingly documented and quantified" social sciences "are no match for" the power of Woolf's "closely knit and subtly balanced" work (p. 624). Italian feminists in the '70s named their cultural center in Rome the Virginia Woolf Center. German literary feminists call their newspaper *Virginia*. *The Norton Anthology of Literature by Women: The Tradition in English* (New York: W. W. Norton, 1985), ed. Sandra F. Gilbert and Susan Gubar, opens with a sentence from *A Room of One's Own,* " 'Books continue each other,' " and the editors see their volume as containing "the tradition [Woolf] was subtly defining," as she "advis[ed] her readers to consider contemporary fiction by women 'as if it were the last volume in a fairly long series' " (p. xxvii). In three volumes of literary criticism published between 1985 and 1987, Virginia Woolf's criticism—often, but not only, from *A Room of One's Own*—figures significantly in one-third of the essays. These are *The New Feminist Criticism: Essays on Women, Literature, and Theory,* ed. Elaine Showalter (New York: Pantheon, 1985); *The Poetics of Gender,* ed. Nancy K. Miller (New York: Columbia University Press, 1986); and *Feminist Issues in Literary Scholarship,* ed. Shari Benstock (Bloomington: Indiana University Press, 1987). Carolyn Heilbrun, introducing *The Poetics of Gender,* writes, "Virginia Woolf was mentioned more often than any other single figure at the conference" (p. viii). To make my point, I am deliberately ignoring (with the exception of the reference from Marcus) the enormous outpouring of Woolf criticism itself.

3. Nancy K. Miller uses this term in "Arachnologies: the Woman, the Text, and the Critic," in *The Poetics of Gender,* p. 274.

4. See Mary Anne Ferguson's "No More Squeezing into One," in *Face to Face: Fathers, Mothers, Masters, Monsters—Essays for a Nonsexist Future,* ed. Meg McGavran Murray (Westport, Conn.: Greenwood Press, 1983), pp. 257–71.

5. I am grateful to Margaret Ferguson and Jean Ferguson Carr for the idea that Eliot's "metaphor of the monument buries the question of reception," since its use allows Eliot to "avoid any sense of possible disagreements among readers about what constitutes either the 'ideal order' or 'the really new.' "

6. Woolf, *A Room of One's Own,* p. 114.

7. Ibid., p. 146; italics mine.

8. Consider, for example, the late Joan Kelly's use of "double vision" to describe the enabling feminist consciousness; and the starting place for Sandra Gilbert and Susan Gubar's *The Madwoman in the Attic.* Also, in another variant, Elaine Showalter, in "Feminist Criticism in the Wilderness" (*Critical Inquiry* 8, no. 2 [Winter 1981]; republished in *The New Feminist Literary Criticism),* defines women's writing as a " 'double-voiced discourse' that always embodies the social, literary, and cultural heritages of both the muted and the dominant" (p. 199). "Doubles" and "Doubling" and "double readings" are, in general, very significant in contemporary feminist literary theory: see, just to take two more examples, Nancy K. Miller's essay already referred to above; and Naomi Schor's "Reading Double: Sand's Difference," in *The Poetics of Gender,* pp. 248–69.

Virginia Woolf returns to this idea in other language in *Three Guineas.* She is, of course, addressing men: "It would seem to follow then as an indisputable fact that 'we'—meaning by 'we' a whole made up of body, brain and spirit, influenced by memory and tradition—must still differ in some essential respects from 'you,' whose body, brain and spirit have been so differently trained and are so differently influenced by memory and tradition. *Though we see the same world, we see it through different eyes"* (London: Hogarth Press, 1938, pp. 33–34; italics mine).

9. I did not read *To the Lighthouse* then, but at the close of my last semester, Ruth Weintraub, a professor of political science, gave me a copy of *Orlando,* a reward for daring—as an English major—to take her senior course in public administration. I read it then conventionally, as a history of English literature, albeit an entertaining one.

10. *The Letters of T. S. Eliot,* ed. Valerie Eliot, Vol. I (New York: Harcourt Brace, 1988), 29 March 1919, p. 280.

11. Ibid., 7 November 1922, p. 593.

12. Ibid., 31 October 1917, p. 204.

13. I am indebted to Margaret Ferguson and to Jean Ferguson Carr for a list of those Woolf pieces that Eliot did publish: "Character in Fiction," the talk that became her (expanded) essay "Mr. Bennett and Mrs. Brown" (1924); a sketch, "In the Orchard" (1923); an essay, "On Being Ill" (1926); and her collaboration with S. S. Koteliansky on the translation of Dostoyevski's "Plan of the Novel 'The Life of a Great Sinner' " (1922).

14. Eliot, "Tradition and the Individual Talent," in *The Sacred Wood: Essays on Poetry and Criticism* (London: Methuen, 1920), p. 54.

15. Woolf, *A Room of One's Own,* pp. 50–52.

16. Ibid., p. 88.

17. Eliot, "Tradition and the Individual Talent," p. 49.

18. I am grateful to an anonymous reader for this supportive comment.

19. First published in Spring 1951 in *The Kenyon Review,* reprinted in *T. S. Eliot: A Collection of Critical Essays,* ed. Hugh Kenner (Englewood Cliffs, N.J.: Prentice-Hall, 1962), p. 143; italics mine. This perspective, viewed in the context of the mass of misogynist criticism that Gilbert and Gubar review in *No Man's Land,* will be discussed later in this essay.

20. Woolf, "On Not Knowing Greek," in *The Common Reader* (London: Hogarth Press, 1925), p. 59. Woolf, who has been studying Greek, writes, "It is obvious in the first place that Greek literature is the impersonal literature" (p. 39).

21. Woolf, *A Room of One's Own,* p. 68.

22. Ibid., pp. 170–73.

23. During the spring of 1976, I gave four lectures (at Brandeis, the University of Cincinnati, Ohio State University, and the University of Chicago) that opened with a description of that early lecture, but that went on to describe the work that Ellen Moers and Mary Anne Ferguson had begun in their respective books, and my own views of "women writers and the literary canon." "Feminism and the Study of Literature" was published first in 1976 in *The Radical Teacher,* and then in a collection of my essays, *Myths of Coeducation: Selected Essays, 1964–83* (Bloomington: Indiana University Press, 1984), pp. 188–205.

24. Since 1985, when The Feminist Press moved into New York City at the invitation of Chancellor Joseph S. Murphy, its name has been changed to The Feminist Press at The City University of New York.

25. In the 1950s and '60s, working on a dissertation at Harvard while teach-

ing there and elsewhere, Elaine Hedges read nineteenth-century fiction by American women, all accessible from Widener Library. She has continued to draw on this work as an advisor to The Feminist Press, as well as in her own scholarship. See also *No More Masks: An Anthology of Poems by Women,* ed. Florence Howe and Ellen Bass, with an Introduction by Florence Howe (New York: Anchor Books, 1973); a new edition is in preparation. *Images of Women in Literature,* ed. Mary Anne Ferguson, was published first in 1973. There have been three subsequent editions—1977, 1981, 1986—and a fifth edition is now in preparation. Such critical curricular work as Ferguson's produces what a reviewer praised as a "tradition in flux," with subsequent revisions documenting "significant changes in our study of women in literature."

As a young girl in Omaha, Nebraska, Tillie Olsen had read "Life in the Iron Mills" in a bound edition of *The Atlantic,* where it had first been published. Only half a lifetime later, in 1958, when reading *The Letters of Emily Dickinson* in the San Francisco Public Library, did Olsen discover that the author of this novella was a woman. When Olsen heard about The Feminist Press in 1970, she offered not only the story, but also the research and criticism of Davis that she had done at the Radcliffe Institute in the early 1960s. A new edition of *Life in the Iron Mills,* expanded with the addition of two more stories by Rebecca Harding Davis, was issued in 1985. See *Silences* (New York: Delacorte Press, 1978).

26. "Tillie Olsen's Reading List," in *Women's Studies Newsletter,* I: 2, p. 7; I: 3, p. 3; I: 4, p. 2; II: 1, pp. 4–5.

27. The Afterword to the first edition was written by Paul Lauter. In 1987, a second edition was issued with an Afterword by Nancy Hoffman and a Foreword by Alice Walker.

28. These essays appear in *In Search of Our Mother's Gardens: Womanist Prose* (New York: Harcourt Brace Jovanovich, 1983). In 1979 The Feminist Press published Walker's anthology of Hurston, *I Love Myself When I Am Laughing . . . and Then Again When I Am Looking Mean and Impressive: A Zora Neale Hurston Reader.*

29. Lillian Robinson, *Sex, Class, and Culture* (Bloomington: Indiana University Press, 1978; New York: Methuen, 1986). The essay called "Who's Afraid of a Room of One's Own?" was written in 1968 and appeared in *The Politics of Literature,* ed. Louis Kampf and Paul Lauter (New York: Pantheon, 1972). Many of the essays in Marcus, *Art and Anger: Reading Like a Woman,* were written in the early '70s, as lectures, and published by the mid-'70s.

30. One might add to the list of feminist anthologies and critical collections at least two others: *Images of Women in Fiction: Feminist Perspectives,* ed. Susan Koppelman Cornillon (Bowling Green: Bowling Green University Popular Press, 1972), and *The Authority of Experience: Essays in Feminist Criticism,* ed. Arlyn Diamond and Lee R. Edwards (Amherst: University of Massachusetts Press, 1977).

There is still no detailed history of this unusual era of publishing. See Florence Howe, "A Symbiotic Relationship," in the *Women's Review of Books,* February 1989, for a brief review of the connections between the growth of women's studies and the development of feminist publishing. There is also still no published account of the ineffable influence of Tillie Olsen on the appearance of most of the anthologies and books cited above, although a collection of essays on the influence of *Silences* is in preparation, edited by Elaine Hedges and Shelley Fisher Fishkin. The Feminist Press continues to acknowledge its debt to Olsen, as I have personally, and as have Ferguson, Murray, Edwards and Diamond, Walker, Marcus, and the late Ellen Moers.

31. Elaine Showalter, *A Literature of Their Own: British Women Novelists from Brontë to Lessing* (Princeton: Princeton University Press, 1977), p. 11.

32. Discussions about a volume of "black women's studies" began at meetings of the Modern Language Association's Commission on the Status and Education of Women in 1973, and at meetings of the Reprints Committee of The Feminist Press in subsequent years. Discussions about a volume of "lesbian studies" began a year or two later. Both volumes were published by The Feminist Press in 1982: *All the Women Are White, All the Men Are Black, But Some of Us Are Brave: Black Women's Studies,* ed. Gloria T. Hull, Patricia Bell Scott, and Barbara Smith; *Lesbian Studies: Present and Future,* ed. Margaret Cruikshank. Both volumes are being revised for reissue.

33. Showalter, *A Literature of Their Own,* pp. 11–12. Germaine Greer, "Flying Pigs and Double Standards," *Times Literary Supplement,* 26 July 1974, p. 784.

34. Ellen Moers, *Literary Women: The Great Writers* (New York: Doubleday, 1976), p. xiii.

35. Ibid., pp. 43–44; 3–4; 7.

36. Ibid., p. 63.

37. Ibid., p. 66.

38. Ibid., p. 39.

39. Mary Helen Washington, *Invented Lives: Narratives of Black Women, 1860–1960* (New York: Anchor Books, 1987), p. xviii.

40. Ibid., p. xx.

41. Ibid., p. xxvii. Cf. Emily Dickinson's "My Business Is Circumference," and Tillie Olsen's *Silences,* p. 247.

42. See Barbara Smith, "Toward a Black Feminist Criticism," first published in 1977, and reprinted many times. It can be found in *But Some of Us Are Brave: Black Women's Studies* (see note 32) and in *The New Feminist Criticism* (see note 2). See also Barbara Christian, *Black Women Novelists: The Development of a Tradition, 1892–1976* (Westport, Conn.: Greenwood Press, 1980) and *Black Feminist Criticism: Perspectives on Black Women Writers* (New York: Pergamon Press, 1985); Erlene Stetson, ed., *Black Sister: Poetry by Black American Women, 1746–1980* (Bloomington: Indiana University Press, 1981); Hortense J. Spillers, "A Hateful Passion, a Lost Love," *Feminist Studies,* IX: 2 (Summer 1983); Deborah McDowell, "New Directions for Black Feminist Criticism," in Showalter, ed., *The New Feminist Criticism.* Only Hazel Carby, who critiques Smith, Washington, and McDowell, is "critical of traditions," complaining that "reliance on a common, or shared, experience is essentialist and ahistorical"; see *Reconstructing Womanhood: The Emergence of the Afro-American Woman Novelist* (New York: Oxford, 1987), pp. 6ff., 16.

43. See the new series of nineteenth-century black women writers by Oxford University Press, published under the general editorial direction of Henry Louis Gates, Jr.

44. See Barbara Grier, *The Lesbian in Literature,* 3rd ed. (Tallahassee, Fla.: Naiad Press, 1981). The first edition of this bibliography appeared in 1967, edited by Gene Damon (Barbara Grier) and Lee Stuart. See also Lillian Faderman, *Surpassing the Love of Men: Romantic Friendship and Love between Women from the Renaissance to the Present* (New York: William Morrow, 1981); Bonnie Zimmerman, "What Has Never Been: An Overview of Lesbian Feminist Criticism," in Showalter, ed., *The New Feminist Criticism.*

45. Zimmerman, "What Has Never Been," p. 219.

46. Faderman, *Surpassing the Love of Men,* pp. 405–6, 41.

47. I am indebted to an anonymous reader for this sentence.

48. I am indebted to Jane Marcus for this quotation from Virginia Woolf's "How It Strikes a Contemporary," *The Common Reader* (London: Hogarth Press, 1925), p. 304. See Marcus, *Art and Anger,* p. 82, which also contains the following parenthetical sentence: "(T. S. Eliot uses a similar idea in 'Tradition and the Individual Talent' to enforce reactionary patriarchal ideas.)"

49. Marcus, *Art and Anger,* p. 82.

50. Gelfant, in this volume, p. 197.

51. Marcus, *Art and Anger,* p. 222.

52. *The Madwoman in the Attic: The Woman Writer and the Nineteenth-Century Literary Imagination* (New Haven: Yale University Press, 1979) was received generously by reviewers of all persuasions. A recent feminist essay by Nina Baym challenges the volume's feminist premises: see Baym, "The Madwoman and Her Languages: Why I Don't Do Feminist Literary Theory," in *Feminist Issues in Literary Scholarship,* ed. Shari Benstock (Bloomington: Indiana University Press, 1987), pp. 45–61.

53. Sandra M. Gilbert and Susan Gubar, *No Man's Land: The Place of the Woman Writer in the Twentieth Century,* vol. 1: *The War of the Words* (New Haven: Yale University Press, 1988), p. xi.

54. Ibid., pp. 156–57.

55. Several feminist critics, including Gilbert and Gubar, for example, have focused on Harold Bloom's mocking prediction "that the first true break with literary continuity will be brought about in generations to come, if the burgeoning religion of Liberated Woman spreads from its clusters of enthusiasts to dominate the West. Homer will cease to be the inevitable precursor, and the rhetoric and forms of our literature may then break at last from tradition." See Susan Rubin Suleiman's response in "Pornography and the Avant-Garde," in Miller, ed., *The Poetics of Gender,* p. 132.

56. I am thinking of what Jane Marcus calls the "false battle between European theory and American practice," but I am also convinced of the importance of recovering thousands of texts—and reading them and their contexts—for (and before) the spinning of theory that attempts to generalize about them. See, for example, Toril Moi, *Sexual-Textual Politics: Feminist Literary Theory* (London: Methuen, 1985) and Jane Marcus's response, "Daughters of Anger/Material

Girls: Con/textualizing Feminist Criticism," in *Last Laugh: Perspectives on Women and Humor,* ed. Regina Barreca (New York: Gordon and Breach, 1988). For a volume of criticism that attempts to combine materialist and European feminist strands, see *Feminist Criticism and Social Change: Sex, Class and Race in Literature and Culture,* ed. Judith Newton and Deborah Rosenfelt (New York: Methuen, 1985).

57. See Showalter, "Feminist Criticism in the Wilderness," in *The New Feminist Criticism;* Marcus, in "Daughters of Anger/Material Girls"; Schor, in "Reading Double: Sand's Difference," and Miller, in "Arachnologies: the Woman, the Text, and the Critic," both in Miller, ed., *The Poetics of Gender,* pp. 249–69 and 270–98, respectively; Gardiner, in "Gender, Values, and Lessing's Cats," and Newton, in "Making—and Remaking—History: Another Look at 'Patriarchy,'" both in Benstock, ed., *Feminist Issues in Literary Scholarship,* pp. 110–23 and 124–40, respectively.

58. Gelfant, in this volume, pp. 197, 198–99.

59. Moers, *Literary Women,* p. xiii.

60. In *Silences,* p. 45, Olsen quotes from Woolf's preface to *Life As We Have Known It: Memoirs of the Working Women's Guild,* "Whether that is literature, or whether that is not literature, I will not presume to say, but that it explains much and tells much, that is certain," and then writes the sentence I have used for an epigraph. Olsen has consistently admired Woolf's anti-elitist stance, so different from most of her contemporaries.

61. See Evelyn Fox Keller and Helene Moglen, "Competition: A Problem for Academic Women," and Valerie Miner, "Rumors from the Cauldron: Competition among Feminist Writers," and other essays in *Competition: A Feminist Taboo?* (New York: The Feminist Press at The City University of New York, 1987).

62. See the new *Longman Anthology of World Literature by Women, 1875–1975,* ed. Marian Arkin and Barbara Shollar (New York: Longman, 1989). Further, The Feminist Press at The City University of New York has in hand 2,000 pages of manuscript, representing 140 women writers of India from 600 B.C. to the present, translated from ten of India's seventeen major languages, edited by Susie Tharu and K. Lalita, to be issued as two volumes.

63. Estelle C. Jelinek, ed., *Women's Autobiography: Essays in Criticism* (Bloomington: Indiana University Press, 1980); Domna C. Stanton, ed., *The Female Autograph* (New York: New York Literary Forum, 1984); Sidonie Smith, *A Poetics of Women's Autobiography: Marginality and the Fictions of Self-Representation* (Bloomington: Indiana University Press, 1987); Shari Benstock, ed., *The Private Self: Theory and Practice of Women's Autobiographical Writings* (Chapel Hill: University of North Carolina Press, 1988); Bella Brodzki and Celeste Schenck, eds., *Life/Lines: Theorizing Women's Autobiography* (Ithaca: Cornell University Press, 1988); The Personal Narratives Group, eds., *Interpreting Women's Lives: Feminist Theory and Personal Narratives* (Bloomington: Indiana University Press, 1989).

64. "Biographical and Literary Afterword" to *Life in the Iron Mills and Other Stories* by Rebecca Harding Davis (New York: The Feminist Press at The City University of New York, 1972, 1985), p. 158.

65. Afterword to *The Girl* (Minneapolis: West End Press and MEP Publications, 1978), following p. 148.

66. Jane Marcus tells the following story of an encounter with T. S. Eliot in 1960. She had heard him lecture on "criticism" at Harvard that year, and had written an essay for Walter Jackson Bate's criticism class that marked Eliot as "political" and "ideological," and very "conservative." Her teaching assistant, today a well-known literary critic, gave her a C and remarked that great critics were not ideological. Later that week, knowing of Jane's interest in Eliot, a friend called her when she saw Eliot and Valerie Eliot in a Cambridge Schrafft's. Jane arrived, introduced herself, was invited to have a cup of tea, showed Eliot her essay, saw him read her opening sentences, and had the pleasure of hearing him say, "Of course all criticism is political." When Jane told the T.A. that Eliot was proud of being "Right Wing," she changed the grade.

67. "The Intellectual Status of Women," Appendix III in *The Diary of Virginia Woolf, Vol. II: 1920–1924,* ed. Anne Olivier Bell (London: Hogarth Press, 1978), p. 342.

PART ONE

The "Cypher": A Trope for Women Writers and Characters

MARGARET W. FERGUSON

Running On with Almost Public
Voice: The Case of "E. C."

She was the only daughter of a rich lawyer; she was precociously
bright but not beautiful; she was married at fifteen to an aristocrat who
wanted an heiress's dowry. He was Protestant, as were her parents; she
converted secretly to Catholicism in the early years of what proved a
stormy marriage. Most of what we know about this female contemporary of Shakespeare (she was born around 1585 and died in 1639)
comes from a biography written (anonymously) by one of her daughters
who became a Catholic nun in France. This daughter does not, however,
mention the single fact about her mother that might be of greatest interest to modern feminist critics and historians—namely, that this
woman was evidently the first of her sex in England to write an original, published play. Her name was Elizabeth Cary and her play was entitled *The Tragedie of Mariam, Faire Queene of Jewry*. It was printed in
London in 1613. Mary Sidney, countess of Pembroke, had translated
Robert Garnier's *Marc Antoine* in 1592, and Cary's play is clearly indebted to that aristocratic experiment in Senecan closet drama. But
Cary's interest in the drama and in women's relation to it goes far beyond that of any female English writer we know before Aphra Behn.
According to her daughter, Cary "loved plays extremely" and for a time
at least managed to go occasionally to the London theater.[1] Her authorship of *Mariam*, along with an early play now lost and a later one on the
history of Edward II, makes her the first woman in England to attempt
substantial original work in a genre socially coded as off-bounds to
women, authors and actresses alike.[2]

Cary's play was never performed on stage. Whether or not it was
published with her permission, much less at her active request, is a question I wish I, or anyone, could answer.[3] Having that information would

make it considerably easier to accomplish one of my chief aims in this essay: to assess the feminist political significance of this play, both in its own time and in ours. More empirical information about the circumstances of the play's publication would be useful because the question of a woman's right to assume a "public" voice is both central to the drama and unanswered within it. That unanswered question, central not only to this play but also to Renaissance debates about the nature and proper behavior of womankind, underlies the lack of consensus among the play's (few) readers about its ideological statement. *Mariam* seems at times to mount a radical attack on the Renaissance concept of the wife as the property of her husband; but the play also seems—or has seemed to some of its readers, both feminist and nonfeminist—to justify, even to advocate, a highly conservative doctrine of female obedience to male authority.[4] I don't intend to make a case for or against either of these interpretations; I hope, rather, to show how, and to begin to show why, the play's ideological statement is so mixed, so contradictory.

The Tragedie of Mariam tells the story of the marriage between King Herod and his second wife, the royal-blooded Jewish maiden Mariam. Like many other Renaissance dramas about this ill-fated match, *Mariam* is based on a narrative in Josephus's *Jewish Antiquities* (ca. 93 A.D.), which was published in an English translation by Thomas Lodge in 1602.[5] Evidently following Lodge's Josephus quite closely, the author nonetheless revises her source significantly. She compresses, amplifies, and transposes material in order to observe the dramatic unities; and she alters the characterization of the heroine and other female figures, as well as the portrait of the troubled marriage between Mariam and Herod, in ways that are both more extensive and more ideologically charged than critics have noted.[6]

The prefatory Argument describes the events which occur prior to the play's action: "Herod the sonne of Antipater (an Idumean), having crept by the favor of the Romanes, into the Jewish Monarchie, married Mariam the [grand]daughter of Hircanus, the rightfull King and Priest and for her (besides her high blood, being of singular beautie) hee reputiated Doris, his former Wife, by whome hee had Children."[7] The play opens at the moment in Josephus's narrative when Herod has been summoned to Rome by Caesar to answer for his earlier political association with Mark Antony, who had helped him acquire Judea. Having overthrown Antony, Caesar is likely to punish Herod, and indeed a rumor of his execution reaches Jerusalem, bringing joy to many who had suffered under his tyranny and bringing relief mixed with sorrow to his wife. Her ambivalent reactions to the news of Herod's death become even more complex when she learns from Sohemus, the man charged by Herod to guard her during his absence, that orders had been given that she should be killed in the event of Herod's death. Outraged by Sohemus's revelation of her husband's jealous possessiveness and grieving still for the brother and grandfather Herod had murdered in order to secure his claim to the Judean throne (as Mariam's mother, Alexandra, continually reminds her), Mariam is unable to rejoice when Herod does unexpectedly return from Rome at the beginning of Act 4. She not only fails to show the proper wifely pleasure at seeing him but she also refuses to sleep with him. His sister Salome, who hates being placed in a subordinate position both by Mariam and by the Jewish marriage laws which prevent women from suing for divorce, schemes to get rid of her husband, Constabarus, and Mariam too. Fanning Herod's anger at his unresponsive wife by "proving" that Mariam is engaging in adultery with Sohemus and is at the same time plotting to poison Herod, Salome convinces the still-infatuated king to order Mariam's death by beheading. After the execution, which is described by a messenger, Herod spends most of the final act regretting, as Othello does, the loss of his "jewel." Unlike Othello, however, this jealous husband created by a female playwright laments not only his innocent wife's death but, specifically, the loss of her too lately valued powers of speech.[8]

Contexts of the Play

According to its first printer, *The Tragedie of Mariam* was written by a "learned, vertuous, and truly noble Ladie, E. C."[9] The scholarly detective work done by A. C. Dunstan for the 1914 Malone Society reprint of the play (there was only one edition) persuasively identified E. C. as that Elizabeth Cary whose father was a wealthy lawyer named Lawrence Tanfield and whose husband, Sir Henry Cary, became Viscount Falkland in 1620.[10] According to the biography of Cary by her daughter, Sir Henry married his wife (in 1602), "only for [her] being an heir, for he had no acquaintance with her (she scarce having spoken to him), and she was nothing handsome" (*Life*, p. 7). The same text traces Elizabeth's gradual conversion to Catholicism and its drastic consequences on her status as a social and economic subject. The biography is a crucial but problematic document in my case; a rhetorically complex instance of didactic religious discourse (the "exemplary Catholic life"), the biography, like Cary's play, raises questions by its very mode of material existence about the effects of gender as well as class on the social construction Michel Foucault has called "the author function."[11] The text of the *Life*, according to its nineteenth-century Catholic editor, was "corrected" by the unnamed female author's brother; his name is given to us (Patrick Cary) and he is said to have "erased" from his sister's biography of his mother "several passages which he considered too feminine."[12]

This enigmatic mark of censorship is one of many reasons why we need to approach both Cary's play and the *Life* as parts of a larger social text that can be only very partially reconstructed—and interpreted—by the modern reader. The traces of the social text which impinge most insistently on Cary's writing, and her daughter's, pertain to the set of prescriptive discourses and legal, economic, and behavioral practices surrounding the concept of female chastity and epitomized in the famous Renaissance formula that wives should be "chaste, silent, and obedient."[13] This triple prescription, the core of a set of theories richly elaborated, and also variously challenged, in texts ranging from domestic conduct books and educational treatises to sermons and works of (so-called) imaginative literature, might be called an ideological topos.[14] The topos that Cary's play at once summons into formal being and re-acts against manifests itself in Renaissance texts both as abstract opinions about women's proper behavior and as "protonarrative" material fashioned into ballads ("The Cucking of a Scold," for instance), prose fictions like Deloney's *The Pleasant and Sweet History of Patient Grissell*, and numerous plays ranging from Shakespeare's *The Taming of the Shrew* and *Othello* to the anonymous *Lingua; or, The Combat of the Tongue and the Five Senses for Superiority* (1607), in which Lingua, dressed as a woman, sows deceit until she is imprisoned in the house of Gustus (Taste), where "thirty tall watchmen prevent her from wagging abroad."[15]

The "chaste, silent, and obedient" topos also informs the English common law doctrine of the *feme couvert* as elaborated, for instance, in a handbook entitled *The Womans Lawyer*: "Women have no voyse in Parliament, they make no lawes, they consent to none, they abrogate none. All of them are understood either married or to be married."[16] The normative woman thus constructed in legal discourse was also the object of Juan Luis Vives's influential educational program for young women. In his *De Institutione Feminae Christianae*, written in 1523 for Mary Tudor and printed eight times in English translation before 1600 as *The Instruction of a Christian Woman*, Vives invokes the authority of Saint Paul to support the view that "it neither becometh a woman to rule a school, nor to live amongst men or speak abroad, and shake off her demureness and honesty, either all together, or else a great part; which if she be good, it were better to be at home within and unknown to other folks, and in company to hold her tongue demurely, and let few see her, and none at all hear her. The Apostle Paul . . . saith: Let your women hold their tongues in congregations. For they be not allowed to speak but to be subject as the law bideth."[17] As this passage suggests, Vives is more concerned with a woman's conduct than with her education; "the notion that a woman's chastity is constantly endangered," as Gloria

Kaufman observes, "occupies most of Vives's attention and delimits his view of the formal education girls should receive."[18]

It seems both important and difficult to analyze this ideological topos of gender, which constitutes "woman," with particular reference to the property of chastity, as a class or group opposed to "man," in relation to the marxist conception of opposing social classes. The difficulty derives partly from the fact that this topos serves the interests of different classes and groups in the early modern period—particularly the aristocracy, the gentry, and the urban middle classes—in rather different ways and by means of a differential social positioning of men and women within each class. Moreover, the ideological topos works in still different ways when cross-class marriages are at issue.[19] The economic and ideological value of female chastity varies accordingly, with the result that certain logical fissures open in the very concept of chastity. These fissures may have been particularly visible to those who, like Cary, experienced a change in their social status.

The Tragedie of Mariam subjects the concept of female chastity to severe scrutiny and goes a long way toward unraveling the logic which binds "chastity" to "silence" and "obedience." That unraveling owes much to the ambiguity of Cary's class position, an ambiguity intensified in her case, as in many women's, by the institution of marriage. The only daughter of a lawyer who rose in social status to become Chief Baron of the Exchequer and his wife, Elizabeth Symondes, evidently a member of the lower gentry, Cary was married to a nobleman who, like many of his kind, needed funds to pay his debts and maintain his family's estate.[20] Marriage in the Elizabethan and Stuart periods was generally a prime avenue for the interpenetration (if not the harmonious blending) of what we may loosely call "aristocratic" and "bourgeois" economic interests and values. Cary's marriage was a paradigmatic instance of such interpenetration, illustrating it, indeed, in complex double measure because Cary's mother had apparently come down the social ladder by marrying Tanfield.[21] Elizabeth herself, following the more common social pattern for women, rose through her marriage to Sir Henry. The son of the Master of the Royal Jewel House, Sir Henry was, according to Kenneth Murdock, "a 'compleat courtier' of the new type soon to flourish under James I and Charles I. Such men observed the external forms of the old chivalric supporters of the throne, but their motives smacked of the increasingly capitalistic atmosphere of the time, and service at court was for them as much a profit-making enterprise as a duty imposed by family or tradition."[22]

The marriage between Elizabeth and Henry brought increased social prestige to her father and a valuable dowry—as well as the prospect of a large future inheritance—to her husband. Rightly anticipating, however, that his son-in-law would lack bourgeois virtues of self-restraint (Sir Henry was constantly in financial straits, and part of his wife's dowry may have been spent on ransoming him home from the Netherlands, where he had been taken prisoner early in the marriage), Lawrence Tanfield supplemented the dowry payment by settling a jointure on his daughter as an independent provision for her and her children.[23] Such jointures, usually settled on a bride by the groom's father to provide income in the event of the husband's death, occasionally worked to give not only widows but wives some control of property, even though the common-law doctrine of coverture forbade it.[24] When, however, Elizabeth Cary sought to exercise control over her jointure later in her marriage—ironically, by mortgaging it to help her husband, who needed funds to take up the post of Lord Deputy of Ireland in 1622—her father was evidently outraged: he disinherited her. His decision, which dramatizes the extent to which daughters were tokens in what Eve Kosofsky Sedgwick has called "homosocial" exchanges between men, may have been reinforced by the fact that he learned of Elizabeth's secret conversion to Catholicism at about this time.[25] She had evidently been brooding about that conversion since the early years of her marriage; her daughter writes that "when she was about twenty, through reading, she grew into much doubt of her religion" (*Life*, p. 9). At about the same time, according to the *Life*, she "writ many things for her private recreation, on several subjects and occasions, all in verse" (9). A "Life of Tamberlaine" (now lost) is mentioned as the best of these literary endeavors; *Mariam*, however, is not mentioned at all.

When Cary wrote *Mariam* (sometime between 1603 and 1612, during the early years of her marriage), she chose a plot in which the husband is of a different religion and a somewhat lower birth than the wife. Cary, however, stresses much more than Josephus does the discrepancy between the husband's bloodline and the wife's. Mariam's mother indignantly insists, for instance, that Herod "did not raise" her sons' status by marrying Mariam because "they were not low, / But borne to wear the Crowne in his despight" (1.2.154–55). And Mariam taunts Salome with her "baser" birth, prompting her to protest, "Still twit you me with nothing but my birth" (1.3.241, 48).[26] Cary's choice of plot, especially when seen in conjunction with these and other changes she makes in Josephus's narrative to emphasize Mariam's queenly status and also her possible political ambitions (Cary's Herod, unlike his prototype, fears that his wife may aspire to usurp his place on the throne [4.4.1494]), suggests that the play represents a gender-marked version of a common Renaissance fantasy, itself a species of what Freud called the "family romance": the dream of being more nobly born than one actually is. The class relation between Mariam and Herod is in fact an inversion of that which really obtained between Cary and her husband, and the inversion provides a historically specific fictional frame for the play's central conflict, which arises from the heroine's refusal to become wholly the "property" of her lord. The frame is historically specific not only because it is arguably shaped by the author's dissatisfaction with her subordinate position in her own marriage but also because Mariam's exceptionally noble birth, which is pointedly described in Cary's prefatory Argument as bringing Herod *"in his wives right* the best title" to the Judean throne (my emphasis), obliquely allies Mariam with those royal women of recent English history—Elizabeth and Mary Tudor and Mary, queen of Scots—who were political figures in their own right and who were legally exempted from the rule of female "coverture" even if they married.[27]

Cary's play therefore might be said to "rewrite" the class story of her own marriage without, however, directly challenging the fundamental concept of class hierarchy; indeed, she explicitly ratifies that concept by equating Salome's baseness of birth with baseness of character. The rewriting, which also stresses the problem of an interfaith union, allows Cary to explore the dilemmas of an allegorical version of herself, a woman who desires at once to obey and to defy that code of wifely duty which subtended the property and class system of seventeenth-century English society.[28] Although Mariam challenges that system much more ambivalently than Herod's sister Salome does when she forcefully protests the sexual double standard with regard to divorce, it is worth noting that Salome's insistence on women's right to pursue their desires is not simply condemned by the play but is instead recast, with its "lustful" motives expunged, by Mariam's ultimate insistence on dying rather than breaking an oath she has made not to sleep with her husband.[29]

Before turning to look closely at the play itself, I should comment briefly on the fact that its very existence in the world—its existence as an ambiguously "public" object, printed but not perhaps by the author's will, and written in the oxymoronic and elitist subgenre of Senecan closet drama—points to Cary's problematic relation to dominant ideologies of both class and gender. Noblemen of Cary's era did not, by custom, write for the public, or for money. The custom existed, however, in some tension with one of the prime tenets of humanist ideology— namely, the "nobility" of the classical ideal of literary fame.[30] For noblewomen, the custom discouraging publication was even more binding than it was on men; but a classical education, however altered to suit the alleged needs and capacities of the weaker sex, instilled in some women, as it did in some men too, a desire for fame that conflicted with the rules of social decorum. Cary, who according to her daughter learned early to read Latin and Hebrew as well as numerous modern European languages (*Life*, pp. 4–5), was clearly vulnerable to the contradictions which pertained to the act of publication throughout this period. An insight into this arena of contradiction is afforded by Sir John Davies, who evidently served as Cary's childhood handwriting instructor and who in 1612 urged her and two other ladies to publish their work.[31] In a poem dedicating his *Muses Sacrifice; or, Divine Meditations* to "The Most Noble, and no lesse deservedly-renowned Ladyes, as well Darlings, as Patronesses, of the Muses; Lucy, Countesse of Bedford; Mary, Countesse-Dowager of Pembroke; and Elizabeth, Lady Cary, (Wife of Sr. Henry Cary)," Davies praises the last named as the creator of a drama set in Palestine and encourages her—or so it initially appears—to show her work to the public and to posterity:

> Cary (of whom Minerva stands in feare,
>   lest she, from her, should get Arts Regencie)
> Of Art so moves the great-all-moving Spheare,
>   that ev'ry Orbe of Science moves thereby.
> Thou mak'st Melpomen proud, and my Heart great
>   of such a Pupill, who, in Buskin fine,
> With Feete of State, dost make thy Muse to mete
>   the Scenes of Syracuse and Palestine.
> Art, Language; yea; abstruse and holy Tongues,
>   thy Wit and Grace acquir'd thy Fame to raise;
> And still to fill thine owne, and others Songs:
>   thine, with thy Parts, and others, with thy praise.
> Such nervy Limbes of Art, and Straines of Wit
>   Times past ne'er knew the weaker Sexe to have;
> And Times to come, will hardly credit it,
>   if thus thou give thy Workes both Birth and Grave.[32]

The problem inherent in the logic of Davies's encomiastic rhetoric is that by praising a member of a class at the expense of that class (the "weaker Sexe") he implicitly places the exceptional woman in the double-bind situation so often discussed by modern feminists: achievement is bought at the price of dissociation from what the culture considers to be one's nature.[33] Moreover, by erasing the fact of prior female achievement even as he urges Cary to publish so that history will not forget *her*, Davies testifies to a problem wryly noted by the seventeenth-century American poet Anne Bradstreet. Evidence of female achievement, she suggests, may well be simply ignored in an ideological climate that presupposes female inferiority:

> For such despite they cast on Female wits:
> If what I do prove well, it won't advance,
> They'll say it's stoln, or else it was by chance.[34]

Davies further complicates his exhortation to female publication by suggesting that it may involve a derogation of noble status in general and, in particular, a danger to female chastity. "You presse the Presse with little you have made," he chides his "Three Graces," but the phrasing surrounds publication with an aura of unseemly sexual importunity which thickens when Davies goes on, in the next stanza, to personify the Press both as a noble damsel in distress, in need of rescue from the low-born versifiers who have "wrong'd" her, and as a woman already so sullied that she is by implication worthy only of scorn from "great hearts":

> [Y]ou well know the Presse so much is wrong'd,
> by abject Rimers that great Hearts doe scorne
> To have their Measures with such Nombers throng'd,
> as are so basely got, conceiv'd, and borne.

The syntax creates a momentary ambiguity about whether "great Hearts" are the object or subject of "scorn" when they approach the press, and the stanza also conjures visions of sexual danger or blood-line contamination. The lines can therefore hardly be read as unequivocally encouraging a noblewoman to "presse the press" with her writing, since in so doing she is implicitly linked either with a fallen woman or with one who has deserted her sex altogether to assume the aggressively masculine sexual role suggested by the verb *press*. The advice to publish is tied to a covert argument for remaining aloof from a scene of illicit sexual traffic: she who submits her creative offspring to the press is likely to be taken for an adulterous mother of bastards. Better to let the poetic children go to the grave unknown to the world than to allow one's noble (and by implication restrained, controlled) "Measures" be "throng'd" by "basely got" Numbers (Davies, p. 5).

Davies's message to his noble female readers is not utterly distant in spirit from that which Sir Edward Denny, Baron of Waltham, sent to Lady Pembroke's niece, Mary Wroth. Outraged because he suspected an unflattering allusion to himself in Wroth's prose romance *Urania,* published in 1621 when the widowed author was in great need of money, Denny wrote her an insulting poem. Unpublished but widely circulated among his friends, it portrayed the female author as a monstrous creature:

> Hermaphradite in show, in deed a monster
> As by thy works and words all men may conster

> Thy wrathful spite conceived an Idell book
> Brought forth a foole which like the damme doth look.
>   . . . leave idle books alone
> For wise and worthyer women have written none.[35]

Denny's harsh advice to Lady Mary that she should cease writing for public consumption evidently had an effect: she soon promised to withdraw her book from circulation.[36]

We have no way of knowing whether Davies's ambiguously encouraging verses contributed in any way to the publication of Cary's play in 1613. Indeed, we can't even discover whether it was Cary herself or one of her friends or relatives who made the decision to publish. There is a cryptic remark in the *Life* about some verse by Cary "stolen" from her sister-in-law's bedroom, printed, and afterward by the author's "own procurement called in" (9). Elaine Beilin has speculated that the "stolen" item may be the prefatory sonnet found in only two known copies of *Mariam*, the sonnet addressed to Cary's "worthy Sister, Mistris Elizabeth Carye" and hence an item which could identify the play's author to the public.[37] If Beilin's hypothesis is right, it is interesting that Cary would have recalled the sonnet but not the play; perhaps she wanted it published but was unwilling to go so far in defying custom—and her husband's strong views on women's proper behavior as "private" beings—as she would have had she publicized her authorship.[38]

The absence of any mention of *Mariam* at all in the *Life* of Cary and her daughter's obvious unwillingness to be known herself as a named author testify to the force of cultural strictures against women's publishing. And ideologies of gender were evidently often reinforced by those of class and religion to maintain the taboo against a privileged woman's "pressing the Press" with her writing. In rare cases such as Cary's, something might be published despite the taboo. But it probably affected the literary work's mode of material existence more often, and more substantially, than modern critics have tended to acknowledge. Recall that Cary's son Patrick "erased" certain passages from his sister's biography of his mother because they were "too feminine." What might Cary herself have "erased" from her play, following her conscious or unconscious judgment or that of other readers during the years when the play was evidently circulating in manuscript? The question can't, of course, be answered, but it's not altogether idle: the problem to which it points is that of censorship—a major theme in Cary's play.

The Text (As We Have It)

The heroine of Cary's play is torn between the demands of wifely duty, which coincide at least intermittently with her feelings of love for the tyrannical but infatuated Herod, and the demands of her conscience, which are initially defined in terms of family loyalty and voiced through the figure of Mariam's mother, Alexandra. She hates her son-in-law because, to secure his claim to the throne of Judea, Herod had not only married the royal-blooded Mariam but murdered her brother and grandfather. The nature of Mariam's dilemma shifts, however, as the play progresses, partly because her long soliloquies, like Hamlet's, work to dissolve binary oppositions. Also like *Hamlet,* Cary's play gives us characters who mirror certain aspects, and unrealizable potentials, of the central figure. At first glance, Cary's two major foil characters seem to come from a medieval morality play: on the one hand, there is Salome, Herod's wicked sister who works, Vice-like, to plot Mariam's death; on the other, there is Graphina, a slave girl loved by Herod's younger brother, Pheroras. Virtuous, humble, obedient, she seems to embody the ideal of womanhood prescribed in Renaissance conduct books.

The ethical opposition symbolized by these two characters—an opposition that emerges, specifically, as one of different modes of speech—is, however, also shot through with complexities. Salome's structural resemblance to the morality Vice figure is partly occluded when she is made to speak crudely but eloquently against the injustice of Jewish law, which gives (rich) men but not women the right to divorce (1.4); and Graphina—the only character whose name is not found in Josephus's text or in Lodge's translation of it—becomes more opaque the more one studies her brief appearance in Cary's text (2.1).[39] She is strongly associated with the feminine virtue of modest silence, but the dramatic presentation prevents us from conceiving of that virtue as a simple alternative to the "vice" of female speech, either Salome's or Mariam's. Pheroras tells Graphina that he prefers her to the bride Herod had designated for him because that "baby" has an "Infant tongue" which can scarcely distinguish her name "to anothers eare" (2.1.562–63). The "silent" Graphina evidently has won her lover's admiration for her powers of speech: "move thy tongue," he says, "For Silence is a signe of discontent" (2.1. 588). She obeys. The strange little scene queries the logic of the "chaste, silent, and obedient" topos by suggesting first that womanly "silence" may function just as erotically as speech in a nonmarital relation (the conduct books never consider this possibility) and second that a certain kind of speech signifies the same thing that "silence" does in the discourse of wifely duty—that is, compliance with the man's wishes: Graphina tells her lover only what he wants to hear, when he wants to hear it. She may therefore be said to figure a mode of "safe" speech, *private* speech that neither aims at nor produces offense. Cary's invented name for this character might, on this line of interpretive speculation, be significant: the name evidently plays on the Greek word for writing, *graphesis.*

If the figure of Graphina represents for Cary the possibility of both a nontransgressive mode of discourse (like private writing?) and a mutually satisfying love relation, neither of those possibilities is available to the play's heroine. The first words Mariam speaks, which are also the play's first words, epitomize the problem:

> How oft have I with publike voice run on?
> To censure Rome's last Hero for deceit:
> Because he wept when Pompeis life was gone,
> Yet when he liv'd, hee thought his Name too great.

These lines, which are spoken in soliloquy and initiate a complex parallel between Mariam's situation and that of Julius Caesar,[40] link the theme of female public voice immediately with the idea of transgression ("run on") and the idea of "censure." The question mark after the first line seems at first merely an oddity of seventeenth-century "rhetorical" punctuation. But the question itself, voiced at the play's threshold moment by a female character whose "unbridled speech" eventually plays a major role in her husband's decision to censor her voice definitively, is not by any means simply rhetorical. It is, we might say, complexly rhetorical—for several reasons. To make it the kind of question that obviously requires the affirmative answer "very often," the reader must "run on" over the line's end and its punctuation. The structure of the verse creates for the reader a slight but significant tension between pausing—to respect the seemingly self-contained formal and semantic unit of the first line—and proceeding, according to the dictates of the syntactic logic which retrospectively reveals the first line to be part of a larger unit. The verse thereby works to fashion a counterpoint between formal and semantic strains. We pause on the theme of "running on," we run on to encounter the theme of censure (as "censorship" and "critical judgment" both). The lines work not only to anticipate the drama to come (deploying the strategy of the "pregnant" opening most famously used in *Hamlet*) but also to mark the play, for Cary herself and perhaps for her first "private" readers, with something we might call the woman author's *signature*.

That signature consists not of a name but of a Chinese box set of questions about the logic of the Pauline injunction against female public speech and the cultural rule of chastity that injunction ostensibly supported. Like a lawyer presenting ambiguous fact situations to a judge, in the opening speech Cary invites us to consider whether the play text itself is "covered" by the law: Is *writing* a form of "public voice"? Is a *drama* not necessarily intended for performance on the public stage a legitimate form of female verbal production? Is a *soliloquy*—by theatrical convention, a "private" speech overheard (overread?) by an audience—legitimate? In short, the play opens in a way that seems designed to test, but not overtly to disobey, the rule proscribing "public voice" for women. Here we have a written representation of a female character soliloquizing, as if in private, about a prior event of (ambiguously) culpable public speech—ambiguously culpable because the comparison with Caesar's speech "degenders" Mariam's prior speech act, although the issue of gender, and a potential male audience's response to the speaker's gender, is clearly on the heroine's (and the author's) mind. Mariam goes on to transform the figure of Caesar from an (imperfect) model for a speaker to an authoritative model for an audience or judge. She suddenly apostrophizes the "Roman lord" with an aggressively defensive apology for exhibiting a fault (rash judgment) commonly ascribed to the daughters of Eve but also characteristic of many male rulers, including Julius Caesar:

> But now I doe recant, and Roman Lord
> Excuse too rash a judgment in a woman:
> My sexe pleads pardon, pardon then afford,
> Mistaking is with us, but too too common. (1.1.5–8)

Mariam's opening lines arguably address a problem that has to do not only with female speech in general but with the play's own mode of material existence—indeed, its *right* to exist in the world. The act of writing, for oneself or for an audience of family and friends, would seem—like the dramatic form of the soliloquy—to occupy a shady territory between private and public verbal production. Because of the ambiguous status of writing, Cary could in one sense have applied Mariam's opening question to herself and answered it with a decorum the fictional character lacks. "How oft have I with publike voice run on?" "Never." But that answer would not have satisfied the culturally constructed censoring power that the play text ascribes chiefly to the figure of the tyrant-husband but also to the chorus and, at certain moments, to the heroine herself, speaking, evidently, for an aspect of the author's own conscience or superego.

According to her daughter, Cary "did always much disapprove the practice of satisfying oneself with their conscience being free from fault, not forbearing all that might have the least show or suspicion of uncomeliness or unfitness; what she thought to be required in this she expressed in this motto (which she caused to be inscribed in her daughter's wedding ring): *Be and seem*" (*Life*, p. 16). This passage, which attributes to Cary a rule of spiritual and social conduct as fraught with problems as the rules Hamlet formulates for himself, might be paraphrased as follows: never be satisfied that you really are as virtuous as you may seem to yourself—but always be what you seem. The difficulty of putting such a principle into practice is dramatized, in Cary's play, by the fact that the chorus formulates one version of this rule in order to condemn Mariam for following (and articulating) another version of it.

The chorus's speech occurs at a pivotal moment in the plot: at the end of Act 3, just before Herod's first appearance on stage and just after Mariam learns, through her guardian, Sohemus, that Herod is alive. The rumor of his death in Rome had prompted Mariam's opening soliloquy detailing her mixed emotions about him and had also prompted the various intrigues—by Salome, by Mariam's mother, Alexandra, and others—which are described and partly enacted in the first half of the play. Through talking with Sohemus, Mariam has just learned of Herod's secret orders that she should be killed if he dies. Sohemus has both disobeyed those orders and broken his oath to keep silent about them—a double transgression that Salome will subsequently exploit to fulfill her desires to rid herself of her husband, Constabarus, and to bring about Mariam's downfall. In this same scene, Mariam has announced to Sohemus her "solemne vowes" to abandon Herod's bed (3.3.1136). Despite Sohemus's prudential advice to the contrary, she refuses to be reconciled sexually with her husband. Mariam's oath arises from her commitment to an ethic of uniting her "being" with her "seeming": she has told Sohemus that she will not use sexual wiles to disguise her true feelings about Herod, nor will she speak in a way that hides her thoughts: "I scorne my looke should ever man beguile, / Or other speech, then meaning to afford" (3.3.1168–69). It is such words of principle—and the principle that generates such words—that Sohemus laments thus after Mariam has left the stage:

> Poor guiltles Queene! Oh that my wish might place
> A little temper now about thy heart:
> Unbridled speech is Mariam's worst disgrace,
> And will indanger her without desart. (3.3.1184–87)

His lines anticipate, albeit with more sympathy for Mariam, the chorus's criticism of her in the subsequent speech, which I shall quote in full:

> Tis not enough for one that is a wife
> To keep her spotles from an act of ill:
> But from suspition she should free her life,
> And bare her selfe of power as well as will.
> Tis not so glorious for her to be free,
> As by her proper selfe restrain'd to bee.

When she hath spatious ground to walke upon,
Why on the ridge should she desire to goe?
It is no glory to forbeare alone,
Those things that may her honour overthrowe.
But tis thanke-worthy, if she will not take
All lawfull liberties for honours sake.

That wife her hand against her fame doth reare,
That more then to her Lord alone will give
A private word to any second eare,
And though she may with reputation live.
Yet though most chast, she doth her glory blot,
And wounds her honour, though she killes it not.

When to their Husbands they themselves doe bind,
Doe they not wholy give themselves away?
Or give they but their body not their mind,
Reserving that though best, for others pray?
No sure, their thoughts no more can be their owne,
And therefore should to none but one be knowne.

Then she usurpes upon anothers right,
That seekes to be by publike language grac't:
And though her thoughts reflect with purest light,
Her mind if not peculiar [i.e., "private"] is not chast.
For in a wife it is no worse to finde,
A common body, then a common minde.

And every mind though free from thought of ill,
That out of glory seekes a worth to show:
When any's eares but one therewith they fill,
Doth in a sort her purenes overthrow.
Now Mariam had, (but that to this she bent)
Beene free from feare, as well as innocent. (3.3.1219–54)

Angeline Goreau finds in this speech testimony to the "social hegemony" of the idea of female modesty in seventeenth-century England.[41]
Assuming that the chorus speaks unequivocally for the author's own
opinions, Goreau concludes that Cary here ratifies a definition of chastity not only as abstinence from illegitimate sexual activity but also as a
virtue that involves divesting oneself of "power as well as will." By thus
reinterpreting chastity as passivity, Cary "sets up an infinitely expanding
architecture of self-restraint, often more far-reaching and effective than
any form of external censorship might be."[42]

Goreau is right to stress this feature of the chorus's speech, but
she fails to consider the ways in which both the rhetoric of the speech
and its larger dramatic context render this extreme prescription of wifely

self-censorship problematic. The chorus, indeed, offers contradictory statements about the precise nature of the error Mariam has committed. According to the second stanza, the error involves indulging in, rather than refraining from, something that is characterized as "lawfull" liberty. When the chorus goes on to specify the error as a fault of *speech,* however, its "lawfull" status seems to disappear. By stanza five, the error is the distinctly illegitimate and usually masculine political one of "usurping upon anothers right." There is a corresponding contradiction in the chorus's views of the "virtue" it is advocating. In the third stanza, which stresses the duty of relinquishing desires for speech and fame, the virtue being advocated is quite distinct from the possession of physical chastity; the woman may be "most chast" even if she does grant a "private word" to someone other than her husband. By stanza five, however, the "redefinition" of chastity that Goreau remarks has occurred: "her mind if not peculiar [private] is not chast." Which formulation about chastity are we to take as authoritative?

Interpreting the chorus's speech becomes even more difficult when we try to read it—as Goreau does not—in its dramatic context, as an ethical prescription for this particular heroine. The final lines seem to suggest that Mariam's tragic fate could have been averted had she refrained from speaking her mind to anyone other than her husband. But the play's subsequent development makes this notion absurd: it is precisely because Mariam speaks her mind—not only to others but also, and above all, to her husband—that she loses her life. She articulates in Herod's presence a version of the same principle we have heard her assert to Sohemus: "I cannot frame disguise, nor never taught / My face a looke dissenting from my thought," she says, refusing to smile when Herod bids her to (4.3.1407–8). It is, however, not wholly accurate to say she brings on her death by transgressively speaking her mind. The problem is that she *both* speaks too freely *and* refuses to give her body to Herod—its rightful owner, according to the chorus. She censors the wrong thing: his phallus rather than her tongue.

The problem of her sexual withholding is addressed by the chorus only obliquely, in the form of the (apparently) rhetorical question "When to their Husbands they themselves doe bind, / Doe they not wholy give themselves away?" By the end of its speech, the chorus has evidently suppressed altogether the crucial issue of Mariam's denial of Herod's sexual rights. The strange logic of the speech anticipates that of Herod's later accusation of Mariam: "shee's unchaste, / Her mouth will ope to ev'ry strangers eare" (4.7.1704–5). The equation of physical unchastity with verbal license, expressed through the provocative image of the woman's mouth opening to a man's ear, alludes, perhaps, to anti-Catholic propaganda against Jesuit priests as Satanic corrupters of women and of the institution of confession, where male "strangers" received women's secrets. The image of a female mouth promiscuously opening to a male ear rewrites Mariam's fault as one of double excess or "openness," whereas what the play actually shows is that Mariam's verbal openness is a sign of sexual closure. Her behavior entails a "property" crime in certain ways more threatening than adultery is to the ideological conception of marriage because it takes to a logical extreme, and deploys against the husband, the concept of female chastity.

Neither the chorus nor any other character in the drama can clearly articulate this central problem in Mariam's behavior. The chorus concludes by asserting that Mariam would have been "free from feare, as well as innocent," if only she had been willing to forbear filling "any's ears but one" with her words. The pronoun *one* evidently refers here, as it does in the earlier phrase "none but one," to the husband. If, however, we grant that the play as a whole makes it extremely hard to read the chorus's question about whether women should give themselves "wholly" away in marriage as requiring a simple affirmative answer, then it becomes necessary to ask, as Catherine Belsey does, whether the term *one* might alternatively refer to the wife herself.[43] Since Mariam is in danger because she speaks to her husband—and against his sexual will and his property rights—perhaps Cary's point, if not the chorus's, is that if a wife has such thoughts she "would be wiser to keep them to herself, precisely because in marriage they are no longer her own" (Belsey, pp. 173–74). But in Mariam's case, such silence or self-censoring would not have any practical efficacy unless it were accompanied by sexual surrender and its psychic corollary: the split between being and seeming which Mariam terms "hypocrisy." The chorus's ethical precepts begin to look at best incoherent, at worst cynical, a dark twisting of the "be and seem" motto into a prescription for wives to seem as others think they should be. Belsey suggests, indeed, that with this speech "the transparency of the text falters as it confronts its own theorization of its challenge to marital absolutism" (174). Although I'm less sure than she is that the text is ever "transparent," I agree that there is a peculiar opacity in the chorus's speech against a wife's right to use "publike language."

That opacity, I think, has something to do with the fact that the chorus's speech is the moment in the drama where Cary most directly interrogates her play's own right to exist. However we construe the injunction that wives should reveal their thoughts to "none but one," it is clear that the chorus draws around the wife a circle of privacy so small that she would err by *circulating* a manuscript, much less publishing it. Had Cary obeyed the rule of privacy set forth by her chorus, she might possibly have written a play, but we would not be reading it. Even the act of writing, which generally requires some will and ambition, comes under implicit attack in the chorus's portrait of the ideal wife who "bare[s] herself of power as well as will" and who is urged to relinquish in particular all desire for "glory." The chorus's speech exposes the logical implications of the legal doctrine of coverture, which held that "the very being . . . of the woman is suspended during the marriage."

The *Life* of Cary by her daughter provides three interesting and ideologically complex glosses on the chorus's speech. "He was very absolute," the *Life* says of Sir Henry, "and though she [Elizabeth Cary] had a strong will, she had learned to make it obey his. The desire to please him had power to make her do that, that others could have scarce believed possible for her; as taking care of the house in all things (to which she could have no inclination but what his will gave her)" (14). The *Life* also tells us that Cary often resorted to sleep to cure depression; she could sleep "when she would" (17), which seems a near analogue for the paradoxical ideal of willed willessness projected by the chorus's speech. And finally the *Life* recounts that Cary gave to her eldest daughter a principle of behavior that contains a significant exception to the absolutist doctrine of wifely obedience: "Wheresoever reason and conscience would permit her, she should prefer the will of another before her own" (13).

Cary's exception has analogues in numerous Protestant works that challenged the doctrine of absolutist royal sovereignty by positing for the individual (male) subject a limited right of passive disobedience to the prince or magistrate on grounds of Christian conscience. Moreover, Cary's statement (as reported by her Catholic daughter) corresponds with certain statements by both radical Protestant and Catholic theorists on the wife's right to disobey her husband—the sovereign's domestic representative and analogue in the little body politic of the family—if his commands should conflict with God's. In an article on recusant women in Renaissance England, Marie Bowlands mentions the case of Margaret Clitherow, who "asked her confessor whether she might receive priests and serve God without her husband's consent. She was told that the less he knew the better, and that nothing could override her duty to serve God."[44] Bowlands also cites a passage from the Catholic *Treatise on Christian Renunciation* which advised women that "your husbands over your soul have no authority and over your bodies but limited power."[45]

During this turbulent era of British history, such formulations appear with enough frequency to justify us in saying they comprise an ideological topos of "minority dissent." Articulated by Catholic and Protestant writers, male and female, such statements clearly drive a wedge into the apparently hegemonic social rule linking female chastity with silence and obedience. The dissenting female voice, historical or fictional, invokes religious principles to redefine chastity in a way that dissociates it from obedience to (certain) figures of male authority. Consider, for instance, the speech of Milton's "Lady" to her would-be king and seducer, Comus: "Thou canst not touch the freedom of my mind / With all thy charms, although this corporal rind / Thou hast immanacl'd, while Heav'n sees good" (*A Maske* [1637], ll. 663–65); or consider the speech of a beleaguered heroine in an anonymous play of 1620: "Tho my body be confin'd his prisoner, / Yet my mind is free" (*Swetnam the Woman Hater Arraigned by Women*, 2.1.97–98).[46]

The language Mariam uses to justify her course of action—resistance to the sexual demands and other wishes of a husband who is also her king—clearly belongs to this religious tradition of minority dissent: "They can but my life destroy, / My soule is free from adversaries power" (4.8.1843–44), she says after Herod has falsely accused her of adultery and, spurred on by Salome, proclaimed his intention to execute her. Although the chorus continues to argue that Mariam should have submitted to Herod's authority—thereby paying her marital "debt" and winning "long famous life" (4.8.1939)—Elaine Beilin is surely right to argue that the play's final act reconceives (and simplifies) the conflict between the chorus's perspective on wifely duty and Mariam's by presenting the heroine's death as an allegorical version of Christ's crucifixion.[47] Josephus had shown Mariam meeting her death with noble fortitude, but Cary adds to her source numerous details that give Mariam a specifically Christological heroism. The messenger who describes her death to Herod in Act 5 apostrophizes her as "your heavenly selfe" and goes on to compare her to a phoenix, a traditional symbol of Christ. A parallel between Mariam and Christ is also implied by the suicide of the butler who had been suborned by Salome to accuse Mariam of seeking to poison Herod. Cary's butler, like Judas, hangs himself from a tree in remorse for his betrayal; in Josephus, there is no mention of the butler's death.

Cary further revises her source by specifying the mode of Mariam's death. Josephus simply says that Herod ordered her executed, whereas Cary places considerable emphasis on the "fact" that she is beheaded. This detail, unremarked by Cary's critics so far as I know, seems an overdetermined allusion—to Christ's harbinger, John the Baptist, beheaded by Salome; to a recent queen of Scotland, Mary, whose son ruled England when Cary wrote her play and who was in the eyes of many English Catholics a victim of Protestant tyranny; and also, perhaps, to Anne Boleyn, killed by a royal husband who had broken with the Catholic church to divorce his first wife and who was explicitly likened to the tyrant Herod by some of his disapproving subjects.[48] Infused with rich but warily coded theological meanings, Cary's play surrounds Mariam's death with an aura of mysterious sanctification altogether absent from Josephus's narrative.

There is, however, a price for such sanctification, with its implicit justification of the ethical path Cary herself would eventually follow: the path that led her to defy her husband's authority on the grounds of conscience. In the play's final act, Mariam is not only absent from the stage but also represented, through the messenger's account of her last moments, as a woman who has somehow learned to bridle her tongue. On the way to her execution, she is cruelly taunted by her mother, who, after having urged Mariam throughout the play to despise Herod, now suddenly—evidently to save her own skin—condemns Mariam for "wronging" Herod's princely authority (5.1.1986). Enraged at the report of Alexandra's behavior, Herod asks, "What answere did her princely daughter make?" The messenger replies, "She made no answere" (5.1.1992); and he goes on to stress Mariam's new virtue of silence by remarking that she died "as if . . . she were content" after "she some silent prayer had sed" (2026–27). The wickedness associated with the female tongue and with women in general, according to Constabarus's misogynist tirade against the sex to which Salome belongs (4.6.1578–1619), is here symbolically transferred from Mariam to her mother, who takes Mariam's place as the object of Herod's censoring wrath: "Why stopt you not her mouth? where had she words / to darke that, that Heaven made so brighte?" (5.1.1979–80), Herod asks the messenger; and the reader remembers that Herod has just exercised his power to stop Mariam's mouth. Once he has done so, in what seems to me the play's most complex and ambivalent irony, he suddenly starts to value Mariam's words with passionate desire: "But what sweet tune did this faire dying Swan / Afford thine eare: tell all, omit no letter" (5.1.2008–9), he says; and again, in an exchange that seems designed to effect a kind of wish-fulfilling revenge on the tyrannical censorious husband, he exclaims: "Oh say, what said she more? each word she sed / Shall be the food whereon my heart is fed" (2013–14). To which the messenger replies, reporting Mariam's words, "Tell thou my Lord thou saw'st me loose my breath." "Oh that I could that sentence now controule," Herod responds, ostensibly referring to his own "sentence" of death. His remark might also, however, refer to Mariam's utterance: by killing her, he has after all lost the power to control her speech. His "word," as he says later, made her "bleed," but it cannot bring her back to life.

It seems significant that Cary only imagines Herod coming to value Mariam's voice at the moment when the disputed property of her body is absent both from the stage and from the narrative "present": "Her body is divided from her head," the Nuntio asserts, and the graphic image of the dead and sundered woman (which occurs nowhere in Josephus's text) highlights the price Mariam has paid for her freedom of conscience. Through its characterization of Mariam, the play offers two different models, neither very satisfactory from a modern feminist perspective, for a woman's ability to exercise her will: according to both models, which might be called the domestic and the religious respectively, the will is exercised with the ultimate aim of losing it or, rather, of adopting, as an object of desire, the effacement of personal desire. Cary's heroine, unable to choose the first model by subordinating her will to her husband's, opts instead for an extreme version of the second, a martyr-like death: "Now earth farewell, though I be yet but yong, / Yet I, me thinks, have knowne thee too too long" (4.8.1902–3). In so choosing, Mariam, like Richard Wilbur's nuns "keeping their difficult balance," finds an uneasy compromise solution to the conflicting behavioral models provided by Salome on the one hand and Graphina on the other: by the former's example of aggressive rebellion against patriarchal rules and the latter's example of passive subservience to a man (rewarded by his romantic adoration).

How are we to assess Mariam's compromise solution from a modern feminist perspective informed by an awareness of the social and imaginative options open to a woman like Elizabeth Cary? Although Cary's representation of Mariam, like Cary's daughter's representation of her mother, shows us women *behaving* in ways that anticipate the "principled disobedience" characteristic of some radical Protestant women during the English civil wars, neither of the Cary texts shows a heroine explicitly justifying independent female behavior. The radicalism of these texts, in so far as we may call it that, occurs chiefly in small details of plot and, in the case of the play, through oblique intertextual allusions, moments of rhetorical tension, and the words of female characters such as Salome, Alexandra, and Herod's first wife, Doris; in other words, what is radical must be inferred or teased out by a reader who assumes that an emphatic "no" may mean a "yes"—a reader, in short, sympathetic with psychoanalytic modes of interpretation and also aware that the censorship so often constitutive of the female author's text may derive not only from what we call the "unconscious" but also from direct social pressures or from that combination of the two known as internalization.

Sympathetic though we may be with the covertly radical dimension of Cary's play and her life story, we nonetheless need to remark that other seventeenth-century women, both historical and fictional, were considerably less oblique than Cary and her daughter in arguing for and / or in demonstrating some form of female independence. One has only to think of the lively and complex heroine of Middleton's and Dekker's *The Roaring Girl* (1611) or the Protestant radical Katherine Chidley; the latter, in her *Justification of the Independent Churches of Christ* (1641), writes: "I pray you tell me what authority the unbeleeving husband hath over the conscience of his beleeving wife. It is true he hath authority over her in bodily and civill respects but not to be a Lord over her conscience."[49] On the spectrum suggested (very incompletely) by such examples, Cary's play appears quite conservative in its statement about women's social being. That conservatism derives from many sources—above all, I think, from the fact that the ideologies of gender, religion, and (privileged) class worked together, in the case of Cary's play, to limit its potential either to reach a broad audience or to make a clear critique of women's status as a male property category.

Consider again the play's contradictory mode of existence as a published Senecan closet drama. Intriguing as it is that this female-authored play was published at all—and evidently with Cary's acquiescence, if not with her active approval—the fact remains that it had a limited and mainly elite readership.[50] Like the Judith Shakespeare imagined by Virginia Woolf, Cary was barred from significant participation in the world of the London stage. Had she been able to write for the public theater, instead of being simply an occasional member of an audience in the city and a closet dramatist at home, her play itself might have been differently constructed; it would surely have reached a wider audience in her own day and later. As the case of Shakespeare amply testifies, access to the commercial stage bears no necessary relation to the articulation of progressive political positions. Such access, however, which opens a play to scrutiny from members of different classes, did frequently serve in Renaissance England as an enabling condition for the development of certain politically radical interpretations of drama. And such interpretations may or may not have been intended by an individual author.

Cary's gender alone would have served to keep her away from the London stage, but her gender and class aspirations and religious beliefs all worked together to create *Mariam's* extremely ambivalent ideological statement about women as male "property." That statement concludes with, though it's not fully constituted by, Mariam choosing (under great duress) to turn her critical rebellious energies inward to self-reproach and upward toward a transcendental religious ideal of chaste female martyrdom. Cary thus rejects the option of turning Mariam's energies outward to some form of collective action by allying her heroine's rebellion against Herod with the "base-born" Salome's critique of the sexual double standard in divorce laws. The vilifying of Salome is of course dictated—but only in part—by generic conventions and by the historical plot Cary inherited; I would argue, however, that Cary's own class position and biases contribute substantially to what she does with Salome. Even more than Herod, Salome is implicated in Cary's use of her drama to rewrite the social story of her marriage. For Salome stands in relation to Mariam as Cary stood in relation to her own husband and mother-in-law; the latter's dislike of Elizabeth, vividly recorded in the *Life,* may well have entailed open or veiled insults about base birth like those which Mariam directs at her sister-in-law.[51] If, as I am suggesting, a desire to ennoble herself and take revenge on the family into which she had been married against her will underlies Cary's identification with the "pureblooded" Mariam, that desire contributes to the play's occlusion of the similarities between Mariam's and Salome's situations as rebellious wives. And the separation between Mariam and Salome, drawn in terms of their social status, contributes in turn to the sharp distinction the play draws between the (religiously valuable) idea of female freedom of conscience and Salome's advocacy of female freedom to pursue one's sexual desires. By vilifying Salome's character and opinions as "base," Cary ultimately ratifies the ideological "truth" proclaimed by the authoritative voices of the Counter-Reformation church (and most Protestant sects as well), by the voices of men in the English middle and upper classes, and by the voices of almost everyone who participated in the Renaissance debates on the nature of womankind. That "truth" is that, whatever one may think about the qualities of a woman's mind or soul, her body is base and in need of governance.

The limits of Cary's choices—and her heroine's—are complex products of a specific set of historical circumstances *and* of an individual psyche capable, to some degree, of interrogating, and even defying, the "customs" rooted in the material and ideological aspects of gender, religion, and class. The complexes of social facts to which those three abstract terms refer have changed enormously since the seventeenth century. Nonetheless, the heuristic interest of Cary's case for late-twentieth-century feminists may well lie in the challenge it offers for thinking about how modern ideologies of gender, radical or conservative, continue to be formed—and deformed—by forces of class and religion that are partly, but not wholly, within our powers to understand and to alter.

NOTES

For invaluable help in the preparation of this essay I would like to thank
Elaine Beilin, David Kastan, Joseph Loewenstein, Mary Nyquist, Mary Poovey,
and David Simpson. I would also, and above all, like to thank my mother, Mary
Anne Ferguson, in whose honor the essay was written.

1. The quotation about loving plays is from *The Lady Falkland: Her Life,* ed.
Richard Simpson (London: Catholic Publishing and Bookselling Co., 1861), p.
54. The *Life,* by one of the four of Cary's daughters who became nuns, exists in
a single manuscript found in the English Benedictine convent in Cambray and
later moved to the Imperial Archives at Lille. Subsequent references to this work
will be given in the body of the essay.

2. For useful discussions of Cary's life, writings (many of which are evidently
lost), and status as the first Englishwoman to publish an original play, see Nancy
Cotton Pearse, "Elizabeth Cary, Renaissance Playwright," *Texas Studies in Language and Literature* 18 (1977), 601–8; Sandra K. Fischer, "Elizabeth Cary and
Tyranny, Domestic and Religious," in *Silent But for the Word: Tudor Women as
Patrons, Translators, and Writers of Religious Works,* ed. Margaret P. Hannay
(Kent, Ohio: Kent State University Press, 1985), pp. 225–37; Elaine V. Beilin,
"Elizabeth Cary and *The Tragedy of Mariam,*" *Papers on Language and Literature*
16 (Winter 1980), 45–64 (rpt. in *Redeeming Eve: Women Writers of the English
Renaissance* [Princeton: Princeton University Press, 1987]); and Betty Travitsky,
"The *Feme Covert* in Elizabeth Cary's *Mariam,*" in *Ambiguous Realities: Women
in the Middle Ages and Renaissance,* ed. Carole Levin and Jeanie Watson (Detroit: Wayne State University Press, 1987), pp. 184–96. See also the introductory material to the selections from Cary's works in *The Paradise of Women,* ed.
Betty Travitsky (Westport, Conn.: Greenwood Press, 1981), pp. 209–12; in *The
Female Spectator,* ed. Mary R. Mahl and Helene Koon (Bloomington: Indiana
University Press, 1977), pp. 99–102; and in *Kissing the Rod: An Anthology of
Seventeenth-Century Women's Verse,* ed. Germaine Greer et al. (New York: Farrar,
Straus & Giroux, 1988), pp. 54–55.

3. The fact that the play was entered in the Stationers' Register (Dec. 1612)
and licensed by the Master of Revels leads its modern editor, A. C. Dunstan, to
surmise that it "can hardly have been printed without the author's knowledge
and at least acquiescence" (*The Tragedie of Mariam,* 1613, Malone Society Reprints [Oxford: Horace Hart for the University Press, 1914], p. ix). See below,
note 37, for a discussion of the cryptic comments in the *Life* on Cary's (possible)
relation to the press.

4. Angeline Goreau's view of the play as univocally conservative is discussed
later in this essay. In *The Tragedies of Herod and Mariamne* (New York: Columbia
University Press, 1940, p. 90), Maurice Valency states that "the author sides
throughout with Herod," having "a low opinion of women in general."

5. For persuasive evidence of Cary's reliance on Lodge, whose conversion to
Catholicism in the late 1590s may have sparked Cary's interest in his work, see
A. C. Dunstan's introduction to *Mariam,* pp. v–ix. See Valency, *Tragedies,* and

also Gordon Braden, *Renaissance Tragedy and the Senecan Tradition* (New Haven: Yale University Press, 1985), for information about other versions of the Herod and Mariam story on the Renaissance stage.

6. To study Cary's revisions of Josephus, which are more complex than this essay can indicate, I have used both the Loeb Classical Library bilingual edition of the *Antiquities of the Jews* (Book 15 is in vol. 8 of the Loeb *Josephus,* trans. Ralph Marcus, ed. and completed by Allen Wikgren [Cambridge, Mass.: Harvard University Press, 1963]), and Thomas Lodge, *The Famous and Memorable Works of Josephus* (London: Peter Short, 1602; copy in the Beinecke Library, Yale University).

7. Quoted from Dunstan's edition of *Mariam,* "The Argument," no page. All subsequent quotations of *Mariam* are from this edition, which is full of textual problems I have not sought to correct. A new, annotated edition, prepared by Margaret W. Ferguson and Barry Weller, is forthcoming from the University of California Press.

8. For brief discussions of the verbal and structural parallels between *Mariam* and *Othello* see Margaret W. Ferguson, "A Room Not Their Own: Renaissance Women as Readers and Writers," in *The Comparative Perspective on Literature,* ed. Clayton Koelb and Susan Noakes (Ithaca: Cornell University Press, 1988), pp. 93–116, and Braden, *Renaissance Tragedy,* pp. 167 and 248, note 11.

9. Quoted from Dunstan's edition of *Mariam,* which reproduces the title page of the 1613 quarto, printed by Thomas Creede for Richard Hawkins.

10. There were several women named Elizabeth Cary (also spelled Carie, Carey, Carew, or Carye) alive in the late sixteenth and early seventeenth centuries. Dunstan himself, in an early study, misattributed *Mariam* to Elizabeth Spencer Carey, a relative of Edmund Spenser's, in his *Examination of Two English Dramas* (Königsberg: Hartungsche Buchdruckerei, 1908), p. 10. See Dunstan's introduction, pp. v–ix, for the attribution to Elizabeth Tanfield Cary. Dunstan is less persuasive in his argument that the play *had* to have been written before 1605. I agree with Elaine Beilin that the dating is problematic; see her discussion of the conflicting pieces of evidence in "Elizabeth Cary and *The Tragedy of Mariam,*" esp. note 6.

11. Michel Foucault, "What Is an Author?" 1969; trans. in *Language, Counter-Memory, Practice,* ed. Donald F. Bouchard (Ithaca: Cornell University Press, 1977), pp. 113–38. Foucault has nothing to say, however, about the peculiar problems that have historically attended the notion of *female* authorship.

12. Quotations from p. vi of Richard Simpson's Preface to the *The Lady Falkland: Her Life.*

13. See Suzanne W. Hull, *Chaste, Silent & Obedient: English Books for Women 1475–1640* (San Marino: Huntington Library, 1984); see also Peter Stallybrass, "Patriarchal Territories: The Body Enclosed," in *Rewriting the Renaissance,* ed. Margaret W. Ferguson, Maureen Quilligan, and Nancy Vickers (Chicago: University of Chicago Press, 1986), pp. 123–42; Margaret W. Ferguson, "A Room Not Their Own," pp. 96–103; and Ann R. Jones, *The Currency of Eros: Women's Love Lyric in Europe, 1540–1621* (Bloomington: Indiana University Press, 1990), pp. 1–18.

14. My concept of the ideological topos is indebted to Fredric Jameson's notion of the *ideologeme* but differs from it by focusing on gender as well as class conflict; see Jameson, *The Political Unconscious: Narrative as a Socially Symbolic Act* (Ithaca: Cornell University Press, 1981), p. 81 and *passim*.

15. *Lingua* is available in R. Dodsley, *Old Plays*, ed. W. C. Hazlitt (London: Reeves and Turner, 1874), vol. 9. The quotation is from Catherine Belsey's discussion of this play in a fine chapter on "Speech and Silence." She remarks that it was republished five times before 1657 (*The Subject of Tragedy: Identity and Difference in Renaissance Drama* [London: Methuen, 1985], p. 181).

16. For the legal theory of the married woman as *feme couvert* or *covert*, see Travitsky, "The *Feme Covert* in Elizabeth Cary's *Mariam*." Blackstone defines the theory thus: "the very being of legal existence of the wife is suspended during marriage, or at least is incorporated and consolidated into that of the husband: under whose wing, protection, and cover, she performs everything," in *Commentaries of the Laws of England, Book the First* (Oxford, 1765), p. 442, quoted in Mary Poovey, *The Proper Lady and the Woman Writer* (Chicago: University of Chicago Press, 1984), pp. 6–7. The passage from T. E.'s *The Womans Lawyer; or, The Lawes Resolutions of Womens Rights* (London: John More for John Grove, 1632) is cited in Belsey, *The Subject of Tragedy*, p. 153.

17. Juan Luis Vives, *De Institutione Feminae Christianae*, quoted from the translation by Richard Hyrde (1540) in *Vives and the Renascence Education of Women*, ed. Foster Watson (New York: Longmans, Green, 1912), pp. 55, 56.

18. Gloria Kaufman, "Juan Luis Vives on the Education of Women," *Signs* 3 (1978), 891–96, quotation from 895. See also Valerie Wayne, "Some Sad Sentence: Vives' *Institution of a Christian Woman*," in *Silent But for the Word*, ed. Hannay, pp. 15–29.

19. On the frequency and economic motives of cross-class marriages, see Poovey, *The Proper Lady*, p. 11, and also the (much contested) book by Lawrence Stone, *The Family, Sex and Marriage in England 1500–1800* (London: Weidenfield and Nicholson, 1977). For a discussion of Stone's work in the context of recent scholarship in family history, see R. B. Outhwaite's Introduction to *Marriage and Society: Studies in the Social History of Marriage* (New York: St. Martin's Press, 1981). See also James Fitzmaurice, "Elizabeth Cary's *Mariam* and Jacobean Marriage," unpublished paper.

20. For information about Cary's parents and husband see, in addition to the *Life* by her daughter, two biographies that draw heavily on that text: Kenneth Murdock, *The Sun at Noon* (New York: Macmillan, 1939), and Lady Georgiana Charlotte Fullerton, *The Life of Elizabeth Lady Falkland 1585–1639*, Quarterly Series, vol. 6 (London: Burns and Oates, 1883).

21. As Nancy Cotton Pearce observes, the Cary-Tanfield marriage "raised Tanfield from the upper middle class into the gentry, and the Tanfield fortune raised Henry Cary from the gentry into the peerage" ("Elizabeth Cary," p. 602). The editor of the *Life* notes that Elizabeth Symondes was the "[d]aughter of Giles Symondes, of Claye, Norfolk, by Catherine, daughter of Sir Anthony Lee, Knight of the Garter" (p. 4). My hypothesis that Elizabeth Symondes—

descended on her *maternal* side from gentry—married somewhat "down" is based partly on the *Life*'s description of Tanfield as the son of a "younger brother" without much to pass on to his children (p. 1). The biographer also writes that Elizabeth Symondes objected to her husband's decision "to provide for himself by following his profession," relying on his "own industry" (p. 1). Working in a profession was often regarded as demeaning by members of the gentry. Cary's mother seems, moreover, to have acted like a snob in the eyes of the inhabitants of Great Tew, where the couple lived; the *DNB* entry for Sir Lawrence Tanfield cites a complaint that "she saith that we are more worthy to be ground to powder than to have any favour showed to us" (19:137; quoted in Beilin, "Elizabeth Cary," p. 49).

22. Murdock, *Sun at Noon,* p. 8.

23. Mahl and Koon note that the ransom payment "reduced the family fortunes to the extent that Sir Henry was in financial straits for many years afterward" (*Female Spectator,* p. 100). The *Life,* p. 8, says that Sir Henry's *father* raised the ransom, but this is evidently a slip for father-in-law, the provider of Elizabeth's dowry. Sir Henry's own father, as the *Life,* states on p. 1, died when his son was still a child. On the jointure settled on Elizabeth by her father, see *Life,* p. 15.

24. Elizabeth Cary's case seems to contradict Miriam Slater's contention that the term *jointure* always referred to the groom's father's counterpart to the dowry given by the bride's father ("The Weightiest Business: Marriage in an Upper Gentry Family in Seventeenth-Century England," *Past and Present* 72 [1976], 28). More research needs to be done by feminist historians and legal scholars on the incidence of the jointure in general and in particular on its use by wealthy families to circumvent the common-law doctrine of coverture. In his chapter on women in English law in *La Femme* (Recueils de la société Jean Bodin pour l'histoire comparative des institutions [Brussels: Editions de la Librairie Encyclopédique, 1959–62], 12:135–241) F. Joüon des Longrais remarks that during and for some years after Queen Elizabeth's reign privileged women were more able than they had been in the previous era to retain some property rights by means of prenuptial contracts, often enforced through the relatively new institution of equity courts (p. 236).

25. On "homosocial" exchanges, see Eve K. Sedgwick, *Between Men: English Literature and Male Homosocial Desire* (New York: Columbia University Press, 1985). When Elizabeth's father disinherited her for using "her" jointure in a way he considered imprudent, he settled the estate on her eldest son, Lucius, or, in the event of Lucius's death, on the next eldest son, thus ensuring the continuity of the patriarchal line. On the disinheritance, see the brief account of it in *Life,* pp. 15–16, and the supplemental information (mostly conjectural) in the editor's Appendix, p. 127.

26. Josephus once mentions Mariam's "jeering" at Salome and her mother for their "low birth" (*Jewish Antiquities* 15:219, Loeb ed. 8:105), but he does not reiterate the point as Cary does nor does he have Herod admit after Mariam's death that he has cruelly "overthrowne" the "royall line" of Judea, the blood of which line ran in "her purer vaines" (5.1.2120–22).

27. The so-called "Queen's privilege" allowed royal women to be legally treated, even if married, as *feme sole* [*sic*] rather than *feme couverte* (*La Femme*, 12:147). On royal women as the "exceptions" that in most respects proved the patriarchal rule of women's subordinate status see Ferguson et al., *Rewriting the Renaissance*, p. xxix, and the essays therein by Louis A. Montrose, Shelia ffolliott, and Constance Jordan. Cary's fascination with historical figures of royal women is even more evident in her later play, *The History of the most unfortunate Prince, King Edward the Second* than in *Mariam*. In *Edward*, evidently written in 1627, first published in 1680, and long attributed to Sir Henry Cary, Elizabeth Cary rewrites previous versions of the history from a perspective sympathetic to Edward's wife, Queen Isabel. The play was eventually pubished in *The Harleian Miscellany* (1808) and reprinted by AMS Press (New York, 1965).

28. Travitsky, Beilin, Fischer, and Pearce have discussed *Mariam* as a refraction of Cary's personal difficulties in reconciling her "independent" spirit (Travitsky, *Paradise*, p. 216) with her conception of wifely duty.

29. See Salome's soliloquy in 1.4, where she vows to be the "custome breaker" who will "Shewe my Sexe the way to freedomes doore" (319–20). Mariam herself argues for the validity of the Mosaic law of divorce in a tense conversation with Herod's first wife, Doris; see 4.8.1861–64. Although Mariam ostensibly justifies divorce here only for the man, her actions suggest that she desires a similar right for herself.

30. On the conflict between the humanist notion of noble fame and the scorn for "clerkly" labor characteristic of the feudal nobility, see Margaret W. Ferguson, *Trials of Desire: Renaissance Defenses of Poetry* (New Haven: Yale University Press, 1983), pp. 19–20.

31. Davies's fondness for his erstwhile "Pupill," as he calls her, may help explain why he includes her with two higher ranking and wealthier ladies. Although Cary's relative poverty makes her an unlikely source of patronage, Sandra K. Fischer rightly observes that Cary was "quite renowned as a hostess and leader of intellectual coteries" ("Elizabeth Cary and Tyranny," p. 230). See Pearl Hogrefe, *Tudor Women: Commoners and Queens* (Ames: Iowa State University Press, 1975), p. 135, on other poets who wrote flattering dedicatory verses to Cary both before and after her marriage.

32. This and subsequent citations to Davies are from *The Complete Works of John Davies of Hereford*, ed. Alexander B. Grosart, 2 vols. (n.d.; rpt. New York: AMS Press, 1967), 2:5, "The Muses Sacrifice" (separate pagination for each poem). The reference to a play set in Syracuse is to a lost drama apparently written earlier than *Mariam;* see Dunstan's Introduction, p. viii.

33. For acute analyses of the double binds affecting the woman of unusual achievement, see Mary Anne Ferguson's Introduction to *Images of Women in Literature,* 4th ed. (Boston: Houghton Mifflin, 1986) and her "No More Squeezing into One," in *Face to Face, Fathers, Mothers, Masters, Monsters: Essays for a Nonsexist Future,* ed. Meg McGavran Murray (Westport, Conn.: Greenwood Press, 1983), pp. 257–71. See also Patricia Labalme's Introduction to her collection of essays *Beyond Their Sex: Learned Women of the European Past* (New York: New York University Press, 1980) and many of the essays in that volume,

including especially Margaret L. King, "Book-Lined Cells: Women and Humanism in the Early Italian Renaissance."

34. Anne Bradstreet, "The Prologue," stanza 5, quoted from *The Works of Anne Bradstreet*, ed. John Harvard Ellis (Gloucester, Mass.: Peter Smith, 1962), p. 101.

35. Denny's poem is quoted by Josephine Roberts in "An Unpublished Quarrel Concerning the Suppression of Lady Mary Wroth's *Urania*," *Notes and Queries* 222 (Dec. 1977), 533. I am indebted to Ann Rosalind Jones for bringing this poem to my attention; see her "City Women and Their Audiences," in *Rewriting the Renaissance*, p. 301.

36. Maureen Quilligan argues that Wroth's written offer to withdraw her book (in a letter to the Duke of Buckingham) is not accompanied by any hard evidence that she actually did stop its publication. See Quilligan, "The Constant Subject: Instability and Female Authority in Wroth's *Urania* Poems," in *Soliciting Interpretation: Literary Theory and Seventeenth-Century English Poetry*, ed. Elizabeth Harvey and Katherine Maus (Chicago: University of Chicago Press, forthcoming).

37. Beilin, "Elizabeth Cary," p. 48, note 6. Cary later dissociated herself from the "worn-out form of saying I printed it against my will, moved by the importunity of friends"; her statement occurs, however, in a letter dedicating to Queen Henrietta Maria of England a work of Catholic polemic (by a man) for which Cary served as a translator, not an author. See the prefatory letter to her *Reply of the Most Illustrious Cardinal of Perron to the Answeare of the Most Excellent King of Britain*, 1630; quoted in the Appendix to the *Life*, p. 172.

38. For evidence of Sir Henry's conventional views on women's duty as "private" beings see, for instance, his letter of 5 April 1626 complaining of his "apostate" wife's "over-busy nature" and lamenting that she refuses to retire "quietly" to her mother's country house (in *Life*, Appendix, p. 132).

39. "With one exception," as Dunstan notes in his Introduction to *Mariam* (p. xii), "the names of all the characters are taken from Josephus." The exception is the name of the slave woman loved by Pheroras. Josephus and Lodge mention a "Glaphyra," wife to a certain Alexander, near the part of the narrative in which Pheroras's story appears; even if, as Dunstan surmises, Cary's "Graphina" was suggested by "Glaphyra," the coinage is nonetheless more purposive, I think, than critics have allowed.

40. As Germaine Greer notes (*Kissing the Rod*, p. 56), Cary alludes here to Plutarch's account of Caesar weeping when he learned of the death of his popular rival, Pompey. The anecdote, which appears in both the "Life of Caesar" and that of Pompey, emphasizes the irony of Caesar's grief: he had, after all, ardently desired and indirectly engineered Pompey's murder. Cary's analogy works to imply that Mariam is Herod's political rival and also that her desires somehow *caused* his (supposed) death in Rome, where he has gone, ironically enough, to answer to Julius Caesar for using murder as a means to the throne.

41. Angeline Goreau, "Two English women in the seventeenth century: notes for an anatomy of feminine desire," in *Western Sexuality: Practice and Precept in Past and Present Times*, ed. Philippe Ariès and André Béjin, trans. Anthony Forster (Oxford: Blackwell, 1985), p. 105.

42. Angeline Goreau, *The Whole Duty of a Woman: Female Writers in Seventeenth-Century England* (Garden City, N.Y.: Doubleday, 1985), p. 13.

43. Belsey, *The Subject of Tragedy,* p. 173.

44. "Mr. John Mush's Life of Margaret Clitherow," quoted in Marie Bowlands, "Recusant Women 1560–1640," in *Women in English Society 1500–1800,* ed. Mary Prior (London: Methuen, 1985), p. 165.

45. Henry Garnet, *Treatise on Christian Renunciation,* quoted in Bowlands, "Recusant Women," p. 165.

46. The quoted lines come from John Milton, *The Complete Shorter Poems,* ed. John Carey (London: Longman, 1971), p. 209, and *"Swetnam the Woman Hater": The Controversy and the Play,* ed. Coryl Crandall (Purdue: Purdue University Press, 1969), p. 73.

47. Beilin, "Elizabeth Cary," pp. 58–60. See also Sandra K. Fischer, "Elizabeth Cary and Tyranny," esp. pp. 235–37.

48. There is complex evidence, in literary sources and in polemical religious and political tracts, for an overdetermined topical allegory in *Mariam,* an allegory toward which I can only gesture in this essay. I am grateful to Peter Rudnytsky for helping me trace allusions to Henry VIII in Cary's text. The evidence suggests that many English Catholics criticized Henry VIII by figuring him as a type of Herod-the-tyrant, a composite character which, like its morality play predecessor, often conflated the identities of three different biblical Herods— Herod the Great, slaughterer of the innocents; Herod Antipas, who judged Christ and ordered John the Baptist's death; and Herod Agrippa. I'm indebted for this information to Rebecca W. Bushnell's fine summary of scholarship on the medieval Herod figure and her analyses of various humanist Herod plays in *Tragedies of Tyrants: Political Thought and Theater in the English Renaissance* (Ithaca, N.Y.: Cornell University Press, forthcoming), chap. 3. For depictions of Henry-as-Herod that seem particularly important for Cary's *Mariam,* see Nicholas Harpsfield, *A Treatise on the Pretended Divorce between Henry VIII and Catharine of Aragon* (written ca. 1530), Camden Society, New Series, 21 (London: Nicholas Pocock, 1878; rpt. New York: Johnson Reprint Corp., n.d.), p. 249, comparing Henry to Herod as lascivious adulterers; and George Buchanan's play *Baptistes sive calumnia* (1578), in which Buchanan uses John the Baptist's story to criticize the fate of one of the most famous victims of Henry VIII's struggle to legitimize his divorce from Catherine. As Buchanan himself remarked when he was facing the Inquisition in Portugal, "I represented the accusation and death of Thomas More . . . and I provided a portrait of tyranny at that time" (quoted in Rebecca W. Bushnell, *Tragedies of Tyrants,* chap. 3). Further support for my hypothesis of a complex topical allegory, rooted in Catholic writings in the years after the "Anglican Schism," lies in a sixteenth-century report that Robert Garnier represented Mary Stuart in his characterization of Cleopatra in *Marc Antoine.* See Gillian Jondorf, *Robert Garnier and the Themes of Political Tragedy in the Sixteenth Century* (Cambridge: Cambridge University Press, 1969), p. 29.

49. Katherine Chidley, *Justification of the Independent Churches of Christ* (London: W. Larner, 1641), p. 26.

50. As Gordon Braden observes in *Renaissance Tragedy*, the Herod and Mariamne story was enormously popular on the Renaissance stage, but the line of drama in the Senecan style favored by Lady Pembroke remained "a fairly elite and circumscribed affair" (pp. 166–67, 171).

51. See *Life*, pp. 7–8, for Elizabeth Cary's strained relation with her mother-in-law, a woman who "loved much to be humoured" and who took Elizabeth's books away when she failed to be sufficiently humble and attentive.

JEAN FERGUSON CARR

The Polemics of Incomprehension: Mother and Daughter in Pride and Prejudice

She was a woman of mean understanding, little information, and uncertain temper.

—Jane Austen, *Pride and Prejudice*

Stupidity (incomprehension) in the novel is always polemical: it inter-
acts dialogically with an intelligence (a lofty pseudo intelligence) with
which it polemicizes and whose mask it tears away.... at its heart
always lies a polemical failure to understand someone else's discourse,
someone else's pathos-charged lie that has appropriated the world
and aspires to conceptualize it, a polemical failure to understand generally accepted, canonized, inveterately false languages with their lofty
labels for things and events.

—Mikhail Bakhtin, "Discourse in the Novel"

My first epigraph depicts the fictional mother, Mrs. Bennet in Jane
Austen's *Pride and Prejudice* (1813), who is identified by her exclusion
from the realms of sense and power, and is contained within her comic
role.[1] As such, she stands in uneasy relationship to her daughter, Elizabeth, who both shares her mother's exclusion and seeks to dissociate herself from her devalued position by being knowing and witty where her
mother is merely foolish.

My second epigraph, from Bakhtin's *The Dialogic Imagination*, raises
questions about the social functions and effects of what is perceived as
knowing discourse and what is perceived as meaningless babble.[2] What
is usually identified as intelligence is the force that constructs the social
order, creates canons, names names, and decides what is acceptable. It is
central, focal, organizing. This "authoritative word," what Bakhtin terms
"the word of the fathers," "permits no play with the context framing it,

no play with its borders, no gradual and flexible transitions, no spontaneously creative stylizing variants on it. . . . One cannot divide it up— agree with one part, accept but not completely another part, reject utterly a third part" (pp. 342–43). Stupidity appears as a weakness that has no place in this proper order, that does the wrong thing and uses the wrong words, is unacceptable or embarrassing. Judged by the unity of the father's word, it seems incoherent or unproductive. Yet such "stupidity (incomprehension) in the novel is always polemical" (p. 403), interacting dialogically with authoritative discourse to disrupt its proper names and categories.

Incomprehension exposes the father's words to play, to jokes. The prototypical literary character who deploys such incomprehension is the fool, whose nonsense reveals gaps in the seamless authority of the father's word, for "by his very uncomprehending presence he makes strange the world of social conventionality" (p. 404). Yet as Freud argues in *Jokes and Their Relation to the Unconscious,* the naïve's "effect" depends on our conviction that he is unaware of (in Freud's terms, "it is not present in him" or he "does not possess") the inhibitions that govern most social discourse, or else he will be judged "not naïve but impudent." If we are not so convinced, "we do not laugh at him but are indignant at him."[3] The fool is a professional who plays the part of a naïve. His power is instrumental, defined not in terms of what he can "possess" for himself but by the effect he has on those in power. Fools exemplify what Freud calls a *"misleading [misverständlich] naïveté,"* representing "themselves as naïve, so as to enjoy a liberty that they would not otherwise be granted" *(Jokes,* p. 184). As long as liberty is something that is "granted," as long as fools do not expect to be made kings, the power of the father remains fundamentally intact.

Yet there is a type of incomprehension whose polemical effects are not finally so easily contained. Its social and literary prototype is the figure of the mother, who shares her child's exclusion from the languages of adulthood and power, and who has an interest in exposing the restraints imposed by patriarchy. A mother like Mrs. Bennet of *Pride and Prejudice* is not in a position to understand the polemics of her incomprehension. In the patriarchal culture in which Austen wrote, such an exposure must be indirect and guarded, or even unaware of its own threat and seriousness. The mother cannot afford to get her own jokes, nor can others accept the implications of her comedy. Her comedy hovers uncomfortably between unawareness and impudence, between triviality and threat. Unlike the fool, her "stupidity (incomprehension)" may not be sanctioned by the novel's explicit directives. It is often understood as simply ridiculous, even by the novel's other outsiders.

It is a critical commonplace to laud a fool's ability to "teach" authoritative speakers to laugh at their rigidity or to expose the faults and follies of a society's discourse.[4] But Mrs. Bennet is primarily defined not in such a direct relationship with authoritative speakers, not as "wife" who challenges "husband," but in her displaced role of mother who guides and restrains her children according to conventions that she herself need not comprehend and has not authorized. Her comedy is constrained by this dual role, by the effect of her foolishness on the children who must grow up under patriarchy. Yet stupidity is *always* polemical even when it is not explicitly understood, even when it is not incorporated into the novel's thematic designs. It may function not as a local challenge to individual failures of perception but as a sign of a general ideological confusion. The mother's position can be neither dismissed nor acknowledged. She persists at the margins of the novel as an irritating, troublesome, and yet indispensable figure.

In *Pride and Prejudice,* as in many nineteenth-century novels, the mother's function is misleadingly represented. Mrs. Bennet *is* a "woman of mean understanding, little information, and uncertain temper," but this representation serves complex interests. To accept her as merely a figure of ridicule is to prevent any investigation of those interests, to ignore the ways in which this novel, in Pierre Macherey's words, is "haunted" by what it cannot say. We must, instead, conduct a double reading, attending not only to what Macherey describes as "that which is formally accounted for, expressed, and even concluded" but also to what is left unspoken or implicit.[5] We need to attend to the novel's resistances, to what is produced only to be quickly dismissed. We thus "make strange" not only the ideology figured in the novel's social world but the ideology guiding the author's representations of social relations and conventions. We thereby consider tensions that remain tacit, that are neither authorized nor expunged, but that make the novel's resolution of social conflicts unfinished or overdetermined. Such a double reading extends our literary interests outside of the novel's social world to the exchanges between the novel and its formative culture. By reading doubly we question the insistence with which cues are delivered and the ways in which constructions are buttressed. We consider what is at stake when certain details are treated as error or as slips of the pen.

Mrs. Bennet is denied the prerogatives of a comic literary tradition: she does not win pleasure for her comedic scenes, forgiveness for her foibles, or credit for her effect on the social world. With an energy that seems excessive, given her slight role in the narrative, she is ridiculed both by powerful characters and the narrator. She is harshly criticized for a role she does not fulfill, for serious effects she does not achieve. She marks a lack of adult feminine power in the culture, a lack felt strongly by the young women she is supposed to educate and protect, and she is blamed for the excesses of the patriarchal culture. This essay explores what unspoken interests produce such a contradictory role for Mrs. Bennet. What interests are served by novelistic insistence that this character does not matter, that she is one-dimensional, that she has no effect? And how does such insistence coexist with the nagging, unsettling effect of the "trivial" character, with the threat she seems to pose to the social world of the novel, to her husband and daughters, to the possibility of women's discourse? Why should Mrs. Bennet's outbursts be found intolerable rather than humorous or socially productive?

Adrienne Rich calls the relationship between mothers and daughters in nineteenth-century fiction "the great unwritten story."[6] Mothers are thoroughly erased from these novels—rejected by their daughters, who wish to distance themselves from the socially conforming and repressed circumstances of their mothers, and disposed of by authors, who write them out of the story by imagining them as dead, bedridden, or left behind while the daughter journeys to Bath. They are, all too often, dismissed or ignored by critics who accept their marginalized status. The few mothers who do appear vanish into narrow stereotypes, both social and fictional. They are either dutiful and selfless or silly and self-indulgent, more likely to humiliate their daughters than to become role models or friends. They are not even given the dubious recognition afforded in twentieth-century fiction of being powerful, damaging adversaries.[7] Mothers are treated as wayward children, likely to say embarrassing things in front of company, needing to be cajoled and pampered, but not a very serious force—for good or ill.

As Nina Auerbach has argued, most nineteenth-century heroines strive to escape the "community of women," which "may suggest less the honor of fellowship than an antisociety, an austere banishment from both social power and biological rewards" (p. 3). They reject the more confined social world their mothers occupy to challenge the expectations of their fathers, brothers, or lovers. The great plot concerns not mothers and daughters but courtship,[8] which leads the heroine away from her mother and ends, conveniently, before marriage or childbirth, before the heroine must find a way to reconcile herself to that woman's world she earlier rejected. Through the ritual of courtship the heroine demonstrates her difference from her parents, especially her mother, whose concern with social rules, respectability, or safety is challenged, if not rejected. Yet the liberation of young, unmarried heroines leaves other women subject to patriarchy. The heroine (or the woman writer) is understood as the one woman who can negotiate the perils of the patriarchal world.

In *The Madwoman in the Attic*, Gilbert and Gubar discuss the "absence of enlightened maternal affection" in Austen's novels, which produces mothers "who fail in their nurturing of daughters" and daughters who are "literally or figuratively motherless." The relationship of mother and daughter is defined by "matrophobia—fear of becoming one's mother" (pp. 125–26). As a result, a mythical "mother-goddess" replaces the problematic social mother and becomes the figure of a feminine tradition that has been "dismembered, dis-remembered, disintegrated" under patriarchy (p. 98).[9] To "remember" and "become a member" of this "shattered tradition that is her matrilineal heritage" (p. 98), the nineteenth-century woman writer/heroine must "kill" the images imposed by patriarchy, the social mothers whom the dutiful daughter is supposed to reflect and reproduce.[10]

One of the ways the daughter seeks to liberate herself is through sharing the male characters' perception of the mother as comic. The situation could have been presented as tragic or wasteful—for the mother, who has no relationship with those around her, and for the daughter, who suffers from the lack of a significant guide. Imagining the mother as a "joke" seems to mitigate this loss and allows the daughter to move beyond what her mother desired or imagined. Yet Freud warns that there is no such thing as an innocent joke, that all jokes are tendentious.[11] Certainly the representation of the mother as comic is tendentious, ultimately working against the daughter's own interests. However much she gains by differentiating herself from a ridiculous mother, she cannot afford to trivialize the position she herself may occupy. Her own possibilities are finally implicated in the mother's position.

Mrs. Bennet occupies just such an uncomfortable position in her culture and in relation to her daughter Elizabeth. She is repeatedly characterized as trivial, static, or uninfluential, the antithesis of Lizzie's complexity and change. Modern readers have willingly accepted such cues and seen her as a dehistoricized trope, as "simply unformed matter," "the embodiment of the unthinking life-force that works through women," or "a transparently scheming boor" who, "like the life force, will persist, as foolishly as ever."[12] Mrs. Bennet holds none of the valued positions of mothers in her culture: she has little influence over the domestic realm and is absent from her daughters' scenes of confession and self-discovery. Elizabeth can "hardly help smiling" at Lady Catherine's concern that Mrs. Bennet has been "quite a slave to your education" (p. 199). Although Mrs. Bennet seems inescapable, constantly interrupting conversations and intruding where she is least wanted, she is ignored and countermanded by her husband and elder daughters. The narrator concludes the first chapter with an invitation to dismiss her as a static character of little interest. Having introduced Mr. Bennet as "so odd a mixture of quick parts, sarcastic humour, reserve, and caprice, that the experience of three and twenty years had been insufficient to make his wife understand his character," the narrator adds: "*Her* mind was less difficult to develope. She was a woman of mean understanding, little information, and uncertain temper. When she was discontented she fancied herself nervous. The business of her life was to get her daughters married; its solace was visiting and news" (p. 53). Although Mrs. Bennet is dismissed (p. 262) as a woman whose "weak understanding and illiberal mind" have lost her the "respect, esteem, and confidence" of her husband—and, by implication, of her daughter, the narrator, and readers—she is a constant enough force in the novel to evoke such strong criticism.[13] She is a serious handicap to her eldest daughters' romances and a serious instigator of her youngest daughters' folly.

Like Dickens's Mrs. Nickleby, who spoke "to nobody in particular . . . until her breath was exhausted,"[14] Mrs. Bennet's language reveals her self-absorbed inattention to her family's needs. She invariably misconstrues her effect on listeners, imagining specific insult from Darcy's general views about the country and city (p. 89) and missing the contempt with which the Netherfield ladies greet her comments (pp. 90, 144). She dwells in a land of "delightful persuasion" (p. 144), where she alone chooses how to interpret others' behavior. As when she bursts forth with her "exuberance" about Lydia's last-minute marriage, she cannot be shamed nor can her present feelings be disrupted with concern about the past or future.[15] Her well-rehearsed discourse on her "poor nerves" preempts her daughters' chances to complain or suffer publicly. After Lizzie rejects Mr. Collins, Mrs. Bennet recasts the entire episode as an attack on her. She does not imagine what the unpleasant scene may have cost Lizzie, nor does she consider how her daughter may have felt in rejecting a man her mother supports. Her complaints admit no co-sufferers and need no audience: "nobody is on my side, nobody takes part with me, I am cruelly used, nobody feels for my poor nerves" (p. 153). Although she vows never to speak to her "undutiful children" again, she babbles on, lost in a self-contained grievance: "Not that I have much pleasure indeed in talking to any body. People who suffer as I do from nervous complaints can have no great inclination for talking. Nobody can tell what I suffer!—But it is always so. Those who do not complain are never pitied." Her complaints earn her no pity from her daughters, who "listened in silence to this effusion, sensible that any attempt to reason with or sooth her would only increase the irritation" (p. 154).

Although Lizzie is in some ways allied with her mother in a struggle with patriarchal powers, she does not willingly admit the allegiance. Embarrassed by her mother's failures and inadequacies, she can neither laugh her off as comic nor fully dissociate herself. Lizzie never speaks her criticism to her mother, treating her as someone beyond conversation or reform, beyond the improvement of sensibility evoked in the novel. Yet she clearly feels the burden of the association and struggles to convince others of their differences. Her mother has a surprising power to silence the heroine, who speaks out in every other situation. At Netherfield, in front of the critical audience of Darcy and Miss Bingley, Lizzie trembles "lest her mother should be exposing herself again. She longed to speak, but could think of nothing to say" (p. 90). She is all too aware of how powerful and final the response to such exposure can be; it is after such an outburst in front of the Netherfield set that "the mother was found to be intolerable" (p. 68). Physical distance does not shelter her from her identity as daughter of "such a mother" (p. 187),[16] and she suffers from the disturbing effects of Miss Bingley's reminders of their "dear friend's vulgar relations" (p. 83). It does not require her mother's presence, but only the "thought of her mother," to make her lose "confidence" in an argument with Darcy (p. 219). Lizzie's concern about exposure—her mother's and, more to the point, her own—shows her tenuous social position, her vulnerability to being judged by her rank or family rather than by her words, her fear that even her words will prove too daring, too revealing.

Lizzie's intense discomfort around her mother seems reciprocal: she is the "least dear" (p. 145) of Mrs. Bennet's children, the one chosen by Mr. Bennet to confound his opinion of women as "silly and ignorant" (p. 52). Such comments suggest that Lizzie has risen above the devalued position of her mother, both personally and socially. Yet Lizzie shares more with her mother than her father or the narrator acknowledges or than she herself can recognize. Her disvalued fictional role allows Mrs. Bennet to voice more radical discontents than can the heroine of the novel. She is "beyond the reach of reason" in her diatribe against entailing an estate away from her daughters "in favour of a man whom nobody cared anything about" (pp. 106–7)—a complaint Elizabeth Bennet might well make if she were not too rational, too worldly wise. Lizzie shares her mother's shock at Charlotte's engagement to Mr. Collins, although she "recollected herself" (p. 165) in time to address her friend with guarded politeness. Like her mother, Lizzie allows herself "agreeable reflections" about what it would mean for Jane to marry Bingley, but whereas Lizzie keeps her dreams private, her mother speaks "freely, openly" (p. 140), causing her daughter to try "in vain . . . to check the rapidity of her mother's words, or persuade her to describe her felicity in a less audible whisper" (p. 141). Although Elizabeth has claimed she does not care what Darcy thinks of her, she "blushed and blushed again with shame and vexation" (p. 141) in watching his contempt for her mother's expressed social expectations. The aspiration of rising through marriage is thus displaced onto her mother's vulgarity, although Lizzie too has imagined Jane marrying into a fine house: "she saw her in idea settled in that very house in all the felicity which a marriage of true affection could bestow" (p. 140). Nor can Lizzie openly support her mother's eagerness to arrange for dinners or balls, contrivances necessary to promote the futures of five dependent girls. The calculation needed to achieve a secure marriage cannot be articulated except as comically disvalued speech.[17]

Mrs. Bennet, whose outbursts are a constant source of anxiety for her elder daughters, is regularly interrupted by her husband, her priorities ridiculed or diverted. Irked at her long tale about a ball and dancing partners, Mr. Bennet dismisses his wife's story and its mode of telling as designed only to irritate him (p. 60). That his daughters' futures depend on such slight details as who dances with whom and in what order, that they too must learn to read minute social signs, is of no concern to Mr. Bennet. As Nina Auerbach has argued, it is Mrs. Bennet who "forges her family's liaison with the outside world of marriage, morals, and money that eligible men embody. . . . While the mother builds connections, the father retreats from the business of marriage to his library" (p. 36).

Such nonchalance, such silence is the prerogative of the powerful, and in *Pride and Prejudice* it is permissible only for propertied men. Mr. Bennet regularly gains the upper hand by not answering his wife's addresses, and Darcy similarly maddens the importunate Miss Bingley. Mr. Bennet teases his family by postponing word that he has visited the new bachelors in town, and Darcy chooses when and how to impart the information he controls about Wickham and Georgiana. But when Jane or Lizzie is silent, the unusual behavior is noted and has serious consequences, causing Darcy, for one, to conclude that Jane is cold or Lizzie hostile. In her chapter on women's conversation in *The Women of England* (1838), Sarah Stickney Ellis codifies the "uses of being silent" for

women, suggesting that a woman's silence and speech are alike secondary, functioning "rather to lead others out into animated and intelligent
communications, than to be intent upon making communications from
the resources of her own mind."[18] Woman's silence is thus very different
from the silence of authority which, as the inverse of Bakhtin's "word of
the fathers," need not be repeated to make itself felt. The women in
Pride and Prejudice work to fill up silences, to repair the suggestion that
they have no purpose, no presence. At Netherfield, the ladies, whose
"powers of conversation were considerable" when the men were out of
the room, are reduced to nervous stratagems to persuade the men to
break the silence they instill (pp. 99–102). The struggle is described as a
contest, and Miss Bingley's failure to "win" Darcy "to any conversation"
shows the imbalance between men and women speakers. Lizzie comments on this contest, suggesting that "our surest way of disappointing
him, will be to ask nothing about it." She thus appears to control the
situation, to have seen through and assumed for herself the power of
silence that Miss Bingley, described as "incapable of disappointing Mr
Darcy in any thing," cannot manage.

But Lizzie's silence is only an imitation of Darcy's power to withhold
his words, since she must explain that she is doing it and must perform
the very role in the scene she hopes to evade, that of speaker who waits
for Darcy's response. When Darcy is "surprise[d] at her silence," Lizzie
tries to validate her silence as something she has determined to enact,
not merely a product of her social position. She does so with a complicated speech that she expects will "affront him": "Oh! . . . I heard you
before; but I could not immediately determine what to say in reply. You
wanted me, I know, to say 'Yes,' that you might have the pleasure of
despising my taste; but I always delight in overthrowing those kind of
schemes, and cheating a person of their premeditated contempt. I have
therefore made up my mind to tell you, that I do not want to dance a
reel at all—and now despise me if you dare" (p. 96). Lizzie claims her
silence as a powerful privilege, affording her time in which to *determine,
know, delight,* and *make up her mind*. Yet she must speak to defend her
silence, and her actions all respond to expectations that are beyond her
control to change. She can refuse to dance, but she cannot alter the nature of dancing and conversing, nor can she alter her position as one
who must first be invited, who can only startle "in reply." The social
discourse is preconstituted.

The less powerful speakers in such scenes are regularly marked as
"crying" out their speech, as breaking the decorum of a scene in which
Darcy's words need only be "said" to have impact and to gain attention.
Women are thus required to speak in excess if they are to be heard at all,

but such excess marks their speech as negligible. Mrs. Bennet is described by the narrator as "sharp" in defense of her five daughters, as indulging in "raptures" and "exaggeration." Although her words are necessary to safeguard a minimal social and economic standard for the Bennet girls, she must "rail bitterly" to make her point. And Lizzie has constantly before her the warning of Lydia, whose energies to procure her own desires are described by the narrator as "put[ting] herself forward," as full of "high animal spirits, and a sort of natural self-consequence," full of "assurance" that makes her "insist" rather than "cry," and "very equal therefore to address Mr Bingley on the subject of the ball, and abruptly remind[ing] him of his promise" (p. 91).

Lizzie can only differentiate herself from these censured women by explaining at length how her words are to be taken. She does not have Darcy's luxury of silence or her father's indulgence of privacy. As she experiences in her painful encounters with Lady Catherine and Mr. Collins, she is drawn into public discourse despite every attempt at resistance. When Mr. Collins dismisses her careful rejection of his proposal as "merely words of course," the "usual practice of elegant females," Lizzie cannot extricate herself from the social construction he has imposed. "I know not how to express my refusal in such a way as may convince you of its being one," she says. "Can I speak plainer?" Her only recourse is to refer him to her father, "whose negative might be uttered in such a manner as must be decisive" (pp. 148–50). Similarly, although she struggles to mark off some prerogatives for herself in her conversations with Lady Catherine (telling her, "*You* may ask questions which *I* shall not choose to answer"), she cannot end the scene. She can deny that Lady Catherine is "entitled" to know her mind and can refuse to be "explicit," but she must continue to speak to reject further attacks. Even as she insists, "I have nothing farther to say," she is provoked into a string of defensive replies ("I will make no promise of the kind"; "I must beg, therefore, to be importuned no farther on the subject"; "I have said no such thing"). Her defeated reaction afterward—"to acknowledge the substance of their conversation was impossible"—reflects more than an unwillingness to confide in her mother; it also suggests how powerless she is to control the "substance" of conversations (pp. 364–68).

Lizzie has been warned about the limits on women's discourse by an offhanded remark of Miss Bingley's. When Lizzie recommends that they "punish" Darcy by teasing or laughing at him, Miss Bingley protests that laughter would only serve to "expose ourselves . . . by attempting to laugh without a subject" (pp. 101–2). Lizzie rejects such an "uncommon advantage" for her male peer, refusing to allow him to conceal himself from the considerable power of her laughter. Yet, although Lizzie "wins" this scene by appearing to reject the conventions of male–female difference, Miss Bingley's comment raises a disturbing problem about women's discourse in Austen's realm. Lizzie's power to laugh depends on having a "subject"; without it her humor will seem as absurd and self-absorbed as her mother's. Although she seems more in control than her mother, Lizzie can neither end nor begin a scene of her own volition. If Darcy does not raise objections for her to correct or mock, her laughter will be seen as having no substance, no social effect; it will emerge not as valiant independence but, like her mother's, as ignorant blindness of serious realities.

The treatment of her mother as comic allows Lizzie, and Austen, to displace the implicit challenge against social limitations with a parental battle that is simpler to fight. The daughter challenges restrictions voiced by a mother who has had no role in creating those rules. Her resentment toward her mother suggests an inability to confront her father's authority and responsibility, but it also gives her the chance to practice rebellion in a less threatening context.[19] Mrs. Bennet's embarrassing outbreaks concern Lizzie partially because they proclaim what she must conceal and partially because the reception of these remarks shows Lizzie the contradictory proscriptions for women. Her mother has warned Lizzie (with a "cry") to "remember where you are, and do not run on in the wild manner that you are suffered to do at home" (p. 88). But Lizzie is caught in a bind: she must be guarded in her words and tactful in her wit if she is to win Darcy (she must always remember she is not "at home"), yet she can win him only by seeming independent and daring (by not allowing him to determine where her home shall be). She vacillates between an astute political analysis and a repression of such insights. When, for example, Darcy confesses he has been attracted by the "liveliness" of her mind, she suggests it might more accurately be termed "impertinence" (p. 388). But she is careful to teach her prospective sister-in-law how "impertinence" gets translated into a permitted or even valued quality: "[Georgiana's] mind received knowledge which had never before fallen in her way. By Elizabeth's instructions she began to comprehend that a woman may take liberties with her husband, which a brother will not always allow in a sister more than ten years younger than himself" (p. 395). Lizzie instructs Georgiana in a mild, affectionate version of sexual politics, but even such casual reminders indicate how careful women must be in determining what is allowed and what will be censured. Lizzie does not presume that Darcy's fondness raises her to a permanent position of "liberty"; even after they have declared their love, she is guarded in her speech, "check[ing]" her "long[ing]" to tease him by remembering "that he had yet to learn to be laught at, and it was rather too early to begin" (p. 380).

Lizzie is also cautious about making explicit the power relations between men and women. She counters her sister Jane's belief that "women fancy admiration means more than it does" with a caustic "and men take care that they should." But when Jane pursues the issue of what is "designedly done," Lizzie demurs from the extremity of her views—"without scheming to do wrong, or to make others unhappy, there may be error, and there may be misery"—and finally offers to be silent before she offends by "saying what I think of persons you esteem. Stop me whilst you can" (pp. 174–75). In the very next chapter, however, she rearticulates the political awareness to her aunt Gardener, who has attributed the failure of Jane's romance to "accident." "These things happen so often!" her aunt has concluded, and Lizzie sharply responds: "An excellent consolation in its way, but it will not do for *us*. We do not suffer by *accident*" (p. 178). She ultimately admits her father's complicity in Mrs. Bennet's ridiculed position, but even a private acknowledgment of this insight seems dangerous and must be carefully contained. Although she "had never been blind to the impropriety of her father's behavior as a husband" and "had always seen it with pain," she "endeavoured to forget what she could not overlook, and to banish [it] from her thoughts." It is only the public disaster of Lydia's seduction that allows her to blame her father as well as her mother for the "disadvantages which must attend the children of so unsuitable a marriage" (p. 262).

Lizzie is trapped between the equally unpleasant expectations of the "good" and "bad" daughter. The fall of Lydia, the bad daughter who is her mother's favorite, is instructive, since it reminds Lizzie of the danger of being judged as "fanciful" or "wayward." Mrs. Gardiner has warned Lizzie to be a good daughter, not of her mother but of her father: "you must not let your fancy run away with you. You have sense and we all expect you to use it. Your father would depend on *your* resolution and good conduct, I am sure. You must not disappoint your father" (p. 181). But Lizzie can see what society's "good sense" wins, what a good daughter can expect for herself. She is greatly unsettled by Charlotte's "sensible" marriage and has little sympathy with the "composure" with which both Jane and Charlotte repress their desires and observations. She also has the example of Miss Bingley, who has constructed herself as the perfect product of social rules, as exceedingly careful to do whatever it takes to win herself a powerful husband and house. In the fabulous world of *Pride and Prejudice,* it is Lizzie, the "bad" daughter, who succeeds and is allowed to laugh at her competitor and to outrank her sensible friend and sister. The happy ending rewrites the historically more likely outcome, the coopted marriage of Charlotte or the ridiculed position of her mother.[20] The heroine wins propriety and wealth through daring and rebellion made palatable to her world through her partial adherence to its rules. She succeeds by publicly being a "bad daughter" to her unworthy mother, but she also succeeds by evading the sense and directives of patriarchal culture.

Pride and Prejudice marks the beginning of a time, as Judith Lowder Newton has argued, of "general ideological crisis, a crisis of confidence over the status, the proper work, and the power of middle-class women" (p. 1). The ambivalent role of the mother, who in Austen's novel is both powerful and negligible, becomes a more conventional trope as it is codified and rationalized by a proliferation of advice books, novels about women's struggles, and treatises on the Woman Question. It is, therefore, productive to compare how the "foolish mother" is positioned in a novel in which the role is still implicit and how that position is solidified in a novel like Hardy's *Tess of the D'Urbervilles* (1891). By the end of the century, in *Tess*, Hardy presents a daughter passionately condemning her foolish mother, blaming the mother for the daughter's tragedy. Such a scene is unmentionable in Austen, and not only because of the differing conventions of polite discourse.

By 1891 it was relatively uncontroversial to represent the mother as scapegoat for cultural disorder. When Tess discovers that there is "danger in men-folk," it is her "poor foolish mother" she blames for not having warned her.[21] The mother's failure in the personal realm is given broad-ranging cultural implications. Tess's mother has seen their fall from "nobility" as merely a "passing accident" rather than the "haunting episode" that ruins her child's expectations (p. 162). Her foolishness thus becomes a historical emblem—of the peasantry's failure to understand the threat of the aristocracy and of the urban world, of the failure of the "past" to understand the demands of "the modern age," of the failure of seeing "accident" or "nature" as a sufficient cultural explanation. And it apparently makes sense to trace all these powerful failures to a mother who has not taken her responsibilities seriously enough: " 'O mother, my mother!' cried the agonized girl, turning passionately upon her parent as if her poor heart would break. 'How could I be expected to know? . . . Why didn't you warn me? Ladies know what to fend hands against, because they read novels that tell them of these tricks; but I never had the chance o' learning in that way, and you did not help me!' Her mother was subdued."

The implication is that ladies have an undue advantage over the daughter of a "poor foolish mother," an advantage which Tess sees as literary but which could more accurately be seen as the advantage of wealth and class. The mother's "simple vanity" becomes the focus for her daughter's anger, which cannot find its more appropriate targets, both individual and cultural. But when the novel has Tess blame her mother for not "telling" her of worldly dangers, and when such an accusation "subdues" the mother into a proper acceptance of guilt, there has been an important ideological manipulation of the role of mother. It is contradictory to locate the fault in not "telling"—in words—rather than in the "wrong doing" of men or the class inequities that make ladies better prepared to negotiate the perils of adult life. *Tess* thus provides a scapegoat for the powerful social transformations that affect the lives of women, for which daughters must be prepared. The mother, who is at best a commentator on the social realm, has taken the place of initiator, guardian, or betrayer.

Mid-nineteenth-century advice books, like the influential series by Mrs. Ellis—*Wives of England, Daughters of England,* and *Women of England*—similarly imply that mothers are the source of broad cultural changes that disrupt the family and the lives of their daughters. They charge women with the responsibility for correcting and upholding moral standards for man, who is "confused by the many voices, which in the mart, the exchange, or the public assembly, have addressed themselves to his inborn selfishness or his worldly pride [and ...] stands corrected before the clear eye of woman, as it looked directly to the naked truth, and detected the lurking evil of the specious act he was about to commit" (*The Women of England,* p. 42). The blame for continued "selfishness" or confusion, for worldly pride or lurking evil, then rests not on the "confused" man but on the woman who fails to oppose him, to provide him with a "clear eye" in which to see his faults. In an 1832 essay on the "Education of Daughters," Lydia Maria Child cites as a "true, and therefore an old remark, that the situation and prospects of a country may be justly estimated by the character of its women" and stresses the important transmission of such influence from mother to daughter.[22] Such pronouncements suggest a cultural concern over what is perceived as women's and, more explicitly, mothers' responsibilities and failures. They also stress the narrow range of possibilities afforded mothers, in which the mother's behavior is always a failure, incapable of satisfying incommensurable demands. Deborah Gorham describes the mother-daughter relationships figured in Victorian literature and art as inevitably producing two outcomes: "one in which the mother fulfilled her maternal functions, and one in which she would not or could not do so" (p. 47). To be a "good" mother according to the culture's proscriptions was to be a failure in her daughter's eyes. But to be a "bad" mother was also to be a failure, to embarrass or commit her daughter to living outside the system of social rewards and approval only the father could bestow.

By working to institutionalize the "proper" discourses of women, to teach the emergent middle class how to be "good" mothers and "dutiful" daughters, nineteenth-century advice books suggest that the relationship between mother and daughter was not seen as "natural" or as the province of individuals, but as requiring considerable institutional support and guidance. The aim was not to create self-fulfilled individuals but to acquire facility in approved social functions. In *Women of England,* Mrs. Ellis warned against encouraging young women to be too "striking" or to stray from their proper "station" as "relative creatures": "If, therefore, they are endowed only with such faculties, as render them striking and distinguished in themselves, without the faculty of instrumentality, they are only as dead letters in the volume of human life, filling what would otherwise be a blank space, but doing nothing more" (p. 108). To be part of social discourse, to avoid the marginality of being a "dead letter," a "blank space" in the "volume of human life," young girls must learn to function in predetermined ways, to fulfill the "instrumentality" established as their role and use in culture. Like their mothers, like Freud's child, they must learn to accept what is "granted" to them by an authority they work to uphold. It would be difficult for a mother to speak from such a proscribed position, and it would be painful for a daughter to hear such words. Austen's Mrs. Bennet makes the position and its restrictions visible and laughable; she "fails" to become an appropriate function and thus remains outside approved social practices. Her daughter "succeeds," but she too is implicated in her mother's exclusion from the social world. The novel "forgets" the bleakness of women's prospects in its exuberant ending, but at the cost of banning the mother from its view and of suspending the objections she voiced.

NOTES

This essay is dedicated, with love and admiration, to my mother, Mary Anne Heyward Ferguson, who, unlike Mrs. Bennet, has been a wise comprehender and a supportive instigator of her daughters' efforts. An early version of this essay was presented at a Wellesley College symposium, "Mothers and Daughters in Literature," in February 1982.

1. Jane Austen, *Pride and Prejudice,* 1813 (New York: Penguin, 1972), p. 53.

2. Mikhail Bakhtin, *The Dialogic Imagination,* ed. Michael Holquist, trans. Caryl Emerson and Michael Holquist (Austin: University of Texas Press, 1981), p. 403.

3. Sigmund Freud, *Jokes and Their Relation to the Unconscious,* 1905, ed. and trans. James Strachey (New York: W. W. Norton, 1963), p. 182. Freud wrote:

"weil eine solche bei ihm nicht vorhanden ist," "er besitze diese Hemmung nicht," and "lachen nicht über ihn, sondern sind über ihn entrüstet" (Sigmund Freud, *Der Witz und Seine Beziehung zum Unbewussten* [Leipzig and Vienna: Franz Deuticke, 1905], p. 156).

4. Bakhtin locates the effect of incomprehension, not within the novel or in any specific character's ability to "teach" others, but in the novelist's awareness of multiple discourses: "A failure to understand languages that are otherwise generally accepted and that have the appearance of being universal teaches the novelist how to perceive them physically as *objects,* to see their relativity, to externalize them, to feel out their boundaries, that is, it teaches him how to expose and structure images of social languages" (*The Dialogic Imagination,* p. 404).

5. Pierre Macherey, *A Theory of Literary Production,* trans. Geoffrey Wall (1966; London: Routledge and Kegan Paul, 1978), pp. 80, 83. Macherey argues that such a double reading seeks "the inscription of an *otherness* in the work, through which it maintains a relationship with that which it is not, that which happens at its margins" (p. 79).

6. In *Of Woman Born: Motherhood as Experience and Institution* (New York: W. W. Norton, 1976), her influential analysis of American cultural attitudes toward motherhood, Rich claims: "This cathexis between mother and daughter—essential, distorted, misused—is the great unwritten story" (p. 225). See also Signe Hammer, *Daughters and Mothers: Mothers and Daughters* (New York: Quadrangle/New York Times Book Co., 1975); and Nancy Chodorow, *The Reproduction of Mothering: Psychoanalysis and the Sociology of Gender* (Berkeley: University of California Press, 1978). In her review essay on "Mothers and Daughters" (*Signs* 7 [1981], 200–222), Marianne Hirsch discusses the reasons for the historical "silence" and "the subsequent centrality of the mother–daughter relationship at this particular point in feminist scholarship" (p. 201). Her essay provides an extremely useful survey of recent studies that are "attempts to prove that the story of mother–daughter relationships has been written even if it has not been read, that it constitutes the hidden subtext of many texts" (p. 214). See also *The Lost Tradition: Mothers and Daughters in Literature,* ed. E. M. Broner and Cathy N. Davidson (New York: Frederick Ungar, 1980), a collection of essays on this issue. Studies that discuss the nineteenth-century scene in particular are: Patricia Meyer Spacks, *The Female Imagination* (New York: Avon Books, 1972); Françoise Basch, *Relative Creatures* (New York: Schocken Books, 1974); Ellen Moers, *Literary Women* (New York: Doubleday, 1976); Elaine Showalter, *A Literature of Their Own* (Princeton: Princeton University Press, 1977); Lynne Agress, *The Feminine Irony* (New York: University Press of America, 1978); Nina Auerbach, *Communities of Women* (Cambridge: Harvard University Press, 1978); Sandra M. Gilbert and Susan Gubar, *The Madwoman in the Attic: The Woman Writer and the Nineteenth-Century Literary Imagination* (New Haven: Yale University Press, 1979); Judith Lowder Newton, *Women, Power, and Subversion: Social Strategies in British Fiction* (Athens: University of Georgia Press, 1981; rpt. London: Methuen, 1986); and Deborah Gorham, *The Victorian Girl and the Feminine Ideal* (Bloomington: Indiana University Press, 1982).

7. In "The Female World of Love and Ritual: Relations between Women in Nineteenth-Century America," *Signs* 1 (1975), 1–29, Carroll Smith-Rosenberg suggests that "taboos against female aggression and hostility" may have been "sufficiently strong to repress even that between mothers and their adolescent daughters" (p. 17). But she also challenges the modern assumption that hostility between generations, "today considered almost inevitable to an adolescent's struggle for autonomy and self-identity," is an essential, ahistorical fact. Patricia Spacks explains the omission of mothers as a stylistic version of an unchanging resentment: "In nineteenth-century novels women express hostility toward their mothers by eliminating them from the narrative; twentieth-century fiction dramatizes the conflict" (*The Female Imagination*, p. 191).

8. Ellen Moers calls courtship "a dreadful word" in Austen, "for it implies something a man does to a woman, and can include adultery." She prefers "marriageship," and argues Austen saw marriage as "the only act of choice in a woman's life" (*Literary Women*, p. 70). Gilbert and Gubar concur that marriage is "the only accessible form of self-definition for girls in [Austen's] society" (*Madwoman in the Attic*, p. 127).

9. See Gilbert and Gubar, *Madwoman in the Attic*, pp. 97–104. Moers describes women writers as "an undercurrent" literary tradition (*Literary Women*, p. 42); Showalter discusses the "covert solidarity that sometimes amounted to a genteel conspiracy" between women novelists and readers in the nineteenth century (*A Literature of Their Own*, pp. 15–16).

10. Showalter discusses the "remarkable frequency" with which nineteenth-century women writers identified with the father at the "loss of, or alienation from, the mother" (ibid., p. 61). "[M]ost mothers in middle-class families were more narrow-minded and conventional than the fathers, who had the advantages of education and mobility. . . . The daughter's nonconformity would increase the strains in her relationship with her mother and lead her to make greater demands upon her father for love and attention" (p. 62). Susan Peck MacDonald argues that the "absence of mothers" in Austen's novels derives "not from the impotence or unimportance of mothers, but from the almost excessive power of motherhood." The mother's power to "shield her daughter from the process of maturation" must be met by a "psychological rift" with the mother ("Jane Austen and the Tradition of the Absent Mother," in *The Lost Tradition*, ed. Broner and Davidson, pp. 58, 64). See also my discussion of Louisa Gradgrind's negotiation of her father's system and her mother's ineffectual resistance, in Jean Ferguson Carr, "Writing as a Woman: Dickens, *Hard Times*, and Feminine Discourses," *Dickens Studies Annual* 18 (1989), 159–76.

11. "Jokes, even if the thought contained in them is non-tendentious and thus only serves theoretical intellectual interests, are in fact never non-tendentious. They pursue the second aim: to promote the thought by augmenting it and guarding it against criticism. Here they are once again expressing their original nature by setting themselves up against an inhibiting and restricting power—which is now the critical judgment" (Freud, *Jokes*, pp. 132–33). See also Sigmund Freud, *A General Introduction to Psychoanalysis*, 1924, trans. Joan

Riviere (New York: Washington Square, 1952), in which he discusses slips of the tongue and other comical errors: "They are not accidents; they are serious mental acts; they have their meaning" (p. 48).

12. The first two depictions are by Douglas Bush in his 1956 article "Mrs. Bennet and the Dark Gods: The Truth about Jane Austen," rpt. in *Twentieth-Century Interpretations of* Pride and Prejudice, ed. E. Rubenstein (Englewood Cliffs, N.J.: Prentice-Hall, 1969), p. 113, and the last two by Mark Schorer in his introduction to *Pride and Prejudice* (Cambridge: Houghton Mifflin, 1956), pp. xiii, xxi.

13. Nina Auerbach argues for the "equivocal" nature of Austen's discussion of "direct female power" and cites Harriet Martineau's "oblique apology" in *Society and America* (1837) that English girls would obey such a "foolish mother" (*Communities of Women*, p. 50).

14. Charles Dickens, *The Life and Adventures of Nicholas Nickleby* (London, 1838–39), ch. 11.

15. On Lydia's return, Austen describes Mrs. Bennet as "disturbed by no fear for her felicity, nor humbled by any remembrance of her misconduct" (p. 320). Nina Auerbach discusses Mrs. Bennet as curiously vague about the details of domestic life, but sees Lizzie as "beyond a certain point devoid of memory": "if she shares nothing else with her mother, her faculty of nonremembrance confirms Mrs. Bennet's perception of the nonlife they have had together" (*Communities of Women*, p. 43).

16. In her essay on Charlotte's prospects, "Why Marry Mr. Collins?" in *Sex, Class, and Culture* (1978; rpt. London: Methuen, 1986), Lillian Robinson discusses Lady Catherine's harsh reminder that although Lizzie's father is a gentleman she is not "the daughter of a gentlewoman as well" (p. 185).

17. Judith Lowder Newton discusses *Pride and Prejudice*'s subversion of the issue of economic concerns by its association with Mrs. Bennet, "a woman whose worries we are not allowed to take seriously because they are continually undermined by their link with the comic and the absurd" (*Women, Power, and Subversion*, p. 70). See also Lillian Robinson's discussion of the economic difference the heroines would experience as daughters and as wives (*Sex, Class, and Culture*, p. 198).

18. In *The Women of England, Their Social Duties, and Domestic Habits* (London, 1838; rpt. Philadelphia: Herman Hooker, 1841), Mrs. Ellis begins her chapter on "the uses of conversation" with what she admits is the "somewhat paradoxical" discussion of silence, the "peculiar province of a woman" which derives "from her position in society" (p. 101). In *The Wives of England: Their Relative Duties, Domestic Influence, and Social Obligations* (London, 1843; rpt. New York: D. Appleton, 1843), she provides a fitting example of the authority of men's silence and the contingency of woman's speech. She advises men to leave the discipline of servants and children to their wives "because the master of a family with whom it rests to exercise real authority cannot so well unbend, and make himself familiar with the young people under his direction, the claims of this part of the community are strong upon the wives of England" (p. 235). The

husband retains "real" power by being silent but allows his wife to "unbend" in speech; her exercise of domestic power is granted on the condition that she make herself "familiar" to a "part of the community" that remains "under" the "master."

19. A sociolinguistic study of mother–daughter relationships comments on the use of "indirection" by mothers to signal "to their children that a directive is meant more seriously than its surface structure suggests." They cite the view that "indirection occurs because mothers are less willing to demonstrate power openly than are fathers. They see in the mother's use of indirect means in controlling her children evidence of her discontent with the superordinate position of power which is available to her as a mother, but not elsewhere in her life." Their study suggests that such a doubled discourse both acknowledges and attempts to circumvent the disparity in social power of men and women, and its use arises from the mother's inexperience with power and her unwillingness to claim it openly. See Ruth Wodak and Muriel Schulz, *The Language of Love and Guilt: Mother–Daughter Relationships from a Cross-Cultural Perspective* (Amsterdam: John Benjamins, 1986), pp. 35–36. Wodak and Schulz discuss indirect means of control or instruction as a sign of the mother's need to domesticate her authority, to make it appear less intrusive or insistent, less like a usurpation of male prerogatives, but they also cite it as a manipulative practice which preserves the mother's power in a realm beyond critique, "because indirection denies the child a chance to respond" (p. 37). As is evident in the interviews, the mother's linguistic claim to power often arises from her borrowing of patriarchal languages. The signal to serious portent, or to powerful command, is achieved by moving outside the language used by mothers to children, by using those social discourses that remain the province of fathers—logic, proper language, or an approved state language. They provide many examples of such "metaphorical code switching (a switch from one register to another)": for example, American mothers' attempt to "convey seriousness by switching from a diminutive name to the child's full name" or Norwegian mothers' movement "from their local dialect into Standard Norwegian to emphasize a command" (p. 36).

20. See Lillian Robinson's discussion of the ending as improbable, "outside the realm of [Lizzie's] own and Jane Austen's imaginings" (*Sex, Class, and Culture,* p. 188).

21. Thomas Hardy, *Tess of the D'Urbervilles* (New York: W. W. Norton, 1979), pp. 69–70.

22. Lydia Maria Child, "Hints to Persons of Moderate Fortune," in *The American Frugal Housewife: Dedicated to Those Who Are Not Ashamed of Economy* (Boston, 1832; rpt. Worthington, Ohio: Worthington Historical Society, 1965), p. 1.

KAREN LAWRENCE

The Cypher: Disclosure and
Reticence in Villette

"It kills me to be forgotten, monsieur," Lucy Snowe tells M. Paul near the end of *Villette*.[1] Through much of the novel, however, Lucy cultivates the oblivion she here resists. "Unobserved I could observe," she tells us early on (p. 198). Lucy's first words in the novel are: "Of what are these things the signs and tokens?" (p. 7); indeed, she seems first and foremost a *decoder* of signs, an interpreter of *other* people and events. One can say that Lucy's development is marked by an increasing desire to signify, to mean something to someone.

And yet this notion of development as an increasing desire to signify is problematic, as is the idea, central to some feminist readings of Lucy, that Lucy's development is measured by her willingness to play a central role in her own story and to abandon her status as pure observer.[2] For throughout Lucy's story (the events of her life) and her narrative (the writing of her story), she displays dual impulses to be overlooked and to signify. She captures these dual impulses in the fascinating figure of herself she provides the reader late in the novel: she calls herself a "cypher," someone "to whom nature had denied the impromptu faculty; who, in public, was by nature a cypher" (p. 515). The word *cypher* can denote both meaning and absence of meaning. Among its definitions are, according to *Webster's New Twentieth Century Dictionary:* "a person or thing of no value or consequence, a nonentity"; "a secret or disguised manner of writing meant to be understood only by the persons who have the key to it"; "the key to such a code"; "an intricate weaving together of letters, as in the initial of a name, or a seal"; and in arithmetic, "a zero, which, standing by itself, expresses the absence of any quantity, but increases or diminishes the value of other figures, according to its position." Lucy chooses an ambiguous symbol that can suggest she is *less* significant than others (a nonentity), *secretly* significant (a code), *more* significant (a key), or significant *depending upon her relation to others,* and possessing the power to make others variously significant as well.

What are we to make of the fundamental ambiguity of this self-articulation? Lucy's primary meaning in calling herself a cypher seems to be the first *figurative* definition—"a person or thing of no value or consequence, a nonentity." In *The Madwoman in the Attic,* Gilbert and Gubar use the word *cypher* in much the same way to demonstrate how women have been overlooked in literary history, particularly in the nineteenth century.[3] In using this figure, then, Lucy paradoxically articulates herself as a nonbeing; the cypher is a figure that refuses to "figure" Lucy, to give her a face or a body. Like her "cloak of hodden grey," the figure covers the person of Lucy. In assigning herself a figure like the cypher, Lucy deliberately obscures her intelligibility, her body, and her signature.

In calling herself a "cypher" *in public,* Lucy refers specifically to her insignificant presence in person. As plain a Jane as her literary predecessor, Jane Eyre, Lucy runs the risk of being overlooked, relegated to a place of nonsignificance. But in articulating herself with a figure that covers, Lucy causes us to wonder if invisibility is not also a strategy like the "cloak of hodden grey," specifically a strategy to avoid being textualized or read. Lucy's use of the word *cypher* refers to the only one of its meanings to shun associations with language or sign. All other meanings of the word besides "nonentity," Lucy's primary meaning, involve writings, signs, textuality. Lucy calls herself a cypher in public, an insignificant person, overlooked—that is to say, not one who becomes a sign or text to be read by someone else. Further, by saying she lacks the "impromptu faculty" in person, Lucy stresses that she does not articulate herself in person or speech extemporaneously and on demand. In diametric opposition to the "Juno" at the concert Lucy attends, who is "a sort of mark for all eyes" (p. 299), Lucy as plain protagonist does not serve as an icon of beauty, a sign that automatically signifies "woman" to be viewed, to be the center of attention. The representation of woman as image—i.e., as spectacle, object to be looked at, vision of beauty—is pervasive in our culture, and the history of the visual arts confirms the position of woman as object rather than subject, spectacle rather than spectator, "other" rather than constitutive consciousness.[4]

The history of the novel is different from that of the visual arts in the sense that woman as subject (consciousness) and spectator ("focalizer," to use Gérard Genette's term) has been depicted by both male and female writers. But one of the striking aspects of Lucy Snowe as protagonist is the degree to which she is primarily a viewer rather than viewed object, an interpreter rather than the erotic, mysterious "other" to obsess the male gaze and fantasy. Although she does become a character in plots of both ambition and love and begins to be a focus of attention in each,[5] it is worth noting that Lucy's "invisibility" is not wholly wished away in the course of the narrative, for it affords a sense of power related to her skills as narrator: "It was not perhaps my business to observe the mystery of his bearing, or search out its origin or aim; but, placed as I was, I could hardly help it. He laid himself open to my observation, according to my presence in the room just that degree of notice and consequence a person of my exterior habitually expects: that is to say, about what is given to unobtrusive articles of furniture, chairs or ordinary joiner's work, and carpets of no striking pattern" (p. 135). Two points are worth noting here: Lucy's plainness allows her to reverse the gaze, to observe the "mystery" of the male rather than provide the feminine mystique. Secondly, in the degree of her unobtrusiveness, she becomes a kind of fly-on-the-wall focalizer gaining access to vision by virtue of her insignificance. The power in these possibilities helps to qualify Mary Jacobus's statement that "Lucy's invisibility is an aspect of her oppression."[6] Gaining access to the dramas of others, developing her powers to observe and interpret, Lucy becomes an observer who often sees what others cannot. She witnesses "spectacles" where others see nothing, as when she sees a "full mournful and significant . . . spectacle" in the interaction of the King and Queen of Labassecour, a scene that "seemed to be wholly invisible" to others (p. 305).

Thus, instead of being a mark to be deciphered, Lucy presents herself as nontextualized, resisting the male as viewer who would interpret her. Although, as critics have pointed out, Lucy represses her feelings unhealthily, particularly at the beginning of the story, her emotional reticence does not eliminate the real power that develops by means of her "invisibility."[7] Like the biblical Vashti, who refused to display herself for the male gaze, Lucy Snowe avoids the fate of spectacle and becomes spectator instead.[8]

Another way to put it is to say that Lucy's resistance to being textualized stems partly from the sense that her person, failing to conform to the text that men view as significant enough to interpret, runs the risk of being misread.[9] Lucy begins to understand Graham's limitations as a "reader" of women and recognizes how he misapprehends her own character and nature: "he did not read my eyes, or face, or gestures; though, I doubt not, all spoke" (p. 455). Lucy guards herself against such misapprehension, biding her time until others learn to recognize her significance. Referring to her own physical plainness, Lucy describes herself all dressed for the fete: "We become oblivious of these deficiencies [i.e., physical plainness] in the uniform routine of daily drudgery, but they *will* force upon us their unwelcome blank on those bright occasions when beauty should shine" (p. 183). Lucy's self-deprecatory reference to the "unwelcome blank" ironically anticipates the responses of certain male critics who were loath to spend so much time with the "ugly" heroines of Brontë's books; but it also reinforces our sense of the process by which the cypher as blank becomes cypher as sign, only when her "public" is educated enough to read her. The elaboration of Lucy's meaning occurs with reluctance on the part of Lucy and with difficulty on the part of those who encounter her.

As an alternative to the perils of interpretation Lucy faces *in person,* she turns to writing, to self-articulation in her own autobiographical text. In calling herself "a cypher" *in public,* Lucy seeks to limit her insignificance to the realm of her person and to suggest an alternate world where her image might be better articulated and, hence, better understood. This alternative "Lucy" is alluded to earlier in the novel, in a kind of psychomachic dialogue between Lucy and her Reason over the possibility of writing to Graham to express her feelings. Lucy's Reason cautions against such a writing, and when Lucy objects that she had *talked* to Graham without incurring Reason's censure, Reason replies: "'Talk for you is good discipline. You converse imperfectly. While you speak, there can be no oblivion of inferiority—no encouragement to delusion: pain, privation, penury stamp your language.'" Lucy rejects this self-image of impoverishment; she counters that "where the bodily presence is weak and the speech contemptible, surely there cannot be error in making written language the medium of better utterance than faltering lips can achieve?" (p. 327). Her writing, then, gives her access to power, a means of signifying herself in a different way. Her "heretic narrative" indeed offers an alternative to the inarticulateness of her speech, marked with privation, and the nun-like silence of her presence.[10]

In her narrative, she "textualizes" herself in her own way; she writes the script and therefore controls to a greater degree the circulation of her own sign. Just as in life Lucy schools the characters around her to interpret a female text different from those they have read before, so in writing she schools her readers to understand her significance. She does this partly, as Brenda Silver says, through covert strategies by which she encodes significance and provides clues for deciphering. Interestingly, then, the sign of Lucy Snowe and the text that elaborates that sign into narrative evoke *cypher* in some of its other definitions. In her narrative, Lucy constructs herself as a sign worth interpreting for readers able to see significance where others see only a blank. Silver's interpretation, among others, implies that a total revelation of Lucy is possible for the initiate who may find a "key" to the code of the text.[11] Indeed, Lucy's own opposition between speech and writing might seem to support the promise that Lucy will be revealed in her written text. But Lucy defers her own significance in writing as well as in person; her narrative, like her person, refuses to tell all. While Lucy's myth of binary oppositions suggests that the cypher applies primarily to her speech and presence, in fact the narrative, too, in its expressiveness and reticence, defers ultimate meaning.

The myth of full self-presence in writing as opposed to speech reverses the logocentrism that Derrida has traced in Western metaphysics—"lack" for Lucy is stamped on her face, on her person, but is presumably completed in her writing. Yet the text as a whole deconstructs this opposition, showing that no medium fully reveals presence or conceals significance. Lucy's cypher-like face ultimately cannot retreat from textuality; however much Lucy sometimes strives to remain out of circulation as a sign, at the very least her person and speech are "stamped" with deprivation, her presence bears the mark of a lack. Analogously, her autograph, in the narrative of herself that she constructs *in writing,* is never fully revealed in the text.

In her study of Brontë, Karen Chase says, "both [*Jane Eyre* and *Villette*] seem to offer the transparency of a confession, until one thinks to ask who has confessed. The speaking voices are distinctive and memorable, but the speakers seem to disappear."[12] I would say, first, that it is not as "voice" but as autograph that we apprehend Lucy's text and that the "disappearance" of Lucy is not attributable wholly to the passivity and lack of desire Chase sees in her. As I have been trying to show, Lucy's cypher-like reticence derives partly from defensiveness and partly from a kind of feminist refusal to be viewed conventionally. But further, in turning the cypher into a narrative, Brontë shows that Lucy's "lack" is not the Lacanian "lack" which, as Luce Irigaray remarks, sees woman as unrepresentable because she lacks the phallus, the key to the symbolic.[13] Rather, Brontë presents the enigma of Lucy Snowe not from the male point of view but as a complex, shifting nexus of meaning and deferral of meaning that, like the sign itself, never refers to an ultimate and stable identity. Lucy doesn't "disappear"; increasingly, we begin to understand that the cypher as blank is the cypher as a mysterious sign of meaning never fully disclosed in this text. Like the French language that remains untranslated, hence undomesticated in the text, Lucy remains, as Mary Jacobus says, a foreigner in her own text.[14] Lucy's autobiography does not fully divulge her essence; her meaning, like retrospective narrative itself, leaves only a trace, but an important trace nevertheless.[15]

Lucy's ambiguous sign contrasts with the myth of the fully adequate letter or autograph purveyed by Paulina in reference to her lover, Graham. After receiving a letter from Graham containing a proposal of marriage,

Paulina examines his seal and his autograph, his "cypher" as decorative signature. In telling Lucy about her love for Graham, Paulina goes on to say: " 'Graham's hand is like himself, Lucy, and so is his seal—all clear, firm, and rounded—no slovenly splash of wax—a full, solid, steady drop—a distinct impress: no pointed turns harshly pricking the optic nerve, but a clean, mellow, pleasant manuscript, that soothes you as you read. It is like his face—just like the chiselling of his features: do you know his autograph?' " (p. 542). Lucy's extended signature in the form of her narrative is also a "distinct impress," but in its textualization of Lucy it does anything but provide "a clean, mellow, pleasant manuscript"; it is anything but a "full, solid, steady drop."

Implicit in my discussion of the cypher is an argument that although "specularity" and viewing are of major importance in this novel they cannot be divorced from the activities of reading and writing—that is, from textuality. Spying, viewing, observation, and voyeurism are all central activities in this mysterious narrative, but they are integrally connected to the reading of significance and the *writing* or tracing of significance in the story and the narrative. Within the story, experience is seen as a marking of the self and is related to what Brontë calls "impressibility"—the ability to be marked or changed by one's experience, to be *impressed* in the sense not only of recognizing significance but of being *altered* by it, one's self engraved by the writing of experience. Of Dr. John, Lucy says, "*impressionable* he was as dimpling water, but, almost as water *unimpressible:* the breeze, the sun, moved him—metal could not grave, nor fire brand" (p. 372). The imagery of impression suggests that experience is engraved on one's face (and thus is expressed as "character"). In contrast to Graham's, Lucy's face, by the end of the novel, displays to her lover, Paul, the undeniable impress of their relationship.

> "Well," said he, after some seconds' scrutiny, "there is no denying that signature: Constancy wrote it; her pen is of iron. Was the record painful?"
>
> "Severely painful," I said, with truth. "Withdraw her hand, monsieur; I can bear its inscribing force no more." (P. 698)

The "writing" of experience on one's "character" is painful, Lucy reminds us—a refrain that I will discuss later in the context of Lucy's resistance to the disturbance of story.[16] And when Lucy desires to see Paul after her visit to Rue des Mages, she feels his countenance will offer "a page more lucid, more interesting than ever; I felt a longing to trace in it the imprint of that primitive devotedness, the signs of that half-knightly, half-saintly chivalry which the priest's narrative imputed to his nature" (p. 577). As Lucy's description indicates, her reading of the signs impressed on Paul is also a writing or "tracing." Referring to the overwhelming effect on her of Vashti's performance, Lucy says it was "set down in characters of tint indelible" in what she calls the "book of [her] life" (p. 373). It is only a step from this idea of memory as trace to the writing of the narrative: Lucy writes her story with "white cap on white hair"; as with Lucy herself as sign, we sense an elsewhere of meaning, a sense that writing is a textual memory, never fully capturing any "subject."

From this overall consideration of impressibility and the link between character and writing I would like to move to the narrative of *Villette* as a difficult process of transforming the blank page into a mark of significance, of elaborating the cypher into story.

I have been suggesting that, from Lucy's point of view, to make the "unwelcome blank" a subject for narration can be painful and risky. *Villette* begins with a kind of resistance to its own story. In describing herself at the beginning of her story, Lucy tells us that she "liked peace so well, and sought stimulus so little, that when the latter came I almost felt it a disturbance" (p. 7). A comparable resistance to the disturbance necessary for narrative to begin marks the opening of the novel. Two useful terms from D. A. Miller will help to clarify the nature of the resistance I wish to describe. Miller is concerned with what he calls the "impulses" that underlie the structure of narrative; he seeks to focus on the "underlying impulsions in the narratable."[17] Miller's theory, like the Freudian theory of Peter Brooks,[18] is based on a metaphor of desire expressed in the narrative and its reading. For Miller and Brooks, a story is generated out of some kind of unfulfilled demand. For Miller, "narratable" instances are those of "disequilibrium, suspense, and general insufficiency from which a given narrative appears to arise" and the "nonnarratable" is the "state of quiescence assumed by a novel before the beginning and supposedly recovered by it at the end" (p. ix). The nonnarratable, then, is that which fails to generate a story.

According to Lucy Snowe, decorum has it that the face of the plain heroine, Lucy's "unwelcome blank," is not under ordinary circumstances made visible or legible. In other words, it is ordinarily an insufficient subject to generate a story. And *Villette* begins, as numerous critics have pointed out, with Lucy's saying very little about herself and much more about those around her. But the idea of the text's resisting its own story goes further. Lucy begins her narrative with a description of the kind of quiescence that Miller posits as preexisting the plot. She presents a general picture of an Edenic world of domesticity at Bretton. In this world Lucy is a favored child by virtue of her status as "one child in a household of grown people" (p. 5). Lucy figures this happy world as the "full river" of time, "gliding" through a plain (p. 6). It is as if events do not as yet make an impression on the page; no scene is yet imprinted in the narrative memory. The narrative memory is, like Graham, as "unimpressible as water." As Peter Brooks says, time is constitutive of the novel form; meaning "unfolds" through time (p. 92). At the beginning of *Villette,* Lucy gives us a figure of time in which time fails to signify meaning, to be impressed, to be disturbed from quiescence. Like the cypher as a figure that refuses to figure the protagonist, this full river of time refuses to figure a plot.[19] It is as if the narrative liked "peace" and "feared disturbance" as much as Lucy Snowe.

Presumably, Lucy shows us an unfallen world from which the plot will depart, for the general picture gives way reluctantly to the specific scene of Polly Home's arrival. Polly's intrusion jostles Lucy into life and the text into plot. It is thus very self-consciously that the plot begins with an intruding *letter,* as if Brontë were enacting a very self-conscious inscription of the blank page. Lucy thinks the letter might be "from home"—an occurrence that would seem to return the story to the nonnarratable by sending Lucy back to her mysterious origins. As Peter Brooks puts it, narrative is always in danger of "short-circuit," of a "temptation to oversameness." His Freudian figure for this aborted process is incest: the plot of love would, of course, be short-circuited by the marriage to, as he puts it, "the annihilatory bride" (p. 109). Lucy's "plot" is indeed in danger of short-circuit, and, interestingly, for the woman protagonist omitted from Brooks's deliberately male-centered version of desire, the short-circuit threatens to deprive her of any fictional life at all—to send her back to the mysterious womb from which she came. Again, this novel deliberately, self-consciously, shows us the attraction of quiescence and the inertia that narrative needs to overcome.

But instead of a letter "from home," Lucy receives a letter from "Home"—that is, Mr. Home—announcing the arrival of Polly, "a second guest": Polly is the second guest, reminding us that Lucy is the first. We realize that the tranquil river of time has been a figure that covers over the fact that home is strange for an orphan like Lucy. The tranquil river, the unimpressible medium of time, becomes complicated, for the events it fails to be impressed by are "nonnarratable" not because too insignificant but because too painful. The reader begins to see other disturbing details within the seemingly tranquil opening descriptions. Lucy's favored status as the "one child in a household of grown people" is called into question by her subsequent reference to Graham as "not yet full-grown." The "explanation" that Graham is away at school fails to erase the direct contradiction emphasized by the verbal repetition. Thus, right at the beginning of her story, Lucy is displaced from the secure center of the story by Graham, the young privileged male character most likely to generate a "story" in a novel, a story of both ambition and love, whereas Lucy Snowe is unlikely to generate either. There is no quiescent origin for Lucy Snowe. Her "origins" are clearly vexed from the beginning. Time's full river is a covering figure for a nonexistent utopian "origin." We begin to sense why both Lucy and her text resist story and how the idea of quiescence is more problematic than Miller suggests.[20]

As Gilbert and Gubar have pointed out, Lucy overcomes her resistance to telling her story by telling the story of certain female doubles, beginning with Polly.[21] But Polly's story is interesting not merely by virtue of its thematic or psychological doubling of Lucy, for it is Polly's arrival that stirs Lucy into participating in the watching and interpreting that become her hallmark. Although, as I have suggested, the opening expository paragraphs describe Bretton and Lucy's stay there in general terms, it is not until Polly's crib and chest of drawers are placed in Lucy's room that Lucy herself becomes situated for us in her story— at the sight of these intruding possessions, Lucy says, *"I stood still, gazed, and considered. 'Of what are these things the signs and tokens?'"* (p. 7; emphasis added). And thus begins Lucy's engagement in the semiotic system. Polly gives Lucy something to see and interpret: "During tea, the minute thing's movements and behavior gave, as usual, full occupation to the eye" (p. 19). As the alienated style of the above quotation suggests, Lucy at first defends herself against being truly "impressed" by Polly. Lucy cultivates her own cool detachment and represses any incipient feeling. But throughout the early scenes with Polly, Lucy develops her powers. Polly is interesting *with* and *for* Lucy. As Lucy puts it, Polly "lavishes" her "eccentricities" on Lucy; with Mrs. Bretton, instead, Polly is uninteresting, conforming to the expectation that she will be a perfect little lady. Lucy "ceased to watch her under such circumstances: she was not interesting" (p. 30).

Lucy watches as Polly is inducted further into the gendered world of little girls, but it is the dynamic between Graham and Polly that fascinates Lucy the most. Although Lucy describes Polly as a "neat" little girl who "fingered nothing, or rather soiled nothing she fingered" (p. 38), she does leave a trace on Lucy, a trace recorded as the first important scene in Lucy's story.[22] When Polly leaves Bretton, the story once again threatens to sink into the nonnarratable. Lucy marks the place of this nonsignificance with another metaphor, this time an image of herself gliding over smooth seas as a "bark." "Picture me," she indulges the reader, "as a bark slumbering through halcyon weather" just the way "a great many women and girls are supposed to pass their lives" (p. 46). Again, we encounter an image of the happy self of Lucy Snowe gliding over the seas of time; again, the self-portrait ("Picture me") refuses to picture. In fact, Lucy quickly revises this portrait, telling us of the "ship-wreck" that more accurately, albeit still metaphorically, describes her lonely life. For Lucy the conventional pieties about women's lives are nonnarratable, as she lets us know by briefly toying with this picture and then erasing it. At this point, however, the true circumstances of her painful situation are impossible to narrate. The figure serves as a bandage, marking the place of the pain but covering it over.

Again, Lucy and the narrative retreat into a kind of blankness. After the narrative and Lucy are rescued by Miss Marchmont and tempted to retreat into oblivion at her death, Lucy records her decision to journey to London in the following terms: she says she has "nothing to lose," because the past was a "desert" to her. In effect, this provides another beginning and turns the previous three chapters of the novel into a pro-logue, a dispensable section *before* the real story gets under way. The narrative past as well as Lucy's personal past is dismissed as "nothing," and the narrative is in search of the narratable, just as Lucy searches for some kind of significance in her life.[23] Lucy's journey to a foreign coun-try is her attempt, and the narrative's, to enhance narratability—to heighten the mystery in the telling, as Lucy, the decoder of signs and enigmatic sign herself, encounters the foreign.

It is fitting that in crossing the threshold of a foreign country Lucy should meet the third woman to provide her gaze with an object—the young English girl, Ginevra Fanshawe. For it is against Ginevra's beauty that Lucy's plainness begins to make itself visible and against Ginevra's "incapacity to endure" that we recognize Lucy's particular genius for survival. People like Ginevra, Lucy says, "seem to sour in adversity, like small-beer in thunder" (p. 77). Suited to the romantic plot that propels the "mystery" of the nun in the narrative, Ginevra is less fit for the kinds of "shipwrecks" of events and emotions weathered by Lucy. If Ginevra's beauty and "Englishness" in Labassecour seem to bring her a degree of freedom, she is, ultimately, bound by the kind of romantic role she plays. Although native shrewdness makes her a sometimes canny and refreshing observer of Lucy, Ginevra's narcissism and selfishness prevent her from being a truly convincing interpreter of character and events.[24] She heaps her hazy impressions of the world into her favorite catch-all French word, *"chose,"* as opposed to Lucy's more strenuous attempt to cope with the difficulties of language. Ultimately, although she seems to play a central role in Lucy's narrative as an actor in its main romantic mystery, in Lucy's heart Ginevra fails to carve "the outline of a place" (p. 202).

In Labassecour, Lucy's habitual sense of powerlessness and inarticu-lateness is intensified. As an English girl in Belgium, Lucy is literally deprived of her language. Her situation is emblematic: she is the image of the powerless female, without the keys to the culture or the power of its privileged discourse. After losing her luggage as well as her language, Lucy is forced to appeal to a young, good-looking Englishman who can converse both in French and, as Lucy puts it, in "the Fatherland accents" (p. 83). Later on Lucy reveals that the young Englishman is none other than Graham. When he speaks of her and guides her, Lucy's response is, "I should almost as soon have thought of distrusting the Bible" (p. 85).

However, travel for Lucy alters the terms of both Lucy's anonymity and ambiguity, her roles as both reader and text. On the one hand, her silence and anonymity are increased in this strange land as is the threat of annihilating loneliness; on the other hand, the semiotic stakes increase: Lucy as decoder *and* as sign becomes more active. Lucy, the foreigner, is likely to be scrutinized, to be "read" by others and to impress them with her foreign "character." She quickly becomes an enigma to Mme Beck's watchful eyes, even a secret code. The spying, reading, decoding that are the major activities conducted at Mme Beck's in a sense give Lucy greater existence and power, both as interpreter and sign. From the moment M. Paul is called upon by Mme Beck to "read" Lucy's face upon her arrival (and finds "bien des choses"), Lucy is given greater existence (pp. 90–91). The foreign locale in a sense prolongs narrative, offering, as it does, hermeneutic mysteries far beyond the gothic mystery of the nun in the Rue Fossette. As I have said earlier, however, this increased focus on Lucy as sign to be interpreted is a mixed blessing, for, particularly in a foreign culture, Lucy is misread.

Yet, with all the energy generated by this foreign system of signs, the first volume of the novel ends with a chapter that poses the greatest threat to Lucy's narrative and narratability to be encountered. In despair after a terrifying dream in which she sees herself as totally unloved and insignificant, Lucy seeks out a priest. After speaking with Lucy, he enjoins her to return. Lucy describes her refusal as a choice of writing over silence and heresy over an orthodoxy that would abort the story. It is in this section that she *names* her "heretic narrative," and, although her decision to write has *preceded* the first word of the narrative, this point in the text posits a crucial choice, as if it were occurring at the moment: "The probabilities are that had I visited Numéro 3, Rue des Mages, at the hour and day appointed, I might just now, instead of writing this heretic narrative, be counting my beads in the cell of a certain Carmelite convent on the Boulevard of Crécy in Villette" (p. 228).

This passage posits a very different destiny for Lucy and her text, for what is suggested is not only the return of Lucy to silence but the *erasure of the entire narrative* as well. For a moment the intriguing mystery of the nun in the Rue Fossette threatens to be replaced by a nun whose story does not intrigue, whose privation is nonnarratable. It is here that

Lucy defines narrative itself as *transgression,* a refusal to conform either to the conventional pieties of a young girl's life or to the orthodox piety and self-denial of the convent.

The image of silence, however, is imagined as the outcome of a scene of confession to the priest. This once-and-for-all telling, this confession, would end all telling. As opposed to the audience for the "heretic narrative," this male authority would rob Lucy of her power to make and record impressions. This "father" is the kind of "blocking figure," to use Peter Brooks's term, that threatens to become an impediment to the protagonist's desire. It is worth quoting Brooks, however, to illustrate how gendered his "masterplot" is and how different the kind and outcome of the "blocking figure" in Brontë. Speaking of the hero's desire and ambition as the driving force of the narrative, Brooks says, "ambition provides . . . a dominant dynamic of plot: a force that drives the protagonist forward, assuring that no incident or action is final or closed in itself until such a moment as the ends of ambition have been clarified, through success or renunciation" (p. 39). Brooks speaks of the typical blocking figures in fiction, who provide the impediment upon which narrative thrives for the redoubling of its energy; he also speaks, elsewhere, of the kind of "annihilatory bride" that threatens to halt the story for good. The priest to whom Lucy confesses threatens indeed to be a kind of "annihilatory bride." It is not incest or taboo but orthodoxy and conformity that threaten to abort Lucy's narrative and whatever "ambition" she has. Similarly, Lucy later thinks of the priest as capable of erasing Paul's "fraternal communion with a heretic." "I seemed to hear Père Silas annulling the unholy pact," she writes (p. 600). Thus, orthodoxy and erasure are linked in the figure of "annulment"; the double plots of ambition and love are potentially threatened.

Although Brooks acknowledges the differences in "female plots," in which the protagonist encounters a counterdynamic of "overt and violating male plots of ambition" (p. 39), he fails to account for both the female protagonist's own attraction to silence and the more complicated role that male figures can play.[25] If the Catholic father is a "blocking figure" who symbolizes the potential death of the heretic narrative, M. Paul is a more complex figure who combines blocking and enabling functions. As Lucy becomes intrigued by M. Paul's gruff attention, she comments to herself on the difference between "[her] own and [her] friends' impressions" and those of M. Paul. While Graham sees her as "a creature inoffensive as a shadow," Paul recognizes her passion and imagination (p. 482). He is the one male character who helps draw out the meaning of Lucy Snowe and, in turn, challenges her abilities in tracing his character. And yet the very power of his presence as opposed to

Lucy's threatens to overwhelm her. If she lacks the impromptu faculty, he "possessed it in perfection," a talent that makes Lucy marvel (p. 551). If it is Paul's presence that enables the love plot to continue, it is, as Karen Chase points out, Paul's absence that allows the plot of ambition to thrive: Lucy succeeds as a headmistress *and* writer, in the spaces provided by Paul's absence. The narrative energies that seem to be winding down with Lucy's outburst of passion and confession of love are revived for one last ambiguous chapter ("Finis") by his departure.

Three years pass, and Lucy tells us, "Reader, they were the three happiest years of my life" (p. 711). Paradoxically, Lucy is nourished by his absence: Paul's letters provide "real food that nourished" (p. 713). But although Paul's "full-handed, full-hearted plenitude," unlike Graham's more facile autograph, provides real sustenance for Lucy, it is the distance between them that allows her writing to flourish. The "final evasion," as Mary Jacobus puts it,[26] the return to the covering figure, brings the reader to an ambiguous ending and the same "sunny" quiescence with which the narrative begins: "Here pause: pause at once. There is enough said. Trouble no quiet, kind heart; leave sunny imaginations hope.... Let them picture union and a happy succeeding life" (p. 715). Lucy returns us to herself as writer, "figuring" her story and its arbitrary ending ("enough said"). The space provided by Paul's absence has allowed for the writing of the "heretic narrative"; it allows a space for Lucy to record her experience with "resolute pen." Somewhere between disclosure and reticence, Lucy makes the cypher signify powerfully, although never completely, in a genre in which we are accustomed to seeing a different kind of beauty shine.

NOTES

1. Charlotte Brontë, *Villette*, ed. Herbert Rosengarten and Margaret Smith, Clarendon Edition of the Novels of the Brontës (Oxford: Clarendon Press, 1984), p. 697. Subsequent references to *Villette* are to this edition and appear in the text.

2. See especially "The Buried Life of Lucy Snowe," ch. 12 in Sandra M. Gilbert and Susan Gubar, *The Madwoman in the Attic: The Woman Writer and the Nineteenth-Century Literary Imagination* (New Haven: Yale University Press, 1979), pp. 399–440, and Brenda R. Silver, "The Reflecting Reader in *Villette*," in *The Voyage In: Fictions of Female Development*, ed. Elizabeth Abel et al. (Hanover, N.H.: University Press of New England, 1983), pp. 90–111.

3. Interestingly, Gilbert and Gubar quote a line from a poem by Anne Finch that draws on two meanings of the word *cypher*—"nonentity" and arithmetical "zero" placed next to "male" integers: "Whilst we beside you but as Cyphers stand/T'increase your Numbers and to swell th'account/Of your delights... " (*Madwoman in the Attic*, p. 9).

4. On the history of the visual arts, see John Berger et al., *Ways of Seeing* (London: Penguin, 1972).

5. See Nancy K. Miller's discussion of the two "plots" in women's fiction and the way their inscriptions differ from those in fiction written by men ("Emphasis Added: Plots and Plausibilities in Women's Fiction," in *The New Feminist Criticism: Essays on Women, Literature and Theory,* ed. Elaine Showalter [New York: Pantheon, 1985], pp. 339–60). It is true that Lucy later wants Paul to find her attractive, but by this point he is able to read her character and see her face as expressively "beautiful."

6. Mary Jacobus, "The Buried Letter: Feminism and Romanticism in *Villette*," in *Women Writing and Writing about Women,* ed. Mary Jacobus (London: Croom Helm, 1979), p. 45.

7. See Christina Crosby, "Charlotte Brontë's Haunted Text," *Studies in English Literature* 24 (1984), 701; and Tony Tanner, Introduction to *Villette* (New York: Penguin, 1979), p. 20.

8. Vashti was the queen of King Ahasuerus before Esther. Drunk with wine, Ahasuerus summoned Vashti to the banquet hall to display her beauty to his guests: when she refused, the king divorced her. The actress Vashti, who makes such an indelible impression on Lucy, does perform for the world's gaze, but Vashti is anything but passive object of that gaze. "She stood before her audience," we are told, "neither yielding to, nor enduring, nor in finite measure, resenting it: she stood locked in struggle, rigid in resistance" (p. 369). What Vashti embodies so completely and fully is female power, passion, and rage. The dynamic and potent meaning of Vashti on stage contrasts in Lucy's mind with the more static portraits of women, like Cleopatra, who are worshipped by the male gaze.

9. For an excellent discussion of the "gendered" reading of characters and texts, see Annette Kolodny, "A Map for Rereading: Gender and the Interpretation of Literary Texts," in *The New Feminist Criticism,* ed. Showalter, pp. 46–62.

10. In "The Laugh of the Medusa," Hélène Cixous discusses woman's fear of speaking in public, of exposing her body in public: "Every woman has known the torment of getting up to speak. Her heart racing, at times entirely lost for words, ground and language slipping away—that's how daring a feat, how great a transgression it is for a woman to speak—even just open her mouth—in public" (trans. Keith Cohen and Paula Cohen, rpt. in *The "Signs" Reader: Women, Gender and Scholarship,* ed. Elizabeth Abel and Emily K. Abel [Chicago: University of Chicago Press, 1983], p. 284).

11. Silver, "The Reflecting Reader in *Villette*," pp. 90–92, 104.

12. Karen Chase, *Eros and Psyche: The Representation of Personality in Charlotte Brontë, Charles Dickens, and George Eliot* (London: Methuen, 1984), p. 70.

13. Luce Irigaray, *Speculum of the Other Woman,* trans. Gillian C. Gill (Ithaca: Cornell University Press, 1985), p. 50.

14. Jacobus, "The Buried Letter," p. 43.

15. See "Charlotte Brontë's Haunted Text," Christina Crosby's fine discussion of Brontë's radical critique of consciousness in *Villette*. Crosby focuses on the specularity in the novel, showing how a series of mirrorings and doublings subverts the clear distinctions between the self and the other (p. 715).

16. In the above quotation, it is Paul to whom Lucy attributes the power to inscribe her "character." Although the complexity of the reciprocal process of inscription between Lucy and Paul qualifies the topos of the male writing on the blank page of the woman, Paul is the writing master who aggressively tries to leave his imprint on Lucy. The rhetoric of textuality applied to Lucy's and Paul's relationship is at times almost egalitarian, as when he tells her they have similar "impressions" (I say "almost," because it is *he* who instructs *her* how to read their similar characters in the mirror). On the other hand, Paul often tries to force Lucy to be written on or to write his way, even asking her at one point to be his amanuensis (p. 552). I will return to this crucial relationship later.

17. D. A. Miller, *Narrative and Its Discontents: Problems of Closure in the Traditional Novel* (Princeton: Princeton University Press, 1981), p. ix.

18. Peter Brooks, *Reading for the Plot: Design and Intention in Narrative* (New York: Knopf, 1984). Further citations of this work appear parenthetically in the text.

19. Karen Chase in *Eros and Psyche* discusses the "narrative ataraxy" in the first part of the novel, primarily to comment on its relation to Lucy's passivity (p. 68). My own interest involves broader issues of representation and desire in the narrative.

20. Miller's book is excellent in discussing the playing out of narratable impulse, but I have some difficulty with his idea of "nonnarratable," which, for him, deliberately excludes the "unspoken." There seems a fine line between the quiescent and the repressed which Miller does not discuss.

21. Gilbert and Gubar, *Madwoman in the Attic*, p. 404.

22. Later on in the novel Lucy discovers these early scenes have left an indelible mark on "the book" of Polly's life as well. When Lucy encounters Polly years later, she supposes that the latter has "outgrown the impressions" of her youth. "The deep imprint must be softened away and effaced?" Lucy asks Polly (p. 396). But Polly tells Lucy she indeed remembers everything; Polly turns out to be a woman capable of impressibility but one who lacks Lucy's own power to engrave these impressions in a text.

23. How different is Lucy's sense that she has nothing to lose from that of the typical heroine of the English novel, whose chastity is worth losing, and the preservation or loss of which is worth relating in a narrative. Of course, these early memories are not merely preamble in the narrative, for they leave a marked imprint on Lucy as well as on Polly. If Lucy attempts to put Bretton behind her, tucked away only as a myth of origin, the plot will bring "Bretton" back in the uncanny scene of Lucy's awakening from her illness in the home of Mrs. Bretton.

24. Graham's final disenchantment with Ginevra occurs because she is incapable of truly reading the significance of Mrs. Bretton (pp. 310–12).

25. Nancy K. Miller's "Emphasis Added" provides an important corrective to the androcentric model Brooks offers.

26. Jacobus, "The Buried Letter," p. 54.

PART 2

Autobiography
The Self as Strategy for Survival

NELLIE Y. McKAY

The Girls Who Became the Women: Childhood Memories in the Autobiographies of Harriet Jacobs, Mary Church Terrell, and Anne Moody

"You a woman and a colored woman at that. . . . You can't act like a man . . . all independent like." . . . "You say I'm a woman and colored. Ain't that the same as being a man?"

—Toni Morrison, *Sula*

In an essay entitled "Self-Concept Formation and the Afro-American Woman," Vernaline Watson observes that "the role of the individual as an active participant in his *[sic]* development has been neglected or minimized in most social psychological perspectives on the self-concept" (p. 83). Watson believes that this neglect stems from a widespread uncritical acceptance of the findings of prestigious white social scientists whose categorical research denies the experiences of people outside of their group. From a position of privilege, and without giving consideration to the full meaning of the heterogeneity of our society, they promote the idea that human socialization takes place in an atmosphere in which the self is valued and communal institutions and traditions shape the individual personality to conform to the values of the larger group. Clearly, such a perspective takes no account of the effects of those influences on the socialization of minority-group people, including black women, who come to selfhood in racist, sexist white America and whom the traditions and institutions of the dominant culture do not nourish. Yet, as Watson and others who study black women's experiences note, many in the group develop positive selves, live fulfilling lives, and attain major achievements even in extremely hostile environments.[1] This phenomenon challenges the stereotype that the damage that racism causes to the identities of all black children results in total black self-rejection. Further, it affirms the idea that black people succeed in part by actively

participating in the process of their psychological development, rejecting
the status quo and opposing the values that demean their humanity.[2]
Many black women's autobiographies vividly illustrate this rejection of
conventional social norms and their authors' efforts to create a healthy
sense of self.

In spite of differences among individual Afro-Americans in skin color,
class background, and political and philosophical beliefs, which have particular impact on each separate life, the search for individual and group
freedom is central to the black autobiographical enterprise. As Stephen
Butterfield points out in *Black Autobiography*, beginning with the slave
narratives (exemplars of the basic search for human freedom), black autobiography has been the assertion of a radical "other" in relationship to
the white American self (pp. 1–7). Pre-1863 texts inscribe the ideology
in accounts of the lives of fugitives from servitude who addressed it in
outcries against the inhumanity of physical bondage. Post-1865 narratives focus on making the black self the subject of its own discourse in
the face of racial discrimination and oppression.[3] To further complicate
the issue for women, the black female self shares psychological space
within the experiences of black men and white women, and, like other
groups, is overshadowed by the dominance of patriarchy. Differences internal to black women's experiences, and others between black women's
and men's, and white and black women's experiences, give the autobiographies of black women an especially complex infrastructure that miti-
gates a unified group identity.[4] Yet, within this complicated network of
interrelationships, large numbers of black women are joined in a common (though individual) search for freedom and autonomy as they resist
any identity, conferred by a white- and male-dominated society, that designates them inferior to others.

Childhood remembrances, recorded in autobiography, provide an excellent source for examining how these women understood their own
development toward such radical stances. Psychologists agree that children develop their basic cognitive and conceptual maps of the world at
an early age, and while these may be modified later, they do not disappear. In his book on young radicals against the Vietnam War, Kenneth
Keniston explains it this way: "childhood creates in each of us psychological configurations that summarize the tensions and joys of our early
lives. These configurations are, in one way or another, interwoven into
our adult political commitments. . . . Just as the foundation of a building
limits, but does not determine, what can be built upon the site, so the
legacy of childhood sets outer limits and establishes enduring sensitivi-
ties for later development, but does not dictate it" (p. 76). In this essay,
we need to recognize that for many Afro-Americans (and some members

of other minority groups), the definition, perimeters, and activities of childhood (especially in respect to chronological age) are largely different from those within dominant middle-class society. For the purposes of this essay I define childhood in autobiography as the period from earliest recall to late adolescence, as we generally understand the latter in relationship to chronological age, even though, psychologically, the childhoods of these subjects may have ended years earlier.

Sociologists and psychologists (supporters and detractors) of the black experience agree that large numbers of black youngsters do not have traditional childhoods. One of the characters in Claude Brown's *Manchild in the Promised Land* explains the phenomenon in black Harlem: "they ain't got no kids in Harlem. I ain't never seen any. I've seen really small people actin' like kids. They were too small to be grown, and they might've looked like kids, but they don't have any kids in Harlem, because nobody has time for childhood" (p. 295). An underlying aspect of the lives of children in poor black communities in all parts of the country is how early in life these young people must learn to protect themselves and to survive in a hostile society. In these environments, relationships between parents and their offspring are often more open, honest, and mature than in traditional middle-class American homes. Poor black children assume greater responsibility for themselves and younger siblings at an early age, and in many cases, the earnings of the very young children are an essential part of the family budget. While these experiences are harsh and cruel, especially in light of the middle-class American cult of childhood, and they offer none of the protective insulation of privileged environments, on the positive side, the children's participation in the creative process that determines who they will eventually become lends itself to the development of strong personalities and gives the young people a greater sense of control over their destinies.[5]

This essay examines how three black women who, as adults, took radical private and public stances against the dehumanizing conditions of black people's lives in America recall their actions and responses in the childhood worlds of their memories. My emphasis is on the relationship between their reconstructions of childhood behaviors and their adult public responses to a hostile social world. From their recollections of their early lives we learn that while they were quite young they became aware of and actively resisted the arbitrarily designated boundaries of race, class, and gender, unconscious of the path toward which they were headed. Thus began their searches for independent black female selfhood. Since the women come from different, but equally important, historical periods for Afro-Americans, their social and economic circumstances offer a view of living conditions over a cross section of the larger black American community; and because they were different ages when they wrote their stories, their texts reflect different stages in individual physical and psychological development.

Harriet Jacobs, whose *Incidents in the Life of a Slave Girl* was published in 1861, was a former slave, already in her middle years when she wrote of her childhood experiences in bondage and her pre–Civil War years as a fugitive. Her narrative is a document that cries out against the institution that permitted black men and women to be treated as less than human, and subordinated black women to the sexual whims of white men. According to Jacobs, who enjoyed greater protection than most slave children, during her early years she did not realize she was a slave. After age twelve, however, she spent her life continuously resisting the forces that dehumanized her and all others of her race. Before the emancipation, although she was not formally connected to the abolitionist movement, she engaged in anti-slavery struggles. After January 1, 1863, when chattel slavery was no longer the issue, she devoted most of her time to work among poor southern black people (Jacobs, pp. 223–25).[6]

Mary Church Terrell's *A Black Woman in a White World* appeared in 1940, when she was almost eighty years old and still actively involved in civil rights issues. Her story is a reflection on a long and successful life which combined a sense of public responsibility with family duties. As *Benjamin Franklin: The Autobiography* chronicles the growth and development of the Republic in the eighteenth century, Terrell's book combines the black female personal narrative with her vision of the history of black America from Reconstruction to World War II. Unlike Franklin, however, she could not use the social or political values of the country for her personal or group development, so she questioned the hypocrisy of the rhetoric of the nation's most cherished public documents and struggled to assert her humanity. As a member of the first generation of post–Civil War children of ex-slaves, Terrell belonged to a group that used whatever educational advantages and economic good fortune came its way to enable us to see her as one of those who forged the beginnings of a recognizable black middle class. She is well known for her pioneering work and her long and distinguished record on black women's liberation and other civil rights activities.

Anne Moody published her autobiography, *Coming of Age in Mississippi,* before she was thirty years old. This work documents the early life of a young black woman who came of age as an activist in the recent civil rights movement within a family that, almost a hundred years after emancipation, remained crippled at the intersection of race, sex, and poverty. Of the three women in this study, Moody is the only one who not only received no support from family or close friends for her radical activities, but, like Richard Wright earlier in the century, endured open hostility from those who knew her best because of her rebellion against the status quo. Her book is especially important because of its child's-eye view of twentieth-century poor black life in the deep South and her own herculean efforts to resist the victimization of the poverty and dehumanization into which she was born. Moody's contributions to the civil rights struggle of the 1950s and '60s placed her in a position of leadership in the movement. But unlike Jacobs and Terrell, who pursued public political activities all of their lives, Moody has discontinued such actions since the publication of her book in 1968.

Although the lives of these women are very different from each other, their stories reveal that each, in her memory of early self-concept development, identified and resisted aspects of the social expectations of black people in general and of black women in particular. Such actions, taking place at different historical times, in different ways, and in different parts of the country, give us a useful reference point from which to examine separate modes of growth and the development of radical ideologies of race, class, and gender in black women's autobiographies. For my examination, I use a paradigm of development from Carol Pearson's study of archetypes of the hero in Western culture, *The Hero Within*. Although Pearson points to six stages in men's and women's journey patterns toward individuation, my discussion focuses on three: the Innocent, or the Edenic stage; the Orphan stage, which embodies the fall from innocence and the acquisition of knowledge; and the stage of the Warrior, the time when those who have the courage to fight for themselves can have an effect on their destinies and on events in their larger worlds.[7] Two of the women have experiences that conform to these three stages; for one, the severity of the physical and psychological oppression of her early years left no remembrances of a period of innocence.

Harriet Jacobs spent all of her childhood in slavery in South Carolina. In her narrative, she divided her early life into three parts. In the first, when she lived with and enjoyed the love and security of her immediate family—her mother, father, grandmother, and brother—she was completely unaware of her slave condition. Her parents were mulattoes who were treated as benevolently as the system allowed. Jacobs's father was a skilled, highly valued tradesman; her grandmother, an old and trusted bond servant, reputed for her faithfulness and the quality of her work. The family was more comfortable than many others, and Harriet Jacobs did not experience the oppressiveness of slavery then. This was

the Edenic period of her life, the "fortunate" times. The sudden death of
her mother when she was six made her an orphan in social terms and
propelled her into a psychological fall from innocence. Removal from
her parental home to that of her slave mistress revealed her status to her,
but since she was still humanely treated, she failed to comprehend its
meaning. When Jacobs was twelve, the death of this woman ushered in
the third stage of the slave girl's childhood and ended her "happy days."
Instead of finding herself free, as her mistress had promised before she
died, Jacobs discovered that she was now the property of a five-year-old
girl. This time, removed to the home of the child's lecherous father and
jealous mother, she learned, firsthand, what slavery had in store for her.
This was her second awakening: determined not to be a wholly passive
victim, she took actions that foreshadowed her subsequent struggles
against strong contending forces.

At the age of twenty-nine, Harriet Jacobs made a dramatic escape
from slavery. At age forty-three, when wide expanses of time and place
separated her from the events of her early life, she published *Incidents in
the Life of a Slave Girl* in the hope of kindling "a flame of compassion"
among northern white women for still-enslaved black women. *Incidents,*
like the autobiographies of the other women in this essay, focuses on the
themes of bondage and freedom within a framework of the writer's consciousness of race, class, and gender oppression from an early age.

In her earliest childhood recollections, Jacobs emphasized her happiness and claimed that until she was six years old she "was so fondly
shielded" that she never "dreamed" she was a slave, "a piece of merchan-
dise, trusted to [her parents] for safekeeping, and liable to be demanded
of them at any moment" (Jacobs, p. 5). These years fit perfectly into
Carol Pearson's archetype of the first stage of human development. In
every way, Jacobs was "the Innocent [who] lives in an unfallen world, a
green Eden where life is sweet and all one's needs are met in an atmosphere of care and love" (Pearson, p. 25). One seldom encounters such
terms as "happy childhood" and "fondly shielded" in slave narratives.
No doubt other slave children were unaware of their true condition for a
part of their young lives, but Harriet Jacobs grew up with familial love
and the illusion of parental protection over an extended period of time.
Unaware of her class, she identified authority within her family, and
thus, in her first six years, was separated from the more common slave
child's experiences and gained a greater sense of positive self-worth than
many like herself.

According to Pearson, the fall from innocence to orphan state usually
causes "political, religious, or personal disappointment and disillusionment" (p. 27). Jacobs's fall and the beginning of her orphan stage oc-

curred when her mother died, an event that initiated her into the realities of slave life. The loss of her mother precipitated great personal grief for her and, as she soon discovered, left her bereft of her imagined familial protection and any illusion of personal freedom. Taken from her home and loved ones to the abode of her mistress, she lost the place of pampered child to that of maid-in-waiting, which epitomized her true condition. Thus, her memories of the period include the child's awareness of her connections to the broader social and historical context: to the meaning of slavery. Knowledge withheld from her for six years came rudely flooding in.

Although she was not treated harshly, she sensed her powerlessness, and that of her father and grandmother, against the system. She realized that her father, as much as he loved her and as much as he was deemed trustworthy by the community, could not keep her with him or influence the course of her life. All his life he suffered the humiliation of having the status of property. Repeatedly, his owners refused to permit him to purchase his children out of slavery. As for Jacobs's grandmother, her five children were sold away from her, and in spite of promises to the contrary, she was never able to redeem them. It was not difficult for the grieving and disillusioned Jacobs to see, at the child's level, that the evil in the system made slavery intolerable and beyond compromise. But worse was yet to come. When she was twelve her mistress died. Having assured Jacobs that in her will she would free the child, from the grave she reneged on the promise. The woman Jacobs recorded that she never forgot the outrage and frustration she felt when she discovered this betrayal. Years later, she wished that she could "blot out" from her memory "that one great wrong" (Jacobs, p. 8).

A sense of the injustices in the slave system dominates Jacobs's remembrances of the second and third periods of her childhood. Her major complaints were not the hardships of work or the deprivation of material comforts, but the violation of common decencies toward black people by white people. She presents the adults in her family as well as the other slaves as honest, hardworking, trustworthy, moral human beings whose labor was brutally exploited and whose dignity denied. Had they been born to other circumstances, for industry and responsibility the Jacobses would have been the ideal American family, but their hopes for themselves and their children's freedom were lost to the immorality of slavery. Jacobs's grandmother suffered a worse insult when her owner defrauded her of money she accumulated to purchase her children.

If innocence and ignorance of slavery marked the first years of Jacobs's life, and the second part brought personal knowledge and a political awareness of race and power, then the third added gender to the list and forced her to confront the three issues in respect to the lives of black slave women in America. In this third phase, she is a paradigm of the warrior on a perilous journey toward selfhood and early womanhood. By age twelve, the deaths of her "kind" mistress and her caring and devoted but powerless father changed her world completely—from a benevolent to a hostile place. Alone, and seemingly impotent to affect her circumstances, she seemed to have made a deliberate decision to challenge and resist the system, never doubting that good was on her side and would triumph over evil.

Jacobs knew both the extent of the racial demoralization that all slaves suffered and black women's added vulnerability to sexual abuse by masters and their agents. In addition, the girls/women endured harsh treatment at the hands of the outraged wives of the sexual offenders; unable to vent their anger and humiliation at the actions of their men, these women abused the victims of their husbands' lust. Writing on this problem in recalling her fourteenth birthday, Jacobs observed that two years of living with the Flint family (her owners) had given her the knowledge of what it meant to live in the world as a woman and a slave. She belonged, she said, among those who, because of the place of black women in slave culture, were "prematurely knowing of evil things." In similar terms, Joyce Ladner notes that in twentieth-century urban ghettos girls in early adolescence gain "emotional precocity" that "far exceeds their chronological ages" (p. 52). The knowledge of her sexual vulnerability frightened Jacobs, for she knew that in her master's eyes she was no longer a child and that her slavery meant more than his ability to command her physical labor.

However, fear did not paralyze her: like Anne Moody later, it made her sufficiently angry that she acted. Jacobs's struggles to thwart her master's designs on her, especially between her fourteenth and fifteenth year, have been widely written about and need not be repeated here. In this, "the war of . . . [her] life" (Jacobs, p. 19), her master had the power of the slave codes on his side, and she had the determination not to give in. Given that she had no one to turn to for advice or comfort, her flagrant open defiance of his sexual advances was astonishing. Strong elements of self-worth, handed down to her in her religious grandmother's moral teachings (her grandmother's rigid moral codes precluded the young girl's confiding her troubles in her) motivated Jacobs to obstinate resistance. Literally, she took power to herself and challenged her master to kill her first.[8] Her relationship with another white man who brought no such pressure to bear on her was the climax of her childhood rebellion. The sexual liaison with the other was a fifteen-year-old child's claim to full ownership of her body and the dignity of an autonomous self. She wrote: "there is something akin to freedom in having a lover who has no control over you, except that which he gains by kindness and attachment" (Jacobs, p. 55).

A year later, before she was sixteen years old, Jacobs left childhood behind as she took on the responsibility of a new, younger life. Her first child was a boy. Her second, born the following year, was a girl, and that fact made her "heart . . . heavier than it had ever been before." In a much-quoted evaluation of the slave woman's plight, she wrote: "slavery is terrible for men; but it is more terrible for women. Superadded to the burden common to all, they have wrongs, and sufferings, and the mortifications peculiarly their own" (Jacobs, p. 79). With this in mind, Harriet Jacobs schemed and suffered in her efforts to escape from slavery and to save her children from the kind of childhood she perceived her own to be. She succeeded. Her determined and courageous resisting of the sexual advances of her master, when she was yet a girl, led to her imaginative escape and eventually to a life dedicated to the struggle against black American slavery.

Mary Church Terrell had a very different childhood from Jacobs's, yet her early life followed similar patterns of development. Born in Memphis, Tennessee, in 1863, of parents freed by the emancipation proclamation, she barely escaped slavery. Like the parents of Harriet Jacobs, hers were industrious mulattoes, and freedom enabled them to turn ingenuity and initiative to economic advantage. Unfortunately, her father and mother separated while Mary and her younger brother were very young, but the children did not suffer for love or material comforts. In contrast to the confinements of slavery that Jacobs knew, Terrell, one of the first black women to attend and graduate from Oberlin College, had advantages of class privilege that set her apart from the majority of black children of her generation.

Mary Church's arrival in the world caused some distress for her parents, however. For more than a year, she was a completely bald baby. Women's hair had always been a matter of great importance in female image-making in Western culture, and black women's hair has caused anxiety and discomfort for them ever since they arrived in America. Was Mary Church's hairlessness a pre-birth protest forewarning her own great distress over the social expectations of women? Did the absence of hair on this black woman-child indicate that she would focus her attention on issues of more fundamental concern to the human condition? Did she, inside her mother's womb, decide to make a dramatic protest against how women "ought" to look? In childhood, as in later life, Terrell actively resisted the limitations and expectations that others close to her and those outside of her family sought to place on her.

By all standards except race, Mary Church Terrell's early childhood shared many of the earmarks of a childhood in the white middle class. After emancipation, her parents reordered their lives and acquired a new social standing. Robert Church, son of a slave owner, seemed not to have suffered many of the indignities that large numbers of slaves had. His father neglected to educate him, yet gave him the impression that he had value in himself. After 1863 he engaged in a variety of successful money-making activities, including land speculation. His daughter recalled him as generous, reserved, unusually intelligent, with great business ability and a violent temper. He never spoke of his life in slavery.

But Terrell also saw her mother as a model of independence. The older woman had an entrepreneurial spirit and shared her husband's desire to rise out of the ranks of the underclass. She had artistic talents as well, but because she was a pragmatist, she became a business woman. After her separation from her husband, Mrs. Church, one of the first black women in the black beauty-culture profession, became a great success in the hairdressing business, first in Memphis and later in New York City.

The Edenic period of Mary Church's life, like Harriet Jacobs's, lasted for the first six years of her life. In those years, as she recalled them, she had the security of a home life that inspired her with self-confidence. Both of her parents were hardworking and successful, and even through separation and divorce, they seemed in harmony with themselves and the world. Remembering her childhood, Mary Church noted she had no divided loyalties between her parents, only the confidence that they loved her, wanted the best for her, and shared the responsibility of making the decisions affecting her young life. Her father paid for her schooling and daily living; her mother was generous with clothes and other necessities. A grandmother's "brutal," inhumane stories of slavery and a racist incident on a train when she was five years old invaded the perfection of Mary Church's Eden without having an adverse impression on her. She made no connection between herself, her family, and the old woman's tales, nor did she understand why the conductor on a train going North roughly tried to eject her from a reserved-for-whites compartment. This period, as for Jacobs, was one of pure innocence for Mary Church.

Mary Church journeyed beyond Eden and into her orphan stage when, at age six, she went to school in Yellow Springs, Ohio, because her parents wished to protect her from the racially segregated, inferior,

Memphis school system.[9] But if they shielded her from poor education, they could not save her from the deep-seated racism of peers and teachers elsewhere. Awakening to the knowledge of her racial identity was difficult for Mary Church, although not the same horror it had been for Jacobs: there were positive buffers between herself and the reality of her place in the world. While Jacobs left home to take up service in the home of her mistress, in Yellow Springs Mary Church lived with family friends, and made a rapid and successful adjustment to her new home. For two years she attended a model school then moved to a regular public school. She reported that, in general, she loved school, learned German from an Antioch College student, and was happy at home and with her friends. In the autobiography she noted the picturesque beauty of the place, and the famous spring that gave a yellow tinge to everything over which it flowed. She named it the "John Brown Spring" in honor of that man's courage in standing up for the humanity of slaves. In those years she also learned to appreciate the majesty of nature.

On the negative side of that experience, Mary Church acquired racial awareness in two particularly painful events in school, a ritual ground for black children's awakening to racism at the hands of white children or grown-ups.[10] The incidents in which she learned of her identity as a black person in a white world and a woman in a society in which gender defines one's roles mark her real loss of Eden and the beginning of her orphan stage. At age eight, in the model school, fair-skinned Mary Church discovered from her white classmates that she was racially different from them and that her difference made her less attractive and less desirable than they. Here, for the first time, she faced race and gender as negative aspects of her life. The unattractive black girl will become an unattractive woman, and an unattractive black woman has no place in the social world.[11] Previously sheltered and pampered, this child faced difficult realities. More than sixty years later, Terrell recalled that that experience "indelibly impressed" her racial identity on her.

Further loss of innocence and another awakening came to Mary Church in a history class in which she learned that she was intimately connected to the slave heritage. When Jacobs moved to the home of her slave mistress at age six, her recognition of her servitude precipitated her knowledge of her connection to the broader history of her people. Living within the slave community also gave Jacobs another advantage over Mary Church: in her predicament she could identify with her family and loved ones. She could feel grief for herself and the lot of her people without suffering a loss of personal worth. On the other hand, the unprepared Mary Church, surrounded by those racially different from herself, felt only alienation from them and great shame for herself. Of the impact of this knowledge she wrote: "I was stunned. I felt humiliated and disgraced, ... I had never thought about my connection with slavery at all. But now I knew I belonged to a group of people who had been brutalized, degraded, and sold like animals. This was a rude and terrible shock indeed. ... I was covered with confusion and shame" (Terrell, p. 21).

For all her shame, like Jacobs, Mary Church did not internalize a sense of worthlessness, even from this shock. Her final encounter with a negative racial incident in school launched her into her third stage of childhood, heralding the beginning of her life as a warrior. In this, again like Jacobs, she took power to herself and moved forward from defensive to offensive action by refusing to take the role of the stereotyped "darky" servant in a school play. This pre-adolescent show of resistance looks toward her college career and her refusal to conform to conventional policies there, and beyond that to her long career in civil rights and feminist activities.

At Oberlin College, Mary Church added gender consciousness to her increasing awareness of racial consciousness, and the battle moved from the private to a more public sphere. As a young child, she knew that women could have independent careers. Since both of her parents approved of her educational ambitions, she took no stock in privileged middle-class views on the subject. Consequently, in college, Mary Church ran into difficulties by refusing to enroll in the Literary Course, designed for women, and insisting on taking the more rigorous Classical Course, designed for men. Although her parents supported her decision, many students (including women) did not. Her friends tried to dissuade her and advised her that a too-highly educated woman, especially a black one, would encounter difficulties in finding a husband.[12] Nevertheless, she remained adamant and graduated from the "gentlemen's course" wearing a "wonderful black jet dress," the gift of her mother. The young women who dared to challenge the conventions and chose to take the "gentlemen's course" always "dressed in sombre black" for their graduation.

But the tension over her education did not end with Mary Church's graduation. Although Robert Church fully supported his daughter's wishes in her course of study, he was not prepared for her subsequent decision to take a position as a teacher. Since he was financially able to do so, he encouraged her to travel abroad for as long as she wished, until she was ready to marry. She, on the other hand, wanted a life of "usefulness" and was determined to enter work that "could promote the welfare of [her] race" (Terrell, p. 60). She understood that her father wanted her to be a lady, to take advantage of opportunities for genteel leisure that black women never had and only a few could yet afford. But she was not willing to accept his ideas of her privileged social role. Once she began to define her place in the world as a black person with a sense of autonomy, she linked her role as a woman to that persona, for both were indivisible in the quest for the full black female self. She acted on this principle for the rest of her life.[13]

Anne Moody was born in Mississippi in 1940, the year that Mary Church Terrell published her autobiography. Her mother, father, and later her stepfather, sharecroppers and menial laborers, were so defeated by racism and economic failure that they could not support her optimism or her educational or social ambitions. Thus, her early struggles against the triple oppression of poor black women was a solitary endeavor that took place at home and abroad. The ascendency of the civil rights movement in the South, beginning in the 1950s, parallels her growth and development toward consciousness of the conditions of black life in that region. Her commitment to the movement during the later '50s and the early '60s is the ultimate declaration of her rejection of the subordinate position that tradition decreed as her place in the world.

Unlike Jacobs and Terrell, Anne Moody had no consciousness of an Edenic period in her life, only of the physical and psychological fears encumbering her and those around her. In rural Mississippi, subsistence living and fears of racial violence leave no room for black or white innocence. Moody's family, long-time residents of the area, were paralyzed by the despair of the lot they inherited.[14] Moody's four-year-old impressions of her landscape were of how dismal, depressing, and degrading it was for them. For blacks the legacy of slavery, almost a century later, was poverty, fear of whites, and powerlessness within the social system. In place of the Eden of the childhoods of Jacobs and Terrell, Moody recalled a nightmare when she wrote of her earliest childhood memories: "I am still haunted by dreams of [that] time. . . . Lots of Negroes lived on [this] place. We all lived in rotten wood two-room shacks . . . ours . . . looked just like the barn with a chimney and a porch but Mama and Daddy did what they could to make it livable" (Moody, p. 12). Thus, she experienced no fall, no sudden awakening to a knowledge of her condition, no personal or political disillusionment that stripped away her innocence, for she was never innocent.

In the absence of stability or an illusion of parental protection, impermanence, delapidation, and the sense of social impotence are her reality. Moody, eldest of six children, had only a vague memory of a time when her mother seemed beautiful: "slim, tall, and tawny skinned with high cheek bones and long black hair," vivacious and happy in spite of the difficulties (Moody, p. 18). She recalled more poignantly how a husband's desertion, anxieties over poverty, the physical difficulties of field work and the equally back-breaking domestic work in white people's homes, along with frequent pregnancies and the burdens of many children robbed her mother of her charms, her physical attractiveness, and the joy of living. Thus, in her earliest childhood memories, Moody accumulated a storehouse of knowledge regarding the plight of poor black women and their children in rural Mississippi. At age four, poverty and physical abuse were not abstract terms to the child whose staple food was beans or who cowered in the presence of an eight-year-old male caretaker who constantly beat her. Nor was responsibility an incomprehensible concept for the five-year-old charged with taking care of herself and her younger sister all day while her parents worked in the fields. At the age of nine, when millions of pre-adolescent American children received small allowances or did odd jobs at home or in their neighborhoods for small fees, to learn the meaning of money, Moody went to work and realized her earnings were a necessary part of her family's income. Her mother's unhappiness also impressed her. Only twice did she recall the older woman seeming otherwise: once, shortly before her second marriage, and again, immediately following the birth of the first child she bore for her second husband. Moody was a young teenager by then and recorded, from an unobserved place, her mother's aura after the birth: "Her face looked different, I thought—so calm and young. She hadn't looked young for a long time. Maybe it was because she was happy now. She had never before been happy to have a baby. . . . For a long time I stood there looking at her. . . . I wanted to think she would always be that happy, so I never would be unhappy again either. Adeline and Junior [the younger children] were too young to feel the things I felt and know the things I knew about Mama. . . . They had never heard her cry at nights as I had or worked and helped as I had done when we were starving" (Moody, p. 57).

Having no experience with innocence, Anne Moody entered the warrior stage of her development at roughly the age at which Jacobs and Terrell came to their first awareness of themselves as part of a group separate from and unequal to the dominant group. As noted earlier in this essay, Joyce Ladner observes that children exposed to these conditions experience rapid emotional development: they learn to protect themselves from the hostile forces in their environments much earlier than those in more sheltered circumstances; they take responsibility for their futures considerably earlier than others in their peer group. By age seven, having observed the hierarchical differences between white and black people all of her life, an angry Moody began to question the rationale for white superiority and black inferiority. Moody's recollections of black adult reactions to her questions were similar to those Richard Wright, asking the same questions a quarter of a century earlier, received. Out of fear that the children might speak out of turn in racially dangerous situations and thus endanger themselves and the community, frustrated adults refused to discuss these problems with their children.[15] Like Wright before her, Moody responded to the silence with greater anger and more confusion.

By the time she was a young teenager, open violence against blacks by individuals or groups of whites, including the death of Emmett Till in her neighborhood, raised unbridled fury in Anne Moody and marked her as a danger to the frightened black community. Their fears for their lives not only prevented them from supporting her in her activities or mounting opposition to their oppression, but caused them to view her as a pariah. She, in turn, saw the black adults whose lives intersected with hers as cowardly—passive in their acceptance of the injustices they suffered and in their refusal to discuss their condition. She considered them participants in their oppression. In college, away from her hometown, to which she could not return on pain of death, she found the civil rights movement gave her an opportunity for leadership and activity that expressed her outrage at the impotence of black people in the face of the oppression that stripped them of all human dignity.

As a girl growing up in a community beleagured by race, Moody was also conscious of gender roles as an added burden of black women. She knew that white and black women had fewer options for self-determination and more potential for physical and emotional abuse from the men of both races. In the white community, where she worked from age seven, much of her interaction was with women. Some treated her kindly and encouraged her to seek a better life; others made her even more aware that race and gender conspired to lock her into a subordinate position for the rest of her life. Their conscious, overt treatment of her as an inferior, and sometimes as the sexually promiscuous, immoral black woman, made that clear. In this way, Moody learned of the gulf that separated white and black women in much the same way as Harriet Jacobs did. Black women suffered the same economic exploitation as black men, and in addition, they were often the objects of the sexual lust of white men and of the anger and contempt of white women.

Within her family and the black community as a whole, Moody saw another kind of black women's oppression. Most of the women she knew were burdened with too many children and lacked means of providing for them adequately. The men often deserted when the burdens were greatest, leaving the women to raise the children by themselves or to seek the help of other men, which in turn increased the sizes of already too-large families. Uneducated, black women in rural Mississippi were tied to poverty and oppression by race and gender. Moody's recognition of this double oppression of black women created additional conflicts between herself, her mother, and her stepfather. This only increased her anger. In addition, her ambitions to have a life other than that of her mother, particularly her rejection of labor on the land, increased the tensions between mother and daughter. As a result, the closing years of Anne Moody's childhood, the years between twelve and fourteen, were marred by rifts that eventually separated her physically and emotionally from blood kin and the community in which she was raised.

In her early painful realization of the meaning of the black experience, issues of class place Moody's remembrances of childhood closer to those of Harriet Jacobs than to Mary Church Terrell. On the other hand, in the absence of black support and reinforcement for her ideals and her desires to change her situation, her story differs significantly from either woman's.

The backgrounds and times of these women were different, yet they distinguished themselves by breaking out of the boundaries others set for black females in white America. In reconstructions of childhood, they reveal that resistance to those boundaries began before they were fully aware of the meaning of their actions. Unimpressed by attempts to protect them from the insults of a hostile world, refusing to conform to familial efforts to define the courses of their lives, the women chose identities and actions that defied society's expectations. Later, they used autobiography to explain vital connections between childhood and adult actions, and to show us why they became who they were.

Refusing to be contained by their race or gender or class, these three black women enabled themselves and others to act with self-determination, and to take an active role in the development of positive self-concepts. Harriet Jacobs, born a slave, experienced the full impact of that institution on the lives of black women, yet her sense of herself and her struggle for freedom belie the slave mentality. To Jacobs goes all the credit. She made herself. Encouraged even by the grandmother she deeply respected to accept her position as a slave and trust in Providence for release from her trials, she disregarded the older woman's advice and devised her own weapons for survival and self-confirmation. Later, a sympathetic community rewarded her courage by helping her to escape. A biography of her, being prepared by Jean Yellin, promises to bring to light even more remarkable achievements of this remarkable woman.

Mary Church Terrell narrowly escaped a slave's birth, and the economic situation of her family shielded her from the worst assaults of segregation and racism during Reconstruction. Living in the North, with adequate financial resources, she found life considerably easier than it would have been in the South. But escape from the racist traumas of that region meant permanent separation from her parents when she was still very young. Nothing in her autobiography suggests anxieties on this level, yet it seems unlikely that the separation did not have psychological effects on her. In a different way, like poor children in contemporary urban ghettos, she drew on internal resources to gain the confidence to stand up for herself, even against her father. Independently, she identified herself with personal achievement and with work for the uplift of those of her race who were less fortunate than herself.

As a child, Anne Moody experienced some of the worst aspects of the poverty and powerlessness of black life in America. Early in her life, she began to question the social structure that defined her as inferior to white people. Unlike Jacobs, who had no parents to turn to because they were dead, or Church Terrell, who was separated from hers, Moody sought answers to the knotty problems of race from her mother. Although the answers were either never forthcoming or unsatisfactory when they came, she persisted in seeking them. She recalled her impatience and anger with the black community for what she saw as apathy and acceptance of a subordinate racial and economic position. But unlike Richard Wright, who turned similar frustrations into alienation from and disparagement of the black community, she translated her emotions into action in the civil rights movement.

For Terrell and Moody, place and economics were as important to their experiences as time was in their separation from the experiences of Harriet Jacobs. But in spite of time, place, and circumstances, their stories reveal that even as children the three women believed that they had ultimate control over their lives. The question for us might be: What was childhood for them? None enjoyed the luxury of the Western storybook period of life. Their environments forced them to grow up and to learn to take care of themselves by making crucial decisions about their lives when they were very young. We might agree with Claude Brown's friend that many black women and men in America have no childhoods, only periods of young lives marked by degrees of innocence and partial knowledge of the true state of their American existence. All who survive are warriors beginning very early in their development; consciously or unconsciously they are the major architects of their concepts of themselves. Often they are alone on the journey to self.

At the center of each of these black women's autobiographies is a rebel with a moral cause that joins her to a tradition of women resisting and transcending the oppression of race, class, and gender. For Jacobs, Terrell, and Moody, childhood was not a period of parental indulgence, but the training ground on which they discovered themselves as black female persons. In this period we first observe the vision that enabled these girls, in the face of seeming powerlessness, to empower themselves in ways that foreshadowed the women they became.

NOTES

1. Vernaline Watson, "Self-Concept Formation and the Afro-American Woman," in *Perspectives on Afro-American Women*, ed. Willa D. Johnson and Thomas L. Green (Washington, D.C.: ECCA Publications, 1975), p. 83. The writings of such well-known social scientists as Erik H. Erikson, who discuss stages of human development, address issues of identity formation from this exclusionary perspective. Conversely, American life had always been oppressive for black women and men, for whom the supportive institutions of the larger society are usually roadblocks to positive self-development. For some recent historical studies on the situation for black women in slavery and beyond, see Deborah Gray White, *Ar'n't I a Woman? Female Slaves in the Plantation South* (New York: W. W. Norton, 1985); Jacqueline Jones, *Labor of Love, Labor of Sorrow: Black Women, Work and the Family from Slavery to Present* (New York: Random House, 1985); and Angela Davis, *Women, Race and Class* (New York: Random House, 1981). Also see Watson, "Self-Concept Formation," p. 88.

2. See Kenneth B. Clark, *Prejudice and Your Child* (Boston: Beacon Press, 1963); Abram Kardiner and Lionel Ovesey, *The Mark of Oppression: Explorations in the Personality of the American Negro* (New York: W. W. Norton, 1951).

3. Stephen Butterfield, *Black Autobiography* (Amherst: University of Massachusetts Press, 1974), pp. 1–7. All critical studies of black autobiography make this point. For other book-length discussions of this claim see William Andrews, *To Tell a Free Story: The First One Hundred Years of Afro-American Autobiography* (Urbana: University of Illinois Press, 1986); Frances Foster, *Witnessing Slavery: The Development of Ante-Bellum Slave Narratives* (Westport: Greenwood Press, 1979); and Sidonie A. Smith, *Where I'm Bound: Patterns of Slavery and Freedom in Black American Autobiography* (Westport: Greenwood Press, 1974).

4. See Hazel Carby, *Reconstructing Womanhood: The Emergence of the Afro-American Woman Novelist* (New York: Oxford University Press, 1987), and Deborah McDowell, " 'The Self and the Other': Reading Toni Morrison's *Sula* and the Black Female Text," in *Critical Essays on Toni Morrison*, ed. Nellie Y. McKay (Boston: G. K. Hall, 1988), pp. 78–89, for discussions of differences affecting a unified black female identity.

5. Kenneth Keniston, *Young Radicals: Notes on Committed Youth* (New York: Harcourt, Brace & World, 1968), p. 76; Claude Brown, *Manchild in the Promised Land* (New York: New American Library, 1966), p. 295. See also Joyce A. Ladner, *Tomorrow's Tomorrow: The Black Woman* (New York: Doubleday, 1971), pp. 44–66; and Robert Coles, *Children of Crisis* (New York: Little, Brown, 1964).

6. Harriet Jacobs, *Incidents in the Life of a Slave Girl,* ed. Jean Fagan Yellin (Cambridge: Harvard University Press, 1987). Subsequent references to this book are taken from this text. From Jean Yellin's chronology of Jacobs's life, we learn that in 1863 she distributed clothing and worked as a nurse and teacher among poor blacks in Alexandria, Virginia, and in 1865 she carried relief supplies to Edenton, her hometown as a slave. Yellin's biography of Jacobs is in progress.

7. Carol Pearson, *The Hero Within* (New York: Harper & Row, 1986). Page references to this work appear in the text.

8. For detailed discussions of this and other aspects of Jacobs's life, see Andrews, *To Tell a Free Story,* pp. 239–63; Carby, *Reconstructing Womanhood,* pp. 45–61; Valerie Smith, *Self-Discovery and Authority in Afro-American Narrative* (Cambridge: Harvard University Press, 1987), pp. 28–43; and Yellin's Introduction to Jacobs, *Incidents in the Life.* See also Frederick Douglass, *The Narrative of the Life of Frederick Douglass, An American Slave, Written by Himself,* ed. Benjamin Quarles (Cambridge: Harvard University Press, 1960), pp. 104–5. After successfully resisting an unfair whipping, Douglass feels transformed from a "brute" into a man who was no longer "a slave in fact," regardless of the law. Jacobs has a similar psychological response when she defies her master.

9. See Mary Church Terrell, *A Colored Woman in a White World* (Washington, D.C.: Ransdell Inc., 1940; rpt. New York: Arno Press, 1980). Subsequent references to this text are taken from this edition.

It is not unusual for young black children to leave home, sometimes alone, for faraway destinations. Maya Angelou discussed this in *I Know Why the Caged Bird Sings,* the first volume of her autobiography. At age three she and her brother, Bailey, age four, with tags on their wrists, traveled alone by train from Long Beach, California, to Stamps, Arkansas, to their paternal grandmother. Angelou writes: "I don't remember much of the trip.... Negro passengers, who always travelled with loaded lunch boxes, ... [fed us] with cold fried chicken and potato salad" (p. 4). Angelou further comments that thousands of frightened black children cross the country each year traveling to or from their "newly affluent" northern parents or to grandmothers in the South.

10. In James Weldon Johnson's *The Autobiography of An Ex-Colored Man,* the protagonist's entire life changes when at age nine he learns from a teacher that he is not white. Maya Angelou also recalls, in *I Know Why the Caged Bird Sings,* how devastating it was for an entire class of young black elementary school graduates to discover that their education was over at this juncture, while their white counterparts would go on to training that would make them professionals. In contemporary life, the inadequacies of segregated education and white harassment of black children in white schools confirm how much black children learn about their inferior place in the world from white teachers.

11. For one painful example of the problems of "unattractive" black women, see Wallace Thurman, *The Blacker the Berry* (Macaulay, 1929; rpt. New York: Macmillan, 1970).

12. In 1891, in "the most notable event in colored society in years," Mary Church married Robert Terrell, a teacher and lawyer who later received five

appointments to a judgeship in the municipal court in Washington, D.C. The Terrells led active political lives which appear to have complemented each other. He died in 1925. She continued her civil rights and women's rights activities until her death in 1954.

13. Mary Church Terrell was one of the founders of the National Association of Colored Women and of the NAACP. She was president of the former from 1892 to 1898. Among her many activities from 1892 to 1953 she addressed the National American Woman Suffrage Association in 1898 and the International Congress of Women in Zurich in 1919, organized voters, and picketed the White House and places of public accommodation in Washington.

14. Anne Moody, *Coming of Age in Mississippi* (New York: Dell, 1968). Subsequent references to this text are taken from this edition. Moody remembered constantly moving from one place to another. By the time she was fourteen years old, and until her mother remarried, the family lived in six different two-room shacks. They slept in one room, cooked and lived in the other. Bedroom walls were usually covered with loose paper held up with thumbtacks. Sometimes they lived with relatives in even more overcrowded quarters. Other times they stayed in places provided by white employers.

15. In *Black Boy* (New York: Harper & Row, 1945), Richard Wright reported several whippings from his mother when as a child he questioned race relations in the South.

JEAN M. HUMEZ

"We Got Our History Lesson": Oral Historical Autobiography and Women's Narrative Arts Traditions

Most students of women's literature are familiar with Virginia Woolf's story of the life and death of Shakespeare's sister Judith. Though "as adventurous, as imaginative" as her brother, and acutely aware of an inborn gift for fiction, Judith Shakespeare "was not sent to school." She discovered through painful experience her inability to make a place for herself in the public, male world outside the family, where poets like her brother were writing for the stage. And so she killed herself, says Woolf, and left us nothing but silence.

Powerful as it is, Woolf's myth of Shakespeare's sister helps perpetuate a questionable set of assumptions about what the Western cultural heritage is and how it has been created. It assumes that there is one single high culture of great literature, largely created by individual male artists of inborn genius, like Shakespeare. It asks us to believe that, because women were unable to escape the private family and gain access to this public culture, they have had no way to use their narrative imaginations, their "gifts for fiction." The Judith Shakespeare story is an important contribution to the rhetorical and conceptual tools of twentieth-century women writers and feminists, but the assumptions on which it rests help to create the unhistorical illusion of women's cultural silence. If cultural historians are to construct a fully inclusive and historically accurate picture of all women's creative heritages—as well as those of men without access to a high degree of formal education—we will need to look not only to sources outside the relatively small body of writings generally acknowledged as Literature but also to sources outside writing itself, to the traditions of the spoken arts. This is true for women of the dominant racial, ethnic, and social-class groups in any given culture. It is even more true for those whose access to literacy and to public literary discourse has been doubly closed off by social subordination based on class, race, or ethnicity.

Walter J. Ong has argued that "more than any other single invention, writing has transformed human consciousness."[1] By divorcing language from its original context in the immediate, personalized, face-to-face interaction of speech, writing forces us to use language in radically different ways, to invent new ways of supplying contextual meaning. Because writing frees the culture as a whole, as well as the individual mind, from the burden of storing and carrying its precious accumulated thought in the most memorable forms, writing allows for the development of analytical thinking, and encourages innovation and experiment. Writing makes possible the distance between knower and known that is necessary not only for the development of abstract thought and science but also, Ong says, for the kind of enlarged self-knowledge that can come only through extended introspection.

Because writing confers such obvious political, cultural, and economic advantages on peoples and individuals, traditionally oral cultures exposed to writing experience great pressure to adopt literacy and its associated values. But in so doing, people who have inhabited an oral world face the loss of many of the values and perspectives of their culture. Exchanging an oral culture for one based on writing can be particularly painful for those who must take on the language of a culturally dominant group as well. In a passionate essay, "Speaking in Tongues: A Letter to Third World Women Writers," Gloria Anzaldúa expresses the continuing sense of alienation of the linguistically colonized, as well as the anger of a woman of color who has endured the kind of literary education designed by and for white Anglo-American males. She nevertheless testifies to the power of writing: "to write is to confront one's demons, look them in the face and live to write about them." She urges her sisters to transform writing into a tool for self-expression by the culturally colonized: "Throw away abstraction and the academic learning, the rules, the map and compass.... Write with your eyes like painters, with your ears like musicians, with your feet like dancers.... Don't let the pen banish you from yourself."[2]

As societies shift from total reliance on speech to deepening dependency on writing, women typically come later and less completely to the written word than do men. This was certainly true in the history of the European/American West, and it is also generally true as traditional societies all over the world modernize, adopting Westernized technologies and often a sexual division of labor created in the industrialized world. Thus any distinctively female use of literary forms or style is very likely to reflect women's longer and fuller immersion in the world of the spoken word, as well as gender-specific spoken-arts traditions developed in relation to family, social, and work roles.[3]

In the Anglo-American West, the written forms to which women first turned after acquiring minimal literacy are the private and semiprivate genres of writing: diaries, letters, and autobiography.[4] These genres are of great interest to literary historians as we construct a picture of women's contributions to culture, but they represent only a small part of the expressive traditions women have created. The great majority of the world's peoples—and of these, a disproportionate number of women—still live in what Ong has called a "primary oral" culture, relatively unchanged by the kind of thought and expression made possible and necessary by high literacy. As Elizabeth Meese has written, "the only literature of many women in the world today is oral literature."[5] In order to appreciate the verbal artistry of this majority—as well as to understand more fully the history of women writers in the West—we need to know more about the special characteristics of the world of the spoken word. Most basically, we need to understand the living spoken-arts traditions, not as mere ancestors of literature, but as powerful and worthy cultural rivals, which offer different but not necessarily lesser ways of experiencing and ordering reality.

A first step in incorporating the spoken arts into a comprehensive study of women's cultural heritage is to be aware of the different aesthetic values characteristic of spoken-arts forms—values that derive from the transient, context-dependent existence of the spoken word. According to Ong, spoken arts tend to produce a style that is "additive, rather than subordinative"; "aggregative," or clustering, rather than "analytic"; and "copious," "redundant," or "generous" rather than spare. This is because of the impermanence of any utterance—its inability to be called back and re-examined at one's leisure—and the resulting burden placed on the memories of both speaker and hearer to organize the meaning of a long utterance over a span of performance time. The spoken-arts forms of a "primary oral culture" will also generally display a kind of reasoning based on accumulated direct experience, rather than on deductive logic, and an embeddedness in specific situations, an absence of generalizing. Most obviously and yet also elusively, spoken-arts forms rely on the extra expressive resources of live performance to convey their full meaning—particularly the dimensions of sound and sight. Frequently performer and audience are well known to each other, and this knowledge provides an essential context for interpretation of face-to-face spoken-arts performances. It is virtually impossible, therefore, to "translate" spoken-arts performances into equivalently powerful and effective written texts.[6]

A second prerequisite for including women's spoken-arts traditions on a continuum with literary traditions is a fresh consideration of the kinds of speech forms that should be included in the category "spoken arts." Several years ago, the folklorist Marta Weigle called for a radical reconceptualization of the spoken-art forms, to include the more private and domestic forms associated with women (and frequently stigmatized or trivialized as a result) on an equal basis with the more public, performance-oriented forms, such as heroic poetry, frequently restricted to males: "Myth narration and gossip may simply be two kinds of meaningful storytelling, each with its own style, both equally valuable to two different groups of people within the same culture."[7]

Since Weigle wrote this critique, much provocative, if still preliminary, work has been done on women's religious and secular spoken-arts traditions by folklorists, anthropologists, and sociolinguists.[8] One debated question has been the extent to which women's separate spoken-arts forms are socially or psychologically empowering. For example, anthropologist Susan Harding has seen women's gossip practices in one Spanish village as conveying a kind of power that "operates as much, if not more, to control their own behavior as that of men" (p. 368). On the other hand, literary critic Patricia Meyer Spacks has seen gossip as a traditional female form of verbal play that can contribute to intellectual and emotional growth and psychological well-being: "By talking about the concerns of other people's lives, the talkers grow to understand their own more fully" (p. 26). Recent anthropological and folkloristic studies have also argued that women's observed capacity to adapt to difficult new circumstances, such as cultural uprooting and aging, is greatly enhanced by their eclectic repertoire of spoken arts evolved in the context of domestic and neighborhood life.[9]

Those who have studied women's storytelling repertoires and behavior in traditional communities especially emphasize the importance of the surrounding context of family roles. A woman in such a community may have a repertoire of stories that can be elicited in a setting with no adult males present; but in mixed company, and particularly when she is acting in a familial role as wife and mother, she may defer to male high spirits or even monitor the storytelling behavior of males in ways she sees as appropriate to her role.[10]

Stories that are specifically told in the presence of children or younger kin, with no adult males present, may very well constitute the most important exception to the general rule, enunciated by Ong, that women's spoken narratives tend to be "conversations rather than platform performances."[11] In such a social context women's traditional family roles, as well as the absence of performance-oriented males, can provide both the strong motivation and the authority required to talk uninterrupted—which is, of course, necessary if one is to move beyond conversation to narrative "performance."

Kathryn L. Morgan's *Children of Strangers: The Stories of a Black Family* is a highly illuminating and suggestive study of women's oral storytelling traditions in the context of one specific Afro-American family.[12] Morgan presents and analyzes stories told by four generations of women in her family about her maternal great-grandmother, Caddy, who was once a slave. She records not just the stories themselves, but the different responses of the different members of the younger generations as they heard them, at different times in their lives. As Morgan shows through this procedure, such stories were not a static body of received doctrine, always told the same way, but a changing, ever-reinterpreted legacy, an ongoing conversation among the generations about the origins and meaning of the evil of racism and about strategies for living whole lives despite its many menaces.

Such direct observational studies of women's actual storytelling behavior within specific social contexts are clearly essential to constructing an accurate picture of the spoken-arts ancestors of women's literary traditions. Yet students of literature also contribute to our understanding of women's vocal-arts traditions through the consideration of written sources. Autobiographies, fiction, and even poetry by women writers should be examined for what they can tell us about women's spoken-arts traditions in specific cultural and historical settings.

Almost every novel, short story, and memoir by a woman writer is full of textual representations of women's talk emerging out of specific social contexts. Though obviously invented, the monologues, dialogues, and group conversations in fiction necessarily derive ultimately from the writer's experience and observation of real-life talk. If we overcome our fear of violating one of the ultimate academic taboos—that against using literature to study life—and agree to treat fictional representations of women's verbal arts with some delicacy and care, we open up an enormously rich body of source material for the study of female talk traditions.[13]

Halfway between literature and talk stands an odd, semiliterary genre whose claim to represent real-life speech behavior may be less problematic than that of fiction: the oral-historical autobiography. Such texts are the products of creative exercises in what Ong would call "secondary orality": "a new orality sustained by telephone, radio, television, and other electronic devices that depend for their existence and functioning on writing and print."[14] In recent years there has been an enormous outpouring of such texts based on interviews with women and for several reasons these can be an invaluable resource for studying and teaching about women's spoken-arts traditions.

First, for those of us who are, by our situation in colleges and universities, immured in a narrow world of high literacy, they provide an unusual window on women's traditional verbal arts. Second, they illuminate cultural and social-historical contexts that have not yet been systematically studied by our colleagues in folklore or anthropology. Third, and perhaps most valuably, they enable us to hear (although in a recomposed form) intimate talk that originally took place in the private world of personal conversation, often within actual families. Most women are still producing most of their self-expressive talk within family settings or in close friendships and neighborhood and workplace networks. Thus it is extraordinarily interesting and valuable to find ways (within the bounds of ethics) of overhearing such talk from any of these settings.

Books like this enable teachers and students of women's literary history to hear the voices—or, more accurately, the secondary-oral representations of such voices—of women with gifts for fiction who do not conceptualize themselves as writers. They give us a literature that translates into permanent, public form a certain kind of private or domestic conversation that we could not possibly have heard without it—in fact, one that might not even have occurred, had there been no way to capture and translate it. If we have good information about the process by which such texts came into being, we can learn from their use of language just as we would from other, more obviously or purely literary narratives.

These oral-historical autobiographies are the result of an invisible process of negotiation between two people: a specific interviewer, at a particular moment of her life, engaged in a friendly contest of wills with a specific woman, also of course at a particular moment in a very different life. The contest is over final control of the meaning of the life story they are generating together. The interviewer's interests, questions, assumptions, and physical presence as an auditor stimulate the woman being interviewed to tell some stories and not others, and to interpret those stories she does tell in ways that she might not have done, had she been telling them to beloved contemporaries or to polite strangers, or even had she been thinking with a pen in her hand, alone in a room of her own, contemplating a faceless public.

The recomposition process used to turn the transcribed speech into effective written narrative is quite similar to the process any writer uses in turning a first draft into a final one—with two important differences. First, the editor is working not with her own first thoughts on a subject, but with someone else's; and second, the thoughts were originally shaped not by the silent imagination guiding the pen, but by a speaker responding to the presence of another person. The "copious, redundant, generous" speech elicited in an interview dialogue format must be transformed into an economical and orderly written monologue that recreates the sound of the unpremeditated, informal speaking voice. Great masses of detail must be reorganized into coherent subunits and units that will seem "natural" to a reader accustomed to texts with clearly demarcated beginnings, middles, and ends. Redundant or finally incoherent textual material must be pared away, and central themes must be pointed out with purely literary devices, such as chapter titles.

Although the process of editorial recomposition will of necessity impose some of the aesthetic values of the world of writing, this will have greatest impact on the large-scale organization of the text. The smaller-scale embedded stories frequently require less editorial interference to achieve written coherence. The editor may omit false starts and condense associative branching-off into other stories or topics, but will conscientiously preserve the essential elements of oral storytelling—its characters, sequence of actions, and the explanatory voice of the narrator giving background or drawing the moral. Though we may lose details of performance style essential for a sociolinguistic study, we can still appreciate the fundamental narrative strategies of the storyteller. Thus such "talk-story" texts—to borrow an evocative term from Maxine Hong Kingston's description of her mother's narrative arts—can help students of women's literature reconstruct the spoken-arts substratum of women's narrative writing.[15]

Lemon Swamp and Other Places: A Carolina Memoir is the life story of Mamie Garvin Fields, constructed out of conversations with her granddaughter, Karen Fields.[16] This text, an exceptionally good example of the kind of oral-historical autobiography that emerges from cross-generational female conversation and storytelling, is obviously valuable to the cultural historian as a source of a wide variety of historical information on the southern black community of the first half of the twentieth century. It is of special interest to anyone who wants to learn about the history of American racism and race relations from a southern black woman's perspective. But for the purpose of this essay, my emphasis will be on the value of this book as a rich example of the kind of female-centered storytelling situation we need to know more about—the one which engages an older woman's narrative skills in a most serious way.

When called upon by a younger, female member of her family to review her past life, a woman must construct its present meaning, not just for herself but in order to fulfill an obligation to instruct succeeding generations. She has the opportunity to help ensure that a coherent idea of her self, incorporating her own perspective on her experience, remains in their memory after her death.[17] At the same time, with a tape re-corder present, she agrees to allow an audience beyond the family—and in this case even beyond the private world of the southern black com-munity—to hear about her experience. She agrees to reveal in print a complex range of feelings and ideas that would otherwise have been kept strictly in the domestic and community realm.

In the introduction to *Lemon Swamp* Karen Fields tells us that the storytelling process in this case was initiated by the grandmother, Mamie Garvin Fields, in several letters to her granddaughter. Mamie Fields was in her eighties, living, as she had for most of her life, in Charleston, South Carolina. Over the next several years, despite the geo-graphical distance between granddaughter and grandmother, the project evolved into a full-scale life history, based on the letters, a series of phone conversations, many tape-recorded interviews, and finally a sum-mer's editing and rewriting, during which the two women lived to-gether in the younger woman's apartment in Massachusetts. Karen Fields describes the growth in mutual understanding—sometimes inad-vertent and painful—that occurred when they discovered their different agendas for the book.

The differences in perspective that the younger Fields attributes to regional and age differences between herself and her grandmother also correlate quite closely to the differences Ong has described, between a world-view primarily shaped by spoken expression and one heavily in-fluenced by, and in many ways dependent on, high literacy.

> I began my part of *Lemon Swamp* with a mental map showing historical events and processes, a map strongly colored with discrimination, vio-lence, economic pressure, and deprivation of civil rights. . . . I tended to operate with a Northerner's "sociologism" about the South, that is, with an abstract scheme lacking the texture of lived lives. By contrast, my grandmother dealt in actual people and places, in the choices that she or her neighbor confronted, in what a man or woman did given a particular circumstance. . . . She was not trying to convey "how black people fared in Charleston over the first half of this century," but "how we led our lives, how we led *good* lives. . . . " (P. xx)

At some point Karen Fields also realized that, because of their very dif-ferent stages of life, she and her grandmother held very different expec-tations of the psychological functions of the *Lemon Swamp* project: "Looking back with my grandmother, I was trying to relegate childhood shocks about Dixie to their proper place. Looking back with me, my grandmother was determined to pass on a heritage. I focussed upon the past, therefore; she, upon the future" (pp. xix–xx).

Thus *Lemon Swamp* is the product of an intimate, but prickly, ex-tended conversation between women of different generations, different political philosophies, different regional loyalties. Each had an important personal stake in interpreting the bare facts of one woman's life. Karen Fields's questions and conversational responses have been edited out of the final text, making it an extended chronological monologue. But the introduction has made us aware of the granddaughter's presence as a discreetly silent, but psychologically insistent, audience. Her modern northern perspective, her contemporary experience of black political movements, her sixties-influenced thinking cannot be ignored by the storytelling grandmother if she is to accomplish her purpose of being heard and understood, of passing on a heritage.

Karen Fields's introduction also serves to situate Mamie Garvin Fields in relation to the worlds and attitudes of the spoken and written word. As a southern black woman living in a segregated city, in touch with many relatives still living in the country, Fields is a member of a relatively small, close-knit community and is undoubtedly exposed to a cultural heritage in which speech arts of many sorts played a major part. As a relatively secure and, indeed, privileged member of that community, she has some access to the larger, less intimate, often intellectually stimulating, but also white-dominated world of high literacy. The elder Fields herself takes care to emphasize her strong family heritage of literacy—clearly of great importance to her sense of personal and family self-respect, given that she grew up as a black southerner during the immediate post-Reconstruction period, when access to literacy, as to other forms of political, social, and economic power, was routinely denied to most poor blacks.

The book begins the way Mamie Garvin Fields began the whole project—by telling the story of the family's great-great uncle, a slave who was educated at Oxford along with his young master (p. 2). Fields also tells how one of her uncles, a seminary-educated Methodist minister, would correspond with her when he was away riding circuit, trading playful verses and correction of her written English for family and local news (p. 3). The same uncle kept diaries while on the road, and Fields read and remembered these as "full of stories," one of which she can still recall: "My favorite one tells how the Spirit came down into one of his congregations. A hush came among the people, then a rushing, and they knew that they were in the Presence" (p. 3). Writing and reading were obviously deeply associated for Fields with this loving and prideful family-based education. But Mamie Garvin Fields also had access to two separate kinds of oral traditions—one primarily Euro-American and the other primarily Afro-American.

As an upper-middle-class black student at Claflin University, she was taught formal rhetoric—the art of oratory based on a study of the classics—on the assumption that this first or second generation of educated blacks "would be leaders . . . and to do that, we had to speak well" (p. 101). Karen Fields does not give us much information about Mamie Garvin Fields's public speaking during her life as a community leader. But she is credited with an unshowy competence in various spoken arts: "Our grandmother talked less than some but more effectively than many, with a special knack for speeches, prayers, and the dry rejoinder" (p. xvi).

Throughout her life, Mamie Garvin Fields clearly admired the educated person who could deliver a good speech—one that could move people to action. One of her most memorable and fully dramatized stories is about the night when she heard Mary Church Terrell deliver a speech so stirring that the local black women's organization was fired up for immediate community activism. She lovingly evokes the jam-packed church audience on the hot night, and the way Mary Church Terrell strode back and forth, and used both her voice and her silence dynamically:

> Above all, we must organize ourselves as Negro women and work together. She told the story about a letter that a Southern white man sent to England, insulting us all, which was the cause of starting the Federation. "Let us turn in our numbers to face that white man and call him *liar,*" she said, and she had a wonderfully resonant voice. Every word could be heard clearly from the very front pew downstairs to the very last one in the gallery. When she raised her voice to say "LIAR," you could almost feel it on your skin. . . . The women hardly knew what to do when Mrs. Terrell got through speaking. We felt so stirred up, nobody wanted to wait till morning to pick up our burden again. Everywhere you might look, there was something to do. (Pp. 189–91)

Lemon Swamp allows us only fitful glimpses of Mamie Garvin Fields's knowledge of traditional Afro-American oral arts of the late nineteenth- and early twentieth centuries. These would have included church-based forms, such as religious song, traditional formulaic testimonial and extemporaneous preaching, and prayer; a whole array of verbal art forms developed in close relationship with work and family life, such as lullabies, curses and chants, ghost stories and animal tales, and children's rhymes; and playful and less respectable forms associated with street life and working-class entertainment, such as the blues and the dozens.[18] As a respectable, urban, middle-class matron, passionately committed to education and what was then called "racial uplift," she would probably have disapproved of some or all of the less respectable spoken arts and musical forms.[19] However, one important part of Afro-American oral tradition she clearly knew well and valued highly: community-history storytelling aimed at children.

Fields's childhood memories suggest that her own skills, repertoire, and sense of purpose as a storyteller in *Lemon Swamp* were developed through experience with many models, inside and outside the family. She remembers both women and men telling about how the black community had created viable institutions during and after slavery days, despite determined opposition from white neighbors. For example, she retells in summary version one story of the acquisition of a church building, formerly owned by whites, by a black independent congregation immediately after slavery. She evidently remembered this as a suspensefully rendered, wonderfully moving tale which she heard told many times as a child. She comments ruefully on her own second-hand rendition, "I wish I could tell this part of the story the way the people who were there used to tell it, because back in 1866, when all this happened, those old folks didn't know whether they would get their church or not." Nearing the climax, she attempts to evoke the entire scene of the remembered performance: "Uncle J. B. loved to quote from James Weldon Johnson at this place in the story," she says, and supplies the quotation (p. 36).

The fragmentary evidence in *Lemon Swamp* does not reveal whether the men of the community had a more dramatic, performance-oriented storytelling style than women would typically employ in mixed company, as the folklore studies cited above would lead us to expect. But children of both sexes certainly listened to storytelling by both men and women, and probably acquired the essential outlines of a large repertoire of black history stories from both.

We get one glimpse of an all-female storytelling situation dating from about the turn of the century. This example illustrates very nicely how women's stories might frequently emerge out of work performed in their family roles, with children present. A group of women and children were cooking for a picnic—held in a park outside town, because blacks were not allowed access to the city parks in those days. The husbands and fathers had not yet arrived from town after their morning's work, so in order to distract the children from hunger while the food was prepared, Fields's Aunt Harriet told a story brought to mind by the cooking rice. The story was about covert resistance, about how the women, forbidden as slaves to eat the expensive rice processed by their labors, nevertheless contrived to steal it for their families by wearing clothing knotted up to catch the grains as they fanned off the husks (p. 59).

Such a memory dramatizes the extent to which storytelling for children in the post-Reconstruction South had to fulfill multiple important functions simultaneously: entertainment, instruction in community history, and formation of attitudes necessary for survival in a hostile world. This story also depicts the women slaves as cunning and heroic, and therefore teaches not only racial and cultural pride, but gender pride as well, to the young female listener. It would be wonderful to know how many such female-centered slave stories were part of the repertoire with which Fields grew up.

Black community history stories were also an important component of the informal schooling that Fields remembers receiving from a neighborhood school founded by her cousin, Lala Izzard. Miss Izzard took the children on long walks through areas of the city informally known to be for whites only, teaching a black perspective on southern history through her storytelling. On these walks through segregated Charleston, the "right" questions would arise naturally, Fields remembers: "We wanted to know why the people along the Battery had such big houses. Who were those people? How did they get the money to build such great big houses? So we found out about the Revolutionary War, the Civil War, how people made money during slavery. We also found out that Charleston had 'aristocrats' and ordinary white people" (p. 53). Looking back on this informal education, the elder Fields thoroughly appreciates its subversive potential: "So although we couldn't stop on the Battery or use the park, we visited it anyhow. We got our history lesson. We got our 'sociology' lesson. And at the end we got our recreation. All that was Lala's doing" (p. 55).

Such imaginative and affirmative teaching through storytelling stands in stark contrast, in Mamie Garvin Fields's memory, to the segregated Charleston elementary schools she also attended, where black children were treated with contempt and white women taught by rote the Rebel version of southern history. Not surprisingly, Mamie Garvin Fields grew up to become a teacher herself, and many of her stories of her own adult experiences feature herself as the inheritor of the teaching strategies and purposes passed down by her cousin Lala.

The great bulk of the stories in *Lemon Swamp* are personal experience narratives: stories in which she herself figures as the central character. In ways beyond recovery, traditional Afro-American storytelling plots and styles may have influenced her procedures as a personal-experience storyteller, just as she may have been influenced by her reading. But, working from a text alone, we cannot analyze these stories in direct relation to oral tradition. Rather, we will consider the implications of their themes and plots for the creation of an impressive fiction of character, a version of the grandmother's self which instructs in different ways the older woman looking forward, the younger woman looking back, and the reader who has never met either one. Although in analyzing these stories I will inevitably refer to Mamie Garvin Fields as the storyteller or narrator, the final fiction of self is a fully collaborative joint creation of the two kinswomen, carved by the hands of both out of the raw materials provided by their conversations.

The most memorable and resonant of *Lemon Swamp*'s personal experience stories can be grouped into a relatively small number of thematic/tonal types. To review these briefly is to see what the two Fields women, despite their differences in perspective and experience, were able to agree on as the most important lessons to be learned from the elder Fields's life.

Inevitably, many stories center on how a southern black woman lived with segregation and the color bar—clearly the burning issue for Karen Fields, who acknowledges her preoccupation with segregation in the Introduction. At one point, unable to remember whether the steamer she took on her first trip North was segregated, the grandmother tries to remind the granddaughter that segregation should not be allowed to become an obsessive focus: "Anyhow, don't have the idea that just because Jim Crow was all round us, we never thought of anything else" (p. 142). Yet explaining to her northern granddaughter how her generation managed to live with segregation is also clearly a central concern for Mamie Garvin Fields in this project.

Segregation stories are told in two highly contrasting moods. First are the ironic, sometimes even broadly comic, stories, which tend to turn on the absurdity rather than the cruelty of the system and to picture whites as to a greater or lesser degree trapped or made ridiculous by their own efforts to deny the humanity of other people. The southern whites in these stories are laughably ill-educated: they speak in a heavily caricatured rural southern dialect while the black characters generally speak standard English. Though fools and boors, the whites in these stories are also dangerous. They are as uncivilized, and therefore potentially as violent, as jealous children, but with considerably more power to hurt. Very often the story of interaction with them illustrates the necessity of withholding information, remaining silent. To keep silent, the stories suggest, is wisdom: it conveys a deceptive impression to an enemy or potential enemy without overtly lying, and therefore in some sense controls the meaning of the interaction.

One good example of this type is the story about the time, in her early married life in a new town, when a white sewing-machine salesman came to her door and offered to sell her a used machine—one that another woman couldn't finish paying for. While Fields silently hesitated, the salesman left the house and returned right away with the machine. The elder Fields comments: "He must have taken it from somebody right there in the neighborhood. And for all I know, with the ways they had, he might just have walked in and picked it up off her table, pulling her goods out from under the needle. I wouldn't have put that past him. Goodness! He couldn't know all I was thinking. I guess he just went by what he could see" (p. 171). Thus though an outside witness of this event, and in fact the salesman himself, would probably have thought her the loser in this situation, manipulated into the sale, by providing private information about her silent commentary on the inhumanity of his behavior to the other woman and on his lack of perception about herself, Fields makes sure that her version of the meaning of this encounter gets passed along as the truth to her granddaughter.

Another group of segregation stories, more serious in tone, presents an opposite strategy for coping with the routine humiliations of segregation and white racism. They urge self-assertion and a degree of open defiance of the rules of the game for race relations in the South. They suggest that because most of these rules for behavior with whites are unwritten, they are not always enforceable, and some may not even be real: they may be imagined—the result of the poisonous habit of self-intimidation.

Fields credits her mother with teaching her how to stand up for herself. "My mother could always answer, when white people would try to treat her like a slave servant. I got that from her," she says, before telling a story about a time when her mother demanded respect from the white salesman in a shoe store: "Two things she couldn't take. She couldn't take slavery business, and she couldn't take color business. Both those things were her 'fightin' pieces.' So although she would walk away from most fights with the attitude 'What goes around comes around,' if people joked about slavery or if they got to calling one another black, she got mad. She just didn't like it" (p. 11).

Like her mother, Mamie Garvin Fields would consciously act as a model of inventive self-assertion for others, and in so doing, as she says, "I opened many a person's eyes to the possibility of using their own brain" (p. 111). *Lemon Swamp* contains several stories about times when Fields's assertiveness both put the overly familiar white person in his or her place and helped her accomplish the practical goal she was seeking. One of Fields's most memorable self-assertion stories deals with how she broke a long-standing unwritten rule of the black community of Charleston by "going through the front door" to get her first teaching job, rather than through "the kitchen"—in other words, by refusing the influence of a black power broker who acted as "henchman" to powerful whites (p. 110).

The overriding theme of these stories is the necessity of demanding respect from whites by presenting oneself as highly self-respecting. She tells one initially frightening, but ultimately comic, cautionary tale at her own expense. It is about the one time she broke her own rule always to dress respectably and got into her car to drive her husband to work, wearing her house slippers, with a coat on over her nightgown. Naturally, she was involved in an automobile accident and had to get out and deal with the white authorities. Because of the way she was dressed, she felt unable to defend herself as she would normally have done, and didn't say a word. Fortunately, the other car was driven by a white northerner, so the southern policeman sided with her against the "damn Yankee." She emerged victorious because of the white southerner's comic regional xenophobia. But the serious moral of the story for herself and the younger generation she addresses is clear: "There's no way in the world you can stand up for yourself in your houseshoes—just as you can't get respect in your apron" (p. 167).[20]

Most of the remaining personal experience narratives in *Lemon Swamp* portray Mamie Garvin Fields in one of two heroic female roles. In one type she is the enterprising, energetic woman with business acumen who, though relatively secure socially and financially, nevertheless starts up a small tailoring or hairdressing business in her home, often with a female friend. In an economic system controlled largely by whites, these stories imply, one always needs to have many ways to support oneself and one's family. Though the text does not discuss this point directly, some of the stories suggest to this reader that Fields found the life of a settled, house-bound wife and mother insufficient for her need for action in the outside world. When barred from practicing her profession through either racism or discrimination against married women teachers, she seems to have turned gladly to her dressmaking skills and business acumen for a secondary occupation outside of the family sphere.

In the second group of stories, Mamie Garvin Fields appears in her professional role as a college-educated schoolteacher of the poor. Here she is seen as embattled with enemies of several kinds, and in these stories she is best able to show that self-assertion can be fused with community service to create a model of community-oriented female heroism for the next generation.

A group of memories, pulled together into two chapters, describes her several years in her teaching job on John's Island, one of the sea islands off Charleston. In these she portrays herself as a young college graduate from the city, set down in a "wild" place where she didn't understand the customs. She emphasizes the poverty of the people and their oppression, not only by the neglect of the white authorities supposedly responsible for their education but also by some unscrupulous local black leaders—the minister who seduces and abandons a young parishioner and the root doctor who plays on people's fears to exploit and control them.

The value of *Lemon Swamp* as a book aimed primarily at young women increases, I think, when in the John's Island stories Mamie Fields shows herself grappling not only with her own inexperience and an utter lack of teaching resources, but with internal terrors as well. She describes not only culture shock but personal fear and half-belief when she first encounters John's Island folk religion in the form of the belief in "hag," or witchcraft. In a story remarkably reminiscent of one told by Maxine Hong Kingston about her Chinese mother's nocturnal fight with a ghost, Mamie Garvin Fields describes how she finally conquered her dreams of the visiting "hag":

> The hag always came with his hands wide open, hands cupped and fingers apart, and thrust them to you and back, thrust them nearer and come nearer, like that. I made up my mind, if that witch came, I was going to tear his hands apart and beat him in the face or anywhere I could get, kill that witch that night. And the witch came. Just as I said, I pulled his hands apart. I knocked him down and off the bed. When she came and jumped on me in the bed, as usual, I caught her hand and pulled her fingers apart with all my strength, beat him or her in the face—at the end, it seemed like the lady in the loft. She got out of the bed and ran away.... Do you know that thing never came back? That dream *never* came back. (P. 119)

The stories about her earliest struggles as a young, unmarried teacher are counterbalanced by a group portraying her as an older, more experienced, and self-confident teacher, after marriage and child-rearing. In the two chapters centered on her teaching on James Island, she tells how, in the days before compulsory education, she was able to convince rural parents to send their children to school through adroit manipulation of the truant officer and parent (p. 233). Many stories are about how hard she worked to instill racial pride and what we might call middle-class values like neatness and punctuality in her "wild" pupils and their parents. At the same time, she includes several stories that show ways in which she genuinely respected the poor and learned from them, and how she took advantage of federal programs during the 1930s to benefit her school, even when she had to fight with the local southern authorities to do so. Other stories emphasize how she became a spokesperson for the black teachers with the local white authorities, because she alone was willing either to speak up when possible or to take silent action when speech would have been counterproductive.

It is a heroic self-portrait—not of the highly individualized personal self so much as of the role of dedicated teacher and community leader. Appropriately, to my mind, the final shaping of the stories into a book emphasizes the virtual merging of Mamie Garvin Fields's professional and personal identities. The memoir effectively ends with her retirement from teaching in the 1940s. Karen Fields suggests in an epilogue that the grandmother and granddaughter agreed to regard the period before Mamie Garvin Fields's retirement from teaching as "her day," a time when her experience gave her special authority to speak. In contrast, the period after that time, including the decades of the civil rights movement, could be justly seen as the day of younger people, and not properly the subject of the book (pp. 242–43). What Mamie Garvin Fields had to teach about black cultural identity and freedom (in her granddaughter's view, at any rate) had already been shown and said in her retrospective recreation of her doings and sayings as a teacher, during a time when the teaching of self-respect to southern black children was a radical activity.

Mamie Garvin Fields, like Shakespeare's sister Judith, never wrote a book. But as this edited conversation with her granddaughter shows, the life she lived was not merely one of victimization. Although she frequently chose to wear the mask of silence in public situations, to conceal a dangerous knowledge from a powerful but ignorant enemy, she was never completely silenced. She was fully and proudly literate, yet she did not live in a time and place in which she could conceptualize herself as a writer. The lessons and eloquence of her life story would have remained in the privacy and concealment of the family and immediate community, had she not allowed the conversations with her granddaughter to undergo translation from the world of their talk to the very different language of the printed page. We would do well, as students and teachers with a particular interest in constructing a history of women's writing, to use books like *Lemon Swamp* alongside books like *A Room of One's Own*. They will help us bear truer witness to the diversity of our past and present relation, as women, to the narrative arts of self-expression.

NOTES

1. Walter J. Ong, *Orality and Literacy: The Technologizing of the Word* (New York: Methuen, 1982), p. 78.

2. Gloria Anzaldúa, "Speaking in Tongues: A Letter to Third World Women Writers," in *This Bridge Called My Back: Writings by Radical Women of Color,* ed.

Cherríe Moraga and Gloria Anzaldúa (Watertown, Mass.: Persephone Press, 1981).

3. For Ong's discussion of the ways in which the style of literature in the West was influenced by the education of male professionals and political leaders of Europe in academic rhetoric and learned Latin, and the impact of women's very different schooling on their belated entry into Western literature, see *Orality and Literacy*, ch. 4, "Writing Restructures Consciousness," especially pp. 108–16.

4. See, for example, Elizabeth Hampsten's *Read This Only to Yourself: The Private Writings of Midwestern Women, 1880–1910* (Bloomington: Indiana University Press, 1982); Lenore Hoffmann and Margo Culley, eds., *Women's Personal Narratives: Essays in Criticism and Pedagogy* (New York: MLA, 1985); Margo Culley, *A Day at a Time: The Diary Literature of American Women from 1764 to the Present* (New York: Feminist Press at the City University of New York, 1985); Jean M. Humez, "My Spirit Eye: Some Functions of Spiritual and Visionary Experience in the Lives of Five Black Women Preachers, 1810–1880," in *Women and the Structure of Society: Selected Research from the Fifth Berkshire Conference on the History of Women*, ed. Barbara J. Harris and Joann K. McNamara (Durham, N.C.: Duke University Press, 1984), pp. 129–43; Estelle C. Jelinek, ed., *Women's Autobiography: Essays in Criticism* (Bloomington: Indiana University Press, 1980); and Estelle C. Jelinek, *The Tradition of Women's Autobiography: From Antiquity to the Present* (Boston: G. K. Hall, 1986).

5. Elizabeth A. Meese, "The Languages of Oral Testimony and Women's Literature," in *Women's Personal Narratives*, ed. Hoffman and Culley, pp. 18–26.

6. For a good brief discussion of the different virtues of oral performances and literary versions of the same story, see Roger D. Abrahams, *Afro-American Folktales: Stories from Black Traditions in the New World* (New York: Pantheon, 1985), Preface, pp. xvii–xix.

7. Marta Weigle, "Women as Verbal Artists: Reclaiming the Daughters of Enheduanna," *Frontiers* 3, no. 3 (1978), 1–9; quote on p. 3.

8. The secular spoken arts have received more attention than the religious, but an important article on the latter is Elaine J. Lawless, "Shouting for the Lord: The Power of Women's Speech in the Pentecostal Religious Service," *Journal of American Folklore* 96, no. 382 (Oct.–Dec. 1983), 434–59. On secular spoken-arts forms such as gossip, see Susan Harding, "Women and Words in a Spanish Village," in *Toward an Anthropology of Women*, ed. Rayna Reiter (New York: Monthly Review Press, 1975), 283–308; Patricia Meyer Spacks, "In Praise of Gossip," *Hudson Review* 35, no. 1 (Spring 1982), 19–38; Deborah Jones, "Gossip: Notes on Women's Oral Culture," *Women's Studies International Quarterly* 3 (1980), 193–98; Claudia Mitchell-Kernan, "Signifying, Loud-Talking and Marking," in *Rappin' and Stylin' Out: Communication in Urban Black America*, ed. Thomas Kochman (Urbana: University of Illinois Press, 1972), pp. 315–35; Fern L. Johnson and Elizabeth J. Aries, "The Talk of Women Friends," *Women's Studies International Forum* 6, no. 4 (1983), 353–61; and Susan Kalčik, "'like Ann's gynecologist or the time I was almost raped': Personal Narrative in Women's Rap Groups," in *Women and Folklore*, ed. Claire R. Farrer (Austin: University of Texas Press, 1975), pp. 3–11.

9. For example, folklorist Linda Dégh described a pair of elderly Hungarian-American widows, living in geographical isolation from family and friends outside Gary, Indiana, who were able to create new, hybrid repertoires combining dreams, jokes, personal experience stories, media-inspired ancedotes, and adaptations of traditional lore in long, daily, cooperative storytelling sessions on the telephone (Dégh, "Dial a Story, Dial an Audience: Two Rural Women Narrators in an Urban Setting," in *Women's Folklore, Women's Culture*, ed. Rosan Jordan and Susan Kalčik [Philadelphia: University of Pennsylvania Press, 1985], pp. 3–25). Similarly, in a study of older immigrant Jews in southern California, anthropologist Barbara Myerhoff noted that the women displayed much greater ability to improvise an adjustment to new life circumstances than did the men, and argued that their freewheeling adaptations of a wide variety of vernacular verbal arts played a crucial part in this process (Myerhoff, *Number Our Days* [New York: E. P. Dutton, 1979], especially ch. 7, "Jewish Comes Up in You from the Roots," pp. 232–68).

10. In a suggestive case study of her own rural Pennsylvania relatives, folklorist Karen Baldwin has observed that when she was present, the husband and wife took complementary roles in a domestic storytelling performance. The husband, whose storytelling habits were conditioned by tale-telling competition and display in his all-male work world, generally told even a family history story or personal experience narrative as if it were an entertaining fiction, attempting always to tell a dramatically structured tale, "a story with a point." Meanwhile the wife cheerfully spoiled his dramatic telling in order to make sure that the literal truth was presented to the listener representing the younger generation of the family (Baldwin, "Woof! A Word on Women's Roles in Family Storytelling," in *Women's Folklore, Women's Culture*, ed. Jordan and Kalčik, pp. 149–62). Folktale collector James York Glimm also noted, in a study of a northern Pennsylvania Anglo-American community, that "women would not participate in story-telling sessions, but they would monitor them" (Glimm, *Flatlanders and Ridgerunners: Folktales from the Mountains of Northern Pennsylvania* [Pittsburgh: University of Pittsburgh Press, 1983], p. xxi).

11. The phrase is used to describe the way in which female literary style in the nineteenth-century novel tended to differ from the rhetorical voice of the university-educated male (Ong, *Orality and Literacy*, p. 160). For a suggestive reminiscence about such an all-female storytelling setting, see Rayna Green, "Magnolias Grow in Dirt: The Bawdy Lore of Southern Women," in *Speaking for Ourselves: Women of the South*, ed. Maxine Alexander (New York: Pantheon, 1984), pp. 20–28.

12. Kathryn L. Morgan, *Children of Strangers: The Stories of a Black Family* (Philadelphia: Temple University Press, 1980).

13. One detailed use of a novel's representation of conversation to illuminate male/female speech differences is Muriel L. Schultz's study of Virginia Woolf's *To the Lighthouse*, "A Style of One's Own," in *Women's Language and Style*, ed. Douglas Butterff and Edmund L. Epstein (Department of English, University of Akron: Studies in Contemporary Literature no. 1, 1978). There is a large and growing body of feminist discussion of the way plots developed by women fiction writers may derive from and illuminate gender-specific social experience.

See, for example, Nina Baym, *Women's Fiction: A Guide to Novels by and about Women in America, 1820–1870* (Ithaca: Cornell University Press, 1978); and Elizabeth Abel, Marianne Hirsch, and Elizabeth Langland, eds., *The Voyage In: Fictions of Female Development* (Hanover, N.H.: University Press of New England, 1983).

14. Ong, *Orality and Literacy,* p. 11.

15. Those who have written about oral history interview technique emphasize the importance of the freestanding story as the heart of the interview—in part because when she begins to tell stories, the interview subject is actively structuring the conversation, rather than merely responding passively to the agenda of the interviewer. Thus it seems appropriate to emphasize the centrality of the embedded story in an edited oral-historical autobiography as the material most likely to have been organized by the interviewed woman herself. See Sherna Gluck, "What's So Special about Women? Women's Oral History," in *Oral History: An Interdisciplinary Anthology,* ed. David K. Dunaway and Willa K. Baum (Nashville, Tenn.: American Association for State and Local History, 1984); and Susan H. Armitage, "The Next Step," *Frontiers* 7, no. 1 (1983), 3–8.

16. Mamie Garvin Fields with Karen Fields, *Lemon Swamp and Other Places: A Carolina Memoir* (New York: Free Press, 1983).

17. Margo Culley makes the point that women's diary writing helps the writer integrate past and present images of self and, as much as any autobiographical writing, may be thought to confer some degree of immortality on the writer (Introduction, A *Day at a Time,* pp. 8–14).

18. For a sample of sources on Afro-American folk traditions, see Abrahams, *Afro-American Folk Tales;* Zora Neale Hurston, *Mules and Men: Negro Folktales and Voodoo Practices in the South* (1935; New York: Harper and Row, 1970); and Gladys-Marie Frye, *Night-Riders in Black Folk History* (Knoxville: University of Tennessee Press, 1975).

19. The folklorist Roger D. Abrahams pointed out several years ago that, in some urban Afro-American communities, a firm line is drawn between the worlds of the home (the woman's sphere) and of the street (the man's sphere). Traditional women in such a setting derive much of their sense of self-respect from insisting on their competence in and control of the culture of the home, and equal rejection of the theoretically forbidden culture of the street (Abrahams, "Negotiating Respect: Patterns of Presentation among Black Women," in *Women and Folklore,* ed. Farrer, pp. 58–80). We know from Fields's stories about John's Island that she found some aspects of southern black folk religion both frightening and a factor in maintaining Afro-Americans in ignorance and poverty (see especially chs. 7, 8, and 12, about her years on John's Island and James Island). She also expresses anger at the exploitation of Afro-American people and folkways by the white "researchers" who came to James Island to get material on black religious expression for *Porgy and Bess* (pp. 214–16).

20. On the importance of respect in the ideology of the traditional Afro-American woman, consult Abrahams, "Patterns of Negotiating Respect," or Aretha Franklin's more powerful variation on the theme, "R-E-S-P-E-C-T."

LOIS RUDNICK

A Feminist American Success Myth: Jane Addams's Twenty Years at Hull-House

In his essay "Autobiography and America," James Cox points out that Benjamin Franklin's autobiography established self-generation as the essential myth of the American Dream. Franklin's was the first major American autobiography written in the success-myth tradition to celebrate the self-made man as an embodiment of the most important values of his culture. Able to transcend the impediments of class, past, and family in order to seize the opportunities that brought fame, fortune, and public recognition, he had no need for woman, except as helpmeet and release for his excess sexual energy.[1] The mid-nineteenth-century "cult of true womanhood" encouraged woman to exchange her sexuality for genteel domesticity. The American success myth still did not include her— or her values.

When we examine the broader issue of national character for which the success-myth heroes of autobiography and popular literature were often the paradigm, we find a similar phenomenon. In 1910, when Jane Addams published *Twenty Years at Hull-House,* the debate about national character was at its peak, spurred by the influx of some fifteen million people who emigrated to the United States between 1860 and 1914. Whether the arguments were waged by racists, moderate Anglo-conformists, or (most) cultural pluralists, the qualities of national character held up as the model for assimilation were those of the male Anglo-American.

The generic Anglo-American defined by the scholarly and popular press was idealistic, but practical; passionately devoted to liberty; individualistic; self-reliant, energetic, and aggressive in the pursuit of material well-being; vital mentally and morally. The generic southern and eastern European immigrant created by the same press bore an opposite set of characteristics: he was anti-democratic; immoral; dull-witted; lacking in individuality and ambition; subject to a herd instinct—all traits that can be viewed as pejorative versions of the feminine ideal of purity, passivity, and submissiveness.[2]

On its surface, *Twenty Years at Hull-House* does not seem a threat to this male-defined Protestant typology. Examined more closely, however, the text is more revolutionary. Its values belong to a feminist tradition that has attempted to alter mainstream male definitions of the national character. "These 'feminine' qualities," as Alice Kessler-Harris has pointed out, "nourish the seeds out of which alternative life-styles might have grown. . . . Women, in other words, harbor values, attitudes, and behavior patterns potentially subversive to capitalism."[3] Addams never openly admits such an agenda, but read carefully, her autobiography argues for women as the proponents of an American Dream that is subversive of the capitalist ethos, if not of capitalist economics.

In *Twenty Years at Hull-House*, Jane Addams reshapes the Anglo-American male success myth of popular and autobiographical tradition by redefining its idea of heroism and by transforming its sexual and ethnic base. Hers may well be the first autobiography in American literature written in the success-myth tradition that creates a paradigm of national character and culture that is predominantly female and includes previously excluded racial and ethnic groups. The feminist ideology that permeates her text is not presented as a compensatory set of values. Rather, she absorbs what she perceives as the best elements of the male success myth into a revisioned America that is the potential model for a new world order.[4]

No Progressive reformer understood better than Jane Addams the profound cognitive dissonance Americans experienced as they applied the standards of behavior, work, and values of nineteenth-century, rural, Anglo-America to a twentieth-century, urban, industrialized society suffering from increasing poverty, class divisiveness, political corruption, and crime. No Progressive reformer understood better than she the national tragedy resulting from the ways in which many Americans were resolving this dissonance, as new immigrants became the scapegoats for fears about the weakening moral fabric of their civilization. Energies that should have gone into a critique of America's capitalist/industrialist order went instead into animus against the working class and the immigrant poor.

What, then, were Addams's autobiographical strategies for reshaping her readers' understanding of American character and culture? How did she transform the ethos of an older America, in which success was a matter of hard work, thrift, and individual initiative; poverty was attributed to faulty character; and women achieved success by marrying wisely?

In order to answer these questions we need to examine closely the artistry of *Twenty Years at Hull-House*. Until quite recently, Allen Davis's discussion of the text in his biography of Jane Addams has been the only analysis that looked at the autobiography for anything more than information about Addams's reformist ideals and her work within the settlement house movement. In the scholarship about American autobiographies, it is, with rare and recent exception, mentioned in passing, if at all. And yet it is a literary achievement, among its other virtues, which demonstrates its author's right to be admired as an artist of ideas, along with her other accomplishments.[5]

That Addams self-consciously crafted her life story becomes evident when one examines the earlier versions, published in a three-part series for the *Ladies Home Journal* in 1906. In her *Journal* articles, Addams is tentative about asserting her motives for settlement work. Whenever she is asked to recall these, she tells her readers, she always finds herself "at a loss for a reply." Many of the same anecdotes appear in both texts, but here they are not organized within any particular scheme, as she focuses on how she started Hull-House and on what she and her colleagues have accomplished. While *Twenty Years at Hull-House* also offers information on their achievements, that information is embedded within an aesthetic and philosophical framework.[6]

Gerda Lerner once asked what would history be like if it were seen through the eyes of women and ordered by the values they define.[7] Jane Addams's central question in *Hull-House* is, "What would America be like if it were seen through the eyes of women and ordered by the values they define?" The strategy by which Addams answers this question is enunciated toward the end of the book when she states: "Life had taught me at least one hard-earned lesson, that existing arrangements and the hoped for improvements must be mediated and reconciled to each other, that the new must be dove-tailed into the old as it were, if it were to endure."[8] This describes her book as well. In it, Addams "dovetails" by mediating and reconciling the old America with the new: pioneers with immigrants; working class with middle and upper classes; material with spiritual well-being; the arts with the sciences; theory with practice; education with work and play; and, most importantly, the domestic sphere with the wider arena of community, city, state, nation, and world, for which it serves as model.

Addams firmly establishes her life story within mainstream American heroic traditions. These legitimize her authority to speak for and to her fellow countrymen and women about the modern world that many of them have trouble comprehending. She begins her life within the familiar bounds of the male heroic journey, distorting some facts and highlighting others. In her first two chapters, she connects her formative years with the best of what she believes the American character has stood for, as well as with America's two most revered heroes: Washington and Lincoln. She certifies her right to the title of "mother of her country" with her very first memory—her confession to her father that she has told a lie and her father's absolving her of guilt because of her honesty.

Mr. Addams, who is linked to Washington as one of the founding fathers of his Illinois community, also fits the heroic image of the pioneer. He is the self-made man who helped to carve a civilization out of a wilderness through hard work, probity, and individual initiative. Rising from miller to banker to leading citizen to legislator and friend of Lincoln, he is, as the primary shaper of his daughter's character, a model progenitor. And Jane Addams is a model child, the weak and awkward "ugly duckling," as she calls herself, who overcomes her physical handicaps to achieve not only local but also national and international renown.

As Allen Davis has pointed out, Addams establishes herself as "the female counterpart of Lincoln," a connection that the press clearly acknowledged when calling her "the mother emancipator." One of her earliest memories is of watching a local troop march off to the Civil War "to die for freedom's sake" (HH, p. 37). She ties herself, Lincoln, and her father to the less dominant strain of the American success myth, which emphasizes equality of opportunity for all and the importance of public-spirited benevolence.[9] Addams recalls the way in which her father worked to create a sense of roots for his pioneer community by establishing the annual celebration of Old Settler's Day. She singles out his honoring a founding mother of the community, a German immigrant whose butter-and-egg money helped to support the building of an access route to the railroad. She is, Mr. Addams announces, " 'one of the public spirited pioneers to whose heroic fortitude we are indebted for the development of this country' " (HH, p. 41).

Throughout her autobiography, Addams interweaves images and motifs that will evoke positive emotional responses from her primarily Anglo-American, middle-class audience. When she creates a paradisical image of her rural childhood, she contrasts its health and freedom for growth with the constriction and misery of urban immigrant life, particularly as it affects children. More typically, she juxtaposes such images in order to help her readers discover ways in which the immigrant experience makes demands of sacrifice, courage, and hardiness like those asked of themselves or their parents as they moved from east to midwest, or from rural areas to the urban frontier. She is particularly astute in drawing her readers' attention to the similarities between pioneering and immigration.

Addams connects the settlement house movement directly to the original settlement of the country by defining "settling" as a migration "from one condition of life to another totally unlike it" (*HH*, p. 45). She sets up an analogue between her father's Old Settler's Day and the Pioneer Day she celebrates each New Year's at Hull-House. On New Year's Day each year, the first settlers of her Chicago neighborhood meet with its newest residents. On one occasion, when an ex-Yankee complains about the "foreign views" that cover the walls at Hull-House, Addams helps him to see the parallel between these and his carrying "yankee notions" to the midwest. Like the immigrants, he and his family eased their transplanting by maintaining their ties to the old world.

At the same time that Addams demonstrates her connections to the traditional values of mainstream American culture, she transforms them. She relates her early childhood dream that the world had ended and that she was left alone to restore it by re-inventing the wheel. The dream is striking, not because she sees herself as a redeemer, but rather because as an active, inventive savior Addams steps beyond the traditional female role of self-sacrificing martyrdom. She presents herself as a young woman who must master the technical skills usually possessed by men. Thus Addams observes the local blacksmith's craft so that she can perform her messianic role properly when called on to save the world.[10] This dream relates to a theme she emphasizes again and again in *Hull-House*. Women cannot lead the way, in a modern industrial society, on mere intuitive good will alone: trained intelligence is a necessity if justice is to be done to and by women.

Nowhere in Addams's descriptions of her own childhood can a reader determine whether the mind and character being formed are male or female. Her father responds to her as a vital, interesting, intelligent being whose sex seems irrelevant to her education. Thus he pays her five cents for every life of Plutarch she reads and twenty-five cents for every volume of Irving's life of Washington. When she asks her father why he is saddened by the death of Mazzini, who is not even an American, Addams receives a lesson a son might have received, a lesson that becomes the cornerstone of her Hull-House philosophy: "differences in nationality, language, creed mean nothing to those trying to fight for principles of freedom and justice" (*HH*, p. 32).[11]

When Addams becomes a student at Rockford Seminary, she insists on a course of study that includes economics, math, and natural sciences. In a rare moment of sarcasm, she tells her readers how a suffragist colleague's career had demonstrated the "efficiency of higher mathematics for women," for she could convince even "the densest legislators of their legal right to define their own electorate" (*HH,* p. 53). In her commencement oration, Addams warns her fellow students about following in the footsteps of Cassandra, the kind of woman whose "tragic fate" was "always to be in the right, and always to be disbelieved and rejected," because she had nothing beyond intuition to support her assertions of truth (*HH,* p. 57). *Twenty Years at Hull-House* is replete with the scientific fact-finding that served as the basis for much of the residents' successful lobbying to establish laws to protect working men and women, consumers, and children.

Addams's presentation of her years at Rockford Seminary emphasizes the beginning of her connection with a variety of female institutions and networks that she later shows are essential to the work at Hull-House. She connects this first generation of college-educated women with pioneer and religious traditions that are nourished on idealistic notions of community, at the same time that she emphasizes her contribution to establishing an equal, if separate, sphere by helping to transform her female seminary into a full-fledged, four-year woman's college. Addams takes on a symbolic leadership role when she recalls debating William Jennings Bryan in an oratory contest in which she claims to have represented "college women in general."[12] Sensitive to the self-deprecating inflections of female discourse, she mentions her college friends' severe criticism of her discouraging habit of dropping her voice in an "apologetic manner" during practice sessions (*HH,* p. 53).

In the chapter on Rockford, Addams also begins to develop the female metaphors that become central to her imaginative reshaping of American culture and society, first noting the adoption by her college class of the "early Saxon word for lady, translated into breadgiver" (*HH,* p. 49). Along with other feminists of her generation, she draws on the traditional sphere of women's work to argue for its natural connection to the realm of "municipal [and later national and international] housekeeping."[13]

While Addams portrays herself as representative of the intelligence, ambition, and idealism that marked the first generation of college women, she also portrays herself as representative of the dislocation many of them experienced as their families attempted to limit their post-college careers to lives of social duties and leisured dilettantism. She starts medical school, but is forced to leave because of ill-health. Suffering from the mysterious neurasthenia that affected many women of her class and education, she is sent off on the traditional rest-cure vacation to Europe. Here she dutifully tours museums and cathedrals, dramatizing vividly the tedium of her class's debilitating idea of culture. After each bout with a museum, she "would invariably suffer a moral revulsion against this feverish search after culture" (*HH,* p. 66).

Culture, Raymond Williams tells us, originally meant the nurturing of human and physical nature. By the late nineteenth century it had come to mean a set of canonized texts and artworks that, to paraphrase Matthew Arnold, were the best that had been thought, written, painted, or sculpted. It was a term appropriated by the Victorian upper class that served both to define their class hegemony and to differentiate them from the presumed barbarism of the lower orders.[14] Addams begins to subvert this elitist concept of culture in her chapter on "The Snare of Preparation," when she draws her readers' attention to the "really living world" of the oppressed working classes of Europe who provide a striking contrast to the dead forms of the past.

Addams's encompassing concept of culture embraces the life-ways of all classes and groups of people. Drawing upon the ideals of the Social Gospel movement, she imagines establishing a "cathedral of humanity" that would integrate the aesthetic, the moral, and the material by being "beautiful enough to persuade men to hold fast to the vision of human solidarity" (*HH,* p. 71). Throughout the rest of her autobiography, she shows how Hull-House became just such a cathedral—one that accepts and promotes a multicultural America, one that revises the canon of its day by supporting and promoting working-class and ethnic literature, drama, poetry, and folk arts along with the more traditionally acceptable Shakespeare and Aristotle.

Addams is empowered to enact this vision only after she has undergone a highly charged conversion experience at the bullfights in Spain. Chastised by her friends for her pleasure in this bloody sport, she realizes the full extent to which her search for European culture has corroded her moral values. Her readers, of course, were primed to accept the image of the American girl as moral innocent.[15] This is not the first or last time in the text that Addams contrasts American decency and democratic fair play with the aristocratic evils of a corrupt European society. She understood very well the American ambivalence toward a Europe at once disdained and courted. When it suits her purposes, she plays on the alternate image, quoting the responses of European visitors who find American society and American cities shockingly laggard with regard to social and labor legislation.

The sexual undertones of this experience, however, are at least as significant as the cultural overtones. For what Addams finds so horrible in the bullfight is the male ritual of homoerotic violence—a glimpse, perhaps, of what the world would be like without women. Bullfighting represents for her a gratuitously and murderously aggressive masculinity. In fact, her language makes it sound as though she has experienced a form of rape. Shocked by the witness of her own "brutal endurance," she is freed from both "passive receptivity" and the "ox-cart of self-seeking" to pursue her true vocation (*HH*, p. 73). She is also freed, it is crucial to point out, from an obligation to heterosexuality, and thus from a patriarchal system that oppresses "weaker" natures.

The bullfight episode is the only sexually unguarded moment in Addams's autobiography. More symbolically than overtly, it suggests the commitment of her erotic self to women, a self which she is careful to exclude from her life story, along with any mention of Mary Rozet Smith, who was her companion and lover for forty years. In *Surpassing the Love of Men*, Lillian Faderman discusses the importance of "Boston marriages" for women who were engaged in the "pioneer experience of living by their brains." But as Carroll Smith-Rosenberg has pointed out, by the first decade of the twentieth century, there was good reason for lesbian women not to make their love public knowledge because of an increasing public obsession with homosexuality as abnormal and obscene.[16]

There are two other exclusions that are crucial to understanding Addams's finding her vocation after eight years of being caught in what she calls the "snare of preparation." Rebecca Sherrick and Phillip Abbott have pointed out that while Addams was indeed "her father's daughter," she had to free herself from his influence before she could succeed in the public sphere. He had, after all, kept her from going to Smith because he wanted her close to home. He died shortly after she graduated from college, and his death was connected to her lost sense of purpose after she graduated. Although her father was linked to the revered martyr Lincoln, he was also linked to a patriarchal way of life she could not condone. Addams also had to break away from the demands made by her stepmother (who is unmentioned in her autobiography) that she devote herself to her remaining family.[17]

Only after Addams is symbolically freed from the "passive receptivity" of subordinating herself to father, husband, family, and European culture can she enact the messianic dream she outlined in her opening chapter: she will now work with other "young people [who] are longing to construct the world anew" (*HH*, p. 74). While that world is not confined to women, it is dominated by them, in a productive, nurturing, and supportive environment. As Blanche Weisen Cook has pointed out, for women leaders like Lillian Wald and Jane Addams, "service to humanity and leadership in public life were constantly refuelled by their female support communities and by personal relationships with women who gave them passionate love and loyalty." This new world will also incorporate the so-called "inferior" races from southern and eastern Europe, who are the most recent immigrants to flock through the golden door into the American Dream. Abbott has noted that "central focus" of Addams's work "is based upon her image of immigrants as a 'household of children whose mother is dead.' Addams saw in the immigrant what she saw in herself, for she too was an immigrant, herself adrift from parental power, from the security of her class and the sorority of her forbears."[18]

Up until "First Days at Hull-House," Addams follows a chronological order centered on her own development as an individual. In her preface Addams says that she has made no effort "to separate my own history from that of Hull-House" at the moment when her work begins there. She then apologizes for having to "abandon the chronological order in favor of the topical," because she can no longer remember the exact sequence of the myriad activities in which she and her colleagues were involved. Although Addams's explanation accounts for the dramatic structural change that occurs in the second part of the book, her decision seems more than pragmatic.

Canonical autobiography insists on the self, particularly in America, and Addams certainly maintains the unique integrity of each individual self, including her own. For Addams, however, these autobiographical conventions must be dovetailed with the concept of the self in relation to society that she believes is necessary for fully realized humanity in a complex, interdependent, modern world. When she ends the focus on her private life and personal development, she thereby displaces the self from the center of autobiographical interest.

In "First Days at Hull-House," the "I" who has been at the center of Addams's text recedes and the "we" of the Hull-House community and its surrounding immigrant neighborhoods take center stage. In an essay on women's autobiographies, Mary Mason points out that "the self-discovery of female identity seems to acknowledge the real presence of recognition of another consciousness and the disclosure of female self is [often] linked to the identification with some 'other.' "[19] It is important to note that the title of Addams's autobiography makes no mention of her name and that the subtitle reads "With Autobiographical Notes." The house—that is, the people who live, work, and learn within and around it—becomes the collective hero of the remaining story.

Addams concludes *Hull-House* with a statement that re-emphasizes the controlling concept of the second part of her life story: "The educational activities of a Settlement, as well as its philanthropic, civic and social undertakings, are but different manifestations of the attempt to socialize democracy, as is the very existence of the Settlement itself" (*HH*, p. 310). This socialization is dependent on a model of personal and community relationships very different from the linear and hierarchical model of the traditional "climb the ladder of success" story.

As Carol Gilligan points out, in discussing the ways in which women often "image" relationships, "The ideal of care is . . . an activity of relationship, of seeing and responding to need, taking care of the world by sustaining the *web* [my emphasis] of connection so that no one is left alone. . . . The experiences of inequality and interconnection, inherent in the relation of parent and child, . . . give rise to the ethics of justice and care, the ideals of human relationship—the vision that self and other will be treated as of equal worth, that despite differences in power, things will be fair; the vision that everyone will be responded to and included, that no one will be left alone or hurt."[20] The web metaphor best describes both the philosophical rationale for the work done at Hull-House as well as the organizational scheme of the rest of Addams's autobiography, which interweaves the social, political, and cultural functions of the Settlement in all their "different manifestations." When one tallies up the local, state, national, and international accomplishments of the women of Hull-House, over the course of the many chapters in which they are noted, one must be impressed by the extraordinary achievements of a feminist cooperative ethic that ultimately incorporates all of humanity within its web.[21]

Addams presents Hull-House as a microcosm of an ideal American society that is run as a feminist collective. In fact, it was one of the most outstandingly successful and longest-lived feminist collectives in American history. As Dolores Hayden notes in *The Grand Domestic Revolution*, the concept of home as a symbol of a reconstructed American society began with mid-nineteenth-century utopian experiments and working women's cooperatives. Hayden writes of the settlement movement: "A new approach to collective domestic life seemed to be emerging, under the leadership of a small group of highly educated women" who "stressed women's collective attempts to improve the public environment and the domestic lives of ordinary people."[22] While men were important contributors, Addams clearly identifies the leadership with women. Hull-House is described as a primarily female space that unifies a heterogeneous body of people in a common mission to achieve a society based on humane values.

Addams makes her case for the social necessity of female values most powerfully in her chapter titled "The Subjective Necessity for Social Settlements." This subjective necessity is based "not only upon conviction, but upon genuine emotion, wherever young people are seeking an outlet for that sentiment of universal brotherhood, which the best spirit of our times is forcing from an emotion into a motive" (*HH,* p. 91). Earlier, Addams had written about the "objective necessity" for social settlements, using as evidence statistics on labor strife, rising crime, and family breakdowns, but she chose not to include this essay in *Hull-House.* For her primary goal here is to transform the consciousness of readers whose response—then as now—to such "objective necessities" was a call for more law and order.

Addams's belief that the unity of humankind can be achieved only by acknowledging its roots in female experience was shared by several feminists of her generation, most notably Charlotte Perkins Gilman. Like many social theorists in Chicago, Addams was probably influenced by Lester Ward's "gynecocentric" ideology, which claimed that women were progenitors of the human race and that males were a "subsequent variation," whose aggressive and competitive natures had proved destructive of human community.[23] Middle-class youth, Addams tells us, have been cut off from "the race life," but they will discover the source of the organic unity that binds all classes and races in "the great motherbreasts of our common humanity" (*HH,* p. 93). This image is rooted for Addams in the primordial archetype of the Great Mother and is also connected with the early Christian church, which she views as essentially female in character. Believing in love as a "cosmic force," the early Christians were "eager to sacrifice themselves for the weak, for children and for the aged; they identified themselves with slaves" (*HH,* p. 96).[24]

Addams places the "subjective necessity" for social settlements within a religious tradition that is tied to "social salvation." She then identifies American democracy and the Social Gospel movement as continuing the ideals of the early church, when it served as the religion of the oppressed: "There was also growing within me an almost passionate devotion to the ideals of democracy," she notes of her decision to join the Presbyterian church, "and when in all history had these ideals been so thrillingly expressed as when the faith of the fisherman and the slave had been boldly opposed to the accepted moral belief that the well-being of a privileged few might justly be built upon the ignorance and sacrifice of the many? Who was I, with my dreams of universal fellowship, that I did not identify myself with the institutional statement of this belief, as it stood in the little village in which I was born, and without which testimony in each remote hamlet of Christendom it would be so easy for the world to slip back into the doctrines of selection and aristocracy" (*HH,* pp. 68–69).[25]

In the remainder of her autobiography, Addams demonstrates the naturally widening gyre of responsibility that such subjective necessity engenders: from the personal commitment of herself and her colleagues to the neighborhood; from the neighborhood to the municipality and the state, which have the power to pass laws affecting the welfare of those who live within their boundaries; to the federal government, which must regulate problems that cross state boundaries; to international organizations in which Americans can act in concert with social reformers from other nations on issues common to the lives of all peoples: health, sanitation, food, labor, and peace.

Addams shows Hull-House, as a model democracy, to be a vital center for the integrated political, economic, social, and cultural life of the city. Socialists, anarchists, and conservatives share the same space and forum. There are lectures on astronomy and evolution, but there are also dances and social clubs. The house serves as an extension of the University of Chicago, as well as a night school for adult immigrants who need to learn English, because the residents do not assume that college culture should necessarily be the norm for all. Their ideal of education for college-bound and non-college-bound alike is Deweyan—that students will be connected "with all sorts of people" by their "ability to understand them as well as by their power to supplement their present surroundings with the historic background" (HH, p. 300).[26] Hull-House provides a stage for the plays of Ibsen and Shaw as well as for the creation of new ethnic theater. It celebrates American holidays and rituals, but it also encourages the preservation of traditions of the many world cultures that make up the neighborhood.

Addams's philosophy of education is epitomized in her description of the Hull-House Labor Museum. It provides immigrant women an opportunity to display their old-world skills within the context of the evolution of manufacturing and places them in the role of teacher, which is important to adults who are so often reliant on their children to interpret for them. The museum gives to crafts the status usually accorded only to the fine arts, at the same time that it contains a series of self-supporting workshops in metal, fabric, and pottery. It is, finally, a living definition of Addams's non-elitist theory of culture: "the Labor Museum and the shops pointed out the possibilities which Hull-House had scarcely begun to develop, of demonstrating that culture is an understanding of the long-established occupations and thoughts of men, of the arts with which they have solaced their toil" (HH, p. 175).

Addams comments that the settlement has been called a sociological laboratory but that she hopes it is something much more spontaneous and human. Her creative ability to dramatize the individual lives of the working-class men and women who frequent Hull-House—they are always neighbors and never clients—is her most persuasive tool in helping her readers to acknowledge their humanity. Addams selects her stories carefully and, on the whole, presents them nonjudgmentally. Her purpose is to cultivate in her readers the kind of imaginative empathy that will allow them to understand the multicultural worlds of her neighbors from *their* points of view: the elderly woman who in boredom and out of desperation peels paint off her tenement walls, until a professor from Hull-House discovers her fluency in Gaelic; the harassed mother who doesn't believe her son, "Goosie," is dead when he is blown off a tenement roof and who begs Addams to give her one day's wages so that she can stay home and hold his dead body; the nursing mother whose breast milk mixes with the slop water she uses to clean the floors of buildings late at night; the Bohemian goldsmith who kills himself with drink because he has no outlet for his creative instincts; the second-generation adolescents whose budding talents as artists and musicians are cut short by tuberculosis; the second-generation adolescents who are driven to crime or suicide from the despair caused by their impoverished lives.

Addams recapitulates the early chapters of her life story in showing how the Hull-House women help their immigrant neighbors along the same route that they themselves have traveled from domesticity to mutual support to social reform, from the belief that their station in life is responsible for their oppression to the recognition that their own combined efforts can change their situation. Thus she cites the "value of social clubs" as "an instrument of companionship through which many may be led from a sense of isolation to one of civic responsibility" (*HH,* p. 253). These clubs, which cross class and ethnic boundaries, also served an important civilizing function for older immigrants and native-born Americans. Referring to an Irish-American woman's admiration for a group of "dagoes" who had spent an evening entertaining her "Social Extension Committee" at Hull-House, Addams provides her readers with an example of how such committees could work to prevent what we have come to call "white flight." Addams's informant says that, as a result of this experience, she will not now be in such a hurry to move out of the neighborhood. Addams tells us, her irony barely in check: "To my mind at that moment the speaker had passed from the region of the uncultivated person into the possibilities of the cultivated person. The former is bounded by a narrow outlook on life, unable to overcome differences of dress and habit... while the latter constantly tends to be more a citizen of the world because of his growing understanding of all kinds of people with their varying experiences" (*HH,* p. 249).

Throughout her discussions of social and civic cooperation, public investigations, and pioneer legislation, Addams demonstrates what recent feminist historians have pointed out about the importance of women reformers' breaking of class barriers by forming gender-based alliances. A particularly interesting example is her description of the federation she chaired of one hundred women's organizations that worked for the municipal franchise for women in Chicago: a church society of Lutheran women whose home countries had given women the municipal vote in the seventeenth century; factory women who wanted more sanitary workplaces; property-owning women who had no say in their taxation; university women interested in "good government" reforms; Russian women who wanted covered markets to protect the cleanliness of the food they purchased; Italian women who wanted public washhouses. As Mary Jo Buhle has noted about such alliances, the women used their "faith in collective sisterhood" to substitute gender consciousness for class consciousness, a consciousness rooted in a belief in "womanly virtue against marketplace capitalism, cooperation overcoming competition, social reconstruction rather than class warfare." Fundamental to the philosophy Addams incorporates in *Hull-House* is her refusal to accept warfare of any sort, including gender or class warfare. Thus she insists that the "labor movement is a general social movement concerning all members of society and not merely a class struggle" (*HH*, p. 158).[27]

Because the immigrants themselves have much to teach their fellow Americans, Addams emphasizes their contributions to the regeneration of America's national character and culture; in fact, it is they who are the true keepers of the spiritual and political flame of the American Dream. Throughout her autobiography, we hear their voices, in wonder and protest, acknowledging how their dream of America as a land of opportunity and democracy has been tarnished by the indifference of Americans to anything but money and social status. A Greek student of architecture carries on his pushcart drawings of the ancient buildings in his native Athens, only to be laughed at by the American customers he tries to interest in them. An Italian workman tells Addams that in America " 'they only made money out of you' " (*HH*, p. 178).

Along with emphasizing the vitality of the various cultural traditions they bring to enrich the new world, Addams demonstrates that the immigrants are the true cosmopolitans of urban America—not in the elite sense of urbane, but in the root sense of being citizens of the world. She finds among them a tolerance and understanding for cultural and racial differences that demonstrates their potential role in solving a race problem that Anglo-Americans have shamefully avoided. The cooperation between Jew and Christian, Russian and Italian, she writes, has engendered an "internationalism in the immigrant quarters of American cities [that] might be recognized as an effective instrument in the cause of peace" (*HH*, p. 217). Thus Hull-House and its surrounding neighborhoods become the locus of her vision of America as the model for the united nations she imagines that the world may one day become.[28]

By the time we reach the final chapter on "Socialized Education," Addams has led us through the various phases of Hull-House's gestation, as it "enlarged for new needs and mellowed through slow-growing associations," all the while that its inhabitants "endeavored to fashion it from without . . . as well as from within" (*HH*, p. 275). From her own socialized childhood and education, we have watched Addams, and later her classmates, colleagues, and neighbors, reach out to their community, to the nation, and beyond. No longer, she has taught us, can America exhibit "the characteristics of a pioneer country, in which untrammeled energy and an 'early start' [are] . . . the most highly prized generators of success" (*HH*, p. 156).

Addams has demonstrated the "natural" evolution of America's leadership, from the eighteenth-century world of our Enlightenment fathers to the early twentieth-century world of our Progressive mothers.[29] The paradigm that she creates in *Twenty Years at Hull-House* is rooted in a compelling vision of an American success myth that celebrates selves who are defined by the community in which they work and play, a community that nourishes individuals who nourish one another. Through the power of her feminist imagination, Jane Addams replaces class, race, and gender oppression with an internationalist vision of social democracy as the foundation for the American republic in the twentieth century.

NOTES

1. See James Cox, "Autobiography and America," in *Aspects of Narrative*, ed. J. H. Miller (New York: Columbia University Press, 1971), pp. 256-74; also Robert Sayre, "Autobiography and the Making of America," in *Autobiography: Essays Theoretical and Critical*, ed. James Olney (Princeton: Princeton University Press, 1980), pp. 146–68. Like Cox, Sayre points out the connection between American autobiographies and the national life, and also like Cox he mentions no women autobiographers. In fact, while admitting that American autobiographers tell mostly "boys' stories" and that we need to look to others to tell what went on inside the American house, he also states that "whether we like them or not, Franklin, Whitman, Douglass and Henry Adams, John Adams and Scott Fitzgerald have been leading architects of the American character."

While scholarship on the American myth and the prophetic mode in American autobiography rarely discusses the works of white women or minority writers, white women and minority writers have an important place within those traditions as they are typically defined. See, for example, William Spengemann and L. R. Lundquist, "Autobiography and the American Myth," *American Quarterly* 17, no. 3 (Fall 1965), 501–19, where they define the myth "as a pilgrimage from imperfection to perfection" whose terms variously include the Puritan typology of the fall and salvation; the Enlightenment formulation of ignorance and the achievement of worldly happiness through reason; and the nineteenth-century reformers' pitting of "predatory individualism" against "collective utopian harmony." In important respects, Addams fits within their definition of both heroic and prophetic modes of autobiographical personae. See also G. Thomas Couser, *American Autobiography: The Prophetic Mode* (Amherst: University of Massachusetts Press, 1979), who claims that the prophet's role "is to offer his society a vision or visionary experience which revises the culture's traditional mythology in such a way as to resolve a communal crisis." Couser notes, only in passing, Addams's search to "add the social function to democracy" in order to answer the question of what it meant to be an American in the new industrial age (p. 9).

For an analysis of the mainstream American success myth see Lawrence Chenowith, *The American Dream of Success: The Search for Self in the Twentieth Century* (North Scituate, Mass.: Duxbury Press, 1974). Chenowith discusses the deleterious influence of such late-nineteenth-century success heroes as Carnegie and the boy heroes who populate Horatio Alger novels. He notes that in the late nineteenth and early twentieth centuries, "the counterpoint between Alger's . . . Carnegie's and Rockefeller's principles indicated the beginning of a process whereby the public was attempting to preserve the success ethic as a philosophy of life while industrial leaders were transforming the dream of success into a corporate ideology designed to justify their power" (p. 36). For a content analysis of the success myth in popular books and manuals, see Richard Weiss, *The American Myth of Success: From Horatio Alger to Norman Vincent Peale* (New York: Basic Books, 1969).

2. See Thomas Hartshorne, *The Distorted Image: Changing Conceptions of the American Character since Turner* (Cleveland: Case Western Reserve Press, 1968). Hartshorne studies both scholarly and popular images of Anglo-Americans and ethnics. See also David Potter, "The Quest for the National Character," and "American Women and the American Character," in *The National Temperament: Readings in American Culture and Society,* 2nd ed., ed. Lawrence Levine and Robert Middlekauff (New York: Harcourt, Brace, 1972), pp. 3–18, 363–78. In "American Women," Potter points out that white Anglo-Saxon men have typically been the norm for discussions of national character and that the city, rather than the frontier, was the place of opportunity for women in the nineteenth century. Jill Conway makes a similar point in "Women Reformers and American Culture, 1870–1930," *Journal of Social History* 5, no. 2 (Winter 1971–72), 164–77. Conway also notes that it was "the essence of Addams' greatness" that she perceived and defined the confusion of a society that was "perplexed by the creation of wealth and leisure, while its predominant values were those of frontier activism and the Puritan ethic" (p. 171).

3. Alice Kessler-Harris, "American Women and the American Character," *American Character and Culture in a Changing World: Some Twentieth Century*

Perspectives, ed. John Hague (Westport, Conn.: Greenwood Press, 1979), pp. 227–42. The discovery of this feminist tradition comprises one of the most important areas of feminist scholarship in the past decade. In *The Creation of Patriarchy* (New York: Oxford University Press, 1986), Gerda Lerner briefly traces the "feminist-maternalists" (of whom Addams is one) from the ideology of republican motherhood, developed at the time of the American revolution, through the nineteenth-century suffrage movement and the Progressive era (pp. 26–29). See also Linda Kerber, *Women of the Republic: Intellect and Ideology in Revolutionary America* (Chapel Hill: University of North Carolina Press, 1980).

Elizabeth Ammons has traced the literary incarnation of this tradition in a variety of nineteenth-century and early twentieth-century women writers. In "Stowe's Dream of the Mother-Savior: 'Uncle Tom's Cabin' and American Women Writers before the 1920s," Ammons notes that "Stowe's manipulation of maternal ideology is adopted and remodeled in illuminating ways in the works of American writers before the 1920s and that, taken together, this body of fiction from Stowe forward constitutes a rich female tradition in American literature. . . . in the tradition that Stowe heads . . . there exists an important and radical challenge to the emerging industrial-based definition of community in the nineteenth century as something organized by work, ruled by men, and measured by productivity" (*New Essays on* Uncle Tom's Cabin, ed. E. J. Sundquist [London: Cambridge University Press, 1986], pp. 156–57). See also Nina Baym, *Women's Fiction: A Guide to Novels by and about Women in America, 1820–1870* (Ithaca: Cornell University Press, 1978), and Jane Tompkins, *Sensational Designs: The Cultural Work of American Fiction, 1790–1860* (New York: Oxford University Press, 1985).

4. Jill Conway and Allen Davis have written of Addams as a self-defined heroine who, in Davis's words, "sought to reinforce her role as a priestess and feminine spiritual leader in America." She affirmed, Davis asserts, "the American myth which made the search for the American dream a secular version of the Christian mission to save the world" (Davis, *American Heroine: The Life and Legend of Jane Addams* [New York: Oxford University Press, 1973], pp. 172, 159). But both Conway and Davis condemn what Conway calls Addams's cultivated "image of a self-effacing, self-sacrificing spiritual woman" that presumably fed stereotypical notions of femininity. Davis notes that it was Addams's qualities of self-direction, autonomy, compromise, worldliness, and business acumen that were responsible for her success, even though her public image was part of the "sentimental love religion" of the 1890s. See also Conway, "Jane Addams: An American Heroine," *Daedalus* 93, no. 2 (Spring 1964), 761–80. I disagree strongly with Conway. However much Addams's public—and her reviewers—insisted on placing her on a feminine pedestal, this is *not* the image she conveys in her autobiography.

The following reviews, which focus on Addams's modesty and saintliness, treat *Hull-House* as a "how-to" manual for social workers and rarely discuss her intelligence or her political savvy: *The Nation* (Dec. 29, 1910); *Literary Digest* (Dec. 24, 1910); *The Survey* (Dec. 3, 1910); *American Review of Reviews* (Dec. 1910); *Annals of the American Academy of Political and Social Science* (July

1911); *New York Times Review of Books* (March 3, 1911); *Political Science Quarterly* (June 1911).

5. For Addams's place within the traditions of female autobiography, see Estelle Jelinek, *The Tradition of Women's Autobiography: From Antiquity to the Present* (Boston: Twayne, 1986). Jelinek's thesis is that women's autobiographies typically depict "a multidimensional, fragmented self-image, colored by a sense of inadequacy and alienation, of being outsiders or 'other'; they feel the need for authentication, to prove their self-worth. At the same time, and paradoxically, they project self-confidence and a positive sense of accomplishment in having overcome many obstacles to their success" (p. xiii). Jelinek notes a more confident self-portrayal in the autobiographies of the reformers of the late nineteenth and early twentieth centuries "whose many life studies constitute a veritable renaissance in women's autobiographical history" (p. 97). Yet, while it may be true that most female autobiographers do not see their identity in heroic terms, nor "see themselves as legends or representatives of their times," this certainly is not true of Addams. Jelinek tends to dismiss heroic female personae by suggesting that they belong to a masculine tradition, but I think her dichotomy is too simplistic and that such self-defined heroic figures as Ida B. Wells and Mother Jones need to be examined more in the light in which I am examining Addams. Jelinek says of *Hull-House* that it "has considerable literary merit as a result of its topical rather than chronological organization, its concrete human interest anecdotes, and its simple, direct, and lucid prose style" (p. 128).

Two recent studies of Addams's autobiography that offer illuminating insights into her intentions as a writer are Rebecca Sherrick, "Their Fathers' Daughters: The Autobiographies of Jane Addams and Florence Kelley," *American Studies* 27, no. 1 (Spring 1986), 39–53; and Phillip Abbott, "Reforming: Charlotte Perkins Gilman and Jane Addams," in *States of Perfect Freedom: Autobiography and American Political Thought,* ed. Phillip Abbott (Amherst: University of Massachusetts Press, 1987), pp. 157–81. See also Herbert Liebowitz, "The Sheltering Self: Jane Addams's *Twenty Years at Hull-House,*" in *Fabricating Lives: Explorations in American Autobiography,* ed. Herbert Liebowitz (New York: Knopf, 1989), pp. 114–55.

6. See Addams's three-part series for the *Ladies Home Journal* (March, April, and May, 1906).

7. Gerda Lerner, *The Majority Finds Its Past: Placing Women in History* (New York: Oxford University Press, 1979), p. xxxi.

8. Jane Addams, *Twenty Years at Hull-House* (New York: Signet, 1910), p. 235, hereafter cited in text as *HH*.

9. Davis notes that Addams "endowed herself with special precocious power and foresight" that is typical of classical heroes and heroines. Throughout his biography, he traces the important changes that Addams made in her life story. Davis quotes from a Boston paper that speaks of Addams as " 'the mother emancipator' " who fought " 'to free men, women, and children from the shackles of discrimination, prejudice, and ignorance' " (*American Heroine,* p. 164). Sherrick explains Addams's emphasis on her place in the Lincoln tradition as part of "her task . . . to convince readers that she was capable of assuming that trust. In forg-

ing the link between her father and the martyred leader, she devised a strategy to accomplish that goal" ("Their Fathers' Daughters," p. 45).

It is interesting to think of these two strains of the American success myth—the dominant school of success that emphasizes manipulation of self and of the physical and material environment, and the more idealistic strain that emphasizes the guarantee of equal rights to a more inclusive human community—in terms of Elaine Showalter's discussion of muted and dominant cultures. In her essay "Feminist Criticism in the Wilderness," *Critical Inquiry* 8, no. 2 (Winter 1981), 197–205, she defines women's writing as "a 'double-voiced discourse' that always embodies the social, literary, and cultural heritages of both the muted and the dominant" (p. 199).

The autobiographies of women—and male minority—leaders seem to fall predominantly within the "muted" tradition of benevolence: Showalter cites, for example, such figures as Dorothea Dix, Helen Keller, W. E. B. Du Bois, and Ida B. Wells. Davis notes that Addams's autobiography was compared to those of Helen Keller and Booker T. Washington, which represent the "other side of the American success myth" from Rockefeller et al. (*American Heroine*, p. 171). I would substitute W. E. B. Du Bois for Washington, who seems to me to belong to a modified version of the Rockefeller school.

10. Jean Humez pointed out to me the significance in this dream of Addams's seeking to acquire traditionally male skills. See also G. J. Barker-Benfield, "Mother Emancipator: The Meaning of Jane Addams' Sickness and Cure," *Journal of Family History* 4, no. 4 (Winter 1979), 395–420. Barker-Benfield interprets the dream partly as Addams's fear of her father's abandonment after the death of her mother and partly as "her wish . . . to stand alone, free particularly of that dominant/dominating figure." Thus she "asserts her own powers by observing and questioning the skilled male." Davis notes Addams's failure to mention the role her stepmother played in her development, while Sherrick points out that Addams barely mentions her mother's death in her autobiography, even though the circumstances of her death were dramatic and heroic. Sarah Addams died, while pregnant with her ninth child, several days after answering a neighbor in need of help. After her mother's death, Addams had nightmares of abandonment; such fears must have recurred after her father's death as well.

11. See Lillian Faderman, *Surpassing the Love of Men: Romantic Friendship and Love between Women from the Renaissance to the Present* (New York: William Morrow, 1981), p. 187, in which she discusses the life patterns of nineteenth-century feminists tied closely to fathers who typically molded their daughters' education and character.

12. According to Davis, contemporary evidence indicates that neither Addams nor Bryan participated in this debate, although she attended it. It is difficult to believe that she consciously claimed credit for something she knew she did not do. This may be a case of projecting her present symbolic status back onto her past.

13. The phrase "municipal housekeeping" is actually Florence Kelley's. See Dolores Hayden, *The Grand Domestic Revolution: A History of Feminist Designs for American Homes, Neighborhoods, and Cities* (Cambridge: MIT Press, 1981).

According to Susan Bell and Karen Offen, this concept was first put forth by feminists in Europe in the 1830s (*Women, the Family and Freedom: The Debate in Documents* [Stanford: Stanford University Press, 1983]). I would like to thank Lucy Knight for pointing this work out to me.

14. See Raymond Williams, *Marxism and Literature* (New York: Oxford University Press, 1977); also Alan Trachtenberg, *The Incorporation of America: Culture and Society in the Gilded Age* (New York: Hill and Wang, 1982), p. 9, where he states that Victorian Americans demonstrated "an evolving consensus of belief that culture indeed represents a higher sphere of activity associated with class privilege and with an older Anglo-Saxon America, a sphere distinct from the crudeness and vulgarities of common life, of trade and labor."

15. Davis points this out in discussing the bullfight episode; he notes that bullfighting was the symbol for the worst of European decadence and brutality (*American Heroine*, p. 173).

16. Faderman, *Surpassing the Love of Men*, p. 206; also Carroll Smith-Rosenberg, "The New Woman as Androgyne: Social Disorder and Gender Crisis, 1870–1936," in *Disorderly Conduct: Visions of Gender in Victorian America*, ed. Carroll Smith-Rosenberg (New York: Oxford University Press, 1985), pp. 245–96.

17. See Sherrick, "Their Fathers' Daughters," p. 46, where she points out that Addams and Kelley linked their lives to their fathers' "while distinguishing carefully between the challenges and issues confronting the two generations. They chose to emulate, rather than duplicate, the men's accomplishments." Abbott speaks of Addams's "double estrangement" as part of a generation of liberated women who could imitate neither their fathers nor their mothers. Like Gilman, he suggests, she succeeded "in reconstructing a personality beyond paternal power through dedication to service" ("Reforming," p. 173). For Addams's relationship with her stepmother, see Davis, *American Heroine*.

18. See Cook, "Female Support Networks and Political Activism," in *A Heritage of One's Own: Toward a New Social History of Women*, ed. Nancy Cott and Elizabeth Pleck (New York: Simon and Schuster, 1979), pp. 412–44; Abbott, "Reforming," p. 173. See also Estelle Freedman, "Separatism as a Strategy: Female Institution Building and American Feminism, 1870–1930," *Feminist Studies* 5, no. 3 (Fall 1979), 512–29; and Mari Jo Buhle, *Women and American Socialism* (Urbana: University of Illinois Press, 1983).

19. See Mary Mason, "The Other Voice: Autobiographies of Women Writers," in Olney, *Autobiography*, p. 210. See also the Preface to *Journeys: Autobiographical Writings by Women*, ed. Mary Mason and Carol Green (Boston: G. K. Hall, 1979). The editors state that the women represented in the volume are making journeys beyond individual concerns to commitment, in the belief that "the journey beyond the self leads not to obliteration but to self-discovery and self-realization" (p. vii).

20. Carol Gilligan, *In a Different Voice: Psychological Theory and Women's Development* (Cambridge: Harvard University Press, 1982), pp. 62–63.

21. To name but a few of the women and their accomplishments: Edith Abbott became dean of the School of Social Service Administration at the University of Chicago, which provided scientific training for women and men entering

public service careers. Grace Abbott headed the Immigrants' Protective League and was the United States' representative to the International Labor Organization. Florence Kelley, one of the prime movers behind the Illinois State Factory Law, was the first state factory inspector and built the Consumer's League. Alzina Parsons Stevens, a working-class woman who became a leading labor organizer, edited a reform paper and worked under Kelley as an assistant factory inspector. Dr. Alice Hamilton pioneered in the field of industrial medicine and became the first woman faculty member at Harvard Medical School. Julia Lathrop headed the first federal children's bureau and worked with Addams and others to establish the first juvenile court in Illinois. And, of course, Addams herself, whose reform efforts in several fields are scattered throughout *Hull-House:* her work on the national woman suffrage campaign; her service on the Chicago school board; her mediation of several labor disputes; her initiatives in helping to found the Women's Trade Union League and the NAACP.

22. Hayden, *The Grand Domestic Revolution,* pp. 151–52. Lucy Knight, who is writing a biography of Addams, has pointed out to me that while the American cooperative movement is not particularly female in origin or practice, "American women took this idea in a novel and interesting direction" (Knight to Rudnick, 18 Jan. 1989). The idea of home that feminist writers and activists have used as a powerful alternative metaphor for conceptualizing the world has also been noted by Baym and Tompkins. Tompkins reads *Uncle Tom's Cabin* as "a blueprint for colonizing the world in the name of the 'family state' under the leadership of Christian women. . . . The home, rather than representing a retreat or refuge from a crass industrial-commercial world, offers an economic ALTERNATIVE to that world, one which calls into question the whole structure of American society" (*Sensational Designs,* p. 144).

23. Rosalind Rosenberg, *Beyond Separate Spheres: The Intellectual Roots of Modern Feminism* (New Haven: Yale University Press, 1982), pp. 36–41. Rosenberg points out that the male mentors of the first generation of women social scientists—George Herbert Mead, John Dewey, and Franz Boas—found the masculine ideal of rugged, aggressive individualism offensive. She also notes that while most nineteenth-century feminists, including Addams, accepted the "evolutionists' beliefs in sexual divergence and the uniqueness of men and women's psychology," that conviction made them believe even "more strongly in the need for greater female power" (pp. 16, 41). On page 41, Rosenberg states that Addams "gave popular expression" to the belief "that social progress depended on the moral insights of women" in her *Democracy and Social Ethics* (1902).

24. See Addams's letter to Ellen Starr about her early religious searchings: "Lately it seems to me that I am getting back of all of it . . . back to a great primal cause, not nature exactly, but a fostering mother, a necessity, brooding over all things" (Addams to Starr, 11 August 1879, quoted in Davis, *American Heroine,* pp. 15–16). Barker-Benfield discusses the importance of the "mother-breasts" metaphor in Addams's self-healing as well as in her social vision. Addams felt the Primal Cause as a "fostering mother," a feeling related to her own early loss of her mother. "She would cure herself by discovering something that had been there all along" ("Mother Emancipator," p. 417). See also Bell Gale Chevigny, "Daughters Writing: Toward a Theory of Women's Biography,"

Feminist Studies 9, no. 1 (Spring 1983), 79–102. Chevigny proposes that women writing about women are partially engaged in a process of self-mothering, recovering "our own history and ourselves, each at least partly in terms of the other" (p. 99). This could equally be true for women autobiographers, particularly so in Addams's case.

25. For the relationship of the Social Gospel movement to Progressive reform, see Henry F. May, *Protestant Churches and Industrial America* (New York: Harper Torchbooks, 1967). May notes that "the ability to justify social change in terms of Christian doctrine has given American progressivism authority, power and a link with tradition" (p. 231), an authority that Addams clearly takes advantage of in her autobiography. Although the Social Gospel was typically aligned with moderate reformism, May is correct in asserting the significance of its break with more traditional forms of Christianity: "To plead for the recognition of human solidarity as a part of Christian teaching, to talk about social sin and social salvation, was to break with fundamental tenets cherished by Protestantism since the Reformation" (p. 231).

26. For the political and social philosophers who influenced Addams, see Rosenberg, *Beyond Separate Spheres;* Jean Quandt, *From the Small Town to the Great Community: The Social Thought of Progressive Intellectuals* (New Brunswick: Rutgers University Press, 1970); and Daniel Levine, *Jane Addams and the Liberal Tradition* (Madison: State Historical Society of Wisconsin, 1971). For two excellent discussions of Addams's concept of culture, see James Dougherty, "Jane Addams: Culture and Imagination," *Yale Review* 71, no. 3 (April 1982), 363–79, and Helen Horowitz, "Varieties of Cultural Experience in Jane Addams' Chicago," *History of Education Quarterly* 14, no. 1 (Spring 1974), 69–86. Dougherty's thesis is that Addams enlarged the concept of culture by uniting the world of art and everyday reality.

27. Buhle, *Women and American Socialism,* p. 70. See also Freedman, who argues that the creation of a "separate, public, female sphere" mobilized women and gave them "political leverage in the larger society" ("Separation as Strategy," p. 513). Addams, however, saw the weakness of a purely separatist strategy, as Kathryn Sklar makes clear in her discussion of the inclusive social vision shared by the women of Hull-House ("Hull-House in the 1890s: A Community of Women Reformers," *Signs* 10, no. 4 [Summer 1985], 658–77). Sklar correctly points out that "although their own communities were essential to their social strength, women were able to realize the full potential of their collective power only by reaching outside those boundaries" (p. 659). For Addams's relationships with and attitudes toward capitalists and radicals, see Liebowitz, "The Sheltering Self," pp. 144–52.

28. Addams's view of the immigrants as redeemers of the American Dream has a fascinating parallel in the autobiography of W. E. B. Du Bois, *The Souls of Black Folk* (1903), where he writes, "there are today no truer exponents of the pure human spirit of the Declaration of Independence than the American Negroes; ... all in all, we black men seem the sole oasis of simple faith and reverence in a dusty desert of dollars and smartness" (*Three Negro Classics* [New York: Avon, 1965], p. 220). Addams, however, does not display an equal admiration

for all ethnic groups. At times in *Hull-House,* she takes a condescending attitude toward the Irish and Italians, in particular. She shows some preference for immigrant cultures that have strong traditions of political democracy (like the Greeks) and education (like the Jews).

29. See Sherrick, "Their Fathers' Daughters," p. 50, where she states that Addams and Kelley believed that "eventually the women would sound a call, not simply for shared participation, but for the transfer of leadership from men to women and the abandonment of rule by force in favor of government by arbitration." One can find these ideals expressed more overtly in Addams's *Newer Ideals of Peace* (New York: Macmillan, 1907) and *Peace and Bread in the Time of War* (New York: Macmillan, 1917).

PART THREE

The "Centrality of Marginality"

NANCY HOFFMAN

A Journey into Knowing:
Agnes Smedley's Daughter of Earth

Daughter of Earth is a novel about the profound destructiveness of not-knowing—of ignorance caused by poverty and isolation. It is also a novel of education. Its protagonist learns to live in the world of the literate, the self-possessed—those with choices. But like many who have made such a journey into knowing, she is haunted by her past, and it shapes her perceptions and actions. As a young child in the dirt-poor Missouri farming country of the 1890s, Marie Rogers is confronted brutally and violently with the stark truth about gender relations and social class in the culture of the frontier. Her only recourse is flight from each exploitative situation. Not until her late teens does she acquire the analytic power of mind to move from gut reaction to the beginnings of conscious understanding of working-class womanhood in the United States. Later her education broadens: She questions her U.S. identity not only on its own terms, but as it appears to non-Western people of color, a perspective the importance of which we are only beginning to realize fully now. But living on the borders between the unknowing silence of the working classes and the glib articulateness of leftist circles, Marie is nowhere at home.

More than any novel I have ever read, this novel demonstrates a painful irony: that the economic and social forces that cause deprivation irreparably maim the heart and the mind even as they strengthen the will to change the world for others. Marie Rogers lives out her life struggling to act as a whole person—to give and receive love in a relationship of equality and to work against oppression—despite the image that inhabits her imagination, the image of the endless horizon where gray sea and sky meet, the image of meaninglessness and despair. Ultimately, she finds meaning and purposefulness in political work, but she remains without intimate companionship, her love relationships poisoned by her uncompromising commitment to sexual equality in a society unable to tolerate it.

First published in 1929 (and reprinted in expurgated form in 1935 with an introduction by Malcolm Cowley), *Daughter of Earth*'s return to print in 1973 with an afterword by Paul Lauter was a consequence of the rebirth of women's activism and, with it, the founding of The Feminist Press.[1] Among the first Feminist Press reprints of "lost" literature by women and quickly a classic, *Daughter of Earth* compares remarkably well with the best of the recent feminist novels written out of the compulsion to understand women's situation; it is also prescient in anticipating the questions raised and the answers given in the new anthropological, psychological, and economic scholarship about women. But, like that scholarship, *Daughter of Earth* looks backward as well, less to a literary tradition than to the radical feminist ideas on the Woman Question of the first decade of the 1900s. Smedley knew and corresponded with, for example, the anarchist revolutionary Emma Goldman, and shares in part the analysis presented in Goldman's essays that women are made "compulsory vessels" in marriage *and* in prostitution; that marriage is "an insurance pact" or protection agreement of a different order than love; and that personal relations are not separate from the social structure, but mirror it.[2] Schooled in feminism, as well as in European Marxist and psychoanalytic practice, and recognizing the contradictions among these perspectives, Smedley used each theory for its explanatory and therapeutic power, but embraced none as credo.

As a literary work, too, *Daughter of Earth* is unusually interesting. Placed beside the best-known novels reflecting U.S. life in the World War I period—*The Great Gatsby, The Sun Also Rises, Main Street, The Sound and the Fury,* or even *Death Comes for the Archbishop*—it forces us to redefine our notions of realism. If Fitzgerald chronicled the underside of the jazz age; Hemingway, expatriate decadence; Sinclair Lewis, the narrow materialism of the midwestern United States; Faulkner, his own emblematically incestuous southern family; and Cather, the harshness of the southwestern desert, each did so with an attention to language and form that blunts the representation of the darker realities. "Her rude pastorals have an expansive nobility," says one critic in praise of Cather.[3] Poverty, ignorance, and class exploitation are never noble in Smedley's drab shacks beyond the tracks or in the Rockefeller-owned mining camps of the west, nor is landscape in any way responsive or nourishing. Indeed, in a haunting image, an inexplicable crack crawls down, up, and around a delicately painted Chinese bowl, marring its once perfect form. If Hemingway's or Cather's novels are like the bowl, Smedley's art is the crack.

While Smedley's realism distinguishes *Daughter of Earth* from the central tradition of U.S. literature, her work does belong within a literary genre. The themes she treats—class conflict, the strait jacket of gender expectation, liberated sexual relations, the pain of childbearing, the search for work, the development of revolutionary politics—appear in the novels of her immediate contemporaries, the leftist women writers of the twenties and thirties. Indeed, Fielding Burke's *Call Home the Heart* (1932), Josephine Herbst's *Rope of Gold* (1939), and Tess Slesinger's *The Unpossessed* (1934), three novels recently published in The Feminist Press's Novels of the Thirties series, explore these themes. But even among her sisters in this special circle, Smedley presents the most radical and daring reading of childbearing: It must not happen. While other novelists present pregnancy and childbirth as inevitable dilemmas complicating the lives of their protagonists and exposing the sex/gender system, Smedley's protagonist aborts two pregnancies. Babies with their dependency arouse her horror, not her longing to nurture. Living in a world where women support children alone, she recognizes that, only unencumbered, might she seek work and demand equality in love. (A comparable protagonist is Zora Neale Hurston's Janie in *Their Eyes Were Watching God,* but Hurston, unlike Smedley, never makes a statement about the barrier children raise to heterosexual equality. Janie has sex but, inexplicably, no children, a lacuna that has troubled readers.)

If thematically *Daughter of Earth* defies convention even among the works of feminist authors, it does so also in its structure. The novel appears to move from mythic to novelistic to autobiographical form roughly in accordance with the movement from childhood to young womanhood to adulthood, and this movement, while psychologically realistic, throws the reader off balance. Convention suggests that the tone and level of narrative detail should remain consistent, but they do not. Regarded in retrospect, people and events of early childhood stand out, not for their narrative continuities, but for their enormous proportion— the grandmother as powerful as "an invading army," a barn-raising, the family's tent swept away by a flooding river, the sounds of physical violence. The middle years are presented more sequentially and, despite their particular twists, conform to novelistic conventions of growing up: departure from home, work, romance, education. The final chapters, in contrast, again defy formula and present so unique a set of circumstances as to resemble a memoir. There are excursions into political analysis, details of meetings, questions from judicial proceedings, office disputes, the pedestrian trials of urban poverty, all told by a narrator on the way to becoming a journalist. These stylistically disparate sections are in part linked by repeated images from the protagonist's unconscious world depicted in standard psychoanalytic language—dreams, symbols such as fire, the horizon, and darkness. Indeed, one fascination of the book is the degree to which it asserts that the painful distortions wrought by gender and class oppression manifest themselves in a troubled sexuality, persisting from the earliest memories of childhood into adulthood. *Daughter of Earth* is a book of unique emotional and political frankness, more likely to change its readers' lives than their aesthetic theories.

I discuss below the novel's themes, then provide briefly an account of Agnes Smedley's work as a teacher, journalist, and revolutionary in the socialist circles of San Francisco, New York, and Berlin; as an observer of the Russian Revolution; as an activist in India's nationalist revolutionary movement; and, most significantly, as a participant-observer of the Chinese Revolution. Smedley was one of a handful of Westerners who lived in China for most of the period between 1928 and 1941.

The weeping of women who are wives—what is more bitter?

Perhaps most powerful and fundamental in the education of Marie Rogers, the name Agnes Smedley gives her fictional self, is the emotional lesson she learned early in childhood: Love expressed in sex enslaves and humiliates women. It is the toll men exact for giving economic protection to their wives. This perception punctuates the book like the refrain in a sad folk song: "The weeping of women who are wives—what is more bitter?" Sleeping in the same room as her parents, Marie is filled with "terror and revulsion" at the sounds from their bed; she learns that male animals cost more than female animals, that her father can beat her mother and desert her because she refuses to tell him how she will vote, and that he can beat her sister and threaten her aunt on a suspicion that they are "carryin' on with men" (p. 34). But the incident that reveals most viscerally the political economy of marriage to the young Marie occurs in the family of a newly married couple to whom she is hired out as a maid. After lying around the house, the wife wants to return to work, but her husband sees his ability to support her as a symbol of his manhood; she is his possession to keep idle at home. Once she is "expectin'," their fights grow more bitter. The following exchange strips bare the marriage contract: " 'Give me back the clothes I bought you,' he bellowed at her one day. 'Damn it, kid, you know I love you!' she begged through her tears—for now she could not go back to work even if she wished" (p. 66).

This revelation—that women become powerlesss as wives and mothers, that they must produce care in exchange for food and clothes, that they must take orders and obey as a condition of the contract—forms for Marie, as yet young and unaware, the kernel of her politics: the same domination she hates in marriage she comes to hate in class relations, in party politics, in Western and Japanese imperialism. But first she must experience—a key word for this novel—woman's struggle to live independently. Like most women, her guides in the endeavor are few (two), and both have their independence still in relation to men. The mythic figure of her great-aunt dominates Marie's imagination—the tall, strong tyrant with the body and mind of a man, the woman who not only controlled her children's love affairs but took a lover as well. But it is Marie's beloved Aunt Helen, a prostitute, who teaches Marie the depths of society's hypocrisy about women. Despised and abused by Marie's father, Helen turns the tables on marriage and exposes the inequalities in the institution. Helen is, in a sense, her own husband; she receives money herself, buys her own clothes, has "nice things," as she calls them. But although Helen can order a man out of her house and has more rights over her body than most women, to Marie she still lives out women's destiny in service to men. When she loses her sexual attractiveness, she loses her livelihood. Encountering her again as an older woman, now working in a factory and learning to shake dice, Marie feels the awfulness of her brief existence: "Such useless pain . . . so useless . . . so useless" (p. 218).

Among the strongest feminist scenes in literature, a series of events seal Marie's pact with herself to avoid the misery of women who are wives. On three separate occasions after her mother dies, Marie chooses to leave her drunken, brutal father and young, vulnerable brothers alone rather than assume responsibility for their care (pp. 133, 148, 185). Here the refusal to serve, obey, and care for anyone—family, father, brothers—comes to the severest test, one about which many readers of this book have felt profoundly ambivalent. How are we to understand a protagonist who reasons that her family is no more to her than any other people; who says, "so deeply did I love them that I even forgot them . . . " (p. 149); who chooses to study rather than to protect and care for; who separates from a comrade and husband because he orders her, weak from an abortion, to "sit up" on a city bus; who becomes a wanderer with the world for her home and the wind for her companion (p. 211)? For a woman, such choices are a form of heroism, uncompromising decisions never to allow love and servitude to be linked, and yet these are choices that repel. May women not love and care for without losing their autonomy? If the first two sections of the novel prepare us to believe that women must reject marriage and the economic dependency it brings, the final third of the novel reintroduces the quest for love. Indeed, the intellectual and emotional task that Marie Rogers sets for herself might be characterized as an attempt to resolve the contradiction between love and autonomy, the theme of much of women's recent fiction.

> *When knowledge and love become one, a force has been created that nothing can break.*

In the final section of the novel, the form and texture change in a way that has been disconcerting to some readers. The gripping drama of Marie's extraordinary coming-of-age among the gamblers, cowboys, miners, adventurers, and wanderers of the west might have ended with her marriage to Knut, the man who agrees to be her equal and companion. But instead, at chapter 6 the novel enters a new phase. If earlier Marie's teacher has been experience and her own sharp wit, now books and the critique of ideas draw her into a world that can both explain her experience and connect it with that of working people the world over. She comes slowly into history; her intellectual awakening coincides with World War I, the growth and repression of the communist and socialist movements, and the Indian nationalist movement of which she becomes a part. No longer is her landscape the western desert and mountains, or even the college campus, but rather an unusual one for fiction—the New York offices of small magazines, the apartments where political meetings are held. Her subject is no longer the weeping of wives—personal stories—but economics, social history, and philosophy. And her primary relationships are not with family and lovers but with teachers and revolutionaries.

We have come to expect in literature by women that daily work and learning will provide a backdrop for the great subject of the novel—relationships. In the final section of *Daughter of Earth,* by contrast, work and learning dominate while lovers come and go in the background (p. 350). The novel enters its most obviously autobiographical phase; it is of a particular place and moment. That readers should on occasion call this section of the novel dull underscores how accustomed we are to novels of private lives, how little, particularly for our heroines, we expect a novel to chronicle the preparation for public life—the life Marie assumes here in the Indian movement and as a socialist writer, and later the life Smedley lives as a journalist and political activist. In the final chapters the question then concerns Marie's choice of the Indian movement as an intellectual and spiritual home, and the tragic irony of the event that poisons her final attempt to fuse knowledge and love, work and personal intimacy.

While Marie's first encounter with an Indian is in a sense by chance—he comes to speak at her school in the west—her attraction to him has a kind of compelling logic. A member of a subjected race, judged and humiliated for his color as well as for his ideas, he is nonetheless willing to speak out for freedom. In his isolation, he illustrates the difficulties of the life Marie is choosing for herself. A woman who has given up her family, who has divorced a companion on principle because he has once spoken to her as a wife, who steels herself against tenderness and weakness, is as much an exile in the United States as is the Hindu. She sees in him her own loneliness, her asceticism, but she does not yet understand the compelling ideas that motivate him, "the use of knowledge for good [social] ends" (p. 256). Indeed, from her first meeting with the Scandinavians, Knut and Karin, she had begun the process of intellectual development. Seeing a play with them, she was suddenly aware of the existence of abstract "ideas"; these differed from the knowledge born of experience or factual knowledge from books. "Independent thought" can be "manufactured" in the course of conversation, she thinks (p. 183). Later, in New York, she castigates herself for her inability to argue—to muster facts, figures, and diagrams—and is enraged by the power of her opponents. Under the tutelage of her gentle though demanding teacher, the Indian Sardar Ranjit Singh, however, she embraces disciplined study and begins to understand its power. Challenged to question U.S. ethnocentrism, she comes to understand, for example, how incomplete is a social history of Britain without the study of India's influence (p. 257). Finally, through Ranjit Singh's eyes, Marie sees her own country and herself, and experiences for the first time discipline and risk for a purpose beyond her own survival. Tested time and again by the Indians—you are too "American," this movement is not an adventure, you will be hunted like an animal—Marie gains physical and intellectual power concentrating "belief and passion" in her work. And she experiences for the first time the bond of love—fatherly, comradely love that suits her because, unlike romance, it liberates rather than enslaves.

That the novel ends in the bitterness and despair of failed romance returns us full circle to the weeping of women who are wives, and this time it is Marie who weeps. Smedley the novelist shapes *Daughter of Earth* to make its final episode the parting of Marie and her Indian second husband, Anand. Marie weeps because neither she nor Anand can endure the censure of their Indian comrades, critical of Marie because *she* was raped prior to marriage by one of Anand's countrymen. Indeed, the failed search for love frames the book, which begins and ends with Marie's recuperative exile from the United States. I take this to mean that, despite the broad sociohistorical canvas on which it is painted, unlike many working-class novels, this one gives full weight to personal psychological need, to the power with which the unconscious shapes our destinies. The ending then provides an ironic commentary on the uses of knowledge and underscores the split between intellect and emotion, the former quality there to be honed and disciplined, the latter out of Marie's control like the horse—"white, lathering, mad" (p. 178)—that gallops off in the moonlight. There is a terrible poignancy in the lines below, which declare that one may use language for understanding— write novels, for example—but words cannot remake the past or heal the scars resulting from what one has lived through:

> I do not write mere words. I write of human flesh and blood. There is hatred and a bitterness with roots in experience and conviction. Words cannot erase that experience. (P. 246)

Where I am not, there is happiness.

If a circular structure binds the story together as a narration, it is bound aesthetically by recurrent images which, presented as the language of the unconscious by the retrospective narrative voice, provide a second story to complement the first. There are the actual events of Marie's life, and there are the psychological mechanisms she uses to endure those events and survive. If, as she tells us, after leaving her father and brothers, after divorcing her comrade-husband, Knut, after her brother George is killed digging a ditch for a sewer, and at other points, she "draw[s] that veil of suppression and forgetfulness" (p. 210) or she wishes her memory "dead" (p. 236), now, to write the novel, she must draw back the veil again. Indeed, the novel itself is the process of remembering. And that memory comes back punctuated by recurrent images.

Marie's mother and her family, for example, are icons of dejection associated with the gaping cracks in the floor (pp. 65, 148), the earth that swallows up its own. The quality of her own freedom and, with it, loneliness exist in the haunting domestic image of the world as a "home" and the wind as a "companion." And in the terrifying scene in which she is raped, the rapist appears in the image of a great swooping bird of prey, the same bird that appears over the gray sea in the opening lines and that might be contrasted with the small gray bird that sings harmlessly in the dawn. But there is one image of terrible power that occurs late in the book and comes to symbolize, as Marie has said earlier, the "bitter harvest that a harsh and distorted society had sown within [her]" (p. 193), the harvest that destroys her love relations. She dreams:

I stood contemplating a bowl in my outstretched hand . . . a beautifully shaped flower bowl, curved gently, broad and low, and about it was painted a wreath of flowers as delicate as all the art of ancient China. So beautiful and delicate it was that I held it far from me to see it shimmer as a ray of sunlight fell upon it. As I stood wondering at its beauty, a crack crawled down the side, to the bottom, up and around to the top again, and the broken fragment rolled over and lay on my palm. I had not broken the bowl . . . nobody had broken it . . . but it was broken, irrevocably broken by something I knew not what. (P. 376)

Here is the magic and the tragedy of *Daughter of Earth*. The bowl recalls the opening pages of the novel: "I belong to those who do not die for beauty," the narrator tells us, "I belong to those who die for other causes—exhausted by poverty, victims of wealth and power, fighters in a great cause. . . . Our struggle is of the earth" (p. 4). While the dream suggests Marie's recognition that she will never experience love—the perfect beauty of the bowl—it suggests as well that the crack is in the nature of things, not in her own control. Because she is strong and of the earth, however, the despair for lost beauty will not prevail.

> *Work that is limitless in its scope and significance, is not this enough to weigh against love?*

In the autobiographical first chapters of *Battle Hymn of China*, written some decade and a half after *Daughter of Earth*, Smedley asserts that friendship, not sex, is the chief bond between men and women.[4] Echoing one theme of *Daughter of Earth*, she declares marriage "at its best an economic investment; at its worst, a relic of human slavery" (p. 8). Comprehending that no society has solved this problem, she reveals that she will dedicate herself to the non-Western world where "people were struggling with the rudest forces of nature to build a new world of their own choosing" (p. 27). The account of her personal life, the narrative that underlies *Daughter of Earth*, ends in 1928 as Smedley's train passes into the Soviet Union, the first socialist country. Before the "rough-hewn" customs station on the Polish border stands a Red Army guard, "silent and watchful, facing the Western world." "In such a position," Smedley muses, "had once stood the men who had founded my own country" (p. 27). Smedley will dedicate the rest of her life to fighting for a great cause alongside people who do not wish to repeat the mistakes of the United States. And she will write always with a special sensitivity to the plight of women everywhere, and with an insistence on women's need for economic independence.

As if the years covered in *Daughter of Earth* are not enough, when one contemplates the courage and the contribution of the decades Smedley spent in China and the Soviet Union, one is astounded. I can only suggest here in the briefest outline the life that was Agnes Smedley's.[5] Book I of *Battle Hymn of China* recounts the years chronicled in *Daughter of Earth* with small variation: the years after her mother's death were spent in "semi-vagabondage" (her word); then Smedley attended Tempe Normal School (now Arizona State University) from 1911 to 1912 and there met the Swedes Ernest and Thorburg Brundin. Ernest became her first husband; brother and sister remained her lifelong friends. Smedley spent the years 1917–20 in New York as a night student at New York University, writing for the socialist paper *The Call* and for Margaret Sanger's *Birth Control Review*. As in the novel, she was arrested as a spy because of her association with Indian nationalists and spent six months in prison in the Tombs, where she wrote her first short stories, *Cell Mates*. (Because the British were U.S. allies in World War I, anyone working against the British—to free India from Britain—was considered a traitor.) However, when she was released from prison, she did not, as in the novel, resume her work in New York; rather she shipped out as a stewardess for Europe with a vague notion of joining Indian exiles in Berlin. The tragic relationship with the revolutionary leader Virendranath Chattopadhyaya, Anand in *Daughter of Earth,* actually took place there. More important, however, than location is Smedley's emotional state. In the novel she conflates the impact of prison and the failed relationship; in actuality, the prison term leads her to flee from the country where her brothers had lived "like animals without protection or education," where she saw middle-class men and women completing school, starting careers with protection and guidance while she slaved by day and strove by night "for some kind of meager education . . . and a shabby hall bedroom" (p. 10). Several years later, the end of her relation with Viren forces her to turn her unhappiness upon herself. Smedley writes of this period, "The circumstances of my youth, combined with the endless difficulties of my life with Virendranath in Germany, drove me to the verge of insanity . . . once I attempted suicide" (p. 4). After two years of psychoanalysis with an associate of Freud's (a woman), and with the writing of *Daughter of Earth,* Smedley regained her equilibrium, but, the MacKinnons (Smedley's official biographers) tell us, "Smedley would never again join a political organization nor become emotionally dependent on a man" (p. xiv).

With the exception of trips to the Soviet Union to rest and regain her health, and to New York to seek, unsuccessfully, a writing job, Smedley lived in China from 1928 to 1941. While she contributed much to the

Chinese revolution, as an organizer and field worker for the Chinese Red Cross and as a nurse in the Red Army, her unique contribution was as a journalist with an independent voice and an unwavering sympathy for the peasants and workers who, like her brothers and sisters, were of the earth. During her first five years in China, Smedley lived in Shanghai and reported for the *Frankfurter Zeitung*, the *Manchester Guardian*, the *Nation*, the *New Republic*, the *New Masses*, and other U.S. journals. One of the few Westerners to understand and seek to explain the complex events sweeping China—the Kuomintang's persecution of Communists, the Japanese imperialist threat, the brutal exploitation of factory workers—Smedley wrote always with her eyes fixed on the daily lives of workers and peasants, and particularly on the foot-bound and large-footed women.

In 1936 Smedley moved to the Communist capital, Yenan, and using her power as a reporter, urged Westerners to see China and the revolution for themselves. Later she marched from Yenan with the Red Army; she reported on that struggle in *China Fights Back: An American Woman with the Eighth Route Army* (1938). After Hankow fell to the Japanese in 1938,[6] Smedley began her most intense and dangerous reportorial mission—several years marching with the Communist-led new Fourth Army. This story is told in her book of war reportage, *Battle Hymn of China* (1943). A section of this book, recounting Smedley's desire to adopt a Chinese boy assigned by the army to care for her, appeared in a collection edited by Ernest Hemingway, *Men at War*. In 1940, her health again failing, Smedley left the army, flew over the Japanese lines to Hong Kong, and returned to her estranged family in San Diego. Through the forties, Smedley continued to write and lecture about China in the United States, to enjoy the many and varied friendships that grew from her years in China with reporters such as Edgar Snow and Jack Belden, and to form relationships with writers such as Katherine Anne Porter and Carson McCullers. Although independent of party affiliation all her life—and sometimes criticized for it—during the political scares of the late forties Smedley was accused in a U.S. Army report of having been a Soviet spy since the thirties. Unable to find anyone who would risk hiring her, she could not support herself, and, with news of the Communist victory in China in 1949, she set out to return there. While awaiting a visa in London, she became ill, and on May 6, 1950, she died during an operation for ulcers, at the age of fifty-eight. Only in China was her death an occasion for public mourning. There her lifelong friends, the writers Ting-Ling and Mao Tun, contributed lead articles about her in the daily papers. The MacKinnons report that in 1960 Chou En-lai opened his first interview in twenty years with

Edgar Snow by saluting Agnes Smedley and Franklin Roosevelt. There is anecdotal evidence that Smedley remains a figure of stature in China. Florence Howe, director of The Feminist Press and editor of this collection, recounts in her Afterword to the Smedley collection, *Portraits of Chinese Women in Revolution*, that, going through customs in China in 1975 with books from The Feminist Press including *Daughter of Earth*, she was stopped by a Chinese official who seemed dismayed by the many volumes. As Howe attempted to describe Smedley as a friend of China and the biographer of Chu Teh, a floor sweeper popped up from behind a counter. His description of "Aganessa Schmedaleya" allayed all suspicion; smiling, the official asked, "You are a teacher?"

"Yes," Howe replied, "I teach about Aganessa Schmedaleya."

NOTES

1. Agnes Smedley, *Daughter of Earth* (New York: Feminist Press, 1987). In 1972 Tillie Olsen gave Florence Howe her copy of *Daughter of Earth* and urged its reprinting.

2. Key Goldman essays are "The Tragedy of Woman's Emancipation," "Marriage and Love," and "The Traffic in Women" from Emma Goldman, *Red Emma Speaks: Selected Writing and Speeches,* comp. and ed. Alix Kates Shulman (New York: Vintage, 1972).

3. Mark Schorer, *The Literature of America: Twentieth Century* (New York: McGraw-Hill, 1970).

4. Agnes Smedley, *Battle Hymn of China* (New York: Knopf, 1943).

5. For many of the details in the following pages, I am indebted to Jan MacKinnon's and Steve MacKinnon's reconstruction of Smedley's biography, which forms the introduction to their collection of Smedley's short pieces, *Portraits of Chinese Women in Revolution* (Old Westbury, N.Y.: Feminist Press, 1976). Smedley's literary estate is in China, uncatalogued and unavailable to the public.

6. See André Malraux, *Man's Fate* (New York: Random House, 1961), for another account.

BLANCHE H. GELFANT

"Everybody Steals": Language as Theft in Meridel Le Sueur's The Girl

In Meridel Le Sueur's *The Girl,* a nameless Girl, the novel's heroine and narrator, undergoes an extraordinary metamorphosis—or more precisely, a series of metamorphoses that change a scared and silent country girl into a woman. At first naive and virginal, she learns the ways of her sex and class, and assumes the responsibilities of her knowledge. She becomes the bearer of woman's secret, the partisan of oppressed people, and the mother of a beatific child—a mythic Mother. Her ultimate transformation, easily overlooked but striking, is from silent witness to storyteller. Like Le Sueur, she retells stories told to her by poor, dispossessed, and mad women whose voices are not usually heard in the world and whose lives, unrecorded in official histories, would be forgotten if not for her words.[1] These words are my central concern. I hope to trace them to their sources within the text and show how, through a process of appropriation and subversion, the Girl acquires a language she finds empowering. At the same time I wish to point out limitations in this language that the Girl does not see but that, I believe, Le Sueur recognizes and tries to overcome by strategies that make her writing linguistically exciting and confused. Confusion, in its etymological sense of melting or pouring together, represents an ideal of unity she attempts to realize by amalgamating discrete and incompatible discourses. The ideal is in itself an amalgam of her utopian dreams of a classless society, of a sexual identity shared by women and men as mothering figures, and of a literature accessible to common people—a poetic language created from proletarian speech.

Ironically, Le Sueur's vision of a reconciliation of difference appears in a text characterized by conflict. Its style is conflicted, its various discourses remaining dissonant despite Le Sueur's attempts to conflate the

rhetoric of proletarian politics with the language of fertility myths, urban working-class vernaculars (male and female), hieratic incantations,
and biblical prophesy. The result is a rich stylistic confusion that makes
The Girl a complicated text to analyze, though it seems superficially simple in plot. On close examination, however, even its plot moves in different directions: in a linear progression that marks the stages of the
Girl's growth to womanhood and social consciousness; and in the circular pattern of loss and recovery of resurrection myths. The result is a
confusion of genres, for *The Girl* is a novel of radical social protest that
contains within its form a feminist jeremiad, a woman's bildungsroman,
and a fertility myth that simultaneously inscribes and denies sexual difference. The history of its episodic production may account in part for
both the overdetermination and the indecisiveness of the text. Almost
four decades intervened between its conception as a record of the lives
of urban working women caught in the Great Depression and its revision and publication. In this interim, Le Sueur accommodated to and
yet resisted the cultural changes she saw taking place. Unlike many leftist
writers of the thirties, she never repudiated the radicalism of her youth;
rather, she sought to consolidate Marxist doctrine with other ideologies
committed to social change—with, for example, the feminism that had
reemerged as a social force while she was revising *The Girl*. Feminism
and radical politics had always been intertwined in Le Sueur's writing,
and as she tried to make them indissoluble in her novel, she produced a
unique text that is both dated, expressive of an aesthetic sensibility of the
thirties, and proleptic, anticipating a call for a generic woman's novel—
for a bildungsroman—and for a woman's language. Since traces of era-
sures made in the early manuscript are visible beneath its revisions, *The
Girl* may also be defined as a palimpsest, a text in which, feminist critics
claim, women writers subversively assert their authority.[2]

The question of authority is mooted in *The Girl*, for in saying that
she was retelling stories told to her, Le Sueur implied that women's storytelling was, distinctively, a shared and collaborative activity. Nevertheless, the novel bears the impression of Le Sueur's political passion and
her literary aspiration as a radical woman writing.[3] In the novel, she
projected her lifelong quest for a language of her own upon a heroine
who was moving, emblematically, from silence to speech. This transition, central to the novel's political and feminist themes, gives a practical
urgency to questions of difference raised in contemporary literary theory. Can a woman, or woman writer, articulate a language marked by
differences attributable to sex? What system of values would structure,
and be structured by, such a language, and what social changes might it
effect? How can a woman exercise the political power of language with-

out sacrificing poetic beauty?[4] These questions are not only applicable to *The Girl;* they are intrinsic, posed within and by the text, and pursued by a protagonist who is self-consciously acquiring language. My discussion of this acquisition—of its process and attendant problems—begins with the long-silent Girl asserting her right to speak.

"Nobody can shut me up" (p. 113), the Girl cries out in a climactic moment that marks her sense of empowerment through speech. Until this moment, she has encouraged other women to speak because she believes they can tell her secrets, dark sexual secrets that an uninitiated girl must know to become a woman. As she begins her narrative, the Girl describes herself listening, scared and enthralled by what women tell; and her notations of their telling—"mamma told," "Belle told," "Clara told"—recur with metronomic regularity. Soon, however, words meant to instruct become obstacles to the Girl's understanding because, she says, "I didn't even know the words Clara spoke" (p. 1). She encounters an unfamiliar vocabulary made up of simple words—colloquial, slangy, idiomatic, and clichéd speech that rushes at her in jazzy rhythms. Women and men speak with the same tin-pan-alley terms and the same toughness, a language of the city's common man that the naive country girl does not understand. She is introduced, for example, to an incomprehensible baseball jargon when her friend Clara tells her "she could 'field' ... [men] ... when they tried to make a home run or a strike, with their too-free paws" (p. 1). Clara's words prepare the Girl for the speech of her lover, Butch. Baseball is Butch's obsession: it figures in his memory as he recalls his winning games; and games become figures of speech as they represent his fantasies of victory. Like Clara, Butch uses baseball idioms that are "Greek" to the Girl, a foreign language that espouses a competitive will to win also foreign to her.[5] Baseball has taught Butch he must "be better than anybody, better than anybody at all." Being better means *beating*. "I like to beat I like to win," he says (p. 5): "I like to beat everybody. I like to beat everybody in the world" (p. 18). Later he tries to include the Girl in his vainglorious vision: "I want to beat everybody down. I want victory. ... I want to beat everyone in the world. ... You like to beat too" (pp. 27–28).

Since the Girl is ignorant about baseball, she has no way of knowing that she is hearing a selected vocabulary, suitable to Le Sueur's theme and expressive of her not-unprejudiced view of male-dominated activities and language. Omitting nouns and adjectives like *home, team,* and *safe* and verbs like *walk* and *catch,* Le Sueur extrapolates words that connote violence: *hit, strike, beat.* When the Girl becomes the object of these verbs, their violence is released and realized. The Girl is struck again and again, by Butch, by Ganz, and by a sexually abusive policeman. She is hit repeatedly. She is beaten by her father, her lover, strangers. Ironically, Le Sueur is choosing words from a nonviolent sport as examples of the violence she finds pervasive in the language of male pursuits—in the vocabulary of prize-fighting (p. 4), of dice or "shooting the bones" (p. 11), and drinking or taking a shot. "Hit me. Go on hit me," Hoinck shouts while playing poker, a game in which cards are slapped down and players bluffed and beaten (p. 82). In a previous game, Hoinck had "hit the other guys in the jaw" and given his wife, Belle, a black eye (p. 20). Now he attacks Belle verbally as though anticipating Butch's physical assault upon the Girl. The violence of the poker game that had been contained by language, held within its verbs, breaks out as *hit* appears four times, along with *struck*. Butch commands these verbs and makes the Girl their object. Her verbs are *touched, loved, helped;* his are *hit, hit, hit, hit.*

As a narrator, the Girl necessarily reproduces the violent speech she hears women and men use; as a character, she appropriates this speech as her own. She begins to talk like Clara, like Butch, Belle, and even the villainous Ganz. Using words that had been "Greek" to her, she conflates verbal codes she had found mystifying and alien—baseball jargon, gangsters' argot, the vocabulary of soldiers—and gives them different, feminine, meanings.[6] In effect she usurps and deconstructs male language, but whether her linguistic strategies succeed in effecting the subversion of male language envisioned by various feminists remains to be seen.[7] Her gradual assimilation of baseball jargon marks the stages of her development from innocence to womanhood. She begins to assert her own identity when she refuses to be goaded into anger by a volley of commands that Butch might be giving to a baseball pitcher, a pool player, or card dealer. He rushes her with his words: "Let's have it. . . . Go ahead hit me. . . . let her fly. . . . Can't you shoot straight girl?" But the Girl resists. "I'm not shooting or hitting or striking," she says, echoing his words while repudiating the actions they represent (p. 49). Later, she expresses her uncertainties about sex in baseball metaphors whose meanings she is changing: "Had Butch won, struck a foul, thrown a home run, made the bases or struck out? . . . Who could tell you, or say anything?" (p. 53). Still later, while Butch is telling her she must have an abortion, she hears the radio announce a home run, and she thinks: *"We won't ever make a home run, ring the bell, beat the race, come in first"* (p. 81, original emphasis). Here she is conflating phrases from different sports and muddling them, substituting *make* for *hit* a home run, and *beat* for *win* a race. This indifference to the phrases she appropriates is less significant than her subversion of their meanings as she makes them signify pregnancy and birth. As though such subversions empower her, she defies Butch in the most significant act of her young life: she allows him to lead her to an abortionist, but then, when he leaves, she runs away. At the end of the novel, as she is giving birth to Butch's baby, she repudiates her dead lover's metaphor for life and the competitive values it had implied. "It ain't a ball game honey," she says (p. 147), assuming a power to name as she names her daughter and the metaphoric game she and Butch have been playing.[8]

Simply stated, the game is stealing. "Everybody steals" (p. 82), Hoinck says in justification of his part in the fatal bank robbery, a plot embedded within the Girl's story that eliminates the male characters in one fell action. If, as Le Sueur claimed, this bungled robbery was based upon a real event, as a fictional strategy it turns the text over entirely to women; and it suggests that hatred of men may be Le Sueur's subtext. Le Sueur reveals this hatred in her characters' sudden outbursts of anger. The Girl's sister says, "O, I'll never marry . . . I hate men" (p. 37); and Clara writes in an unsent letter, "Well I hate all the men" (p. 123). Belle's triumphant shout at the birth of a girl also reveals sexual animosity: "It's a woman . . . No dingle dangle, no rod of satan, no sword no third arm . . . (p. 148). In the robbery scene, Le Sueur expresses her own aversion by dramatizing the destructiveness inherent in the values the men had intended to validate—competitiveness, pride in standing alone, violence as an expression of power. Though they set out together, once they are in the bank, each man acts alone. Each is out for himself: greedy, vengeful. All are losers. Their death is senseless, except as a revelation of their profound failure to act cooperatively, either as a sex or a class. Ganz shoots Hoinck for the stolen money he wants for himself, Butch shoots Ganz in retribution, and Ganz, though he is dying, shoots Butch.

The robbery is more than a scenario of male greed and fatuity, however, for underlying the men's destructiveness is the desperation of a dispossessed working class. "I want a job" (p. 14), Butch says, speaking for all the novel's jobless men including the dead—for his brother Bill, soon to be killed as a strikebreaker, and for Amelia's husband, killed as a strike organizer. Butch boasts that he had worked in a foundry when he was fifteen and would now be a foreman if "the depression hadn't hit." He sees the robbery as a way of getting enough money to lease a service station and become "a boss," a capitalist dream later revealed as impossible in a polarized society where "they hold the cards, [and] you can't win" (p. 99). *Striking, hitting, winning*— ironically, an accretion of Butch's favorite words now tells that he has been depleted and left a loser. His fate indicts a society that Le Sueur believes has stolen from the working class a just return for its labor. Indeed, an epigraph for *The Girl* might be Hoinck's cynical phrase, "Everybody steals." In a society where everyone steals, the rich and powerful most of all, the robbery of jobless, dispossessed men like Butch is a benighted attempt to steal back what has already been stolen. *"Where are the oats, the wheat . . . the wealth of the country?"* Butch cries in his dying delirium. He knows the answer—that there is an elusive, institutionalized "they" who have stolen the land: *"They own the town. . . . They own the earth and the sweet marrow of your body"* (p. 107, original emphasis). Like Butch, Amelia expresses her anguish over the depredations of capitalist society in rhetorical questions. Who is the criminal, she asks impassionedly over Clara's dead body: "Was she a criminal . . . a danger? Clara never got any wealth. . . . She never stole timber or wheat. . . . She never stole anyone's land . . . never got rich on the labor of others . . . never fattened off a war . . . never made ammunitions or guns. . . . Who killed Clara? *Who will kill us?"* (p. 146, original emphasis).[9] Amelia knows that Clara has been seized not because she was a criminal (in fact, she was not) but because those who seized her have power and impunity. To Amelia, real criminality entails robbing a country of its land and resources and working people of their labor, a theft that she believes capitalist society condones and rewards.

Setting the robbery within a story of class struggle, Le Sueur blurs sexual and class differences, indicting capitalist society for dispossessing urban working men and impugning the men, as men, for not working together. Moreover, though she implies that poverty and desperation have motivated the robbery, she suggests another motive revealed as the men adopt the discourse of war. Preparing for the robbery as though for combat, they speak of strategies of attack and defense, maneuvers, and weapons; and they obey the orders of a commander, the nefarious Ganz. "It's worse than a war" (p. 73), Belle cries, seeing no way the men can survive, even with guns, rifles, automatics, shotguns, and revolvers. The language of violence that encodes the robbery includes the names of weapons, such words as *arsenal, dynamite, bullet, battle,* a succession of shots—*shot, shot, shot, shoot,* and a final *dead.* The name *Hitler* also appears, evoked by Ganz whenever the men plan their strategy. As driver of the getaway car, the Girl plays a part in this strategy, and once she becomes absorbed in the male plot she begins to assimilate the argot of a gangster. Though again she deconstructs male language by subverting the meanings of *steal, safe, vault, treasure, loot,* she becomes imbued with the war mentality that underlies the robbery. She had always opposed Butch's combative vision of life, denying that she wanted to be against others, to beat everyone down, to win. She wanted, she said, simply *to be,* to be-long. However, once she is in the getaway car with the fatally wounded Butch, she belongs nowhere. She has become an outsider, alienated from a state that will keep a bank robber in jail forever just "to show how important banks are" (p. 116). Entering into a permanent war with society, she says, "We were against everybody now" (p. 98). The words *against everybody* connote the breadth of the Girl's opposition and of a resisting force she can never overcome. Driving without destination, she realizes, as though for the first time, that she has been up against a social system capable of destroying her if she defies its power.

One consequence of the male plot is the Girl's sense of militancy. She accepts the position of being against as well as with, or, rather, she sees the positions as inseparable, defining an ineluctable class conflict in which she has been caught all along. Butch's death changes her from a woman who works into a worker, a member of a class that has its own discourse. From an inmate in the maternity jail, she hears the words *common people, workers, organizing, demand.* "I looked at the word demand," she says: "It was a strong word" (p. 133). Amelia, the political organizer, adds the word *care.* To the Girl's anguished question, "Who cares . . . ?" Amelia answers, "I care. . . . All that knew what she knew. All that feel the same, they are together" (p. 135).[10] Women who work together and suffer together care for each other as individuals and as a class; and the Girl asserts her identity with this class when she says, "I knew then I was one of them" (p. 136).[11] Thus the Girl converts *Us* and *Them,* a polarity inscribed in crime and war, into the solidarity of working women set against everyone, women and men, who are their oppressors.

As she merges the language of war (acquired in the bank robbery) with the language of labor unionism to which she is being exposed, the Girl finds herself forced to recognize the necessity for violence. For class war is violent. Soldiers appear and guns sound again and again during a strike in which Butch is hurt and his brother Bill killed. In typical confusion, the roles of aggressor and victim seem reversed, for strikers are the assailants, beating Butch bloody for scabbing and shooting Bill to death. Amelia justifies this violence by telling the Girl, "You got to fight for it" (p. 134). She tries to inspire (or indoctrinate) her by recounting the story of her husband's death on a picket line: "It was dangerous . . . he might be killed . . . he said he'd better die fighting than . . . live like a rat" (p. 54). As a text produced in an intensely radical period, *The Girl* calls for action, not merely words, but Le Sueur shows words becoming undifferentiated from actions as they act upon her characters' consciousness. Words contextualize and interpret experiences so that the Girl can see the social origins of her suffering as a member of an economically dispossessed class and as a woman subject to sexual victimization.[12] But

as Amelia draws upon the discourse of war for her political rhetoric, and
the Girl upon the language of bank robbers for metaphors of pregnancy,
they demonstrate that an appropriated language may be deconstructed,
but not destructured: its structure of binary oppositions will remain and
reinscribe difference.[13]

On Easter Day, while she is being held in a maternity jail, the Girl
declares her allegiance to the women united in the Workers' Alliance.
Earlier, on Christmas Day, she had seen men tragically isolated from
each other at a time when they should have joined together. "Each
alone" in a crowd, poor, jobless workers lack power, which the Girl sees
attainable through union based upon brotherhood, the message of the
season that she has translated into class solidarity. Easter and Christmas
become confused in the jail when the women are led to sing a Christmas
song on Easter. This confusion—like others, both stylistic and thematic—signifies an indifference that the text translates into fusion or
union: communality. As Le Sueur fuses the political ideology of *The
Girl*, defined by Marxist doctrine of the thirties, with Christian imagery
and pagan myth, she seems to be seeking, within all the ideologies she
knows and all the forms of discourse she can appropriate, a single expression of communality. Her biblical allusions in *The Girl* universalize
woman's story, sweeping it into a timeless history of oppression and
retribution. *The Girl* begins with an epigraph from Jeremiah and ends
with (unattributed) excerpts from the Song of Songs. The epigraph
sounds the prophetic note to which the conclusion resounds as it foresees an apocalyptic death and resurrection. "Woe! woe! to the Phari-
sees," the fanatically religious Sara cries (p. 139). Meanwhile, the birth
scene represents a marvelous resurrection as Clara comes to life in the
baby that has her face and her name. Greeted joyously as "a girl a
woman a mother"—the unpunctuated words becoming one word to signify one woman—the baby turns "golden as Clara" (p. 148). The birth
signals also a rebirth of social consciousness. The shrouded mimeograph
machine is uncovered and begins to record Amelia's inflammatory accusation. The Girl's words consecrate the machine by comparing it to
"some kind of shrouded altar, like . . . the statues in the church, Friday
before Easter rising" (p. 141). Thus included in the ritual of resurrection, it produces words that are to be a revelation. As Amelia had earlier
promised the Girl, the secret of their dark oppression "buried deep in
our class . . . will come out. It always comes out" (p. 135).

If the miracle of Easter supports a vision of coming revolution, so do
myths of return, particularly the Persephone-Demeter myth that had
long inspired Le Sueur. In the Eleusinian mysteries dedicated to Deme-

ter, the goddess's life-sustaining power is symbolized by the sacred ear of corn that is passed to the initiate, a *Kore* or eternal Maiden—a Girl. Given in secrecy, the corn silently transmits the seed and secret of life.[14] Throughout her story, the Girl has wished to learn this secret, which she believes only women know, only mothers can tell; and after she has safeguarded the stolen seed that her lover and her society would have forced her to destroy, she becomes the secret. Surrounded by ecstatic, cultic "great Mothers," as she calls them (though realistically they are poor, maddened, and ravished women), she enacts the secret of continuity, which is the essence of life, by giving birth to a child of light: "Clear Light, the baby. Clara! . . . Claro clara cleara light yes" (p. 143, original spacing). Eleusinian iconography often associated a child bathed in light with a cornucopia, for in the Eleusinian mysteries, a divine birth, culminating the rites, gave promise of rich harvests and a prosperous future.

Assuming the circular pattern of Christian and pagan resurrection myths, *The Girl* disavows death as finality by ending with a (re)birth.[15] The birth scene joyously celebrates a mother's body: *womb, belly, thighs, hands,* and *breast.* "O, a breast for all" is the Girl's passionate outcry as she hears lamentations for "our little sister [who] has no breasts" (p. 143); and her last triumphant words are, "My full breast of milk." If it is possible for women "to write their bodies," as some feminist theorists claim, then the Girl is doing so, ironically, in a variety of languages inscribed with polarities and hierarchic difference.[16] For she represents her pregnant body in metaphors she had deplored when men used them to justify competitiveness and violence. Now she celebrates her body and her baby by appropriating Butch's dichotomy of winning and losing (thus preserving adversarial relationships) and declares herself a winner. Butch loses because he "was playing the wrong game," making "the wrong hold up, the wrong home run" (p. 134). What is "wrong," she asserts, is not robbery, though it is, obviously, an illegal and potentially violent act, but the kind of robbery that is committed and its consequence. Butch commits the wrong crime and loses his life. She wins by bringing life into the world, an act that fulfills the design of her development as a woman and of the novel as a woman's text. "I had just outfoxed the cops," she says, "the whole shebang, cracked the vault, made my get away with the loot under my belly. And I am the Treasure" (p. 134). The Girl's celebratory outcries in a thief's language (now her own) recur as ballad-like refrains telling how she has "robbed the bank." Her loot is the seed of life, stolen from Butch and now hers: "I had stolen the seed. I had it on deposit. It was cached. It was safe. . . . It was in a safe. I had the key" (p. 85).[17]

In declaring herself a winner and her body a bank, a safe, a treasure, the Girl celebrates a victory made dubious by her enumerations of the body's vulnerabilities, visible in Clara's half-starved, bird-like body, as well as her own, and the mothers' bent backs and sagging bellies. Women's bodies are vulnerable, too, to commodification; they can be seized and used or sold. Clara sells herself on the streets, and the Girl gives herself to Ganz at her lover's brutal insistence. Like sexual brutality, sexual desire, once aroused, seems invasive and lashing; wild, unsatisfied longings make the Girl's flesh feel burdened, "like a tree after a storm, weighted to the ground" (p. 79). Even the vagaries of the seasons do violence to the body. Summer's heat is punishing to the women in a crowded tenement, and winter's wind cold and wolfish. Constantly threatened, the women protect themselves by banding together, warning an initiate like the Girl against dangers she is too naive to know. She is told that her body may be overpowered and forcibly sterilized or raped.[18] Like Persephone, she can be seized and violated—and she is, by Ganz, an underground figure who drives her "into the dark earth."[19] She emerges from the hellish hotel room where she has been brutalized, knowing bitter secrets she can never tell. They are embodied secrets: "they move inside you like yeast" (p. 72).

Vulnerability cannot be translated into communicable language; it is a secret that cannot be told, that limits and constrains the Girl's power of speech, but also complements it. For in telling that she has experienced what cannot be told, the Girl imbues woman's silence, as well as her speech, with value. Speech empowers woman to protest her silencing and to tell of her oppression. But speech makes her a thief and structures her into irreconcilable binary oppositions. Silence offers an escape from an alien(ating) language that is constituted, Le Sueur implies, to define exclusion, division, opposition, Other-ness. During the birth scene, Amelia keeps talking, but the Girl says, "I didn't hear her" (p. 147). As she becomes the unitary being the text envisions—at once girl woman mother—language loses its power to penetrate and divide. Instead of talk, the Girl hears wordless sounds that make silence audible. For the silence that signifies spiritual communion is not soundless. It is heard as "a kind of woman's humming," "a kind of sound like AHHHHHHHH of wonder and delight" (p. 148). Encircling the Girl, the women become one wordless voice or, metaleptically, breath and blowing wind: "They seem to breathe with me, a kind of great wind through their bodies like wind in a woods" (p. 147).[20] The mimeograph machine accompanies these wordless sounds with a "kind of beat" that marks the steady growth of women's solidarity.

As speech gives way to silence in the birth scene, so do metaphors of war yield to images of fluidity, circularity, openness, and giving that critics have considered specifically feminine.[21] They coalesce to represent a complex image of uncontainability that contains the secret the Girl has sought and become. That which cannot be contained is the flow of life represented by the birth of the baby Clara. As her labor pains intensify, the Girl feels her "blood like a river" inside her; and at the moment of crowning, the river breaks and flows: "I felt all the river broke in me and poured and gave and opened" (p. 147).[22] This outpouring of life is reflected in a mirror that had been "empty" when held in front of Clara's lifeless face and is now full with faces that the baby's face reflects: Clara's face, "the tiny face" of the Girl's mother, the faces of all women whose images have been erased from history (p. 148). If the Mother signifies the repressed, then the images appearing in the mirror represent a return of the repressed as the Girl's mother returns and all women turn into mythic Mothers whose bodies are "great mirrors." Speaking of "we" rather than "they," the Girl includes herself in the circle of Mothers whose bent backs and sagging bellies "picture . . . the suffering of all" women. "I got no words" (p. 146), the Girl says as she tries to describe these women. Then remembering the little mirror that Clara had always carried, she likens them to mirrors, and mirrors to memory.[23]

"Remembering always and appearing in everything, great mirrors" (p. 146), the women who move processionally around the dead Clara, presenting her with gifts, prayers, and little songs, perform a complex memorial service. They plan a mass for Clara and a mass meeting that will be her "Memorial." The text's punning play on words (con)fuses religious communion with political mass action and the revolutionary ardor of the masses. Once the Girl relates memory to the mirroring of oppression, Amelia calls for militancy, her words running together with the Girl's as though one voice is speaking. "We got to remember. We got to remember everything," the Girl cries, and Amelia continues, "We got to remember to be able to fight. Got to write down the names" (p. 142). Ironically, this union of voices reveals that divisiveness, seemingly absent from metaphors of silence and fluidity, has been present all along. For as Amelia completes the Girl's statement, she calls for class warfare and also for women to voice their "judgment against the city fathers" (p. 146). "We accuse," Amelia says, blurring the identity of the accused by a confusion of class with sex. Indicting the "city fathers," she equates capitalism with patriarchy, though she knows that within a capitalist class system, women (landladies, bureaucrats, and "stools") can be women's oppressors, and men, as well as women, the oppressed.

Le Sueur epitomizes men's victimization in the loss of their tools and trade. Hoinck, the Girl's father, and Clara's (imagined?) boyfriend— each in his own way becomes dispossessed when he is deprived of his *tool,* a word with murky associations Le Sueur may have meant to evoke.[24] Indeed, Belle implies that social powerlessness is equivalent to castration when she says, "What can a man do without tools?"; "Yes sir, when Hoinck pawned his tools that was the end of us all" (p. 137). Without tools a man "has to lick the boots of crazies like Ganz" (p. 138). A "crazy" like Ganz eludes or confuses the novel's categories, since he exploits and betrays—and kills—those of his own class, men and women alike. Though he may be simply a stereotyped movie gangster, necessary to the robbery plot, he contributes to the thematic tensions created within a text that simultaneously supports and subverts class solidarity and sexual unity—and does so in a discourse of war that expresses and undermines its visions of peace and communality.[25] In fighting for both her class and her sex, while inciting oppressed people, whether men or women, to fight, Amelia also personifies the text's undecidability—or, rather, its ambivalence over the relationship between capitalism and patriarchy, whether each is distinct or both collapse into the same oppressive force. At times Amelia calls for women to unite as a sex that suffers the same pain and suffers together, and at other times she solidifies working men and women as a class aspiring toward an ideal classlessness. She expresses her confused visions of political insurgency in a language that is emotional and militant, but vague, as though she (and Le Sueur) were relying upon vagueness to lessen or obviate the ideological struggle she cannot resolve. Her polemical call to arms resonates to the radical rhetoric of the thirties, but it lacks a radical sense of history and even denies that the causes of injustice can or should be known. A slippery word *it* refers first to an undefinable social agency and then to undefined social dreams. Amelia's desire for militancy, however, is clear, and the Girl marvels at words that seem to her unique and inspired though they are, clearly enough, a set political tirade: "There is no use saying it is this and that, it is men, it is women.... We all got to be alive and not lay down, and *fight* for it. We got to be men and women again and want everything and dream everything and fight for it" (p. 125, original emphasis).

If Amelia's *we* includes men, Meridel Le Sueur's *we,* in her afterword to *The Girl,* is exclusive, designating woman as "the granary of the people." Ideology, as much as commitment to a common language, determined Le Sueur's choice of the word *people.* In the thirties, it had been proposed as an alternative to *the masses,* a term tinged with connotations uncongenial, it was said, to America's working class. *We the People* was, of course, a founding phrase for Americans, and for the radical writer, *people* had the appeal of combining rhetorically an ideal of classlessness with the reality of oppression.[26] In representing "woman" as "the granary of the people," Le Sueur gave *people* a sexual exclusiveness contrary to its ordinary, as well as its ideological, meaning. She mentioned men only incidentally in her "Afterwords" and excluded them from her rushing final words: "women our mothers ourselves who keep us all alive." These words endowed women with the power to give and hold (or withhold) life—a power inherently biological. In the "Afterwords," Le Sueur moves from the biological identity of woman as mother to a metaphor of motherhood as an originating source, not only of an ideological entity (the people), but also of literary production.[27]

The implications of the metaphor become explicit in Le Sueur's definition of the writer's function: "to mirror back the beauty of the people, to urge and nourish their vital expression and their social vision" ("Afterwords," n.p.). This definition, common to radical writers of the thirties, is genderized by Le Sueur's slippage from one infinitive to another as she makes *to mirror* synonymous with *to nourish* and, eventually, with *to mother.* Motherhood connotes control and authority as well as caring, and as a mother-writer who nourishes, Le Sueur claims authority; but she disclaims authorship by saying that the text we have just read "was really written" by the women whose stories it collates. This deferral of authority raises questions about the creative source and language of a mother(ing) text. Like a folk ballad (which it resembles), *The Girl* grows out of a collective telling. A group of women told each other their stories and Le Sueur "took their stories down"; she took also stories the women wrote. By acts of taking, Le Sueur preserved or took care of the women's words, at the same time appropriating them and transforming them into her own ambitious text. In calling *The Girl* a "memorial" to the women whose stories it (re)tells, Le Sueur fuses celebration with elegy. Her novel, she says, is "a hosanna, a shout of joy and strength," raising women's "miserable conditions" to "the level of sagas." At the same time, as it records women's suffering, it is a lamentation that indicts society. Like Amelia's mass demonstration, it becomes "a trial, a judgment . . . an accusation."

In the novel, Le Sueur seems to be projecting upon her women characters her own desire, as a writer, to nuture. As waitresses in Belle's bar, they are always bringing food to others. But even when she is not working, the Girl feeds Butch doughnuts, coffee, hamburgers, and sandwiches warmed against her body.[28] All the women cook and serve, sometimes in choreographed unison as each contributes to a communal stew. Throughout the novel, mothers sustain children, men, and each other with this stew, a simmering mix of anything scavengeable made nourishing by woman's culinary art. A food of the poor, the stew functions semiotically as a designation of class and of women's collective efforts, while it brings to mind the linguistic mix that Le Sueur has created in her quest for words that nourish, a mother tongue. Returning home after her father's death, the Girl listens closely to her mother's painful and revealing words. The words that "hurt" are "FATHER, HUS-BAND," because the mother has no money to put them on a casket and because the "father, husband" has inflicted pain upon his wife and children. Like all the men, he hits, strikes, and beats. As the mother goes on "taling," she describes a delicious lamb stew she had once made out of a whole sheep, her story turning the act of feeding into a sacrament. Listening to her mother's words, the Girl understands that this distraught, penniless woman, smaller and older now, had "something": "she had her life, her children, she knows what it is even if she can't say it right out" (pp. 40–41). The wonder of a mother language is that it communicates even when words are vague and nonreferential: "something," "it." After she leaves her mother, the Girl knows that "it" can be "hard," and "it" can be "good," and she is ready to "be in it like mama" (p. 45).

In seeking constituent elements for a language that could be imbued (like the lowly stew) with sacramental grace, Le Sueur was indiscriminate. She was willing to piece together disparate and discrete fragments of incongruous discourses. If, as some feminists maintain, such piecing together, like weaving, typifies women's work (represented in the novel by the mother's quilting and the women's working on a jigsaw puzzle), it seems also to be Le Sueur's method as a writer. By the end of *The Girl* she had woven into a seamless text(ure) common street speech and the lush language of the Song of Songs. Slang becomes sacramental—an alchemical transformation that is, however, not uncompromised. Le Sueur's puns are destabilizing, turning words with serious religious and political meanings into mere wisecracks: God's divine mansion becomes the Hollywood dream house of Clara's fantasies, and the bosom of Jesus a blasphemous joke. Puns show Le Sueur's desire for unity challenged by her words, chosen precisely because they express divided and contradictory meanings. Like Clara, who "wants only peace and gets only trouble," Le Sueur wants collectivity and communion but creates strife—linguistically by puns and competing discourses, and thematically by conflicts among her incompatible ideologies.

Oddly enough, the incoherencies that result from this inner strife do not interfere with the reader's understanding. Though individual sentences may be illogical and passages contradict each other, what has not been told clearly—like what cannot be told—seems somehow luminous, especially at disjunctive moments when the Girl says, "I got no words." This might suggest that Le Sueur has proleptically realized an ideal of a "mother tongue" characterized by ruptures, disjunctions, repetitions, rhythmic returns—all to be found in Le Sueur's writing.[29] If so, then such language, said to be based upon a pre-Oedipal unity of mother and child, seems incongruous with metaphors of war in the novel that express, and may even produce, a fatal divisiveness. In its failure to eliminate the violence in these metaphors, *The Girl* seems doomed to retell a story of irreconcilable difference and conflict. This is a possibility against which feminists have been forewarned in a much-quoted admonition: "If we keep on speaking the same language together, we're going to reproduce the same history."[30] But since, to Le Sueur, telling means not only retelling but also telling *on*—incriminating, indicting—her text can repudiate the history it reproduces in the very process of telling. Once her women characters refuse to "shut up," they begin to tell on those who want them silenced. In the lingo of her characters, they become "stools." Just as everybody steals in *The Girl*, "Everybody stools." "We're all stools," Ack tells the Girl: "Everybody's got to do it to live, see? . . . Don't you have to live? . . . All right then . . . flea-bitten humanity has got to live and they have got to stool" (pp. 18–19). Some stools—like Ganz and the old whore in the relief agency—are invidious because they betray their own class and sex. But the writer who tells on a system that generates betrayal speaks with a difference. She may reproduce a familiar history of conflict, but she does so from a moral perspective that transforms reproduction into revelation. Such a transformation takes place in the final scene of *The Girl* as secular language reveals its sacred meanings, a daughter's face reveals the mother's eternal presence, and silence reveals what words cannot tell.

In the end, the text realizes a wish for unity by finding in diverse discourses a common aversion to ending. Perhaps a desire for continuity is elemental to biology, religion, myth, and human history. In the novel, it impels a flow of speech that ceases but does not end with the last sentence of *The Girl*. The Girl is still speaking, and the Kore who is yet to speak is already present. "O girl, I said," the final sentence begins, with speech and milk flowing. As a visionary writer, Le Sueur believed that all forms of being belonged within the same endless flow of life; all shared the same desire for renewal or rebirth. In *The Girl*, she claimed that the aspiration of a seed is always the same, whether it is buried in the winter earth, in woman's womb, or in an oppressed people. Birth fulfills this universal aspiration and democratizes it; in the novel, birth can bring forth a kitten and, however incongruous the combination, a new social order.[31] The birth of kittens in the opening scene (remembered by the Girl as she goes into labor) inspires Amelia to political prophesy: "One thing comes out of another one. I say the same with society, one gives birth to another. . . . One dies, another is born."

In its circularities, *The Girl* mimetically reproduces a return of the same from which it draws hope for the future.[32] Le Sueur's visionary dream of return, religious in essence and revolutionary in intent, reveals that nothing is lost forever, and her mythic allusions imply that absence, even when created by violence, is temporary. Though Persephone has been abducted and raped, she returns to earth to be reunited with Demeter. Reunion, like rebirth, occurs within a timeless cycle of loss and recovery, death, and new life. In its final orchestration of images and motifs of different discourses flowing contrapuntally together, *The Girl* suggests that Persephone's re-emergence from the land of the dead (like Clara's return) is consonant with, if not the same as, the resurrection of Christ, the rising up of a submerged lower class, and biological birth.[33] Through this attempted conflation, Le Sueur seeks to realize the novel's religious and political themes, its desire for ultimacy or transcendent truth and for social justice. Ironically, Le Sueur's overdetermination, as she draws upon diverse discourses and ideologies for thematic support, may cause a divisiveness among readers that it is trying to forestall. If few readers will wish to distance themselves from Le Sueur's quest for social justice, some will be alienated by her use of the Demeter-Persephone myth which others admire. The myth has been impugned for fating woman to an "endless breaking . . . on the wheel of biological reproduction";[34] and Demeter has been criticized for compromising woman's strength when she agreed to a conditional, rather than permanent, return of her daughter.[35] However, Persephone's annual descent to Hades is thematically useful to Le Sueur because it allows her to deny that winter's devastations—and all signs of desiccation—can last.

On a winter night, in falling snow and wind, the Girl follows Clara through the city's back streets and sees men turn away from her pitiable solicitations. The Girl studies Clara as never before and says, "We are growing, in a field that is cold, bitter, sour, and no chance for life" (p. 59). In its contradiction, the sentence epitomizes the will of the novel to deny the finality it admits. Self-divided by a binary opposition—no chance for life/growth—the sentence divides the reader's response and suspends the possibility of resolution. But though *The Girl* may be read as a self-subverting text that locates its own points of undecidability, it does decide. *We are growing* prevails as its visionary theme, its political warning, and its main action. It decides affirmatively in spite of all it knows about the cold and bitter fields in which women like the Girl must grow. It decides that stealing can be different when it is transformed into a woman's act of stooling, and that even this ugly, crude word can be subverted into a tribute to the writer who tells on those

who want their oppressive actions kept secret. Just as the Kore symbolizes transformation, so the writer who steals from the proletariat a language that stools upon their oppressors (to use Le Sueur's ideological
terms) represents the transformative powers of art. As a radical writer,
Le Sueur wanted her words to transform consciousness—a necessary
prelude, in her view, to the restructuring of society. A revolutionary restructuring, whether of society or of language, still seems difficult, if not
impossible, to effect. Nevertheless, the novel does achieve, and enact, a
radical transformation, and at least in one way, Le Sueur succeeded in
showing simultaneously a universal sameness that subverted social and
sexual differences and a difference that art created and sustained through
its transformations. For as an artist Le Sueur transformed the speech of
the variously modulated voices she had listened to because she feared
that few others, and none in power, were listening. The voices belonged
to people as anonymous as the Girl, but Le Sueur considered them as
enduring and vital as the utterances of the Kore or Eternal Maiden.
They were voices swiftly silenced by fear, madness, imprisonment,
death. In *The Girl* they are authoritative and resonant, sounding together chorally, running fugue-like after each other, opposing each other
in rapid stichomythic responses, melding into ballad-like rhythms and
refrains—ordinary, colloquial, violently ugly speech transformed into
song. They contain the paradox of difference in sameness. Le Sueur's
words are the same as those spoken by the proletariat, but in her poetic
prose they become different, strange, and unparaphrasable; and they dissolve the confusions they inscribe through their willed assertion of human possibilities. As a testimony of faith, the words *We are growing* are
unequivocal and univocal. Ultimately, *The Girl* expresses belief in universal nurturing powers—of women, of the people, of language and art.
Fusing lowly street speech with the language of religion, politics, and
myth, its prose creates, as Meridel Le Sueur wished, a memorial to the
lives of forgotten women, to an American past we must not forget, and
to a woman writer whose aspiration and art we do well to remember.

NOTES

Since there has been, as yet, little critical discussion of *The Girl,* the notes
amplify various points made in the essay and suggest theoretical and cultural
contexts appropriate to further analysis of the novel that the essay lacks space to
develop.

1. Meridel Le Sueur, "Afterwords," *The Girl* (Minneapolis: West End Press,
1978), n.p. Le Sueur has defined herself as a scribe, saying that she became a

writer "in order to express the lives and thoughts of people who were unexpressed." See Patricia Hampl, "Meridel Le Sueur," *Ms* 4, no. 1 (Aug. 1975), 62–66; and "Meridel Le Sueur," *Publishers Weekly* 221, no. 21 (21 May 1982), 18. As writer of *The Girl*, Le Sueur would answer *Yes* to all the questions asked hypothetically of a woman theorist: "Is she speaking *as* a woman, or *in the place of* the (silent) woman, *for* the woman, *in the name of* the woman?" See Shoshana Felman, "Women and Madness: The Critical Phallacy," *Diacritics* 5, no. 4 (Winter 1975), 3, original emphasis. Jacques Derrida considers the scribe—one who translates the spoken word into written language—a conservator of the power of the bureaucratic state, a role that as a radical writer Le Sueur would wish to reject. See *Of Grammatology*, trans. Gayatri Chakravorty Spivak (Baltimore: Johns Hopkins University Press, 1976, published originally in 1967 as *De la Grammatologie*), p. 92.

2. Assuming that literary history reveals sexual differences discernible to the critic, Sandra M. Gilbert and Susan Gubar define a palimpsest as a text in which a women writer has "managed the difficult task of achieving true female literary authority by simultaneously conforming to and subverting patriarchal literary standards" (see *The Madwoman in the Attic: The Woman Writer and the Nineteenth-Century Literary Imagination* [New Haven: Yale University Press, 1979], p. 1). In *The Girl*, Le Sueur makes no attempt to conceal her subversions by seeming to conform to patriarchal language and values. However, the method by which she produced the novel makes it a palimpsest, if that term means a text whose words have been partially or entirely erased from pages that can then be written over. Le Sueur only partially erased the stories she "took" from St. Paul's dispossessed women in order to produce her 1939 manuscript of *The Girl*, an unpublished work that in the 1970s she revised, but did not entirely rewrite, with the encouragement and help of John Crawford, editor of the West End Press. I wish to express my thanks to John Crawford for sending me a copy of the 1939 manuscript and to professors Mary Childress, William Spengemann, and Diana Taylor-Manheimer for helping me *write over* this essay.

3. Born in 1900, Le Sueur has had a long and involuted career as a writer and reporter, a feminist, and a political activist; her life and work reflect, and reflect upon, the cultural history of twentieth-century America. Much of her writing has yet to be published, and the story of her life, aspects of which she has revealed cryptically in interviews, remains to be told. Her works are reviewed in an anthology published recently and in a Ph.D. thesis that quotes her at length: *Ripening: Selected Work, 1927–1980, Meridel Le Sueur*, ed. and intro. Elaine Hedges (New York: Feminist Press, 1982); and Neala Janis Schleuning Yount, "America: Song We Sang without Knowing—Meridel Le Sueur's America" (Ph.D. diss., University of Minnesota, 1978; Ann Arbor, Mich.: University Microfilms International, 1983). Le Sueur's involvement with the Communist party is described by Linda Ray Pratt in "Woman Writer in the CP: The Case of Meridel Le Sueur," *Women's Studies* 14, no. 3 (1988), 247–64. Le Sueur has written several autobiographical essays and a short account of her parents. See "Corn Village" in *Salute to Spring*, (1940; New York: International Publishers, 1977), pp. 9–25, and in *Corn Village: A Selection* (Sauk City, Wis.: Stanton and

Lee, 1970), pp. 15–29; "The Ancient People and the Newly Come," in *Growing Up in Minnesota: Ten Writers Remember Their Childhoods,* ed. Chester G. Anderson (Minneapolis: University of Minnesota Press, 1976), pp. 17–46; and Le Sueur, *Crusaders* (New York: Blue Heron Press, 1955).

4. Throughout her writing, from her early prize-winning story "Persephone" (1927) to the experimental prose of "Memorial" (1979), Le Sueur has sought to give expression to woman's difference, while asserting, at various times, that difference implies social values men can assimilate, rather than (as some feminists argue) social inequality. Her story "Annunciation" (1935) develops an image of spiraling, of sinuous openings without closure, that various critics consider feminine—though what, if anything, is specifically feminine still remains undecided. Le Sueur began searching for examples of feminine writing decades ago in old immigrant newspapers held by the Minnesota State Historical Society: she was looking, she has said, for the words of working people and farm women, our authentic "storytellers" and "poets" (Hampl, "Meridel Le Sueur," 62, 63). As a reporter, she became intimate with the dispossessed women she interviewed, violating an ideal of objectivity that she rejected as men's way of relating (see "I Was Marching" [1934] in *Salute to Spring,* pp. 159–71; and "Eroded Woman" [1948] in *Song for My Time: Stories of the Period of Repression* [Minneapolis: West End Press, 1977], pp. 19–25). In her quest for a different feminine language, she based the poems of *Rites of Ancient Ripening* (1970) upon Native American chantways (see Blanche H. Gelfant, "Meridel Le Sueur's 'Indian' Poetry and the Quest/ion of Feminine Form," in *Women Writing in America: Voices in Collage* [Hanover, N.H.: University Press of New England, 1984]), pp. 71–91. While Le Sueur's writing provides one context for the study of style in *The Girl,* another would be recent theories pertaining to sexual difference and language, particularly those proposed by and indebted to Jacques Lacan, Jacques Derrida, and Michel Foucault, as well as those articulated by French and American feminist critics.

5. Warren Sussman says that in the thirties games like baseball were a conservative influence in a period of social change. Marshall McLuhan singles out poker as "a game . . . often . . . cited as the expression of all the complex attitudes and unspoken values of a competitive society"; he adds that it was commonly believed "women cannot play poker well." See Sussman, "The Thirties," in *The Development of an American Culture,* ed. Stanley Cohen and Lorman Ratner (New York: St. Martin's Press, 1983), pp. 215–60; and McLuhan, *Understanding Media: The Extensions of Man* (New York: New American Library, 1964), p. 212. In *The Girl,* baseball and poker conserve a structure of competition for dispossessed men who, the Girl thinks, would benefit from class solidarity and cooperation.

6. By making such reassignments, Le Sueur may be demonstrating the arbitrariness that modern theorists have discerned in the relationship between signifier and signified. According to Saussure, arbitrariness does not imply cultural indifference, for a system of signs has a history of production that places it within a cultural context and relates it to cultural values. Though a sign may be arbitrary, it is subject to mutability and to appropriation (see Ferdinand de

Saussure, *Course in General Linguistics*, ed. Charles Bally and Albert Sechehaye, trans. Wade Baskin [New York: McGraw-Hill, 1966], p. 67). Realistically, the impoverished male characters of *The Girl* have little that is appropriable except their language. Butch's poverty is described in the depression song that plays when he and the Girl are together—"I can't give you anything but love, baby" (p. 50). The Girl takes from her lover all that he can give: his seed and his speech.

7. See Luce Irigaray, "The Politics of Discourse and the Subordination of the Feminine," published originally in 1975 as "Pouvoir du discours/subordination du féminin," and republished in *This Sex Which Is Not One* (Ithaca: Cornell University Press, 1985), pp. 68–85. Irigaray visualizes "a language work" that would "*cast phallocentrism, phallocratism,* free from its moorings . . . leaving open the possibility of a different language" (p. 80, original emphasis). Mary Jacobus has applied Irigaray's theories on subversion to George Eliot in "The Question of Language: Men of Maxims and *The Mill on the Floss*," in *Writing and Sexual Difference,* ed. Elizabeth Abel (Chicago: University of Chicago Press, 1982), pp. 37–52. Some of the words the Girl acquires from women have already been subverted. "Crowning . . . I never had heard that" (p. 147), the Girl says, taking possession of a word symbolic of power to express woman's power to bring life into the world and to prevail.

8. Mary Daly has argued that "women have had the power of *naming* stolen from us" and must reclaim "the right to name." This does not mean creating new words, but rather setting "old" male-inflected words in a new "semantic context"—in effect "*castrating*" a "language and images that reflect and perpetuate the structures of a sexist world" (see *Beyond God and the Father* [1973; Boston: Beacon Press, 1985], pp. 7–11, original emphasis).

9. Erving Goffman has raised real, rather than rhetorical, questions about a mental patient's loss of "rights" and "liberties" in "The Moral Career of the Mental Patient" (1959) in *Asylums: Essays on the Social Situations of Mental Patients and Other Inmates* (New York: Doubleday Anchor, 1961), pp. 125–70. If Clara had few perceivable rights, she did have the liberty to wander the streets, to create a satisfying imaginary correspondence (in which she wrote herself letters), and to be with women who cared. Why she is seized and given shock treatments is never explained, but explanations might be inferred from Michel Foucault's disquisitions on the relationship of madness, poverty, and marginality to the punitive powers of a "disciplinary" and incarcerating state (see *Madness and Civilization: A History of Insanity in the Age of Reason,* trans. Richard Howard [New York: Random House, 1973; published originally in 1961 as *Histoire de la folie*]; and *Discipline and Punish: The Birth of the Prison,* trans. Alan Sheridan [New York: Pantheon, 1977; published originally in 1975 as *Surveiller et punir*]). Though individual characters in *The Girl* pose questions in limited ways, the text places these questions within the broad context of power relationships. Thus it achieves an ideological density that contrasts with its easy colloquialism. Even the "Afterwords" thicken the text by noting that one of the Girl's prototypes—one of "our mothers"—was incarcerated in an asylum for thirty years.

10. A recent study that tries to define the specificities of "women's ways of knowing" suggests that Amelia's and the Girl's way of learning and their use of *knew* may be gender-specific. According to this study, the Girl would be a "connected knower" rather than a "separate knower," for she believes that "nobody knew anything that didn't do it" (p. 72) or, in the words of the study, that "the most trustworthy experience comes from personal knowledge" (p. 112). Unlike "separate knowers," who are usually male, connected knowers "gain access to other people's knowledge" through a "capacity for empathy" that allows them to "share" experiences (p. 113) (see Mary Field Belenky, Blythe McVicker Clinchy, Nancy Rule Goldberger, and Jill Mattuck Tarule, *Woman's Way of Knowing: The Development of Self, Voice, and Mind* [New York: Basic Books, 1986]). Sharing stories and shared suffering distribute authority among the women of *The Girl*, so that no one dominates. "I don't believe in leaders," Le Sueur has said, expressing her distrust of "authority" (quoted in Yount, "America," p. 227). Arguing for collective, rather than competitive and hierarchical, relationships and imagining a collapse of Us and Them as binary oppositions, she anticipates Adrienne Rich's ideal of a "woman's consciousness" that would "stop splitting... dichotomies." "The good society," Rich has said, "would be one in which... divisions would be broken down, and there was... flow back and forth.... When I'm in a group of women... I have a sense of real energy flowing and of power in the best sense—not power of domination, but just access to sources" (see "Three Conversations," in *Adrienne Rich's Poetry*, ed. Barbara and Albert Gelpi [New York: W. W. Norton, 1975], p. 119).

11. As a sex and as a class, Le Sueur's women share the same pain and suffering. The Girl tells the stricken Clara, "We suffer together.... I hurt where you hurt" (p. 140). All the women have found pain inseparable from sexual pleasure and the joy of giving birth. Butch's lovemaking leaves the Girl feeling as if she "had been taken like a chicken by the legs and torn apart"; his birth had left his mother "nearly torn to pieces" (p. 52). Suffering reveals women's oppression and provides a basis for their bonding; but the acceptance of suffering as a necessary and even valued aspect of sexual identity raises the specter of masochism that has haunted the study of women. More immediately pertinent to *The Girl* than well-known references to woman's masochism in the works of Freud, Helene Deutsch, and Karen Horney is a question raised by Susan Griffin: "What if all our efforts towards liberation are determined by an ideology which despite our desire for a better world leads us inevitably back to the old paradigm of suffering?" (see "The Way of All Ideology," *Signs: Journal of Women in Culture and Society* 7, no. 3 [Spring 1982], 642).

12. Words also prepare an oppressed class for victimization, Amelia warns: "They get you before you got time to learn anything.... They stuff you with fine words and then they stick you in the stomach like a pig" (p. 136).

13. Jonathan Culler points out that structuralists view "binary opposition as a fundamental operation of the human mind" (see *Structural Poetics: Structuralism, Linguistics and the Study of Literature* [Ithaca: Cornell University Press, 1975], p. 15). If binary oppositions do indeed structure conceptualization and language, then the attempts of contemporary feminists—and of Le Sueur—to

discover means of collapsing oppositional dualities may not succeed in the ways they hope. By insisting upon a "returning, cyclical history," however, Le Sueur concludes that "nothing is lost" and that a belief that radical movements "fail" or "disappear" is merely "a bourgeois illusion" (quoted in Yount, "America," p. 193). Women's attempt to escape binary thinking may seem to fail, but it will reemerge and be renewed, Le Sueur argues, as history traces its cyclical pattern of return.

14. Le Sueur has written a prose poem on corn as the essence of life and "communal love," containing in its chromosome the protein that signifies life and in its bisexuality the paradigm of union or ultimate oneness. The history of corn epitomizes, she believes, an eternal story of abduction, rape, and theft (see "Excerpt from 'The Origins of Corn,'" published originally in 1976 in *New America: A Review*, and republished in *Ripening*, pp. 254–60). Le Sueur's rhapsodic praise of corn may be traced to her knowledge of Native American myths that attribute the origin of life to the Corn Maiden; to her identification with the landscape of the Midwest; and to her desire as an American writer for an indigenous symbol of renewal. In the Eleusinian mysteries, the epiphanic presence of light, birth, and corn was central to the ritual of renewal (see *The Homeric Hymn to Demeter*, ed. N.J. Richardson [Oxford: Oxford University Press, 1974], p. 26). As a British writer, Richardson may be using the word *corn* to mean what we call wheat (or cereal grains generally). For Le Sueur, the word *corn* is strategic as an endlessly exploding symbol that evokes American history and American regionalism, Native American cultures, nurturance, biology, sex, and myth—a melee of meanings she finds inspiring.

15. Though *The Girl* is a short novel, its complex pattern of returns, in which different motifs and refrains recurrently intertwine, creates the impression of a "text that starts on all sides at once, starts twenty times, thirty times, over" and "goes on and on." This is Hélène Cixous's definition of "a feminine text" in the essay "Castration or Decapitation" (p. 53). Other characteristics Cixous assigns to a feminine text also fit *The Girl:* it assumes "the metaphorical form of wandering"; it "can't be predicted . . . and is the text of the unforseeable" (p. 53); and it engages in *"political* and not just literary work" (original emphasis), inventing a form "for women on the march" (p. 52). Moreover, it is "very close to the voice"; its movement is "an outpouring"; it *"takes up the challenge of loss"* (original emphasis); and it creates "the impression of constant return . . . a kind of open memory" (p. 54) (see "Castration or Decapitation," *Signs* 7, no. 1 [Autumn 1981], 36–55, trans. Annette Kuhn. The essay was published originally in 1976 as "La Sexe ou la tête?")

16. "Women are body" and the "body must be heard," Hélène Cixous writes in her much-quoted essay "The Laugh of the Medusa" (pp. 886, 890). Writing, she proclaims, is the way for woman to reappropriate her "confiscated" body and make heard her silenced voice. "Text: my body" (p. 882), she declares cryptically, enjoining women "to write through their bodies" (p. 886). Cixous's description of a feminine style as woman's way of writing, as well as her designation of women as "birds and robbers," provides an interesting theoretical context for reading *The Girl* (see "The Laugh of the Medusa," *Signs* 1, no. 4

[Summer 1976], 875–93, trans. Keith Cohen and Paula Cohen, published originally in 1975 as "Le Rire de la Méduse"). In another well-known essay, woman's body is declared inseparable from her language, memory, and "certainty" (see Luce Irigaray, "When Our Lips Speak Together," published originally in 1977 as "Quand nos lèvres se parlent" and republished in translation in *This Sex Which Is Not One*, pp. 205–18).

17. Earlier the Girl had heard Belle speak of pregnancy as theft: "we steal it everyday, we wait for it . . . till they open the vaults and bring us the seed. If women are to get anything you have to be . . . a thief" (p. 55). As a thief, the Girl steals only from men. With women she shares, having learned sharing from her mother, who would have chopped her body into "little pieces" to feed her family. Her surrogate mothers also give whatever they have: Belle, her heavenly stew and her wisdom; Clara, her food and money; and Amelia, her ideological passion and her past.

18. Long before the appearance of feminist writings on rape—the work of Susan Brownmiller, Susan Griffin, and Annette Kolodny, among others—Le Sueur had translated displays of force in sexual relationships into political terms. In "Eroded Woman," *North Star Country,* and *Rites of Ancient Ripening,* for example, she related the rape of woman to a rapacious exploitation of the land and natural resources, as well as of working people and Native Americans. In *The Girl* she places rape, sterilization of women, and forced abortion within the same discourse of power. Opposition to abortion in *The Girl* may seem incompatible with its feminist themes, but it represents a resistance to the coercive power that pro-choice women see exercised when women are denied control over their own bodies. For a contemporary essay that resonates to many of Le Sueur's feminist themes and shares Le Sueur's view on sterilization, see Adrienne Rich's "Motherhood: The Contemporary Emergency and the Quantum Leap," in *On Lies, Secrets, and Silence: Selected Prose 1966–1978* (New York: W. W. Norton, 1979), pp. 265–66. (Rich's definition of lesbianism has led her to define *The Girl* as a lesbian novel that belongs within the "continuum" of women's history, which Rich sees marked by women's resistance to "male tyranny" (see "Compulsory Heterosexuality and Lesbian Existence," *Signs* 5, no. 4 [Summer 1980], 631–60.)

19. Le Sueur has written a parody of the Persephone-Demeter myth in tough-guy street talk, with Pluto cast as a gangster (Yount, "America," pp. 91–92).

20. Le Sueur translates breathing, an elemental sign of life, into a communal act that fuses individuals into one body, the sign of human solidarity. She ends her journalistic piece on the Minneapolis truckers' strike of 1934 by describing her fusion with the strikers as her body "join[s] . . . with . . . thousands of bodies . . . and [her] breath with the gigantic breath" of thousands (see "I Was Marching," *Salute to Spring,* p. 171). Cixous's injunction, "Inscribe the breath of the whole woman" ("Medusa," p. 880), suggests an emphasis upon individuality that is contrary to Le Sueur's image of all women breathing together as one.

21. Le Sueur has called for women to "make their own language" and structure their art with "something related to woman's body. The round, the circular

imagery" (quoted in Yount, "America," pp. 300, 302). Equating linearity with masculinity and destruction, she has said, "One of the most dangerous concepts we have in modern life is what I call the linear or male view of the world. It is aggressive, progressive . . . the progression of explosion toward a target, to destruction" (quoted in Yount, "America," p. 54). For a discussion of Le Sueur's view of circularity as a feminine form, see Gelfant, "Meridel Le Sueur's 'Indian' Poetry."

22. The breaking the Girl describes produces continuity—a flow—rather than division or an ending. The flow of life dissolves differences between the biological and the symbolic, the circumstantial and universal, a particular girl and the eternal Kore. All become one in the baby Clara.

23. Commonplace details like this emphasize Le Sueur's deliberate use of simple daily experience as the (people's) source of knowing and being. However, the face of the girl woman mother that the Girl sees in the mirror might be interpreted in Lacanian terms *"as an identification, . . .* the transformation that takes place in the subject when he *[sic]* assumes an image" (original emphasis) (see Jacques Lacan, "The Mirror Stage," in *Écrits: A Selection,* trans. Alan Sheridan [New York: W. W. Norton, 1977; formulated originally in 1936], p. 2). Luce Irigaray's response to Lacan and Freud (among others) also suggests ways of analyzing Le Sueur's mirror imagery and its associations with memory and the mother (see *Speculum of the Other Woman,* trans. Gillian C. Gill [Ithaca: Cornell University Press, 1985], published originally in 1974 as *Speculum de l'autre femme).* Reflecting upon her own experience, Le Sueur has discussed the repression of woman as a repression of the unconscious and declared her writing an attempt to recover in language women's buried subjectivity.

24. If Le Sueur had intended to evoke the sexual connotations of *tool,* then the attempt of the Girl's brother to take possession of the father's tools may be interpreted as an Oedipal struggle, as well as a practical effort to get a job.

25. In "The Way of All Ideology," Susan Griffin concludes that an "aspect of ideological structure" is its destructive competitiveness: "Dialogue—which is finally perhaps the form of all thought—must become a war. One must lose and the other win" ("The Way of All Ideology," p. 651). Unlike Griffin, Le Sueur seems to believe that discrete ideologies can reinforce each other, though she shows them coexisting not through cooperation but through indifference as each permits the other to enunciate a position, while the text itself remains simultaneously supportive and subversive of both.

26. Kenneth Burke argued this point before the first Congress of American Writers, in which Le Sueur spoke on "Proletarian Literature and the Middle West" (see Burke, "Revolutionary Symbolism in America," *American Writers' Congress,* ed. Henry Hart [New York: International Publishers, 1935], pp. 87–94). Burke and other participants of the congress recall the furor aroused by his proposal for a change in rhetoric in "Thirty Years Later: Memories of the First American Writers' Congress," *The American Scholar* 35 (Summer 1966), 495–516. Frank Lentricchia has discussed Burke's rhetorical strategy at some length in *Criticism and Social Change* (Chicago: University of Chicago Press, 1983), pp. 21–38. Le Sueur concluded her regional history *North Star Country* (1945) with an accolade to the people as "a story that never ends, a river that winds and falls

and gleams ... emerges to the sea.... The people are ... a long incessant coming alive ... persistent and inevitable" (see *North Star Country,* intro. Blanche H. Gelfant [Lincoln: University of Nebraska Press, 1984], p. 321). Le Sueur's rhetoric is similar to that of Ma Joad in John Steinbeck's *The Grapes of Wrath:* "Us people will go on livin' when all them people is gone.... We're the people that live.... We go on.... We keep a-comin' " (New York: Penguin, 1978), p. 310. *The Grapes of Wrath* was published in 1939, the year that Le Sueur's manuscript of *The Girl* was rejected. In concluding her bitterly denouncing essay "The Dark of the Time" (1956), Le Sueur wrote (in approved party rhetoric): "It is the people who give birth to us all, to all cultures, who by their labors create all material and spiritual values" (see *Song for My Time,* p. 58). For a discussion of the meaning that *folk* had for Le Sueur as both a literary and political term, see Gelfant, Foreword to *North Star Country,* pp. vii–xviii.

27. While Le Sueur speaks of the biological mother, she tries to avoid the Freudian equation of woman's fate with her anatomy. In coalescing noun and verb, so that *mother* becomes synonymous with *mothering* and both with *caring* and *nurturing,* she seeks to collapse binary gender oppositions. Caring, nurturing, and mothering are in her view inherent in a "feminine consciousness" that is distinguishable from the female body. Le Sueur's definition of mother includes men because survival depends upon men and women sharing a "mothering element" that, she believes, sustains all life: "men have got to become mothers and nourishers instead of exploiters and seizers" (quoted in Yount, "America," p. 68). In an essay that distinguishes biological from social discourse, Sara Ruddick introduced the term "maternal thinking," which I find congruent with Le Sueur's "feminine consciousness." Like Le Sueur, Ruddick envisions a future in which men and women can think maternally, and she too foresees that mothering values will prove politically subversive (see "Maternal Thinking," *Feminist Studies* 6, no. 2 [Summer 1980], 342–67).

28. The Girl feeds Butch, but when she says, "I want something to eat ... I'm hungry," he answers bluntly: "I haven't anything to feed you ... I told you that" (p. 78).

29. The play of rhythms and of ruptures in *The Girl* seems to fit Julia Kristeva's descriptions of *le sémiotique,* a potentially revolutionary kind of signifying derived from the pre-Oedipal relationship between mother and infant (see *Revolution in Poetic Language,* trans. Margaret Waller [New York: Columbia University Press, 1984], published originally in 1974 as *La révolution du langue poétique).* In an interview given in 1974, Kristeva designates the male "literary avant-garde" as practitioners of "feminine writing," naming as examples Mallarmé, Malador, Lautreamont, Artaud, and Joyce (see "Oscillation between Power and Denial," in *New French Feminisms,* ed. Elaine Marks and Isabelle de Courtivron [Amherst: University of Massachusetts Press, 1980], pp. 165–67). Le Sueur has acknowledged her literary indebtedness to D. H. Lawrence, saying that the sexuality she saw in his writing inspired her to an expression of woman's sexuality. The issue of difference has murky depths.

30. Irigaray, "When Our Lips Speak Together," p. 205. Posed in various ways, the question of how to create a language that is not inherently oppressive echoes through contemporary feminist criticism (see, for example, Jean Bethke

Elshtain, "Feminist Discourse and Its Discontents: Language, Power, and Meaning," in *Feminist Theory: A Critique of Ideology*, ed. Nannerl O. Keohane, Michelle Z. Rosaldo, and Barbara Gelpi [Chicago: University of Chicago Press, 1982], pp. 127–45; and Madeleine Gagnon's excerpt from "Corps I" [1977], which quotes Annie Le Clerc, *Paroles de Femme* [1974], in *New French Feminisms*, p. 179). Recently, Le Sueur has concluded that nouns institute domination, and she has been experimenting with a "nounless" prose that, she says, has its prototype in Hopi language (see Gelfant, "Meridel Le Sueur's 'Indian' Poetry").

31. Like the trees associated with Amelia, animals, insects, birds enlarge the constricted urban world of the novel and extend its range of discourse. Wolf, rabbit, deer, jackal, hawk, snake, duck, grouse, dog, bird, pig, wasp, buzzard—these creatures suggest through their moiling activity the omnipresence of predator and victim. The Girl describes her mother "chased, like by a pack of wolves" (p. 44); and the mother describes the father pursued by adversity "biting at his heels like a hound dog" (p. 43). The Girl sees Ganz and his gang as "wolves"; she dreams of men with "wolves' faces and long teeth" (p. 46); she has "this feeling you have to hurry, like running in the woods with hunters after you" (p. 44) or else lie "quiet like an animal when hunters are near" (p. 71). In a submerged hunting image, Amelia describes social oppression as a pursuit that ends with devoured bodies (p. 135). Wolves, rats, pigs, and snakes evoke men's vicious aspects, but in his sleek beauty, Butch is a fox. The cat, traditionally a symbol of the feminine, is "a female like us" (p. 16). While the animal images are colloquial, if not clichéd—Ganz is a "rat," the Girl a "scared rabbit"—they emphasize innateness and so tend to subvert the novel's explicit contentions that cultural forces, rather than nature, determine the predatory behavior of a sex or a social class. The animal images also reinforce the Girl's paranoid feelings that someone is "always after me"—not only men, but also "dicks," "policematrons," and women "stools" (p. 127).

32. Le Sueur's emphasis upon the sameness underlying difference, generic to the collective proletarian novel, precludes the argument that poverty is a sign of individual failure. As members of a submerged social class, Butch and Hoinck, different as individuals, make the same gestures: both ritualistically empty their pockets (pp. 21, 86); neither has a cent; both suffer the same poverty. Because their situations are the same, different characters will say the same things, so that the Girl and Belle, clearly distinguished from each other, seem often to speak with one voice. At the same time, a particular character will sound the same motifs on different occasions. Clara's tin-pan-alley recital of "funny things that didn't go together" (p. 55)—pulp magazine optimism, suicidal despair, and rambling woman's advice—identifies her as the same in madness and sanity. To show the pervasiveness of social misery, the same descriptions introduce different scenes: in the spring, the women live in a condemned tenement owned by a woman vacationing in Mexico, and in summer, they inhabit an abandoned warehouse (the same building?) owned by a widow vacationing in Europe.

33. A conflation of different discourses characterizes much of the well-known protest fiction written in the thirties. Various combinations of the language of labor unionism, Marxism, religion, and biology appear, for example, in Michael

Gold, *Jews without Money* (1930); Richard Wright, *Uncle Tom's Children* (1940), and John Steinbeck, *The Grapes of Wrath* (1939). Le Sueur added feminism to this variety.

34. Phyllis Chesler, *Women and Madness* (New York: Doubleday, 1972), p. 240. Chesler concedes that "Persephone's traits of naivete, docility, and conservatism are probably more conditioned than inevitable," but she finds "such traits intrinsically valueless—whether they appear in women or men" (p. 266).

35. See Mary Daly, "Prelude to the First Passage," *Feminist Studies* 4, no. 3 (Oct. 1978), 84. Daly believes that the Demeter-Persephone myth "expresses the essential tragedy of women after the patriarchal conquest," a tragedy that lies in Demeter's compromised agreement to allow Persephone to return to Hades: "it was fatal for her [Demeter] to undervalue the power of her own position and set aside her anger, just as it was fatal that she taught the kings of the earth her divine science and initiated them into her divine mysteries." While Daly objects to men's participation in the Eleusinian mysteries, Le Sueur permits some anonymous men to witness the mysteries of the birth scene in *The Girl*, though she keeps them "kind of hung back" (p. 146). No major male character appears because all have been killed off, so that in the end, "the great Mothers" form a "community of women" (to use Nina Auerbach's phrase) that Daly might approve. Butch is remembered in the birth scene, but only to be declared wrong and ignorant: "O Butch, . . . you didn't know what your mamma knew" (p. 146). Moreover, the infant's "first breath" is the "last breath of Butch": he breathes again at the birth of his child, only to die again.

Daly's separatism would weaken Le Sueur's commitment to a working class that includes men and women as the exploited and oppressed. It would undermine also her universalism, her vision of the circle that encompasses all Being. While the Demeter-Persephone myth centers upon the mother-daughter relationship, it symbolizes, various scholars believe, a universal human fate or, even more cosmically, "the infinity of supra-individual organic life" (see C. Kerenyi, "The Eleusinian Paradox," in C. G. Jung and C. Kerenyi, *Essays on a Science of Mythology: The Myth of the Divine Child and the Mysteries of Eleusis*, Bollingen Series 22 [1949; Princeton: Princeton University Press, 1969], pp. 151–55, quote on p. 153). In the same volume, however, Jung concludes that "Demeter-Kore exists on the plane of mother-daughter experience, which is alien to man and shuts him out" (p. 177). Another explication of the myth both includes and excludes men, marking them as simultaneously the same as women and different. "The separation of Mother and Daughter, the yearning of Demeter for her own girl-child, the Kore, must be characteristic of individual human existence, of men as well as women, but in one way of men and in another of women" (see C. Kerenyi, *Eleusis: Archetypal Image of Mother and Daughter*, trans. Ralph Manheim, Bollingen Series 65 [New York: Pantheon Books, 1967], p. 146). Kerenyi goes on to say that "all human beings and not women alone bear [the same] origin and . . . duality . . . both the Mother and the Daughter—within themselves" (p. 147).

Bruce Lincoln has called Persephone's initiation "a cosmic event in the fullest sense. If ever a Greek woman assumed the role of this goddess at Eleusis or elsewhere, it was not a personal ceremony, but a matter that affected the entire universe" (see "The Rape of Persephone: A Greek Scenario of Women's Initiation," *Harvard Theological Review* 72 [July-Oct. 1979], 233–35). Lincoln concludes that throughout history women's initiation rites have been imbued with cosmic importance. Le Sueur is trying to ascribe such importance to the initiation of a poor proletarian girl who, like Persephone, would have cosmically transformative powers. To believe that a single individual can effect radical transformations may require a mythic, rather than historical, imagination. Le Sueur (con)fuses myth and history to exert pressure upon the reader's imagination.

JANE MARCUS

Laughing at Leviticus:
Nightwood *as Woman's Circus Epic*

Lion and woman and the Lord knows what
—W. B. Yeats

O monsters, do not leave me alone ... I do not confide in you except
to tell you about my fear of being alone, you are the most human
people I know, the most reassuring in the world. If I call you monsters, then what name can I give to the so-called normal conditions
that were foisted upon me? Look there, on the wall, the shadow of
that frightful shoulder, the expression of that vast back and neck
swollen with blood ... O monsters, do not leave me alone.
—Colette, *The Pure and the Impure*

Djuna Barnes's great Rabelaisian comic epic novel, *Nightwood* (1936),
is beginning to excite the critical attention it deserves. As a contribution
to that effort this essay is a feminist interpretation which argues, among
other readings, that *Nightwood* is a brilliant and hilarious feminist critique of Freudian psychoanalysis and a parody of the discourse of diag-
nosis of female hysteria. Using Julia Kristeva's *Powers of Horror,* I argue
that *Nightwood,* in its original title of "Bow Down" and its continual
reference to submission and bowing or lowering of the self, is a study in
abjection and that by its concentration on the figure of The One Who Is
Slapped, the downtrodden victim, it figures by absence the authoritarian
dominators of Europe in the thirties, the sexual and political fascists.
While Kristeva studies abjection as a pathology, I maintain that Barnes's
portraits of the abject constitute a political case, a kind of feminist anarchist call for freedom from fascism. Looking at Nikka's tattoo as a defiance of the Levitical taboo against writing on the body, I see the body
of the Other—the black, lesbian, transvestite, or Jew—presented as a

text in the novel, a book of communal resistances of underworld outsiders to domination. Its weapon is laughter, a form of folk grotesque derived from Rabelais and surviving in circus.

With Mikhail Bakhtin's *Rabelais* as model methodology, I see *Nightwood*'s extravagant language and imagery as a direct descendant of medieval grotesque realism (as *Ladies' Almanack* is certainly a descendant of the Rabelaisian almanack hawked about in Paris street fairs). In this "reversible world," or "world turned upside down," Barnes moves from high to low culture, from opera to circus, and even expands Bakhtin's categories from their body-base in the material to include the mystical and mental grotesqueries which he excluded.

I would also argue that the status of *Nightwood* as a lesbian novel or a cult text of high modernism has obscured the ways in which it is a French novel, indebted as much to Victor Hugo and Eugène Sue as it is to Rabelais. My purpose in reviving *Nightwood* is political. Strangely canonized and unread, it cannot function as a critique of fascism. The revision of modernism in which this essay participates is an effort to read race, class, and gender back into the discussion. Unlike most expatriate writing from this period, *Nightwood* paints the Paris underworld and demimonde with its own colors, not a specifically American palette. Its characters are her modern *misérables,* brothers and sisters to the hunchback of Notre Dame. *Nightwood,* like modernism itself, begins in Vienna in the 1880s. Freud, fascism, Hitler, high art, and the lumpen proletariat haunt the text as a potent political unconscious. *Nightwood*'s hysterical heteroglossia is a perverse and almost postmodern folk-text in which language and its possibility for figuration are as potent and explosive as in Shakespeare or Joyce.

Tattoo as Taboo

> Ye shall not make any cuttings in your flesh for the dead, nor print any marks upon you.
>
> —Leviticus 19:27–28

In order to be pure and symbolic, Kristeva argues, the patriarchal body may have only one mark, the circumcision, which cut duplicates in the symbolic order the natural cut of the umbilical cord, which separates mother and son. The ritual cut replaces the natural cut—"the identity of the speaking being (with his God) is based on the separation of the son from the mother."[1] In political terms, patriarchal identity is established by marking the body to distinguish it not only from the unclean mother but from the polytheistic worshipers of the mother goddess who threaten the tribe. The establishment of marked sexual difference with rigid boundaries differentiates the people of the Bible from other religious cults, like the worship of Dionysus in Greece, where the erasure of sexual difference is the point of ritual activity. (The Jews were neither the first nor the only people to use circumcision, a practice some anthropologists see as a form of menstruation envy.)

Writing on the body, I would argue, is breaking a powerful patriarchal taboo for the inheritors of the Judeo-Christian ethos in which the possession of the Logos is indicated by writing on the holy tablets. If human skin is made into a page or a text, it violates the symbolic order. A body covered with marks is too close to the natural "unclean" state of the newborn's body, with the marks of the "unclean" placenta, the traces of its mother's blood upon it. A tattoo, then, is not only taboo; it is the birthmark of the born-again—the self-created person who denies his / her birth identity. This "monster" is a carnivalesque figure who revels in the taboo-shattering act of making the body a book, dissolving the difference between spirit and matter.[2] (The Levitical taboos include incest and homosexuality, and mark out any aberrant or physically blemished person as unpleasing to God. While the prohibition extends to prevent the union of same and same or human with animal, it also extends to the mixing of things: seeds should not be mingled, nor breeds of cattle; clothing should not be made of linen *and* wool.)

In this context, Djuna Barnes's *Nightwood* might be called "The Lamentations of the Levitically Impure." Leviticus is about separation. *Nightwood* is about merging, dissolution, and, above all, hybridization— mixed metaphors; mixed genres; mixed levels of discourse from the lofty to the low; mixed languages from medical practice and circus argot, church dogma and homosexual slang. Barnes's revision of the Old Testament parallels Joyce's revision of Homer in *Ulysses*. By making hybrids of the sacred texts of Western culture, both writers revitalize high culture by carnivalizing the dead bodies of the old texts, engorging them in a sacred / profane cannibalism. *Nightwood* is also a dangerous novel, if we use Mary Douglas's concept of "purity and danger," for the whole social order of this novel is "impure."[3] The world is turned upside down for carnival; it is the reversible world of the circus, the night world of lesbian, homosexual, and transvestite Paris. Leviticus writes the rules for purity of blood. Ironically, it is Felix, the wandering Jew, marked as impure by a world that has incorporated his culture's ethic of purity and named the Jew himself as impure, who searches hopelessly for a "pure" aristocratic European bloodline: "With the fury of a fanatic, he hunted down his own disqualification" (p. 9).[4] *Nightwood* makes a modernism of marginality. Its danger is that the excluded object of its rage, the white Christian male, might read it. The Aryan superman is absent from the text but his "uprightness" is the ethic which the characters' abjection opposes.

At a party in Vienna in the twenties, echoing Act 2 of *Die Fledermaus*, the characters of *Nightwood* meet. Count Onatorio Altamonte is entertaining "the living statues," collecting for his amusement, as some European aristocrats did, circus people, Jews, transvestites, exiled Americans. I take one passage as my example here but the whole novel encourages close reading. Dr. Matthew O'Connor tells Felix the story of "Nikka the nigger," whose name not only mimics the obscenity of the word, like a Middle European mispronunciation of the American racist epithet, but has a feminine ending. He "used to fight the bear at the Cirque de Paris." His role is savage primitive male battling the beast for the thrill of an effete audience. But O'Connor exposes the myth of the fascist projection of savage sexuality on to the black man:

> "There he was, crouching all over the arena without a stitch on, except an ill-concealed loin-cloth all abulge as if with a deep-sea catch, tattooed from head to heel with all the *ameublement* of depravity! Garlanded with rosebuds and hack-work of the devil—was he a sight to see! Though he couldn't have done a thing (and I know what I am talking about in spite of all that has been said about the black boys) if you had stood him in a gig-mill for a week, though (it's said) at a stretch it spelled Desdemona. Well, then, over his belly was an angel from Chartres; on each buttock, half public, half private, a quotation from the book of magic, a confirmation of the Jansenist theory, I'm sorry to say and here to say it. Across his knees, I give you my word, 'I' on one and on the other, 'can,' put those together! Across his chest, beneath a beautiful caravel in full sail, two clasped hands, the wrist bones fretted with point lace. On each bosom an arrow-speared heart, each with different initials but with equal drops of blood. . . .
>
> "The legs," said Doctor O'Connor, "were devoted to vine work, topped by the swart rambler rose copied from the coping of the Hamburg house of Rothschild. Over his *dos*, believe it or not and I shouldn't, a terse account in early monkish script—called by some people indecent, by others Gothic—of the really deplorable condition of Paris before hygiene was introduced, and nature had its way up to the knees. And just above what you mustn't mention, a bird flew carrying a streamer on which was incised, '*Garde tout!*' I asked him why all this barbarity; he answered he loved beauty and would have it about him." (Pp. 16–17)

O'Connor exposes in his tale ("at a stretch it spelled Desdemona") the white man's projection of desire for the white woman onto the black man, the white's naming of the black's genitals as "rapist," the white man's desire to rape and kill woman. The pun on the word *spell* suggests that his penis is named Desdemona, as O'Connor's penis is named Tiny O'Toole, but *spell* could also be read sexually as "to satisfy" Desdemona or, in another meaning, to take someone's place. The name concealed by Nikka's knickers is Verdi's Desdemona more than Shakespeare's, as Nikka acts an operatic Othello. The miscegenation and murder suggested by Desdemona are also in the tattoo's "confirmation of Jansenist theory," defined by the O.E.D. as the heresy of belief in the eternal battle of good and evil, the belief in the "perverseness and inability for good of the natural human will." There are no margins; every inch of space is covered with drawings and texts, breaking both the Levitical taboo of writing on the body and the taboo on mixing objects, for text and drawings clash with each other, mixing the sacred and profane, the vulgar and the reverenced, the popular and the learned. The texts of each breast and buttock contradict each other as the ferociously oxymoronic frenzy of Barnes's prose style, as well as her painting style, continually yokes opposites together in violent opposition, mocking Levitical prohibitions in an endless play at dissolving and reconstituting difference.

The length of the name Desdemona suggests a gigantic penis and is part of an age-old tradition of sexual jokes. But it also suggests Othello and "savage" jealousy and murder. The reference to Victor Hugo's *Notre Dame de Paris,* with its famous digression on the criminal underworld and the sewers, is in the line "Paris before hygiene was introduced."[5] Hugo's earlier novel *Bug-Jargal* (1818 and 1826) was, like Aphra Behn's *Oroonoko,* a study of a figure of "the royal slave."[6] This figure is a projection of a "phallic negro," the white man's archetypal erotic animalization of the black. The white's spelling of desire on the black's penis, the pricking of the "prick" in what must have been a very painful operation, renders him impotent as a man while it mythologizes him as savage maleness. The black man's body is a text of Western culture's historical projections and myths about race. The angel from Chartres represents the myth of the black as angelic, innocent, and childlike during the early days of slavery; the book of magic refers to Europeans' fears of African religions. The Rothschild rose from Hamburg may suggest money made in the slave trade. The "caravel" suggests a slave ship, and the elegant wrists the ladies who benefited from slavery. In a further description of the tattoo, O'Connor claims that an obscene word runs down one side into the armpit, a word uttered by Prince Arthur Tudor on his wedding night, "one word so wholly epigrammatic and in no way befitting the great and noble British Empire" (p. 16). We may assume that word, *merde,* is the doctor's favorite and the author's, too, since the text is as full of references to bird droppings as Paris itself is.

We know from Barnes's long response to Emily Coleman's essay on *Nightwood* that she expected readers to understand the references to Victor Hugo in the novel and to see it as part of the comic tradition of grotesque realism reaching back through Hugo to Rabelais.[7] In *Les Misérables*, Jean Valjean's fellow convict, Cochepaille, is tattooed with the date of the defeat at Waterloo, 1815. In *Nightwood*, Robin wanders from church "monstrously unfulfilled" with her large monk's feet, and the nuns at the Convent of Perpetual Adoration give her a sprig from their rosebush and show her "where Jean Valjean had kept his rakes" (p. 46). Hugo describes the way in which the basest word in the French language, *merde*, became the finest word as General Cambronne hurls it at his enemy on the battlefield. Hugo says that the expression of the excremental equals the soul, and in a note about the novel he claimed that *merde* was the "misérable de mot," the outcast word, as his *misérables* were outcast people.[8] The fecal motif in Hugo's sewer chapters is continued in Barnes's *pissoir* passages and her description of O'Connor's chamberpot.[9] For Hugo, the person who says "merde" is Prometheus, expressing the obscene laughter of the oppressed. The language of the latrine, which O'Conner speaks in the novel, is regenerative and Rabelaisian, as voiding is cleansing. Gutter language, *fex urbis*, is the voice of outcast people. In these chapters Hugo explores the argot of the underworld, its special culture, and defines it as "verbe devenu forçat," the word become a convict.[10]

Similar convict words are chained together in Dr. O'Connor's speeches, his stories of grotesque and painful suffering, the intensely overdetermined figures banging against the bars of the prison house of language. His swearing, the mixture of prayer, oath, and profanity, the inclusion of the Virgin Mary and shit in the same sentence, goes back to Rabelais, reminding us of Gargantua arriving in Paris and drenching the crowd with urine, his "Mère de ... merde ... shit, Mother of God." Dung and defecation in the Rabelaisian tradition described by Bakhtin are part of carnival's reversal of authoritarian values, the eruption of folk humor in a bawdy acceptance of decay as renewal, of death as part of life. The language of this irrepressible force, as Bakhtin says, privileges the lower parts of the body. Critics who have described *Nightwood* as modernist decadence or the product of perversity have missed its deep roots in folk culture, via Hugo and Rabelais. For Barnes is the female Rabelais, the articulator of woman's body / bawdy language. Like Hugo and Rabelais before her, Barnes writes scatology as ontology. She affirms being by celebrating the Below, the belly, the bowels, the big feet of Robin Vote, and Nikka, who is a natural black man only to the knees.

Nikka's tattooed body, to return to the text, is a cabalistic ritual object put on display at the circus. He fights the bear and reminds us of Eugène Sue's Morok and Hugo's bizarre *L'Homme qui rit,* whose monstrous and maimed characters resemble *Nightwood*'s. The friendship between the bearlike man, Ursus, and the civilized wolf, Homo, reminds us of Robin Vote as "the beast turning human" and the novel's controversial last scene with the dog; and Hugo's circus wagon, as a universe of human, animal, and divine monsters, is an earlier version of the circus world of *Nightwood.* "Garlanded with rosebuds and hack-work of the devil," Nikka's body is also a journalist's page (hack; Barnes as a brilliant journalist and "hack" writer; printer's devil). The tattoos, with their combination of text, vines, flowers, and gothic script are an exact version of the early definition of the grotesque. In *Rabelais,* Bakhtin described the bold infringement of borders in early grotesque art, where forms "seemed to be interwoven as if giving birth to each other," and the uncanny passing of animal, vegetable, and human into one another (p. 32). Nikka's body is like one of Djuna Barnes's drawings for *Ryder,* or *Ladies' Almanack,* which I describe as "Pennsylvania Dutch surrealism" to capture its combination of primitive folk naivete and vitality with mythical beasts, texts, human figures, and grotesque vines.

But the art of tattooing is also a kind of bloody needlework. Thelma Wood, Djuna Barnes's lover and the model for the character of Robin Vote in the novel, was an artist who did silverpoint etchings, an art form which one might call, with its dangerous, uncorrectable pin pricks, a "high art" form of tattoo. These etchings are also tabooed objects, studies of cannibalistic flowers and fetishistic shoes.[11]

In the body of Nikka, Barnes creates an aesthetic of the modernist grotesque, a delicate and exotic refinement of the gross Rabelaisian realistic grotesque and the romantic intellectual grotesque of E. T. A. Hoffmann. Nikka's body as ritual object asserts the unalterable real grotesquerie of the human body. In *The Painted Body,* Michel Thévoz follows Lacan in seeing marking the body as primitive human grappling with the mirror stage of development and identity formation, so that human skin is humanity's "first ground and surface of sign-making."[12] In other words, the body is our first book, the primal blank page on which our ancestors wrote. Anthropological evidence places the most ancient tattoos on the genitals, a tattooed or decorated phallus or voluptuous female body decorated on breast, buttocks, and genital areas among the first human artifacts. Our own bodies were our first works of art, a remaking of the self. *Nightwood*'s project is a remaking of gender and race categories of selfhood and it is preoccupied with skin as a blank page. In Nikka's case, the tattoo so graphically described is another of Barnes's reversals, for Africans seldom used tattoos to mark the body. They used scarification or body painting, while light-skinned peoples, notably Asians, used tattoos. Marking the body seems to enact opposite meanings, a symbolic separation from the mother as in Kristeva's use of the terms *semiotic* and *symbolic*, where *semiotic* means all that Plato excluded from art—circus, carnival, festival, music, laughter, and dance. But it also marks the return of the repressed savage and unconscious desire. *Nightwood*'s language is a perfect example of this "semiotic" in practice.

Thévoz sees the original tattoo as a symbolic mark of the human being's social relation to culture and circumcision as a representation of the taboo against incest with the mother. In Western culture, tattoo has been used to mark the subject as a slave or a convict and has lost its ritual social origins in inclusion rather than exclusion from culture. The modern tattoo is like the mark of Cain, a sign of exclusion. But it also identifies the body with a certain class or group. The meaning of tattoo has changed historically from embodying symbolic law in primitive societies to marking the outlaw in modern societies—hence, the figure of the lesbian in the modern novel feeling she has the mark of Cain on her forehead. (Cain seems to survive as a figure for the prepatriarchal. He is driven out because he will not slaughter an animal for a patriarchal god.) Nikka in *Nightwood* is like a convict in Kafka's *The Penal Colony* whose body has been tattooed by the infernal machine that tattoos each criminal with the text of the law he has infringed. French soldiers in the nineteenth century often tattooed the side of the hand with the word *merde* so that it would deliver a message when they saluted their superiors.

Djuna Barnes was fascinated with maquillage. Body-painting, makeup, extravagant costuming, and cross-dressing were part of the style of what Shari Benstock calls "Sapphic Modernism." Figuring Nikka as abjection, his skin a text on which the dominant culture writes him as other, Barnes writes from the place of exclusion as woman, exile, and lesbian, juggling the double message of the memory of body marking as beautiful and social and its present meaning as sinister and shameful. Thévoz relates the angry or erotic tattoos of modern convicts and mental patients as the outcast's defiance of logocentric society's exclusion of him, hence the body and hair painting of "punk" culture. An answer to the question raised by Nikka's tattoos in *Nightwood* may be found in the barbaric Ilse Koch's collection of tattoos cut from the skin of victims of Nazi persecutions at Buchenwald. Given the Levitical prohibition of writing on the body, these "works of art" were taken not from the bodies of Jews but from other outsiders, and represent the moment when culture ceases to laugh at Leviticus and begins to shudder.

Since so many readings of *Nightwood* situate the reader as "normal" and the characters as perverse and "damned," reading against the grain of the text's privileging of the oppressed as "us," I propose this reading as a sisterhood under the skin with the victimized, as the "fluid blue" under Robin's skin allies her with Nikka. In a similar way, many studies of the Nazis (aside from the brilliant film, *Our Hitler*) emphasize the perversity of individual sadists rather than the complicity of a whole nation in genocide. Such readings deny not only history and reality but the power of art in fiction like *Nightwood* to change us.

Modernism, then, if we take *Nightwood* as its most representative text, is a tattoo on the backside of a black homosexual circus performer. The non-Aryan, nonheterosexual body is a book in which the modern failure to understand or assimilate the difference of race, class, and gender is inscribed. Sexuality, liminality, and color are textualities written on the body in thousands of pinpricks, little dots which make a language of bloody ellipses, a *dot dot dot* or code of absences as presence. The representation of taboo in tattoo is a fierce example of the display of the body as other, a ritual hieroglyphics of pleasure and pain, an invitation to read the body of the Other as a book. What is absent is the Nazi who will burn this book.

If Joyce in *Ulysses* writes ancient and modern patriarchy, mythologizes woman and Others the mother, Djuna Barnes in *Nightwood* laughs at Leviticus, brings all the wandering Jews, blacks, lesbians, outsiders, and transvestites together in a narrative which mothers the Other. While Joyce privileges the fertility of the modern mother goddess and her private parts, Barnes privileges the penis. It is the nonphallic penis that she celebrates, the limp member of the transvestite Dr. O'Connor—who masturbates in church like the Jongleur of Notre Dame doing tricks for the Virgin Mary—and the black man's impotent genitals that bear the white man's sexual burden.

The symbolic phallus as law is absent from *Nightwood*, replaced by the wayward penis of outlaw and transvestite. But its presence is brilliantly conveyed in the person of a woman, Hedvig Volkbein, Felix's mother, who dies in childbirth, not quite convinced by Guido, an Italian Jew masquerading as a German aristocrat, that his blood is untainted. Hedvig is German militarism. With her "massive chic," her goose-step, her "hand, patterned on seizure," she dances in "a tactical manoeuvre" with shoulders conscious of braid and a turn of head which holds "the cold vigilance of a sentry." Like Lina Wertmüller's daring representation of a Nazi concentration camp commandant as a woman in her powerful film *Seven Beauties,* Barnes breaks taboo by representing absent Aryan patriarchal power in the person of a woman. In the film, Italy is to Germany as woman is to man, the Other. So the Italian male is Other to the German woman, feminized by fascism.

Kenneth Burke says *Nightwood* is not political, that it has nothing to do with the Nazis.[13] Burke's discomfort with the seeming anti-Semitism of *Nightwood* is understandable. The scholar working on the text is confronted with T. S. Eliot's editorial cuts of passages that seem overtly homosexual or questionably anti-Semitic. But Djuna Barnes here identifies with all outsiders. She was originally named Djalma, after Eugène Sue's *Wandering Jew.* Sue's Djalma is tattooed by a "thug" in Java during his sleep. His killing of the panther on stage in chapter 14 is surely a source for Robin's scene with the lion in *Nightwood.*[14] But I would argue that the "political unconscious" of *Nightwood* is located in its supposedly irrelevant first chapter, meant to disguise its existence as a lesbian novel.

As *Nightwood* is not only a lesbian novel, its antifascism is apparent only when it triumphs over its own anti-Semitism, when we realize that its characters—Jews, homosexuals, lesbians, transvestites, gypsies, blacks, and circus performers—were all to perish in the Holocaust. Felix Volkbein is named for his role as wandering Jew (and the Yiddish Theatre in New York?), his middle European sadness contradicting the happiness of the Italian "Felix." As "Volkbein" he is the foot soldier of history, the portable slave, the legman of disaster, the unofficial "advance man" of the Paris circus, as Nora Flood is in reality the leg-woman of the Denckman Circus. Like the Roman fragment of a runner's leg in his parents' plush Vienna flat, Felix is "disassociated" from his past. As his ancestor's black and yellow handkerchief reminds him of the medieval Roman circus, where Jews were forced to run around the arena with ropes around their necks, his restless search for "pure" racial nobility to which to "bow down" signifies his internalization of racial difference while underscoring the reality of a Europe in which racial purity has been obscured by mixed marriages and false credentials. The dismemberment and fragmentation of the Roman statues, the runner's leg, the "chilly half-turned head of matron stricken at the bosom" recall early Roman circuses that sacrificed outcast Christians to the lions, medieval circuses where outcast Jews were terrorized, and prophesy with chilling accuracy the Nazi destruction of millions of Jews and other outcasts, devoured by their modern technological lions, the gas chambers and ovens of the concentration camps.

The blond Aryan beast slouching toward Buchenwald is only present in this novel in Hedvig's resemblance to him in 1880, but Felix's uneasiness, his attraction to the Catholic church, his scholarly labors and devotion to the past, to his sick child, and to the topsy-turvy world of the circus are reminders of what was destroyed by fascism's ugly fist. Felix is literally the foot of the folk, the embodiment of Bakhtin's carnivalesque, the preserver of circus culture and history.

Joyce's Night Town with cross-dressed Bella-Bello played against Bloom in a corset, like Tiresias in Eliot's *Waste Land,* suggests emasculation, not the ancient powerful life-force of mythical transvestite figures. Barnes's doctor-transvestite is only posing as a gynecologist, and he identifies with the maternal principle. He lampoons all of the male sex doctors whose own sexual identity was so troubled, from the mad Otto Weininger to Havelock Ellis (who was only aroused by women urinating) to the Freud of the Fleiss letters. Unlike Joyce's Night Town, Barnes's *Nightwood* privileges the female world of night, magic, and ritual in the last scene in the chapel in the forest (Dante's darkwood), suggesting that "culture," in the primitive figure of Robin as racial memory, survives in America as Europe is destroyed by fascism.

The exiled Felix with his monocle reminds one of Djuna Barnes's sketch of Joyce, as *Nightwood* in its static structure reflects Stephen Dedalus's aesthetic of stasis and proves it wrong, for fiction can be just as "impure" while standing still as it can be while wandering. Joyce is recalled in O'Connor's chamber pot, in the naming of Nora, in her flat in the rue de Cherche-Midi, the home of the eye clinic where Barnes visited Joyce after his many operations. Did he give the manuscript of *Ulysses* to the author of *Nightwood* in tribute to a writer of one of the few modernist texts to rival his phallogocentricism? Or, by giving the logos to a woman-identified man, does Barnes rob it of patriarchal privilege? Since O'Connor, "the Old Woman who lives in the closet," defines the female as only the maternal and womb-centered, his is a matriarchal phallogocentrism, a gynologos, not a cliterologos. Molly's "yes" is answered by Robin Vote's "no" to marriage, "no" to motherhood, "no" to monogamous lesbianism. Robin's "no" is a preverbal, prepatriarchal primitive bark, as the novel ends in America and she ritually acts the bear before her Madonna-Artemis, goddess of autonomous sexuality, owner of her body and her self. As Europe bows down to fascism, O'Connor asks, "Why doesn't anyone know when everything is over, except me? . . . I've not only lived my life for nothing, but I've told it for nothing—abominable among the filthy people" (p. 165).

Despite Burke's denial of its political awareness I believe *Nightwood* is the representative modernist text, a prose poem of abjection, tracing the political unconscious of the rise of fascism, as lesbians, blacks, circus people, Jews, and transvestites—outsiders all—*bow down,* as the text repeats, before the truly perverted Levitical prescriptions for racial purity of Hitler.

We might also see the political unconscious at work in the other meanings of tattoo.[15] After the doctor finishes telling the story of Nikka, Felix asks him about Vienna's "military superiority." For a tattoo is

also a military drum signal or call to alarm, as well as a symbolic drama
or masque performed by soldiers by torchlight before a battle, to act out
the victory of valor over the forces of the night. The rosy-faced German
boys the doctor recalls will soon be at the gates of the night world of
Paris. The drumbeats of racial "purity" will sound against Nikka,
O'Connor, and Volkbein. The evening of the living statues and outcasts
at the count's is a museum of soon-to-be-exterminated human types, like
Hitler's Jewish Museum at Prague, meant to be all that was left of Jewish culture after the Holocaust. As Hugo's *Notre Dame de Paris* is an
"antihistorical" novel prefiguring the Revolution, *Nightwood* is an "ahistorical" novel anticipating the Holocaust.

When the living statues are expelled from the party, the scene anticipates uncannily all the Expulsions from the Party of modern European
history. Their refuge is a café in Unter den Linden, the traditional meeting place of homosexuals and political aliens. O'Connor explains the
count's action as fear of impotence: he "suspected that he had come
upon his last erection" (p. 25). The count's erection is a signifier of
order and uprightness. And the remark is uncanny in the light of subsequent political events, as is Frau Mann's lament, "I've an album of my
own ... and everyone in it looks like a soldier—even though they are
dead" (p. 27). The narrator may say with Doctor O'Connor: "Oh, *pa-
palero*, have I not summed up my time! I shall rest myself someday by
the brim of Saxon-les-Bains and drink it dry, or go to pieces in Hamburg at the gambling table, or end up like Madame de Staël—with an
affinity for Germany" (p. 126).

Ritual as Instruction: Barnes Critiques Freud

My voice cracked on the word "difference"; soaring up divinely ...
                                                        —*Nightwood*

Nightwood is problematic for the woman reader and unusual for modernism because it is such tightly closed text and the narration is so distant and detached. Its heteroglossia resides in the doctor's multivoiced
stories of abjection; its carnivalesque is not open to the audience but
stylized and ritualized in the performative mode. The intimacy of a Colette or Woolf novel, in which narration is shared with the reader so that
she feels co-creative in the making of the text, is avoided. The narrative
voice seems to have no gender except in the vitriolic description of
Jenny, which privileges Nora's pain. Jenny Petherbridge, as the most abject character (because her author hates her), might be Barnes's portrait

of the voyeuristic reader or literary critic, collecting other women's clothes and cast-off loves. Strictly cast in this role of "audience" the reader is forced to "bow down" to the text, to replicate the anxiety of abjection. The reader reads at the site of what Naomi Schor calls the "bisextuality" of female fetishism. As a lesbian novel *Nightwood* dramatizes illicit love in patriarchy, and some readers may find Nora's possessive infantilization of Robin as patriarchal as Hedvig's militarism or Felix's fixation on Germany. Despite the fact that its plot is a lesbian love story, *Nightwood* does not write the lesbian body as *Ladies' Almanack* does, nor does it dramatize female desire, except in so far as it voices victimization, sets the alienated subjectivity of all outsiders, and flaunts bourgeois concepts of normality by privileging the private pain of a panoply of "monsters."

The indeterminate desire of transvestite, Jew, lesbian, and black makes the forbidden erotic into a political cry for freedom. Mlle. Basquette, raped on her wheeled board, is the archetypal sexual victim as "basket case," humiliated and used by male sadism as Nikka is abused by male masochism. Racism, sexism, anti-Semitism, and homophobia are challenged by this text. The desire of the disabled like Mlle. Basquette, "a girl without legs, built like a medieval abuse" (p. 26), to enjoy love and freedom *as they are,* rather than to be made "normal," cannot be made into a universal principle of natural law. As Hans Mayer writes in *Outsiders,* "The light of the categorical imperative does not shine for them."[16] As O'Connor says, "even the greatest generality has a little particular" (p. 89). Mlle. Basquette looks like the figurehead of a ship and is raped by a sailor. She is the disabled woman, hostage to men, of Hans Christian Andersen's "The Little Mermaid," as brilliantly analyzed by Nina Auerbach in *Women and the Demon.* There is always another Other.

Such a spectacle of human bondage as *Nightwood* provides, by centering the marginal, articulates the angst of the abject so well that the absent upright, the pillars of society, are experienced unconsciously by the reader as the enemies of the human spirit. Figuring plot as plight in the tradition of the great nineteenth-century French realist fictions of Victor Hugo and Eugène Sue, Barnes modernizes the story of the oppressed hunchback or Jew to include sexual outcasts. As a melodrama of beset perverts, *Nightwood* transcends its models by its refusal to play on the reader's pity. The human dignity of the aberrant is maintained by the narrator's objectivity, the irrepressible comic carnivalesque tone, and the exuberant vitality of obscene language.

The linguistic richness of *Nightwood,* its choked abundance of puns and plays on words, its fierce allusiveness to medieval and Jacobean high and low art, the extraordinary range of its learned reach across the history of Western culture, marks it as the logos-loving match of *Ulysses*. We are not accustomed to thinking of Djuna Barnes as a learned woman, a scholar as well as a writer. Nor does *Nightwood* arrange itself neatly next to other modernist experimental women's writing in an anti-logocentric act. Gertrude Stein robs words of meaning, objectifies them, empties them, and fills them again out of her own ego. Woolf and Colette experiment with an intimate and flexible female sentence. The narratives of Jean Rhys, H. D., or Elizabeth Bowen are inescapably women's novels. If we place *Nightwood* among female antifascist fiction of the thirties—Christina Stead's *The House of All Nations*, Virginia Woolf's *The Years*, and Marguerite Yourçenar's *Coup de Grâce*, it fits thematically. Woolf's novel traces the rise of fascism from the 1880s to the 1930s by concentrating on the origin of fascism in the patriarchal family. Stead condemns capitalism for its collaboration with fascism. Yourçenar brilliantly exposes German militarism and its patriarchal code of honor by privileging the ruthless and ethically bankrupt officer-narrator, leaving the reader the work of judging his self-serving narrative. In light of these antifascist texts, *Nightwood*'s project is to expose Freudian psychoanalysis's collaboration with fascism in its desire to civilize and make "normal" the sexually aberrant misfit. *Nightwood* asserts that the outcast *is* normal, and truly human. Freud and fascism, by labeling deviance, politically and medically, expose the inhumanity of the madness for order in every denial of difference from Leviticus to the sex doctors—Krafft-Ebbing, Havelock Ellis, and Otto Weininger—to Freud himself. Barnes makes us all misfits, claiming that in human misery we can find the animal and the divine in ourselves.

In this reading Nora is the archetypal Dora or female hysteric and Dr. Freud is brilliantly parodied in the figure of Dr. Matthew-Mighty-grain-of-salt-Dante-O'Connor. The lesbian patient chooses as doctor a transvestite whose most passionate desire is to be a woman, whose womb-envy is so strong that it parodies Freudian penis-envy mercilessly. The psychoanalyst's office is a filthy bedroom with a reeking chamber pot. Freud's famous totems, the sacred objects from ancient cultures which people his shelves and tables in H. D.'s famous tribute, are mocked by O'Connor's rusty forceps, broken scalpel, perfume bottles, ladies' underclothing, and abdominal brace. The psychoanalytic structure is ruptured as the patient asks the question and the doctor answers. The doctor is in bed in a granny nightgown and wig, powdered and rouged, and the patient stands by his bed; it is three in the morning, not three in the afternoon. The patient is rational, puritanical, and analytical; the doctor is mad. When Nora complains of heartbreak at the loss of Robin,

Matthew mocks her: "A broken heart have you! I have falling arches, flying dandruff, a floating kidney, shattered nerves *and* a broken heart! But do I scream that an eagle has me by the balls or has dropped his oyster on my heart?" (p. 154).

But he proves to be a brilliant feminist psychoanalyst as he devastatingly deconstructs Nora's dream. Floating in a Chagall-like dreamscape, her grandmother, "whom I loved more than anyone," is in a glass coffin; her father circles the grave, struggling with her death. In the dream she watches, unable to do anything; then her father's body stops circling and drifts immobile beside the grandmother's body. O'Connor detects the absence of the mother in her dream. "'It's my mother without argument I want!' And then in his loudest voice he roared: 'Mother of God! I wanted to be your son—the unknown beloved second would have done!'" (pp. 149–50). The two grandmother incest dreams constitute a revisionary psychological constitution of the female self, which we may call a *nonology*. The *nona*, or grandmother, may well become a young woman's role model and beloved in cases of real or imagined incest, when the mother has not protected the daughter from the father's assaults.

Nora refuses to deal with the relationship between her love for Robin and her own role as daughter in the family. She begs the doctor to tell Robin never to forget her. O'Connor's psychological advice to the upright Nora is that she must bend, bow down, experience the body, and get out of herself in ritual or carnival, let herself go, deal with the animal in herself:

> "Tell her yourself," said the doctor, "or sit in your own trouble silently if you like; it's the same with ermines—those fine yellow ermines that women pay such a great price for—how did they get that valuable colour? By sitting in bed and pissing the sheets, or weeping in their own way. It's the same with persons; they are only of value when they have laid themselves open to 'nuisance'—their own and the world's. *Ritual itself constitutes an instruction* [emphasis added]. So we come back to the place from which I set out; pray to the good God; she will keep you. Personally, I call her 'she' because of the way she made me; it somehow balances the mistake. . . . That priceless galaxy of misinformation called the mind, harnessed to that stupendous and threadbare glomerate compulsion called the soul, ambling down the almost obliterated bridle path of Well and Ill, fortuitously planned—is the holy Habeas Corpus, the manner in which the body is brought before the judge. . . . " (P. 150)

The doctor continually points out to Nora that the rigidity of her American Protestant consciousness, her fear of the body, of drink, promiscuity, and dirt, make her love for Robin destructive, possessive, patriarchal in its insistence on monogamy and control of the beloved. He mocks her romantic possessiveness: "there you were sitting up high and fine, with a rose-bush up your arse" (p. 151).

Like Freud, O'Connor has an inexhaustible fund of case histories of aberrant behavior, and he has a great deal to say about the art of writing. "I have a narrative, but you will be put to it to find it" (p. 97), he tells his "patient." He begs Nora to stop writing letters tormenting Robin: "Can't you rest now, lay down the pen?" Since he has no one to write to, he takes in "a little light laundry known as the Wash of the World" (p. 126), the psychoanalyst as Irish washerwoman, the writer as producer of dirty linen. "Haven't I eaten a book too? Like the angels and prophets? And wasn't it a bitter book to eat? . . . And didn't I eat a page and tear a page and stamp on others and flay some and toss some into the toilet for relief's sake—then think of Jenny without a comma to eat, and Robin with nothing but a pet name—your pet name—to sustain her . . . " (p. 127). Telling one of his homosexual stories in which he claims that like a gourmet he can tell the district and nationality of every penis he encounters, he says, "must I, perchance, like careful writers, guard myself against the conclusions of my readers?" (p. 94).

He rails against American cleanliness, praising "the good dirt"; because a European bathes in "true dust," he can trace the history of his actions. His body is his page. "*L'Echo de Paris* and his bed sheets were run off the same press. One may read in both the travail life has had with him—he reeks with the essential wit necessary to the 'sale' of both editions, night edition and day" (p. 89). Nora's problem is the body/mind split. "The Anglo-Saxon has made the literal error; using water, he has washed away his page" (p. 90). The doctor wants Nora to recognize her animality, to face her desire for Robin as physical, and to stop seeing herself as "saving" a lost soul.

The great writer writes from the body. The dirty bed sheet is the writer's page. Patriarchal culture has traditionally seen woman as a blank page on which to write. So Nora sees Robin and projects herself onto that page. Djuna Barnes's genius lies in her ability to overcome Nora's anxieties, and she is one of the few women writers whose novel was run off the same press as her bed sheets. Contemporary novels, like Gabriel Garcia Marquez's *A Hundred Years of Solitude* or Günter Grass's *The Flounder,* owe a great deal to the fantastic realism of *Nightwood*. Feminist fantastic realism has its own as yet critically uncharted history, but certainly *Nightwood* may be read in the context of Sylvia Townsend Warner's *Lolly Willowes,* Rebecca West's *Harriet Hume,* Joanna Russ's *The Female Man,* and their brilliant successor, Angela Carter's *Night at the Circus* (1985). I have argued in "A Wilderness of One's Own" that these novels often appear after a period of realism in fiction reflecting political activism on the part of women, like Woolf's *Orlando* and *Flush,* where the writer is frustrated at the failure of struggle to change the power structure.[17]

Nightwood differs from its sister texts in its anticipation of historical horror, its proleptic impulse. Women writers have traditionally been forced to wash away from their page any mention of desire. It is as if Djuna Barnes had decided to include in *Nightwood* every word, image, and story women have never been able to tell, to flaunt every possible taboo from the excretory to the sexual, and to invent, in Nora's grandmother incest dreams, her *nonology*—taboos uncataloged even by Freud. Her boldness is remarkable. Even H. D. in her *Tribute to Freud* was sly and subtle in her critique of "the master." She undermines his authority by greeting his dog first, by getting him to complain that she won't love him, by pretending that he treats her as an equal, by claiming that he approves of her relationship with Bryher, by describing him as a fellow student of myth and the collective unconscious. In short, H. D. fictionalizes Freud as Jung. Her tribute is really to woman's power to make the analyst collaborate with her, to save her "abnormality" for her art.

Djuna Barnes's critique of Freud is less directly personal than H. D.'s, but both are part of a modernist feminist insistence on woman-centeredness and partnership between doctor and patient. *Nightwood* challenges not only Freud but the whole history of the treatment of female hysteria. Dr. O'Connor's lies seem to Felix "to be the framework of a forgotten but imposing plan" (p. 30); "the great doctor, he's a divine idiot and a wise man" (p. 31). Matthew says "the only people who really *know* anything about medical science are the nurses, and they never tell; they'd get slapped if they did" (p. 31). (The nurse is a major icon of European modernism. See Barnes's friend Antonia White's brilliant story, "The House of Clouds," and one of many novels about nursing in World War I, Irene Rathbone's *We That Were Young,* rpt. 1989, The Feminist Press.)

O'Connor claims that he is not neurasthenic and pronounces "No man needs curing of his individual sickness; his universal malady is what he should look to" (p. 32). These remarks are part of the slapstick dialogue, with Felix as straight man, which introduces "La Somnambule." Stage Irishman and stage Jew mock each other's racial traits as liars and meddlers, and make fun of doctors. The comic pair then wake Sleeping Beauty, in the person of Robin Vote, "meet of child and desperado" (p. 35). In keeping with the carnival spirit of their "act," O'Connor plays magician, or "dumbfounder," at a street fair and turns his back on the patient to make up his hairy face with her powder and rouge and to steal a hundred-franc note. The reader "watches" this scene as a cabaret act and "reads" it as a pantomime of Sleeping Beauty woken by the wrong prince as well as a classic crooked-apothecary or quack-doctor joke.

The narrator tells us "the woman who presents herself to the spectator as a 'picture' forever arranged is, for the contemplative mind, the chiefest danger" (p. 37). The "picture" of the disheveled Robin flung like a dancer on the bed in a scene like Rousseau's "jungle trapped in a drawing room" emphasizes her legs and feet in men's white flannel trousers and dancing pumps. Extraordinarily cinematic, the scene reverses the reader's picture of Marlene Dietrich in thirties vamp films like *The Blue Angel* or *Blonde Venus* (which even has a gorilla, a "beast turning human"). We remember Dietrich "transvested" from the waist up in male top hat and tails, pointing the contrast to very feminine legs. In a famous essay Kenneth Tynan wrote of Dietrich what might be said of Robin Vote: "She has sex but no particular gender. They say . . . that she was the only woman allowed to attend the annual ball for male transvestites in pre-Hitler Berlin . . . this Marlene lives in a sexual no man's land—and no woman's either . . .she is every man's mistress and mother, every woman's lover and aunt. . . . "[18] In the context of *Nightwood,* one would say every woman's lover and grandmother.

Lesbian subculture in Paris in the twenties and thirties affords many examples of the woman in a tuxedo. (Rebecca West once described Radclyffe Hall and Una Troubridge as looking, in their male attire and cropped hair, like "a distant prospect of Eton College."[19]) As tattoo is a form of the general Levitical taboo against transvestism, Robin's appearance in men's trousers is another version of writing on the body, or rewriting the body. The carnival of cross-dressing destabilizes identity, keeping bisexuality from being anchored to one pole and acting out a "female fetishism," denying Freud's assumption that fetishism is exclusively male. Naomi Schor's argument "that ultimately *female travesty,* in the sense of women dressing up as or impersonating other women, constitutes by far the most disruptive form of *bisextuality,*" applies more fully to *Nightwood* than to any other novel I can think of, though it is characteristic of the lives and work of the whole movement of Sapphic modernism. If "female fetishism is an oxymoron," then one may argue that Djuna Barnes's style itself is a form of fetishism that allows the reader free play in the riddle of sexuality.

Even Robin's skin participates in tattoo and links her to Nikka and to Nora's obsession with her as "purity's black backside." Consoling Felix for the loss of Robin, O'Connor later compares her to a horse whose "hide was a river of sorrow. . . . Her eyelashes were gray-black, like the eyelashes of a nigger, and at her buttocks' soft centre a pulse throbbed like a fiddle. . . . Yes, oh God, Robin was beautiful. . . . Sort of fluid blue under her skin, as if the hide of time had been stripped from her." Robin's "hide," her "flayed body" is "the infected carrier of the past"; she is "eaten death returning" (p. 37), exactly Bakhtin's construction of the material body as the memory of culture. The "fluid blue" under Robin's skin is like Nikka's tattoo. The scene at the circus when Robin is lionized by the lion's eyes reminds us of Mae West's brilliant articulation of female animal desire in the classic thirties film *I'm No Angel*. As a heroine, Robin rescues libido from the exclusive possession of men. The agency of her desire and its refusal to be fixed as the desired object of lesbian lover or husband; contained in motherhood; or controlled by T. S. Eliot's or other critics' reading of her as doomed, damned, or pathologically placed as a medical case study is a textual triumph.

Even Robin's voice (reported, for she only speaks twice) resembles Marlene Dietrich's: "In the tones of this girl's voice was the pitch of one enchanted with the gift of postponed abandon: the low drawling 'aside' voice of the actor who, in the soft usury of his speech, withholds a vocabulary until the profitable moment when he shall be facing his audience" (p. 38). It is precisely that pitch of postponed abandon that characterizes the art of Dietrich. The "low drawl," the slight catch in the phrasing, the way she sang the sensual as if it were a lullaby, and, above all, the sense that every song was sung as if she were remembering it from a long time ago—these are the things that constitute her appeal. So Robin's "soft usury" of speech is related to her archetypal resemblance to the ancient past. There is a nonthreatening animal growl to this voice; O'Connor would call it the voice of the dream prince, the "uninhabited angel," the genderless or empty sign of her body in which child and desperado meet. Robin is a speechless picture for much of the novel, but her outburst at Nora (the fetish talks back?) when she is drunk in the street is telling: "You are a devil! You make everything dirty! . . . You make me feel dirty and tired and old!" (p. 143). She makes Nora give money to an old prostitute: "'These women—they are all like her,' she said with fury. 'They are all good—they want to save us!'" (p. 144). Robin's sisterhood with the downtrodden, crawling in the gutter with outcasts, is the way in which "ritual constitutes an instruction" for her. Her abjection is the reverse of Nora's uprightness, and it is privileged in the novel as the more humane condition. She doesn't want to be saved; she wants to be free.

There is an ironic message for Nora in Matthew's tale of the London "Tupenny Upright": "ladies of the *haute* sewer . . . holding up their badgered flounces, or standing still, letting you do it, silent and indifferent as the dead ... their poor damned dresses hiked up and falling away over the rump, all gathers and braid, like a Crusader's mount, with all the trappings gone sideways with misery" (pp. 130–31).

At the very heart of the novel the twin *pissoir* passages condemn the upright. A woman curses her lover in the toilet: "May you die standing upright! May you be damned upward!" She curses her lover's genitals: "May this be damned, terrible and damned spot! May it wither into the grin of the dead, may this draw back, low riding mouth in an empty snarl of the groin" (p. 95). The rest of this passage anticipates Robin on all fours at the end of the novel: "For what do you know of me, man's meat? I'm an angel on all fours, with a child's feet behind me, *seeking my people that have never been made* [emphasis added], going down face foremost, drinking the waters of night at the water hole of the damned ..." (p. 95). The lesbian curse on the clitoris in the *pissoir* is terrifying. Why does Barnes set it next to the rollicking tales of happy homosexual cruising ("cottaging") and O'Connor's domestication of the Parisian *pissoir* as his cottage ("my only fireside is the outhouse" [p. 91])? What is missing from the casual sex of the men is the possessiveness of "love." (These passages couldn't be written after AIDS.) Yet when Nora seeks solace in the arms of other women, she misses Robin even more. Barnes seems to suggest that the dynamics of lesbian sexuality are different from homosexuality. Matthew longs to be someone's wife while Robin rejects Nora's wifely domestic ways and Nora's infantilization of her. In Latin *infans* means speechless and *Nightwood* creates the sex object as the silent subject.

Between them, O'Connor and Nora try to analyze lesbianism, though she cannot give up her posture, derived from patriarchal conceptions of love, of the abandoned wife. The discussion centers on the figure of the doll as the lesbian's child, Robin's smashing the doll, Jenny Petherbridge's gift of another doll to Robin, and the figure of the prince. Robin says she chose a girl who resembles a boy as a lover from the figures of the prince and princess in romances. "We were impaled in our childhood upon them as they rode through our primers, the sweetest lie of all ... " (p. 137). When the love one has been told to expect never arrives, one chooses the androgynous figure of the prince.

Nora tells the doctor that the doll she shared with Robin was "their child," but she also says, "We give death to a child when we give it a doll—it's the effigy and the shroud" (p. 142). O'Connor tells Nora that she really wanted Robin to *be* a doll, an "uninhabited angel," an object onto which she could project "sexless misgiving." But she does not really listen to him or respond to his analysis. "Do you think that Robin had no right to fight you with her only weapon? She saw in you the fearful eye that would make her a target forever. Have not girls done as much for the doll?" (p. 148). That female "fearful eye" is not the phallic gaze that casts woman as object, but a gendered same-sex form of objectification that is just as abusive. He continues: "The last doll, given to age, is the girl who should have been a boy, and the boy who should have been a girl! The love of that last doll was foreshadowed in the love of the first. The doll and the immature have something right about them, the doll because it resembles but does not contain life, and the third sex because it contains life but resembles the doll" (p. 148). So sleeping Robin is not really the princess but the prince.[20]

The moment when Robin raises her child over her head as if to smash it, but doesn't, and the repeated moment when she smashes and kicks the doll—her "child" with Nora—have an element of the uncanny in them. We may compare the treatment of the doll figure in *Nightwood* to Freud's essay on "The Uncanny." When O'Connor tells Nora that she has "dressed the unknowable in the garments of the known" (p. 136), he is giving a definition of the uncanny much like Freud's definition of a species of the horrifying that is also very familiar. Freud's essay is a peculiar example of the analyst as literary critic, or rather, father of patriarchal aesthetic theory. Like some contemporary theorists, he begins, "I have not made a very thorough examination of the bibliography."[21] He then claims that he himself is not susceptible to the uncanny, but he will nevertheless write the essay since most aesthetic theory deals only with "the sublime." Freud fills the gap with several pages from dictionaries in various languages defining *unheimlich*. *Heimlich* comes to mean not only "homely" in some cases, but its opposite, and magic is associated with it as well as the secret parts of the body. It never occurs to Freud that *heimlich* refers to the female world of the home with safety and comfort provided by woman. The transition of the word's meaning from holy to unholy, from the domestic to the horrific, clearly marks the historical change from male pleasure in the female to his fear of woman, her body and her space. Freud, albeit unwittingly, is one of the best examples of this ideological reversal. While Freud's definition is a workable one, there is a great discrepancy between his definition and his examples, most of which come from E. T. A. Hoffmann's *Tales*.

I maintain that Freud's notion of the uncanny (in examples) is gender biased, that only certain men would experience the uncanny in the cases he cites, and that women do not find these situations uncanny; therefore they are not universal. It seems perfectly reasonable to suppose that male and female versions of the uncanny should be different from each other, and to examine the female versions of the uncanny offered by *Nightwood* in contrast to Freud's analysis. Since women have been the providers of *heimlichkeit*, or domestic bliss, it is obvious that their experiences of the uncanny will be different. Freud, quoting Jentsch, starts his inquiry by finding the uncanny in our doubt as to whether something that appears animate is really alive or whether a lifeless object might really be alive (p. 132) as in waxwork figures or dolls.[22] Freud is at some pains to deny the importance of the figure of the doll, Olympia, in the uncanny effect of Hoffmann's "The Sandman," the first act of Offenbach's opera, *Tales of Hoffmann*. (I wonder if one could read Manet's famous painting, *Olympia*, as another participant in the Freud-Hoffmann doll-making paradigm, the reduction of woman to the passive object of the male gaze. The painting seems to invoke an order of objecthood: white woman/doll, black woman, cat.[23])

Hoffmann's fantastic realism and grotesquerie were a direct influence on Djuna Barnes. While Bakhtin regards Hoffmann as too alienated and morbid to participate in the Rabelaisian folk tradition of grotesque, Djuna Barnes was influenced by, and participates in, both traditions. The romantic concern with the sick self, the move of fairy-tale fantasy from pastoral forest to metropolitan café, the concern with night and dream and Mesmer's experiments with hypnotism, "the science of the soul" as proof of the existence of the supernatural—these concerns come from Hoffmann to Barnes and are part of the intellectual origins of *Nightwood*. "The Sandman" was originally published in *Night Pieces*, and Hoffmann shared Barnes's love of Callot, the seventeenth-century grotesque engraver of creatures part beast and part human. Like Barnes, Hoffmann had an amazon grandmother, and he enjoyed disfiguring the margins of her Bible with figures of satyrs and hell. His portrait of Olympia seems to have come from his mother, described as rigid, cold, hysterical, and given to staring vacantly into space (*Tales*, pp. 18, 19). Nathaniel's obsession with Olympia, the automaton, is based on her passivity: "Never before had he such a splendid listener. She neither embroidered nor knitted; she did not look out of the window nor feed a bird nor play with a lapdog or kitten ... she sat for hours on end without moving, staring directly into his eyes, and her gaze grew ever more ardent and animated" (*Tales*, p. 162). Through the spyglass he buys from Coppelius, Nathaniel sees his real lover, Clara, as a doll and tries to kill her. Eyes are the heart of the story, and Freud insists on reading through men's eyes a tale of fear of castration in the loss of eyes and the hero's relation with his father and Coppelius as a good father/bad father drama.

I suggest that Freud's analysis represses his own interest in the collaboration of Professor Spalanzini with the mysterious charlatan Dr. Coppelius/Coppola ("eye-socket" in Italian) in which he may have seen his own collaboration with the eventually discredited Fleiss, though the part of the body in question was the nose. The two doctors "create" a woman (the womb-envy of the Freud-Fleiss letters is obvious; Fleiss believed that men had cycles like women, and Freud appeared to accept this idea).[24] What is at issue in the story is the male doctors' creation and destruction of the woman patient. Hoffmann's Olympia is a mechanical "La Somnambule." The intellectual history of somnambulism, which meant hypnotism (not merely sleepwalking), is the direct forerunner of Freud's definition of the unconscious. In this history the line between science and charlatanism was very thin. For Fourier, Eugène Sue, Victor Hugo, Mesmer, and Hoffmann somnambulism proved the existence of the human spirit, the collective unconscious or God. This anti-Enlightenment, antimaterialist doctrine of "illuminism" was also the mother of modern socialism; metempsychosis (Joyce's "met him pike hoses") and animal magnetism were some of its tenets as well as an androgynous god, a sexed universe, and a division of the world into animal, human, and angel.[25] Since so many of these ideas animate the world of *Nightwood*, I suspect that Djuna Barnes's intellectual origins are to be found here.[26]

When she labels Robin Vote "La Somnambule," Djuna Barnes is aligning her not with Lady Macbeth but with the innocent heroine of Bellini's opera, *La Somnambula*, whose romantic story was written to prove the existence of the soul to atheists and rationalists. People are not simply living statues, material automatons, it was argued, but animated by spirit. The count in the opera was a "scientist" who proved to the unbelieving folk that the heroine's unconscious spirit caused her to walk in her sleep and that her rational self had no control over her actions. Unlike *Tales of Hoffmann*, *La Somnambula* no longer commands the immense popularity it had in the nineteenth century, largely because intellectual historians have not been willing to see the roots of modern thought, either socialism or psychoanalysis, in these romantic, irrational experiments. At a production of *La Somnambula* in Washington, D.C., in December 1984, the audience laughed through the scene in which the heroine sings of her love for her fiancé while sleepwalking to the count's bed. The unconscious power of her desire is the point of the opera, as it is the point of Robin's nightwalks into promiscuity in *Nightwood*—she retains her innocence, her association with the virgin Diana of Ephesus. This "virginity" of Robin's we interpret as control over her own sexuality. As a sleepwalker she is the collective unconscious of undifferentiated female desire. Felix says she has the "odour of memory"; her speech is "heavy and unclarified"; "there was in her every movement a slight drag, as if the past were a web about her" (pp. 118, 119).

Nightwood plays operatic allusions against circus allusions in a dialectic between folk and highbrow art on the subject of desire. O'Connor introduces Robin to Jenny Petherbridge at the opera, the powerful

Rigoletto, also based on a Victor Hugo plot, in which the father murders his daughter while trying to avenge her rape, refusing to accept the fact that she loves the count who raped her. O'Connor mocks the diva: "there's something wrong with any art that makes a woman all bust!" (p. 103).

Though Felix asks for Wagner's music to be played in cafés, O'Connor turns Wagner's heroic chaste male ideal of brotherhood as well as the medieval patriarchal theme of the quest (which were used to great effect by the Nazis) into a joke (as well as a feminist critique of Wagner): "one woman went down through the ages for sitting through *Parsifal* up to the point where the swan got his death, whereupon she screamed out, "'Godamercy, they have shot the Holy Grail!'" (p. 96). Barnes is taking potshots at the repressive ideal of celibacy for men, which displaces desire onto evil figures of seductive females and which Wagner articulates. The operatic *motives* are also "answered" in the dialogue of the novel with lines from music hall and popular songs. This pastiche of fragmented pieces from the past of Western culture that we now associate with the postmodern is also practiced by Barnes in her painting and drawing, *faux* woodcuts, parodies of the Beardsleyesque, copies of folk-art cartoons in which the faces are made into realistic portraits while the rest of the drawing is derivative, oil paintings on cardboard.

The doctor tells the story of Don Anticolo, the tenor from Beirut who, drinking with a dozen sailors, mourns his dead son, throwing up and down the box of his ashes "no bigger than a doll's crate," recalling Robin smashing the doll. The whole of the chapter called "The Squatter" mimics the opera as well as a *commedia del l'arte* Punch and Judy show. When Jenny dresses up in costume and takes Robin and her guests in old-fashioned carriages to the Bois, the grand masquerade scene is an abduction from the lesbian seraglio, the fighting and scratching of the lovers like a puppet show at a fair, where Punch and Judy are both women, and the child, Sylvia, who is caught in the quarrel, adds a melodramatic *frisson.* Djuna Barnes's father composed operas, including the comic and melodramatic "Allan Castle," whose heroine is stabbed as she poses inside a picture frame, anticipating the "framing" of Nora in *Nightwood,* in the window as she observes Robin with another woman and in the doorway of the chapel in the last scene.[27]

To return to Freud, Hoffmann, and the uncanny, one may say that the (woman) reader (though woman is not a universal category) does not experience a chill when the mechanical doll is smashed and the eyes roll on the floor, whereas some women do have such a response to Robin's smashing the doll in *Nightwood.* The (woman) reader of "The Sandman" knows that Nathaniel will reject Clara precisely because she is not a doll, because she has a mind and uses it to analyze his obsessions as well as to criticize the poem in which he predicts that he will kill her. Hoffmann pictures the patriarchy in the persons of the two doctors, constructing woman as a passive, mindless doll and passing on this "ideal" to a young man who accepts the image, sees through the patriarchy's lens, its dark glass, and cannot relate to a real woman. "The Sandman" is, in fact, about the construction of the male gaze and the Oedipal initiation of the son into the father's dominating I/Eye. Coppola's doll does not move the reader because she is so patently not of woman born, so clearly a creature of male science and male desire. When Robin smashes the doll, the horror is caused by the erasure of the difference between sign and signified. Western culture has socialized girls by giving them dolls to develop their maternal instincts. A doll *is* a baby, they are told. It is precious and must not be broken. The uncanny moment is caused by Robin killing her and Nora's baby, the symbol of their union. The doll signifies as well the unnatural and illegitimate in their relationship.

The smashing of the doll is a recurrent scene in women's writing. The mathematician Sophie Kovalevsky tells in *A Russian Childhood* of her pathological fear of dolls; Jean Rhys in *Smile Please* almost defines her writing self as the doll-breaker. Fear of objectification and abjection seems to be at work here, as well as fear of motherhood. The classic story is Maggie working out her anger deliberately on a doll in George Eliot's *The Mill on the Floss*. Eliot calls the doll "a fetish which she punished for all her misfortunes." She has banged three nails into the doll's head in her fury, and the trunk is "defaced by a long career of vicarious suffering." However, Maggie never really destroys the doll, for in order to go through her ritual of comforting it after she has beaten it, she has to leave it some semblance of resemblance to herself. The doll as a toy or "baby" is a relatively recent cultural phenomenon, but there is a long history of the doll as a magical ritual object. In the Russian version of Cinderella, it is the doll which brings Baba Yaga to save the heroine.

While Freud claims that the doll Olympia is "nothing else but a personification of Nathaniel's feminine attitude toward his father in infancy" and "a dissociated complex of Nathaniel's which confronts him as a person" (p. 139), I suggest that she is Freud's patient, the female hysteric, who is hypnotized and forced into "good" and wooden behavior and eventually destroyed by quarreling male "doctors." Freud claims that one of his patients believed that her dolls would come to life if she looked at them with enough concentration, but that "the idea of the living doll excites no fear at all" (p. 140).[28] For a woman who is socialized to be looked at, who even objectifies herself in the mirror, the uncanny is figured not in symbolic castration of the eyes, for she is the object being gazed at, but in the fear of becoming a living doll or statue, of becoming *only* an object. When Robin and Nora act as *kores (kore* means pupil of the eye in Greek), or living statues of the lesbian as eternal maiden, while they look at a representation of such abjection in the statue with the protruding blank eyes, as pupils (in the other meaning of the word) of the eye, they deconstruct the process of objectification/ abjection of woman. Felix, with his monocle and false portraits of ancestors as blank-eyed actors, returns the gaze of the Aryan at the Jew.

Djuna Barnes's articulation of the female uncanny and its relation to writing in a complex of signs around images of dolls and eyeless statues participates in female modernism's larger interrogation of gender and the writing self under the male gaze, which also includes the problem of the struggle between the needle and the pen. (In "Il vole," set to music by Poulenc in "Fiançailles pour rire," 1939, French poet Louise de Vilmorin writes, "I should like to sew but a magnet/Attracts all my needles.") Jean Rhys uncannily suggests in *Smile Please* the relation of the woman's eye to her "I." "Before I could read, almost a baby, I imagined that God, this strange thing or person I had heard about, was a book. Sometimes it was a large book standing upright and half open and I could see the print inside but it made no sense to me. Other times the book was smaller and inside were sharp flashing things. The smaller book was, I am sure now, my mother's needle book, and the sharp flashing things were her needles with the sun on them." Her nurse forbade her to read and told her a version of the Sandman story:

> "If all you read so much, you know what will happen to you? Your eyes will drop out and they will look at you from the page."
> "If my eyes dropped out I wouldn't see," I argued.
> She said, "They drop out except the little black points you see with."
> I half believed her and imagined my pupils like heads of black pins and all the rest gone. But I went on reading.[29]

The relationship between the woman reader and the woman writer often reproduces the uncanny feeling of your own eyes looking up at you from the page. God/father/book is indecipherable, but in reading a sympathetic writer and in writing for a sympathetic reader, the woman can look at herself and be looked at without fear. The eye of God is the big book, but in the little book the needles (pens) connect with the eyes of the mother as the daughter's mirror. When the book is the mother's eye, the daughter writing finds her "I."

Freud asks, "Who would be so bold as to call it an uncanny moment, for instance, when Snow White opens her eyes once more?" (p. 154). Many women would be so bold. Certainly we may read Nora's dream of her dead grandmother in a glass coffin as her wish to be the prince who wakes Sleeping Beauty or Snow White. Her anxiety is caused by her wish to kill her father, who is already playing that role and standing in her way in the dream. The dream, with its absent mother and hovering father, also enacts the struggle to maintain female connection within the patriarchy, the desire to remove the possessive father and incorporate the magic grandmother, to erase the boundaries imposed by patriarchal culture. Robin, lying prone on the bed, acting as a "picture" for others to look at in the "La Somnambule" chapter, is the proverbial woman patient. Barnes brilliantly parodies the famous scene in which Charcot and a group of upright doctors hypnotize the horizontal female hysteric, by exposing the erotics of the doctor-patient relationship, its voyeurism and quackery.

We see psychoanalysis as circus in Matthew "I am my own charlatan" O'Connor, whose womb-envy is openly expressed: "it was a high soprano I wanted and deep corn curls to my bum, with a womb as big as the king's kettle ... in my heart is the wish for children and knitting. God, I never asked better than to boil some good man's potatoes and toss up a child for him every nine months by the calendar" (p. 91). O'Connor as transvestite-shaman knows by vicarious experience what certain women want. His analysis of Nora and his advice, that "ritual constitutes an instruction," amounts to a feminist critique of patriarchal psychoanalysis: "And do you need a doctor to tell you that it is a bad strange hour for a woman? If all women could have it all at once, you could beat them in flocks like a school of scorpions; but they come eternally, one after the other ... " (p. 101). He recognizes female desire as different from men's and it is difference he urges on Nora. He claims to be "the last woman left in this world" (p. 100) though he is "the bearded lady."

O'Connor's transvestism is a positive force in *Nightwood*. The most powerful representation of the uncanny in the novel occurs when Nora sees him in bed in his flannel nightgown and curly wig and says, "God, children know something they can't tell; they like Red Riding Hood and the wolf in bed" (p. 79). In the typescript of the novel the following lines are crossed out: "with what cunning had his brain directed not only the womanly, but the incestuous garment? For a flannel night dress is our mother."[30] In fragments from the "Go Down, Matthew" chapter Barnes wrote: "What sense is there in saying the girl went wrong at twenty, that she wore a bowler hat by preference when but eight months old and showed a liking for kissing her grandmother's bottom left elbow; it's not that she did so that needs explanation, it's what it seemed like while she was about it."

Children liking Red Riding Hood and the wolf in bed is uncanny because O'Connor is acting the role of Nora's grandmother in the other dream, the version which is "well-dreamt" because Robin enters it "like a relative found in another generation." Nora is looking down into the house "as if from a scaffold" at her grandmother's high room "bereft as the nest of a bird which will not return" (Nora is mocked by O'Connor as "Turdus musicus" or European singing thrush), and Robin is lying below in fear with a disc of light (obviously a spotlight) on her. Nora keeps calling her to come into the "taboo" room but "the louder she cried out the farther away went the floor below, as if Robin and she, in their extremity, were a pair of opera glasses turned to the wrong end, diminishing in their painful love" (p. 62).

The house is *unheimlich* because, though it has all her grandmother's things, it is the opposite of her real room and "is saturated with the lost presence of her grandmother, who seemed in the continual process of leaving it." It is a house of incest, and if Robin enters it she joins the incestuous family. There are two grandmothers, a beautiful feminine one and one "dressed as a man, wearing a billy cock and a corked moustache, ridiculous and plump in tight trousers and a red waistcoat, her arms spread saying with a leer of love 'My little sweetheart.'" Nora had wanted to put her hands on something in this room but in the past "the dream had never permitted her to do so." I suggested that what she puts her hands on is "the plume and the inkwell" and the pictures of her ancestors mentioned in the beginning of the dream, to take up her grandmother's profession of writing.

The costume her grandmother wears is that of the master of ceremonies at the circus, precisely the role of the narrator of *Nightwood.* Robin is in fear because she is being written about. Nora experiences the dream as "something being done to Robin, Robin disfigured and eternalized by the hieroglyphics of sleep and pain" (p. 63), that is, being made into La Somnambule. Nora, as publicist for the circus, is dreaming herself into the male role of master of ceremonies, Djuna Barnes writing this novel as circus. Her grandmother is herself in drag. The grandmother is cross-dressed as herself, the writer. This role of narrator as master of ceremonies at the circus is spelled out in "La Somnambule" in the description of Robin's room as like a jungle trapped in a drawing room: "the set, the property of an unseen *dompteur,* half lord, half promoter, over which one expects to hear the strains of an orchestra of woodwinds render a serenade which will popularize the wilderness" (p. 35).

The performative structure of *Nightwood* is like an eight-ring circus, brilliantly controlled by the grandmother-narrator-*dompteur* as each "act" is performed and the living statues speak their lines. As Paul Bouissac argues in *Circus and Culture,* circus acts progress in a dialectic of control and disturbance, culminating in a triumphant assertion of the performer's mastery. The reader is never allowed to play any participatory role, but is eternally cast as "audience" at the circus or cabaret.[31]

In her dream Nora sees her grandmother as a "wolf" in both senses, and recognizes the ill-fitting male costume she must don as granddaughter-writer; when she constructs the doctor as her grandmother, a fine feminist transference for a workable psychoanalysis begins. Like Felix watching O'Connor's tricks at Robin's bedside, the reader experiences "a double confusion" as the narrator alternates between *dompteur* and "dumbfounder," providing a sideshow and "preparing the audience for a miracle" (p. 35). Barnes's rhetorical tricks are like the magician's feints with back and elbows, "honesties" to distract the audience from his hoax. Is *Nightwood* a hoax or a profoundly humanistic and political novel? When the woman acts the beast and the beast turns human in the last scene, do we laugh or weep?[32]

Bakhtin would argue that Barnes, like Rabelais, does not reverse the world for carnival as political therapy, or release, in the steam-engine model of social behavior; but that Barnes's characters represent the revolutionary potential in folk culture.[33] That is, *Nightwood* reveals that gays and outcasts *have* a culture—a linguistically and philosophically rich culture, encompassing high and low art, opera and circus, psychoanalysis and religion—and that this culture is a vital political force.

Inversion reveals the essence of the particular historical moment that we construct as the "rise of fascism" in the "upright," defining their differences from the abject by race, gender, or sexual practice. At this historical moment the outcasts constitute the essence of human culture. Fascism chooses to eliminate from civilization those very figures who are the symbolic forms of humanity in ancient traditions—circus folk, lesbians, homosexuals, transvestites, and the Jews, who are the recorders of history and culture.

The "splendid and reeking falsification" of the world of carnival and circus in *Nightwood*'s reversals is redemptive. As in Rabelais, the circus folk take royal titles: Princess Nadja, Baron von Tink, Principessa Stasera y Stasero, a King Buffo and a Duchess of Broadback. In carnival, enthronement of the fool implies dethronement of hierarchy. They are "gaudy, cheap cuts from the beast life" (p. 11) as the butcher is a stock figure in old European carnival. (O'Connor compares penises to mortadellas. Carnival parades often featured enormous phallic salamis.) Nadja's spine curves like a lion's and Frau Mann's costume is like Nikka's tattoo:

> She seemed to have a skin that was the pattern of her costume: a bodice of lozenges, red and yellow ... one felt they ran through her as the

design runs through hard holiday candies, and the bulge in the groin where she took the bar, one foot caught in the flex of the calf, was as solid, specialized and as polished as oak. The stuff of the tights was no longer a covering, it was herself; the span of the tightly-stitched crotch was so much her own flesh that she was as unsexed as a doll. The needle that had made one the property of the child made the other the property of no man. (P. 13)

Here the novel's themes converge: circus performer = doll = lesbian. In her 1935 *Fires* Marguerite Yourçenar creates Sappho as an aging lesbian trapeze artist, in a mode described by Susan Gubar as preserving "the utopian grandeur of the lesbian aesthetic project in the modernist period."[34] Memoirs of Paris in the twenties and thirties recall the circus, the elegant trapeze act of Barbette, the Texas Transvestite, the human gorilla.[35] In *Nightwood* the lovers meet at the circus and mix circus figurines with ecclesiastical hangings in their flat, continuing carnival's tradition of mixing the sacred and the profane. Robin laughs in church and goes home to read de Sade on the day she gives birth, and O'Connor masturbates in church as the Transvestite of Notre Dame in one of the novel's most hilarious scenes. Bouissac defines circus as a *language*, "a set of rules for cultural transformations, displayed in a ritualistic manner that tempers this transgressive aspect." It enacts freedom from culture and inverts the ordinary. He claims that "individuals who have not been fully integrated into a culture find it more acceptable to enjoy this type of performance, as do individuals with a marginal or unique status, such as poets and artists."[36] As Lévi-Strauss says, we see the circus as supernatural, a place where human beings can still communicate with animals and with our own "higher powers." One of *Nightwood*'s most fascinating aspects is that it has more animal characters than people, from lions to mouse-meat, cows, horses, fish, and an extraordinary number of birds, adding to its archetypal qualities.

Like the circus, *Nightwood* is polycentric; it makes the reader uneasy with time and history for political purposes. Robin Vote, Nora Flood, and O'Connor (whose names intersect in their *o*'s and *r*'s and *n*'s) are performers of archetypal roles. The hybrid form of the fiction reinforces the hybrid experience of the characters. O'Connor says, "take away a man's conformity and you take away his remedy," and tells of the paralyzed man in a velvet box at Coney Island: "suspended over him where he could never take his eyes off, a sky-blue mounted mirror, for he wanted to enjoy his own difference" (p. 146). Robin is the androgynous ideal, the archetype of the savage virgin Diana, a feminist version of the Noble Savage; *Nightwood* is her "sacred grove." The name "Vote" signifies the suffragettes, often martyrs and victims of police and government brutality. As a young reporter, Barnes investigated the violent forcible feeding of hunger-striking suffragettes by having herself forcibly fed and writing "If I, play-acting, felt my being burning with revolt at this brute usurpation of my own functions, how they who actually suffered the ordeal in its acutest horror must have flamed at the violation of the sanctuaries of their spirit?"[37] A photograph of Barnes, the prone victim, being violated by a group of doctors accompanies the article and echoes the picture of the hysterical woman being hypnotized by Charcot and the French doctors. The image conflates the subordination of the politically independent woman with that of the medical model of the aberrant woman. Barnes experienced forcible feeding as a kind of rape, as many of the brave movement women did. Christabel Pankhurst was figured as Joan of Arc on the front page of *The Suffragette*. Martyrdom, sainthood, the androgynous militant figure of the woman in men's clothes—all were part of the mythology of this feminist modernism, and Barnes draws on its culture for Robin.

But *Nightwood's* uniqueness lies in its language—its billingsgate and, to use a phrase Freud coined for the analysis of dreams in his letters to Fleiss, a nice combination of Yiddish and Greek, its "dreckology," the continual use of animal and human excremental imagery, from "whale shit" to "dinosaur droppings" to bird turds. Djuna Barnes is the female Rabelais. Only ribaldry is powerful enough to carry *Nightwood's* political vision. For she was writing, like Nora in the dream of her grandmother, at what Victor Hugo calls "noir ceur sublime de l'écritoire," the sublime blackness of the inkstand.[38] Despite fascism or political repression, folk art survives among the marginal and in the circus: "Clowns in red, white and yellow, with the traditional smears on their faces, were rolling over the sawdust as if they were in the belly of a great mother where there was yet room to play" (p. 54).

If I am right in reading *Nightwood* as a prophecy of the Holocaust, an attack on the doctors and politicians who defined deviance and set up a world view of us and them, the normal and abnormal, in political, racial, and sexual terms, a world which was divided into the upright and the downcast, the horror which in fact took place is still very difficult for us to contemplate. In Yvonne Mitchell's *Colette: A Taste for Life*, she describes Sarassani, the "great circus king" who invited the European press to performances in Berlin in the early thirties in order to get bookings in France for his troupe of five hundred animals. Djuna Barnes and Thelma Wood may well have been there with Colette and other journalists. Because the circus performers were Jews, Yugoslavs, and negroes, and Sarassani chose expatriation over firing his crew, they were scapegoated by the Nazis. The night before he left Antwerp for South

America, "the tent housing his twenty-two elephants caught fire, and most of them were burned to death."[39]

The abjection Barnes figured in *Nightwood* is mild compared to the murder and dehumanization (including medical experimentation) of the Nazi concentration camps. When American soldiers liberated the camps, the stench of excrement and death overpowered them. They could not identify with the tortured, starved prisoners as fellow human beings. One soldier wrote of them as a "horde of gnomes and trolls. . . . Some hop on crutches. Some hobble on stumps of feet. Some run with angular movements. Some glide like Oriental genies." Another described the emaciated victims as like "huge, lethargic spiders," and others described the "absent-minded apes" of Buchenwald, while many said the scenes were like a bestial circus nightmare.[40] While the soldiers had difficulty identifying with the humanity of the Nazis' victims, civilians refused to believe the newsreel evidence of the massacres. Since people could not deal with the idea of sadism on such an immense scale, involving the whole nation, eventually the press began to focus on individual perverse Germans as perpetrators of the crimes. Interestingly, the press focused on two women, "Irme Grese, the Bitch of Belsen," and "Ilse Koch, the Beast of Buchenwald." It seems to me immensely significant, though it has not been noted before, that the press singled out individual women as symbols of Nazi sadism and cruelty, as objects of hate, when Nazism itself was such a patriarchal ideology, and the crimes were committed almost entirely by men. Ilse Koch is significant for us, for she collected pieces of tattooed human skin from camp prisoners. Did she write on the skin as a direct challenge to Leviticus? Were Felix and Guido among her victims? Certainly Nikka's body as the black backside of Western culture and the mutilated body of Mademoiselle Basquette challenge us to remember the inexpressible horror of the Holocaust. *Nightwood* reminds us that the human condition is a sister- and brotherhood of difference and that ideologies that seek to erase those differences and define only themselves as human are indescribably dangerous.

NOTES

This essay was written in 1983–84 for Mary Lynn Broe's *Silence and Power: Djuna Barnes, A Revaluation*, which has not yet appeared. Because it has been widely cited from manuscript beginning with Shari Benstock's *Women of the Left Bank* (1986) and circulated widely, I resist the urge to revise substantially in reference to subsequent work, and hope it will now enter into a dialogue, however belatedly, with others working on Bakhtin's idea of carnival, the revision of modernism, Kristeva's concept of abjection, and Freud on the uncanny. A version of this paper was given at the 1984 MLA American Literature Division meeting in Washington, chaired by Margaret Homans. I am grateful to the panelists (especially Susan Friedman) and the audience for their response. I am also grateful to Shari and Bernard Benstock and their students at Tulsa and audiences at the University of Wisconsin, CUNY Graduate Center, Northwestern University, the University of Utah, Grinnell College, the University of Houston, the University of Arizona, and Susan Lanser and the Georgetown Critical Theory Conference, 1987. My thanks to Dean William Livingston and the University of Texas for a research grant that allowed me to work at the Barnes collection, McKeldin Library, University of Maryland; Donald Farren and his helpful staff for making the materials needed for this study available to me and for permission to reproduce materials in the collection; as well as to the Author's League fund, Herbert Mitgang, holder of the Djuna Barnes copyright. I am also grateful to Beverly Stoeltje for introducing me to Bakhtin's work and discussions of circus from the perspective of folklore, and to the students in my Feminist Theory Seminar at the University of Texas, especially Lee Mellick, Patricia Rezabek, and Ingeborg O'Sickey.

1. Julia Kristeva, *Powers of Horror: An Essay on Abjection* (New York: Columbia University Press, 1982), p. 100.

2. See Mikhail Bakhtin, *Rabelais and His World,* trans. Hélène Iswolsky (Bloomington: Indiana University Press, 1984).

3. Mary Douglas, *Purity and Danger* (London: Routledge and Kegan Paul, 1966).

4. Quotations are from Djuna Barnes, *Nightwood* (1936), with an introduction by T. S. Eliot, who edited the first London Faber edition (New York: New Directions, 1977).

5. See Victor Brombert, *Victor Hugo and the Visionary Novel* (Cambridge: Harvard University Press, 1984).

6. Aphra Behn is one of the few precursors to Barnes whose work survives. Most women's bawdy humor available to us is oral, as in Bessie Smith and black women's music, but see *Last Laughs: Perspectives on Women and Humor,* ed. Regina Barreca (London: Gordon and Breach, 1988).

7. Emily Coleman's essay with Djuna Barnes's comments and objections is in the McKeldin Library, University of Maryland. The Emily Coleman papers are at the University of Delaware.

8. Brombert, *Victor Hugo,* p. 109.

9. For another analysis of Barnes's excremental imagination, see Louise De Salvo's essay on *The Antiphon* also written for *Silence and Power: Djuna Barnes, a Revaluation* (Carbondale: Southern Illinois University Press, forthcoming).

10. Brombert, *Victor Hugo,* p. 116.

11. Thelma Wood's Berlin sketchbook is in the McKeldin Library.

12. Michel Thévoz, *The Painted Body* (New York: Rizzoli, 1984).

13. Kenneth Burke, *Language as Symbolic Action* (Berkeley: University of California Press, 1968). Burke notes the God/dog reversal in the last scene of *Nightwood.*

14. Eugène Sue, *The Wandering Jew* (New York: Random House, 1940). A full study of the influence of Eugène Sue on Djuna Barnes remains to be done. It is clear that Sue's career as doctor/sailor/writer is a major source for the character of Matthew O'Connor. The description of Morok, the lion tamer, with his beasts, Judas, Cain, and Death, in ch. 1 of *The Wandering Jew* begins with a three-sided chapbook illustration of his conversion from beast to human, a savage fleeing from wild animals, transformed to their tamer in the last picture. It is not difficult to imagine the young Djuna Barnes's identification with outsiders deriving from the novel after which she was named. Her early journalism produced memorable portraits of misfits and outsiders, and the chapbook or broadsheet is an important motif in her writing and drawing.

15. See Fredric Jameson, *The Political Unconscious* (Ithaca: Cornell University Press, 1981). While I find Jameson's categories valuable for this analysis, I must point out that he does not count feminism as part of the political nor does gender appear in his system. For a good discussion of these issues, see Judith Gardiner's review, *In These Times*, 28 Oct. 1981.

16. Hans Mayer, *Outsiders: A Study in Life and Letters* (Cambridge: MIT Press, 1984). Naomi Schor's essay is in *The Female Body in Western Culture*, ed. Susan Suleiman (Cambridge: Harvard University Press, 1986).

17. Jane Marcus, "A Wilderness of One's Own," in *Women Writers and the City*, ed. Susan Squier (Knoxville: University of Tennessee Press, 1984), pp. 134–60.

18. Kenneth Tynan, "Berlin in Person," *TLS*, 28 Dec. 1984, p. 1507. Heinrich Mann, whose novel *The Blue Angel*'s script was taken from, was surely an influence on Barnes in *Unrath* and *Der Untertak*.

19. For feminist discussions of the importance of transvestism to women artists, see Susan Gubar, "Blessings in Disguise: Cross-Dressing as Re-Dressing for Female Modernists," *Massachussetts Review* (Autumn 1981); Sandra Gilbert's "Costumes of the Mind," *Critical Inquiry* (1980); and Shari Benstock's response to and revision of their arguments in *Women of the Left Bank* (Austin: University of Texas Press, 1986). To this debate among feminist critics on the function of transvestism in women's culture, I would add that Barnes's presentation of a male transvestite as hero is a very clever way of privileging the female. Radclyffe Hall's *The Well of Loneliness* (New York: Covici and Friede, 1928) was clearly an influence on *Nightwood*, and I maintain that the structure of *Nightwood* is based on cabaret "acts." *The Well of Loneliness* also gives a guided tour of gay bars in Paris in the twenties. I believe that the novel's title is a play on the name of a well-known homosexual and lesbian club in London in the twenties, called the Cave of Harmony after the club in Thackeray's *The Newcomes*, famous for impersonations, improvisations, and dirty songs. Radclyffe Hall's tour includes Monsieur Pujol of the Ideal, who "collected inverts" and entertained his straight clients with photographs of his customers and a sinister locked leather notebook in which he cataloged his "collection" (pp. 441–42). He tells stories like Dr. O'Connor's, but their object is not the same. At Le Narcisse the Patron is a transvestite who sings both sentimental and lewd songs. At Alec's the whole

"miserable army" of inverts is gathered. He sells cocaine to his "filles" and Stephen is called "Ma Soeur" by a dying young addict of whom she thinks, "It's looking for God who made it" (p. 449). The contrast between Hall's tragic, despairing vision and Barnes's comic approach is instructive. Barnes never reifies her outcast figure into an "it." Yet Angela Ingram points out that Hall's line repeats the earlier scene where the fox is hounded to death as "scapegoat"; she is referring to all outcasts as hounded beasts, a view she and Barnes might have shared.

20. The figure of the lesbian lover as a fairy-tale prince or page is a common one in women's writing. In Antonia White's *Frost in May* (1933; New York: Dial, 1982) the heroine's adored friend in a Catholic girls' school in England, Léonie, is seen as "a young prince, pale and weary from a day's ride, with his lovelocks carelessly tied in a frayed ribbon. . . . Her feeling for Léonie was one of pure admiration, the feeling of page for prince, too cold and absolute to be called love" (pp. 79, 80). Antonia White was part of the Peggy Guggenheim circle at Hayford Hall, where Djuna Barnes wrote part of *Nightwood*.

21. Sigmund Freud, "The Uncanny" (1919), in *On Creativity and the Unconscious* (New York: Harper and Row, 1958), pp. 122–61, quote on p. 123. Page numbers in the text refer to this edition.

22. See Nancy Harrison, "Jean Rhys and the Novel as Woman's Text" (Chapel Hill: University of North Carolina Press, 1988).

23. For "The Sandman," see the *Selected Writings of E. T. A. Hoffmann,* ed. and trans. Leonard J. Kent and Elizabeth C. Knight, 2 vols. (Chicago: University of Chicago Press, 1969). The tales are in vol. 1.

24. See the review of Freud-Fleiss letters in the *New York Times Magazine,* 17 March 1985. As Freud repressed physical evidence of father-daughter incest to write his seduction theory, so Marx rejected earlier nonrational socialisms to create Marxism as a science. Consequently, in each ordering and theorizing of self and history an important component is left out and made other. The real incest victims are neglected after Freud until quite recently. "Other" socialisms were denied by Marxists. For feminist socialisms in pre-Marx English history, see Barbara Taylor's *Eve and the New Jerusalem* (New York: Pantheon, 1983).

25. I am indebted here to a paper read by Gareth Stedman Jones at the University of Texas in March 1985 on the nonrational origins of socialism in French thought. In a typescript of *Nightwood* in the McKeldin Library, after Robin is called "the infected carrier of the past," the phrase "the *magnetized* beastly" is crossed out; clearly it is a reference to the magnetic theory of somnambulism of Mesmer. Bernard Benstock points out that Marx discusses these thinkers in *Capital* (see "Making Capital Out of Vampires," *Times Higher Education Supplement,* 15 June 1984).

26. As I write, the Barnes family papers at Maryland have been opened to scholars. I suspect that both her father, Wald Barnes, and her grandmother, Zadel Barnes, were deeply interested in Fourier, Mesmer, Hugo, and Sue and that the family experiments in living on their farm owed much to the influence of Fourier's ideas.

27. This information was supplied by Nancy Levine; Wald Barnes's novels and musical compositions are in the possession of Kerron Barnes and Duane Barnes.

28. Freud says that the mother of a girl he had cured regarded psychoanalysis itself as "uncanny." Helplessness causes one to feel "uncanny," he argues, and he tells the story of being lost in the streets of a town in Italy on a hot afternoon. Three times, while trying to get out, he returns to the same place, a street where "nothing but painted women were to be seen at the windows" (p. 143). This hardly needs a feminist analysis. Though Freud says he has "drifted into this field of research half involuntarily" (p. 160), I suggest he was writing the male fear of being castrated by the father as a cover for his own guilt at having mishandled his women patients. For a brilliant analysis of the power of the mesmerized woman and of Freud's relation to hysterical women patients, see Nina Auerbach's *Woman and the Demon: The Life of a Victorian Myth* (Cambridge: Harvard University Press, 1982).

29. Jean Rhys, *Smile Please: An Unfinished Autobiography* (New York: Harper and Row, 1979), pp. 20–21.

30. The typescripts of *Bow Down* and *Nightwood* are in the McKeldin Library, University of Maryland. When it is possible to quote from T. S. Eliot's letters, a full study of his cuts and corrections to *Nightwood* should be made with the aim of restoring and publishing the text as Barnes wanted it. While Eliot did have to think of the censor, many passages could be restored. He corrected her French and German, marked out many passages on Jews, on King Ludwig and a scene with the doctor in jail, as well as passages which might be considered obscene. He crossed out on page 202 "You can lay a hundred bricks and not be called a bricklayer, but lay one boy and you are a bugger." He told her to think over whether she wanted to say of Jenny "when she fell in love it was with a perfect fury of accumulated dishonesty," and told her to take out Matthew calling himself a faggot, a fairy, and a queen in the scene in the carriage. He crossed out "and the finger of our own right hand placed where it best pleases" and the McClusky passages on a girlish boy in the war. In the description of the "Tuppenny Upright" he crossed out "letting you do it," but she restored it in 1949. He wanted to change "obscene" to "unclean" on the last page and said he couldn't understand why Robin had candles in the chapel at night. Barnes's penciled note says "Sample of T. S. E.'s 'lack of imagination' (as he said)." Also cut is a homosexual courtroom joke in which the judge asks, "What do I give a man of this sort?" And the clerk replies, "A dollar, a dollar and a half, two dollars." The whole of Matthew's circumcising the regiment scene is cut. The collection also includes Barnes's library. Inside her copy of Eliot's *Collected Poems* she wrote, "He said 'Someday they will say I copied you,'" and in his *On Poetry and Poets* she wrote in 1981, "Mr. E. said of the last act of *The Antiphon* that it was one of the greatest last acts he had ever read. But he did not so write of it."

31. I have discussed this aspect of *Nightwood* in a review of Andrew Field's *Djuna* in *The Women's Review of Books* 1, no. 8 (May 1984). See also Paul Bouissac's *Circus and Culture: A Semiotic Approach* (Bloomington: Indiana University Press, 1976).

32. Note the resemblance of Robin as a beast to the description of Charlotte Brontë's Bertha in ch. 26 of *Jane Eyre:* "What it was, whether beast or human being, one could not, at first sight, tell; it grovelled, seemingly, on all fours; it snatched and growled like some wild animal. . . . "

33. For discussions of carnival, see *The Reversible World: Symbolic Inversion in Art and Society,* ed. Barbara A. Babcock (Ithaca: Cornell University Press, 1978), in particular David Kunzles's "World Upside Down: The Iconography of a European Broadsheet Type" and Natalie Zemon Davis's "Women on Top: Symbolic Sexual Inversion and Political Disorder in Early Modern Europe."

34. Marguerite Yourçenar, *Fires* (rpt. New York: Farrar, Straus & Giroux, 1981); Susan Gubar, "Sapphistries," *Signs* 10, no. 1 (1984). See also Colette's *The Pure and the Impure* for further connections among woman, circus, cabaret, and lesbianism.

35. For a contemporay version of Barbette's story see Albert Goldbarth's prose poem *Different Fleshes* (Geneva, N.Y.: Hobart and William Smith Colleges Press, 1979). Writing of the painter Soutine, Goldbarth says, "No one had ever prayed before in Meat Cathedral," which also recalls Barnes's Rabelaisian use of the butcher motif.

36. Bouissac, *Circus and Culture,* p. 8.

37. Djuna Barnes in the *New York World,* 1914, Barnes Collection.

38. Brombert, *Victor Hugo,* p. 202.

39. Yvonne Mitchell, *Colette: A Taste for Life* (New York: Harcourt Brace Jovanovich, 1975), p. 177.

40. See Robert H. Abzug, *Inside the Vicious Heart: Americans and the Liberation of Nazi Concentration Camps* (New York: Oxford University Press, 1985), pp. 56, 128–29, 132.

PART FOUR

The Tradition of Socially Engaged Literature

NANCY PORTER

Women's Interracial Friendships and Visions of Community in Meridian, The Salt Eaters, Civil Wars, and Dessa Rose

The possibility of friendship between black and white women has been explored in a small but powerful body of recent fiction and in contemporary feminist thought. Although both the literary and the theoretical concerns reflect larger questions of female bonding, for the most part, those literary critics who have written about interracial friendships have not used a feminist psychoanalytic perspective, and those who have used female development theory to understand the unconscious dimensions of women's friendships have not discussed how race, class, and cultural experience affect the dynamics they analyze.

As described by Elizabeth Schultz in her ground-breaking analysis of women's interracial friendships in American novels, black and white writers establish different terms for these friendships and offer contrasting views on their long-term survival.[1] According to Schultz, white women writers develop the dark-skinned friend as mirror or mentor of the white character whose identity and growth are the novel's central concern. The relationship may temporarily nourish the participants; it may even illumine the white person's understanding of racism. However, the friendship itself dissolves by the end of the novel or at best lives on as a faded image in the white protagonist's memory. In Schultz's reading, white writers do not appear sanguine about the durability of black-white friendship in a racist world.

The black and white characters of black writers, on the other hand, appreciate one another as individuals and as members of different races or the relationship ends. Even so, only a handful of black writers suggest that a female interracial friendship might survive the power plays engendered by white privilege. And only in two novels—Alice Walker's *Meridian* and Toni Morrison's *Tar Baby*—is that hopefulness informed by the characters' actual confrontation of racism and its sexual dimension. Such openness of communication between black and white women, Schultz concludes, must develop before forgiveness is possible and change can occur, before perhaps friends become certain friends in literature and in reality.

In recent applications of feminist psychoanalytic theory to women's friendships, theorists focus on the suppressed components and transactions held over from the pre-Oedipal mother-daughter tie.[2] Often unconsciously, women look to one another for nurturance, acceptance, and support—for the love that was once given and perhaps lost. At the same time, however, women anticipate attempts at control and rejection when they differ or grow apart. Similarly, the intersections between women's friendships and experiences imposed by race, class, and cultural perception need to be mapped, for patriarchal racism, with its legacies of white guilt and black distrust, will mute or inflame the submerged issues of longing, fear, and rage when black and white women try to speak to one another in or by means of fiction.[3] Although I appreciate Schultz's concern for the transformations imposed by racism, the issues raised by a psychoanalytic perspective, which suggest a complex relation among text, author, and reader, particularly when women and race are concerned, lead me to question privileging both confrontation as a narrative strategy and permanency of relationship when evaluating an interracial friendship. To see what more might be in the picture I have chosen novels that evolve diverse strategies for constructing the relations among race, class, and gender, and that allow me to consider the applicability of a merged-identity theory to interracial friendships.[4]

Alice Walker's *Meridian,* Toni Cade Bambara's *The Salt Eaters,* Rosellen Brown's *Civil Wars,* and Sherley Anne Williams's *Dessa Rose* depict obstacles to interracial friendship, but affirm its possibility by locating the power of female bonding at the heart of their visions of a transformed human community.[5] As Janice Raymond argues in *A Passion for Friends: Toward a Philosophy of Female Affection,* the central issue of women's friendships is not their private nature but their necessary connections to power in the public realm.[6] By contextualizing relations between black and white women in historical movements for social change—Walker, Bambara, and Brown use the civil rights movement of the 1960s, Williams the black freedom movement in the nineteenth century—this group of novels provides the necessary political connection. Examining the ways that each writer constructs the relations among race, class, and gender expands our understanding of the possibilities for female interracial friendship.

In *Meridian* a young southern black woman, Meridian Hill, encounters the civil rights movement at a point in her life when she is on the verge of defeat.[7] Seventeen, a high-school dropout, deserted wife, mother to a son, estranged daughter, and heir to the Harriet Tubman legacy of "outrageous" black women she has yet to discover, Meridian sits benumbed in front of the television set. News of the bombing in her neighborhood, where young civil rights workers have been staying (the year is 1960), awakens Meridian to "the past and present of the larger world" (p. 67). She joins the workers in their voter registration and direct action campaigns and begins the quest for a new life and identity within a social cause that leads her to Saxon, a black women's college, then to New York, and finally back south again.

The novel, however, does not begin with Meridian's awakening or develop chronologically but instead assembles fragments within Meridian's consciousness in shifting patterns of meaning and association. In the first fragment Meridian is living by herself in a shack in a raggedy southern town sometime in the 1970s. She has turned away from the revolutionary violence contemplated by some of her disillusioned black comrades and has returned to her roots in the southern black community. There she attempts to provide opportunities for education and to organize protest among the populace. But she is ill and tired and in the process of changing her mind about martyrdom. Soon we begin to learn of the stages of Meridian's quest. By the end of the novel we see her pulled back from the brink, healed and secure in her identity as a black woman.

Walker has termed Meridian a flawed revolutionary, but not in a negative sense.[8] Her cracks have developed within a racist and sexist society. In actively countering these forces, she comes into her own as a black woman but at some cost to her health and sanity. Two of the relationships Meridian forms intersect the issues. One is with the young northern black intellectual movement leader turned artist, Truman Held. The other is with the young northern white Jewish student volunteer, Lynne Rabinowitz. The structural and ideological parallels Walker develops between Lynne and Truman in relation to Meridian suggest Walker's chief narrative strategy for constructing the relations among gender, race, and class in the novel. These relationships serve also to "deconstruct" the civil rights movement by exposing discrepancies between its ideology and practice.[9]

Truman is introduced to Meridian's consciousness dressed in flowing white Ethiopian robes and speaking French, the image of a "conquering prince returning to his lands" (p. 95). For all his affectations, Truman proves a good grass-roots community organizer in the South, but his understanding of the right humanitarian moves to make in the cause of social justice does not extend to his personal life. He abandons Meridian after their first sexual encounter and takes up with the privileged white Lynne. After Meridian aborts her pregnancy and is sterilized, he returns in an ardent mood and sentimentally asks her to bear his "beautiful black babies" (p. 113). Although Meridian comes to forgive Truman— their bond sealed in brutal civil rights jailings and finally turned into a tender friendship—Walker does not entirely. When Meridian resumes her quest at the end of the novel, she leaves behind a penitent Truman, who has abandoned his robes, his Volvo, his white girlfriends, and his canvases to carry on Meridian's unglamorous work among the people as part of the re-education of his racial and gendered identity.

If Meridian's relationship with the ironically named Truman reveals the contradictions of sexism (and, in his attraction to the power white women represent, class bias) in a movement for equality, her relationship with Lynne focuses the issue of white racism in what began as a black movement. When Lynne joins the movement as a college student in the summer of 1964, she, like Meridian, is at odds with her heritage and seeking a new community to feel at home in. Walker couples the news that Truman has selected Lynne, originally introduced as one of a group of white girls, with Meridian's poignant reflection, "the one she had liked, Lynne Rabinowitz" (p. 112).

The question of Lynne's likeableness is delicate. She is intelligent and dedicated. In contrast to the inhabitants of the sterile white suburbs of her upbringing, black people of the South strike her as capital A art. Their vibrant culture attracts her, but she also casts a romantic veil over the whole. In her adopted community she commits a number of inter-racial blunders—from wearing skimpy clothing on the street, to setting her foot on the porch of a black household before she is invited, to becoming involved with Truman. Her involvement doubly educates her. She marries Truman and, when he tires of her, she learns of the shadow side of the black experience as she tries to survive the humiliations of the welfare system in New York and loses a child to violence.

The death of Truman and Lynne's child, Camara, is the catalyst that brings Lynne and Meridian together toward the end of the novel. "They waited for the pain of Camara's death to lessen. They waited to ask for-giveness of each other" (p. 177). Meridian feeds, talks with, and sup-ports Lynne in trouble. There is intimacy and mutuality in the scenes. Meridian reads Margaret Walker poems to Lynne. "Lynne, in return, would attempt to cornrow Meridian's patchy short hair" (p. 176). They sit in front of the television set, and as the face of a young black militant appears, they unite in their feelings of love and sorrow, their memories and hopes for the South. It is in this context that Meridian tells Lynne, "I tried very hard not to hate you. And I think I always succeeded." To which Lynne replies, "It ain't easy not to hate the omnipresent honky woman" (p. 178).

The tensions that precede and disrupt the harmonies, however, are fully disclosed earlier in the novel. Lynne's relationship with Truman is the primary cause of conflict. Walker handles the perspectives generously, giving multiple points of view. Truman falls for Lynne, her pink-canopied bedroom, long flowing hair, black leotards, dancing shoes, *New York Times,* sexual eagerness, and all. His hurtful comparisons, which make Meridian feel provincial and ashamed, are not Lynne's fault, but she does know at least some intimate details of Truman and Meridian's relationship, which later in anger and bewilderment she throws up to Meridian. Although the scenes of reconciliation appear toward the end of the novel and seem recent in the reader's mind, there is also a final scene between Meridian and Lynne which appears in an earlier fragment but which occurs chronologically a year later. This scene, racially ugly, casts an ambiguous light over the friendship. Fat, graying, in need of a bath, smoking marijuana, and still in pursuit of Truman, Lynne appears on Meridian's southern doorstep precisely because she knows Truman is there. Meridian tries to assure Lynne that her relationship with Truman is not sexual. Lynne tries to tell Meridian of her rape by one of Truman's friends, a rape that symbolized both personal betrayal and rejection by the movement. Neither can hear the other, and the tension releases the kind of racist language and assumptions that suggest Lynne is woefully deficient in her understanding of Meridian's feelings as a black woman. Racism and its sexual dimension are at least allusively confronted by the women, but even an optimistic reading of the friendship would have to take into account Lynne's on-going obsession with Truman and what the hurt of that breeds in her.

Walker paints a qualified picture of Lynne and of the friendship and would seem to suggest that, before either Lynne or Truman can gather with Meridian by the biblical waters where "truth" can be known (and where, presumably, there is neither "black" nor "white," neither marrying nor being given in marriage), each has to understand what Meridian does about sexual and racial oppression. Until they can live through parts of her experience, their place in the new order of Meridian's individual and collective consciousness is provisional.

Toni Cade Bambara's *The Salt Eaters*, like *Meridian*, is concerned with the healing of a burned-out (angry) civil rights worker and her restoration to a black community that has in part been transformed by her efforts.[10] Set in Georgia, in a city Bambara calls Claybourne, in one of the many images of center and horizon that radiate out from and draw back into the heart of the novel, *The Salt Eaters* opens with a question: "Are you sure, sweetheart, that you want to be well?" (p. 3).[11] The spirit healer Minnie Ransome is talking to the attempted suicide Velma Henry. There is no simple answer. Velma has survived some of the painful experiences of the civil rights movement, such as the long hot march she finished on swollen feet only to be greeted by the sight of the demonstration's black male leader stepping cool and composed from his air-conditioned limousine. In the movement's aftermath she has assumed the burden of another set of contradictions in doing and being all things to keep up the momentum. She is wife to the organizer and philanderer Obie; mother to an adopted son; computer programmer and trouble shooter; and the office manager, fund raiser, bookkeeper, grants writer, staff supervisor, and general peacekeeper between the factions of the Academy of the Seven Arts, a cultural-political organization in the black community. Velma has perfected her own variety of hunger artistry to accomplish this: she lives by not feeling. Now Minnie—spinster, swamp hag, wise woman—sits ready to draw out of her own gut, shake from the fringed edges of her shawl, and conjure out of thin air the silken threads of song, shimmering points of light, and webbed connections among all forms of life to spin a protective cocoon of love for Velma to heal in.

Women are central to Bambara's understanding of healing, even as they are to Walker's. In the background of *Meridian* are black women whose support, actual and symbolic, is crucial to the journey and shapes its meaning. In *The Salt Eaters,* whether engaged, as Minnie and Velma are, in reclaiming the African spiritual heritage from the jaws of the unceasing logic of political action, or caucusing to take over the agenda of a male-dominated meeting, or forming an action committee to tackle the problems of "drugs, prisons, alcohol, the school, rape, battered women, abused children ... [and] the nuclear power issue" ignored by the politicians (p. 198), or arguing the merits of horoscopes versus Marxist analysis, women act together to set the agenda and control the space.

Although Bambara exposes the distortions of sexism and of racism— the white world is primarily represented by the poisonous Transchemical Company on the edge of town—the importance of her novel for a discussion of women's friendships lies in Bambara's reconstruction of cultural difference to represent not inferiority to a presumed superiority but a source of political strength. This she does most concisely by developing the metaphoric Seven Sisters political performing troupe and connecting friendship with political action.

We are first introduced to Cecile and Chezia, from the West Indies; Inez, who is Chicana; Nilde, from the Black Hills; Mai, from San Francisco; Iris, who is Puerto Rican; and Velma's sister Palma—the sisters of the plantain, the corn, the rice, and the yam—on a wild bus ride from an antinuclear demonstration at which they have performed in Barnwell to another appearance at the Claybourne festival. These savvy, bright, creative, meditative women, dressed in their "bossy" political T-shirts, who exchange symbolic hats, work on their camera equipment and tape recorders, polish skits for performance, talk, laugh, and eat together, model the weaving of the texture of women's friendships into an empowering fabric. For all their pride in national identity, they are appreciative friends who seal their bonds to one another with gifts each has chosen from the homeland she has left behind, exchange memories of their mothers, and share hopes and dreams. The troupe, furthermore, is not necessarily fixed in its membership. Mai dreams of organizing caucuses of Asian women all over the globe. Members go and are replaced by new recruits. Their habit of friendship is what Janice Raymond would term *recurrent:* romanticized permanency is not the issue. In conceptual terms, however, the group is as on-going as the necessity of their collective struggle.

Rosellen Brown's new community in *Civil Wars* differs from Walker's and Bambara's, but it too grows out of the "old" civil rights movement.[12] In Brown's novel the failure of integration to bring about equality of relation between black and white people is confronted by the white protagonist Jessie Carll, not in her friendship with Andrea Smith, the black civil rights lawyer who has been her friend from movement days, but in adopting out of necessity the children of her husband's sister and brother-in-law, who are killed in an automobile accident. Trained only too well by their bigoted parents, the children are disdainful, even fearful of blacks. Jessie and her white southern husband, Teddy—movement veterans who stayed on in an integrated, now turning black power, neighborhood in Jackson, Mississippi—handle the addition of Helen and O'Neil to their own two, Andy and Lydia, very differently. At least in part from reading her adopted daughter's diary, Jessie grows to acknowledge and understand the dislocation that moving from one culture to another, radically different, forces upon Helen and O'Neil. (Their home, with its "spotless" kitchen scrubbed by a black woman, bears little relation to Jessie's household, with its movement posters, well-thumbed copy of *Pedagogy of the Oppressed,* and general clutter.) Teddy never does understand. He continues to despise the differences between his political commitments, and the physical dangers and psychological discomforts they entail, and the children's need for a safe space to grow up in. His nearsightedness strains the marriage.

Beginning in the prologue when Jessie recalls the first time she and Teddy made love in the summer of 1964 and he discovered that she was not an ideological virgin like the other student volunteers, Brown constructs her critique of racial-patriarchal power by paralleling the power relations of whites to blacks, men like Teddy to women like Jessie, and parents to children. The issues of guilt and privilege are focused at the beginning of the novel as Jessie, attired in dungarees and sneakers, walks in on one of her son Andy's classmates, a young black boy, guzzling sweet apple wine in her living room beneath the integration posters. Sammy Hines (the name stitched on his brand-new shiny red track jacket) has broken into the house, one of a mounting number of harassments that Jessie believes are calculated to force the Carlls to move out of the neighborhood. Torn between outrage at the violation and guilt—not the least because in confronting Sammy she reverts to schoolmarm behavior and draws a stereotypical response as Sammy rolls his eyes upward and mumbles "yes 'm"—Jessie handles the intrusion (or "bungled burglary," as she calls it) badly. She lets Sammy off the hook but makes him climb ignominiously over the back fence to get away or possibly to be caught by one of the black neighbors. As Andrea later comments, "You got your husband's dumb liberal soft-headed do-good condescension in you. . . . You should have sent that boy to the po-lice" (p. 12).

But the failures in the scene are multiple. As soon as Jessie says to herself "a classmate of Andy's," she realizes the irony of the image: if the boys have exchanged anything in their integrated school, it has been hostility. Sammy lives in the neighborhood, "on the corner behind two or three cars in various stages of decay and cannibalistic dismemberment"; she knows his "mother and grandmother to say hello to," but shares with them no sense of community (p. 6). The neighborhood itself feels oppressive. She is used to violence, she thinks, but not from black people. "*What is this?*" she asks parenthetically, appalled at what is happening and her own strained attitudes.

What has happened is in part the loss of hopefulness about social change, in part the loss of a sense of sustaining community between blacks and whites, the "press of general affection, the sharp quick hugs of the men and the sweaty bosom-to-bosom embraces of the women" that celebrated her marriage to Teddy (p. 19). Jessie does not allow herself the self-indulgence of memory very often. The days of "Earnest White Girls for Integration" are over. Black nationalism is a reality. She and Teddy are "obsolete," she concludes, adrift in their sense of misplaced public ironies that have begun to eat into the fabric of their marriage as well.

The cloth of Jessie and Andrea's friendship proves resistant to the changes. The two women are neighbors as well as friends. Typically Andrea is ahead of Jessie in understanding the issues at stake in any given situation, particularly the issue of white guilt and the distorted thinking and actions it leads to. In this she conforms to the role of black woman as mentor that Schultz comments upon as a limitation of portraiture. Andrea entered the movement as the more or less sheltered and strait-laced daughter of a black college professor. She had adjustments to make to the free-floating sensuality of the movement's youthful subculture. These adjustments may have predisposed her to both realism and tolerance. Jessie, coming from a northern Jewish Communist family, had to adjust to the relatively nonideological character of the movement. Her commitment to integration wars with her self-preservative instincts and her dawning recognition that she, like Walker's Lynne, has to make peace with her own parents and heritage. Andrea marries a white movement worker, now a social worker, and has a child in addition to a law practice. Jessie teaches in an alternative grade school, modeled in part on Mississippi Freedom School principles. A traveling college rep for a textbook company, Teddy allows his political skills to rust, except for misguided and abortive attempts to engineer a demonstration or two.

How Andrea has been affected by the changes in the supportive community ethic and collective strategy is not clear. The point of view is primarily Jessie's. As a character Andrea is developed with few ironies and no inner life. We learn from Jessie that, in order not to appear as though she has argued cases before the Supreme Court, Andrea adopts the black vernacular she was never raised to speak. On the other hand, she wears men's white shirts as a uniform to "ward off attacks on her efficiency." This may suggest that to survive in the professional world she has become "bi-cultural." On the whole she appears an idealized super black woman and friend to Jessie. She takes in Jessie's children when needed, feeds them, allows herself to be called out of meetings when Jessie is in distress, shops with Helen and Lydia, and is generally there for Jessie as Meridian is for Lynne. Above all she sees Helen and O'Neil not as bigots in mufti but as the displaced refugees they are. Toward the end of the novel, however, Andrea confronts Teddy on his assumption that without the inspiration of white (and he means male) leadership there would not have been a civil rights movement, and her anger is clear and targeted.

In the stunning denouement, Jessie and Andy rescue Helen from her attempt to die rather than carry on with a life which has become intolerable, and Jessie envisages leaving behind Teddy (who has already more or less abandoned his family) and taking the children north to New

York "where they would all be new together, and [share] the handicaps all around, the unfamiliarity, the strains, the foreignness" (p. 414). In her vision the burden of dislocation, the abandonment of privilege, which has so divided black and white, man and woman, parent and child in the civil wars of this novel, will be equalized, a model of community-making in collective struggle she may have derived from her experience with Andrea and others in Sheriff Dickie Wing's Indianola, Mississippi, jail where "surviving together, they were shriven" (p. 118).

Rosellen Brown appears to take for granted the possibility that black and white women of good will and common interests and experience may be friends, which, indeed, was one of the social visions of the civil rights movement. Although neither Andrea nor Teddy is included in the new community of single mothers and children Jessie envisages forming in New York, the reader may assume that at least Jessie and Andrea will keep in touch by phone as they have throughout the novel. In her projection of continuity of friendship, Brown differs from those white women writers Schultz includes in her study. The difference may lie in the particular kind of bonding Brown's friendship represents, one born in a shared social vision of struggle, and in the writer's political commitment to interracial friendship. Andrea is, however, in some sense an overdetermined character, which may reflect a degree of discomfort or self-consciousness on Rosellen Brown's part, even as the distortions in Lynne Rabinowitz's character suggest Alice Walker's anger. (Walker has said that as many white readers seem to identify themselves in Lynne as reject the proffered mirror, but to me she is the stereotype of the young mixed-up and whacked-out white woman, which may reflect my own bias.) It seems quite possible that, in the dynamics of enscribing one's racial opposite, particularly within a friendship, the writer faces her own desires and ambivalences—and, of course, so does the reader.

More than the three civil rights novels, *Dessa Rose* offers the richest context within which to examine the anticipations of friendship against the distortions of racism in a particular historical era.[13] Set in the antebellum South, the novel brings together black Dessa, who leads a coffle uprising, and white Ruth, who harbors runaway slaves on a remote plantation in Alabama. Williams accepts the challenge to imagine the language and inner life of a young black woman slave from an era in which the thoughts of even such prominent ex-slave women as Sojourner Truth and Harriet Tubman have been preserved for us only through the writing of white abolitionist intermediaries. Along with that challenge, Williams undertakes the creation of the interior life of a young white plantation mistress whose particular experience has also not made the historical record of diary or letter. (Williams takes on the additional challenge of making credible the psychology of a white proslavery male writer who is obsessed by black women's sexuality.) As Michelle Wallace notes in her review of *Dessa Rose*, Williams overcomes the problem of the narrowness of view each character presents—Dessa's from her experience of slavery, Ruth's from her experience as a southern white woman, Nehemiah's from his patriarchal assumptions and racist ignorance—by adopting the narrative strategy of "a rhetorical play of relative perspective," one that serves her purposes well and from which other writers might learn.[14]

In the prologue, the lyrical memory of the springtime love of two slaves, Dessa and Kaine, returns fleetingly to Dessa in the heat of summer where she crouches, imprisoned in chains in a dark and airless root cellar, awaiting the birth of their child and her own hanging for killing white men in an uprising. In the epilogue, which takes place many years later, Dessa sits surrounded by listening grandchildren and recalls a different love, that for her white friend, Ruth, who is now far away. The novel itself is structured by three symbolic encounters between the black and white worlds of the times that mark the stages of Dessa's passage from slavery to freedom and also the phases of her growth as a black woman with an identity of her own. In parallel development Ruth Sutton moves from being the property of her absentee-landlord husband to a woman who discovers that she can act and live on her own. She too has encounters that define her passage from the enforced childishness and "protected" ignorance of the institution of southern white womanhood to free-standing emotional and economic independence. The intersection of these two women's paths—their points of similarity and difference—is the catalyst for the expansion of each woman's consciousness as she is forced by circumstances to confront, examine, and revise racial myths and images. The bond they ultimately form is sealed through working together to purchase their separate freedom.

The encounter with Nehemiah Adams, a proslavery social misfit who is writing an admonitory book on the origins of slave rebellions that he hopes will gain him a footing in planter society, gives Dessa the opportunity to begin to review her life up to that point. The information that Nehemiah obtains he itemizes as factual.

> The master smashed the young buck's banjo.
> The young buck attacked the master.
> The master killed the young buck.
> The darky attacked the master—and was sold to the
>   Wilson slave coffle. (P. 39)

The story behind the facts is supplied by Dessa's fragmentary recollections of her life as a slave on the Vaugham plantation in Alabama and as part of the chained group who overpower the slavetrader Wilson on the way to market. For Dessa the death of Kaine is the event that opens her to the wider world. In rage and grief she both strikes Vaugham and tries to kill his wife (who tells Dessa her husband must be the father of Dessa's child), is whipped and branded about her genitals and sold to Wilson. In explaining her escape from the coffle, she tells an incredulous Nehemiah: "I kill white mens cause the same reason Masa kill Kaine. Cause I can" (p. 20). We learn from Nehemiah that Wilson, obsessed with the profit to be made from selling Dessa's child, is keeping her alive until she gives birth. Before that happens, however, Nathan and Harker, two of her fellow insurrectionists, spirit her away to Sutton Glen and the colony of fugitive slaves Ruth harbors in exchange for their services in house and field.

Dessa's second set of encounters with the white world begins to reverse the direction of her first. Ill and delirious with postpartum fever, she wakes to the alien touch of cool linen sheets on a soft feather bed (she is in the only one in the house, which is Ruth's) and sees a blurred vision: Ruth breastfeeding Dessa's baby. Is this dream or reality? "A white woman—Is that your enemies?" she asks herself (p. 83). All her past experience would certainly indicate yes. She fears for her baby's life at the hands of this white woman, the first she has seen up close. Her terror magnifies Ruth to Brobdingnagian ugliness.

Ruth, for her part, "had taken the baby to her bosom almost without thought. . . . The sight of him so tiny and bloodied had pained her with an almost physical hurt and she had set about cleaning and clothing him with a single-minded intensity" (p. 101). Her response is "instinctive." As Wallace comments, Ruth has no abolitionist or revolutionary intentions. Dessa's milk is dry. Her desolate face and plight draw Ruth's sympathy almost against her will, certainly against her attitude about malingering slaves. And it is Ruth's coming to identify with Dessa—for instance, seeing the cruel scars on Dessa she realizes that Dessa's is a vulnerable woman's body like her own—that enables her to grow beyond her childlike assumption that blacks are part of the support system of her environment and to see them as human and individual.

The daughter of a Charleston, South Carolina, society family, Ruth had married young a man with pretensions of owning a successful cotton plantation. The enterprise turned into a disaster, symbolized by the half-finished house Ruth lives in with her baby daughter and son. Estranged from her family over the debts of her riverboat gambler husband, whom she has not seen for eighteen months, Ruth rocks and sews and dreams of better days—her life in Charleston and Dorcas, the black woman who raised her. "Mammy" becomes the focus of the first verbal exchange between Dessa and Ruth. Overhearing Ruth, Dessa accuses her of not even knowing Mammy. "I do so," Ruth sputteringly replies. Dessa is thinking of her own lost mother, Ruth of the woman who nurtured and protected her (the fugitive slaves farming Sutton Glen is Dorcas's idea) until she died. Dessa wins her point because Ruth can't immediately recall Mammy's proper name. The encounter, however, expands Ruth's consciousness, as she begins to wonder if Mammy-Dorcas had children and a life other than taking care of her. Williams uses the encounter between the two women over their mammys to symbolic advantage. Although Ruth is shaken by seeing hatred beamed toward her from eyes so like her beloved Mammy's, she eagerly seeks a connection among Dessa, her mother, and Charleston. It is clear that a black woman provided both Dessa and Ruth with the first love they had known and that in quarreling over her the child who lost her mother in each dominates the adult women.

Later in her loneliness Ruth reaches out to Dessa, nestling against her in sleep, and is rejected. What Dessa experiences is revulsion. Williams, though obviously sympathetic, allows no easy leap over the barriers. It is perhaps an open question whether Williams ascribes a longing for attachment to Ruth and the fear of that to Dessa as an articulation of the merging of their identities, or as a separation of the two women's identities; as a reflection of the entwining of conscious and unconscious motives, or as a logical consequence of Ruth's positive experience with Dorcas as a source of love and Dessa's negative one with white women as a source of bodily violation. The question is worth pursuing because the dynamics between Ruth and Dessa, as they struggle toward individuation, very much resemble the conflicts described in feminist psychoanalytic scenarios. In any event, Dessa's rejection of Ruth—after that she sleeps with the other black women in their quarters—is followed by Ruth's developing a relationship with Nathan and Dessa with other black women and Harker.

The trust that begins to grow between the two women as each comes to see the other more clearly is almost ruptured in the third encounter when Dessa comes upon Ruth and Nathan making love. "It was like seeing her nurse Monty for the first time all over again," Dessa thinks. "Can't I have nothing?" she inwardly screams (p. 163). Ruth's association with Nathan transforms her attitudes about black men. Both her sexuality and her understanding of where she stands in the southern scheme of things unfold. Williams, in a sense, gets both women off the hook by providing Dessa with a love of her own, the gentle Harker. But the tension between Dessa and Ruth over Ruth's relationship with Nathan continues and imperils the growth of the friendship. It is finally, however, the trust and confidence that Nathan inspires in Ruth that allow him to put into operation a scheme by which Ruth, dressed as a mistress, and Dessa as her servant travel about the countryside selling Nathan, Harker, and others, who then escape to rejoin the two women in another town to be sold again. In the process, Dessa and Ruth destroy more myths by learning about one another's realities. Dessa, for instance, discovers that a white woman may be raped by a white man and Ruth that any white man can legally call for the seizure and body search of a black woman. They seal their friendship ironically by playing out and transforming their historic mistress-servant roles. And in the end, as both Dessa and Ruth grow into self-defining women, each is able to express her love of the other.

While black and white people in *Dessa Rose* confront and transcend racial and class perceptions to become real to one anther, the ending of the novel is not utopian. Ruth does not join the new order of free blacks in the west, where some "good white men" are invited to eat at Dessa's table. "I guess we all have regretted her leaving, one time or another. She couldn't've caused no more trouble than what the white folks gived us without her. . . . Miss her in and out of trouble," Dessa reflects. And on a deeper level of historical complexity: "Negro can't live in peace under protection of law, got to have some white person stand protection for us. And who can you friend with, love with like that? Oh, Ruth would've tried it; no question in my mind about that. Maybe married Nathan—if he'd asked her . . . but Ruth went East and we all come West . . . " (p. 236). Ruth goes on to make a life for herself in "Philly-me-York—some city didn't allow no slaves" (p. 236)—another empowerment created by the friendship. But this novel that affirms so much that is possible between black and white women hesitates and tips the balance toward separate destinies.

It is tempting for a white reader to greet Williams's extraordinary gift of vision with a sigh of relief. Here is a depiction of a black and white female friendship that withstands the stress of confronting both the psychological and the historical wounds, that accords each woman the dignity—and sometimes the humor—of her own experience and perspective, and generously adds a bonus: the acknowledgment that black women have myths and taboos about white women that do not always stand up to reality. This act of imaginatively bridging the distance between black and white women created by race and class perception in the nineteenth century is repeated in Toni Morrison's *Beloved* in the bonding of two "run-a-ways" from racial patriarchal tyranny, Amy and

Sethe.[15] Sethe decides to trust Amy Denver because she recognizes her "fugitive eyes and a tenderhearted mouth" (p. 78). Amy recognizes in Sethe a slave with a price on her head and a pregnant woman in need of help. She identifies the "chokecherry tree" on Sethe's back with her own whippings at the hands of a white man who was or wasn't her father, and the reader realizes that both Amy's and Sethe's mothers have been white men's property. Amy sings to Sethe the songs her mother sang to her and her "good hands" start the process of healing and then deliver the baby. In a novel in which the past literally haunts the present and comes back to life and light in order to be healed, Morrison carries on Amy's particular spirit in her namesake Denver's ministrations to her murdered sister Beloved. But it is perhaps most of all Morrison's strategy of identifying similarity of class and gender experience across racial lines that makes her contribution to the strategies of interracial female bonding appropriate for mention in this study.

Each novel takes a different approach to the possibility of female interracial bonding and to the construction of the relations among race, class, and gender. Alice Walker's qualified view of black-white friendship is developed in a context in which the parallels between racial, class, and gender oppressions are structurally and ideologically drawn. Toni Cade Bambara strategically excludes white women from her women-of-color sisterhood, but she redefines cultural difference as strength and affirms that female friendships that cross cultural and class lines girder the global community. Rosellen Brown affirms the possibility of an ongoing interracial friendship, modeled on the vision of "black and white together" embodied in the civil rights movement. She conducts her analysis of the race, class, and gender issues that divided that movement, however, in terms of the relations between men and women, parents and children, and blacks and whites generally. Sherley Anne Williams's affectionate friendship bridges the psychological and historical distance between black and white women by negotiating and transforming their roles. Morrison establishes the recognition of gender and class commonalities across racial lines.

These novels as a group affirm different rhythms of female interracial friendship—from the off-again, on-again pattern of harmony and disruption in *Meridian;* to the engaging down-to-earth banter and beat of the Seven Sisters in *The Salt Eaters;* to the supportive friendship in *Civil Wars;* to the remembered friendships of Williams and Morrison. The variety is *not* strikingly different from that found in the literature of friendships between women of the same race. The friendships support growth in the individual and offer models for human relationship in a transformed society—most notably in these novels, women bonding over children and concern for the future.

Precisely because the narratives make accessible for analysis perspectives that are rooted in racial, class, and ethnic experience, the friendships raise issues that illumine the heart of contemporary feminist debate over difference. White guilt and black distrust, particularly prominent in the feminist movement discourse of the past two decades, surface as the writers in this study create their racially opposite characters: Brown's idealization of black Andrea; Walker's mistrust of white women inscribed in Lynne; Bambara's strategic silence about white women who may think they are omnipresent. Williams and Morrison, moving away from the contemporary scene, create nineteenth-century black and white characters for whom identification with one another's circumstances as *women* becomes possible. Perhaps moving the issue of negotiating a friendship between racial opposites to a different era facilitates imagining a friendship based on identification, or perhaps Williams and Morrison signal a hopeful shift in the discourse. In any event, friendships that embody imperfect knowledge and trust, betrayal, anger, jealousy, as well as affection, harmony, and recognition of commonality, energize feminist fiction of dialogue, analysis, forgiveness, growth, and change.

NOTES

I wish to thank Deborah Rosenfelt and Bell Chevigny for their suggestions for improving an earlier draft of the essay.

1. Elizabeth Schultz, "Out of the Woods and into the World: A Study of Interracial Friendships between Women in American Novels," in *Conjuring: Black Women, Fiction, and Literary Tradition,* ed. Marjorie Pryse and Hortense J. Spillers (Bloomington: Indiana University Press, 1985), pp. 67–85.

2. I am thinking here particularly of Luise Eichenbaum and Susie Orbach, *Between Women: Love, Envy, Competition in Women's Friendships* (New York: Viking Press, 1988). Although I found Eichenbaum and Orbach's discussion of women's "merged attachments" useful and have drawn my summary from theirs, the authors do not discuss the impact differences of race, class, and sexual orientation have on their subject.

3. For their conceptualization of the issues surrounding racism and its relation to sexism, and for the necessity of redefining commonality and difference, I am particularly indebted to the discussions of Bell Hooks and Audre Lorde. Bell Hooks, *Feminist Theory: From Margin to Center* (Boston: South End Press, 1984), and Audre Lorde, "Age, Race, Class, and Sex: Women Redefining Dif-

ference," in *Racism and Sexism: An Integrated Study* (New York: St. Martin's Press, 1988), pp. 352–59.

4. For illuminating applications of recent feminist theory to women's friend-ships see Elizabeth Abel, "(E)Merging Identities: The Dynamics of Female Friendship in Contemporary Fiction by Women," *Signs* 6, no. 3 (1981), 418–21, and Judith Kegan Gardiner, "The (US)es of (I)dentity: A Response to Abel on '(E)Merging Identities,'" *Signs* 6, no. 3 (1981), 436–42.

5. I am not using the language of community in the sense of a literary tradi-tion as described by Sandra A. Zagarell, "Narrative of Community: The Identi-fication of a Genre," *Signs* 13, no. 3 (1988), 498–527. *The Salt Eaters,* for instance, is certainly a narrative of community and, as Zagarell might suggest, Bambara's shaping of a "racial community anchored in history and culture" is an explicit goal of her writing. I mean *community* to be taken in the more general sense of a social grouping of people whether that is a family or another kind of community.

6. Janice G. Raymond, *A Passion for Friends: Toward a Philosophy of Female Affection* (Boston: Beacon Press, 1986).

7. Alice Walker, *Meridian* (New York: Harcourt Brace Jovanovich, 1976). Page numbers appear in parentheses in the text.

8. Interview with Alice Walker in *Black Women Writers at Work,* ed. Claudia Tate (New York: Continuum, 1983), pp. 175–87.

9. I am indebted to my colleague and friend Susan Danielson for my under-standing of the civil rights movement in relation to *Meridian* and for many in-sights into the text. Susan Danielson, "Alice Walker's *Meridian,* Feminism, and the 'Movement,'" *Women's Studies* 16 (1989), 317–30.

10. Toni Cade Bambara, *The Salt Eaters* (New York: Random House, 1980). Page numbers appear in parentheses in the text.

11. For a brilliant discussion of structure and meaning in *The Salt Eaters* see Gloria T. Hull, "'What It Is I Think She's Doing Anyhow': A Reading of Toni Cade Bambara's *The Salt Eaters,*" in *Conjuring,* ed. Pryse and Spillers, pp. 216–32.

12. Rosellen Brown, *Civil Wars* (New York: Penguin, 1985). Page numbers appear in parentheses in the text.

13. Sherley Anne Williams, *Dessa Rose* (New York: William Morrow, 1986). Page numbers appear in parentheses in the text.

14. Michelle Wallace, "Slaves of History," *Women's Review of Books* 3, no. 1 (Oct. 1986), 1, 3–4.

15. Toni Morrison, *Beloved* (New York: Knopf, 1987). Page numbers appear in parentheses in the text.

Feminism, "Postfeminism," and Contemporary Women's Fiction

The relationship between women's literature and the rise and fall of social movements may be mapped by the intersections of consciousness, history, and textuality. My own work in the past has focused on the explicitly engaged fiction written during eras of intense political activity like the thirties and, for women, the late sixties and seventies—fiction inscribing the radical consciousness and deliberately intervening in the ideological struggles of its time. Here I want to explore how women's fictions respond to the changes in consciousness and vision that accompany not only the rise but also the decline, revision, or institutionalization of social movements. How do the writers of a more conservative era (some of them, of course, the same individuals who wrote during the full flush of revolutionary optimism) treat the progressive ideas and passions of a passing historical moment—ideas and passions that may seem to have borne too slender a harvest before the frost set in? How do their texts respond to the literary and political legacy of a more radical decade and simultaneously to that radicalism's impasse? How do they revise, modify, incorporate, or interrogate the ideas and texts of their predecessors, sometimes their own earlier selves? And what do they have to tell us, as readers, about the probable and possible directions for further social change?

To explore these questions, I will offer a comparative reading of two groups of contemporary texts that I call, respectively, "feminist" and "postfeminist." Many women's novels in the 1970s and early 1980s inscribed, as the proletarian literature of the thirties did for the left, the ideas, struggles, and visions of the women's liberation movement. Indeed, as Jan Clausen has pointed out, women writers in the United States have had positions of extraordinary influence in that movement, their works often read, not always with happy results, as political statements, even as political directives.[1] But in the mid-eighties, especially since 1985, a new tendency in women's novels emerged—a series of sometimes troubling but potentially instructive revisions of the feminist narratives that dominated women's fiction in the 1970s and early 1980s. I call this tendency *postfeminist*, a word I use to connote not the death of feminism but its uneven incorporation and revision inside the social and cultural texts of a more conservative era. The term, read analogously to terms like *postmodernist* or *postrevolutionary*, acknowledges the existence of a world and a discourse that have been fundamentally altered by feminism.[2] So understood, *postfeminism* can be a useful term of analysis, one with a descriptive power that makes it worth retaining. This essay attempts to define and distinguish between feminist and postfeminist textual politics in women's novels written in North America in the 1970s and 1980s.

The works from which I have derived my generalizations include Toni Morrison's *Sula* (1973), Marge Piercy's *Woman on the Edge of Time* (1976), Marilynne Robinson's *Housekeeping* (1980), and Alice Walker's *The Color Purple* (1982), which I designate "feminist" texts; and Louise Erdrich's *Love Medicine* (1984), Jan Clausen's *Sinking, Stealing* (1985), Margaret Atwood's *The Handmaid's Tale* (1986), Sue Miller's *The Good Mother* (1986), and Anne Roiphe's *Lovingkindness* (1987), which I designate "postfeminist."[3] Almost all these texts have captured both mass popularity and critical attention in the feminist and often the nonfeminist literary/academic community—that is, they have resonated persistently both in popular imagination and in criticism. Four of them have inspired film versions. These novels, particularly those I identify as feminist, have begun to constitute a canon of their own in women's studies circles—reviewed and analyzed in journals, assigned in classes, discussed at professional meetings.

These texts have in common with one another, and with feminist theory, their concern for the indicators of power—gender, race, class, sexuality—that affect women's lives and their privileging of women's consciousness, women's subjectivity, and, therefore, women's agency. I see all these works as part of a larger tradition of socially concerned women's fiction that extends back into the nineteenth century. Yet my reading also locates important differences between the two groups of texts.

Feminist novels take their textual life from an encoding of the dynamic of women's oppression and women's resistance. Many—especially those in the realist mode, the majority mode of American feminist novels—narrate a mythic progress from oppression, suffering, victimization, through various stages of awakening consciousness to active resistance and, finally, to some form of victory, transformation, or transcendence of despair. Feminist novels privilege women's bonding and female friendships; reject, marginalize, or subvert heterosexual love and passion; and interrogate family and motherhood. Their characteristic modalities are the bildung and the utopia. Their characteristic tone compounds rage at women's oppression and revolutionary optimism about the possibility for change.

Postfeminist novels, like postfeminist culture and ideology generally, retain an awareness of male domination in gendered relations. They are, however, less clear about what can be done, and more likely to grieve and worry than to rage and hope. They tend to reinstate (though still to problematize) heterosexual passion and heterosexual love, as well as familial relations, perhaps especially motherhood. They are more skeptical than optimistic, more aware of limits than transgressive of traditional boundaries, more elegiac than "bildungsromanic." They often retain a vision of injustice and a longing to redress it. But the narrative of oppression, growing consciousness, resistance, and transformation is replaced by a multiplicity of plots, and the revolutionary chorus of the feminism of the seventies is replaced by multiple inharmonious voices, often contradicting one another within the same text. Such novels do not by any means reject feminist analysis wholesale but rather find it, implicitly more often than explicitly, insufficient as an account of the diversity of women's experiences or naively optimistic about the possibilities for change, given the disheartening evidence in the eighties of patriarchy's staying power. Often ambiguous, and clearly embodying a retreat from the visionary politics of their predecessors, these novels may nevertheless through their very contradictions help in reformulating a more honest and inclusive feminism.

Three qualifications need stating before I turn to the novels themselves. First, I do not mean to imply that no one today is writing feminist novels. Some novels that do fit my definition of a feminist novel have been published quite recently.[4] Other recent women's novels with feminist themes have been rejected by publishers convinced that they won't sell.[5] And the popularity of works with postfeminist themes, of course, owes a great deal to the power of a few influential editors, publishers, and reviewers, and to subsequent manipulation by public relations departments. Such interventions—a publisher's judgment on what will sell, a reviewer's instinct for what is important and/or trendy, a clever and expensive marketing campaign—are of course crucial to the process of literary production under capitalism.[6] So I am not suggesting that the feminist novel abruptly ended in, let us say, 1984. I am suggesting that some of the most popular and widely discussed women's novels published since then that address women's issues at all represent various departures from their feminist predecessors, and that the nature of their departures can be instructive to feminists.

My second qualification has to do with the inclusion in my feminist and postfeminist canon of various works by women of color. Chikwenye Okonjo Ogunyemi argues in "Womanism: The Dynamics of the Contemporary Black Female Novel in English" that most works by contemporary Afro-American and African women writers are not feminist but "womanist." She defines the feminist novel as an openly propagandistic protest against sexism and the patriarchal power structure.

> A reader can expect to find in it some combination of the following themes: a critical perception of and reaction to patriarchy, often articulated through the struggle of a victim or rebel who must face a patriarchal institution; sensitivity to the inequities of sexism allied with an acceptance of women and understanding of the choices open to them; a metamorphosis leading to female victory in a feminist utopia, or a stasis, signifying the failure to eliminate sexism; a style spiced with the acrimony of feminist discourse.

She argues that while a womanist writer may include some of these characteristics, she will also "incorporate racial, cultural, national, economic, and political considerations."[7] Similarly, my colleague Chinosole, a black feminist critic, has suggested that to include women writers of color under my feminist rubric risks assimilating them under a label to which they themselves may not have assented and obliterating their historical ties to their distinctive racial traditions.

The risks of expropriation and distortion are real. Yet Ogunyemi's distinction between womanist and feminist writers seems less useful to me in distinguishing literary texts from one another than in signaling black women's resistance to assimilation. Many white women writers, particularly those with socialist feminist inclinations, explore relations of power inherent in the intersections of race and gender.[8] More important, any definition of a feminist novel that excluded, let us say, *The Color Purple* from its field of reference would fall absurdly short of adequacy.[9] My approach is synchronic rather than diachronic—that is, rather than exploring the historical roots and chronological evolution of a distinctive group of women writers over time, I look in this essay at a range of works by writers of various backgrounds written in a given moment in history—a moment, I would argue, when few writers have been unaffected by the women's liberation movement and when many— even those who do not count themselves as feminists—present imaginative visions profoundly shaped by feminism even as their visions have further given feminism shape. I mean not to expropriate the work of women of color but rather to acknowledge what should be obvious— the fullness of their participation in contemporary feminist discourse.

The third qualification has to do with the permeability of the categories I elaborate above. Obviously, not even the novels I have selected— and there are many others I could have chosen as exemplary—conform fully in each instance to these paradigms. Both *Sula* and *Housekeeping,* for example—novels I designate feminist—have features I am ascribing to the postfeminist novel. And my assignment of certain of the novels, especially *The Handmaid's Tale,* to the postfeminist camp is probably still more controversial than my effort to define and locate the feminist novel. This is true primarily because feminism has been an articulate social movement, while postfeminism is more a cultural tendency, amorphous and contradictory, a difference textually inscribed in the post- feminist text's greater ambiguity, its greater openness to multiple interpretations about basic issues and values. Still, I am convinced that my paradigm does represent a genuine distinction, one important to the literary history of women's fiction and to the politics of a fragmented but potentially regenerative women's movement.

> Theirs is the money and the power, theirs the poisons that slow the mind and dull the heart. Theirs are the powers of life and death. I killed them. Because it is war.
>
> —Consuelo Ramos in Marge Piercy,
> *Woman on the Edge of Time,* p. 375

The narrative movement from oppression and suffering through consciousness-raising to resistance and finally to a form of victory or transcendence is characteristic of many feminist novels. Piercy's *Woman on the Edge of Time* and Alice Walker's *The Color Purple* represent this narrative movement in its purest form. Ostensibly different in form, one juxtaposing a naturalistic present with a utopian future, one an episto- lary novel set in the rural southern past, the novels narrate remarkably similar stories. As I have argued elsewhere, Walker's novel is a utopian novel set in the past just as Piercy's is a utopian novel set in the future.[10]

Piercy structures the realist parts of *Woman on the Edge of Time,* those set in the present, as a typology of oppression suffered by women. In Piercy's socialist feminist vision, class, race, and gender equally deter- mine the fabric of Consuelo Ramos's suffering and struggle. The brutal male violence of the pimp Geraldo leads to her incarceration in Rock- over; the corrupt opportunism of her white-identified brother Luis (now Lewis) precludes her escape. Most powerful symbols of authority, the white male doctors in the hospital exercise a lethal control over the poor, minority, female, and gay patients, who themselves constitute a typology of the oppressed. In *Woman on the Edge of Time,* the mental health bureaucracy and its machinery of hospitals, drugs, and punitive "experimental" procedures emblematize patriarchy at its worst. Connie's growth in consciousness under the tutelage of her alter ego from the future, the bisexual Indian Luciente, and her eventual engagement in acts of resistance that she defines as acts of war constitute the central drama of the text. The narrative moves Consuelo inexorably toward the recognition and action implied by her words in the epigram to this section. Conscripting readers as participants in the same linear evolution, the narrative enacts the central feminist myth in its purest form—a woman's progress from passivity to action, from weakness to strength, from victimization to agency, from silence to expression, from oppression to liberation. Oppression is the present; liberation, the future. Connie's final incarceration at the conclusion of the novel does not represent a defeat but rather a victory: her poisoning of the symbolic doctors ensures us that the future will be ours, if we, like Consuelo, will fight for it.

The Color Purple moves its hero, Celie, through stages similar to those in *Woman on the Edge of Time.* Suffering and victimization: Celie is raped by her stepfather; separated forcibly from her sister; raped, beaten, humiliated by her husband; always negated and unheard. An awakening of consciousness: Celie recognizes the difference between her relation with Mr.—— and Sophia's with Harpo, with a dawning sense that female passivity is not the only possible response to male domination; her erotic encounter with Shug, a sexual awakening that elides into a political awakening as well, leads her to an understanding of the sexual politics that have deprived her of sexuality, voice, power. Resistance: razor in hand, she considers and rejects violence; finding her own voice, she eloquently curses Mr.——; together, the women laugh spontaneously at the ignorance and rigidity of the men; together, they travel to Memphis and establish a female-centered household in Shug's vaginal pink house with its round bed, Shug the priestess of a female culture of resistance; Celie establishes her economic independence as an entrepeneur sewing comfortable pants for women and men alike. Transformation: a new social order emerges, freer, more humane, more androgynous than the old. The progress of this novel thus reflects, like *Woman on the Edge of Time,* the deepest longings and hopes of feminism for profound social change.

The linear movement of these texts brooks no opposition; they muster all the resources of narrative to enlist the reader in the protagonist-hero's camp. To use Benveniste's categories, as reinterpreted by Catherine Belsey, these works combine features of the declarative texts of classic realism, which construct the reader as a subject who knows, who receives knowledge, with those of the imperative texts of political polemic, those constructing the reader as one who struggles, who identifies with one set of discourses and practices in opposition to another set.[11] Obviously, not all novels directly influenced by feminism inscribe this progress so emphatically. *Sula,* for example, presents a far more ambiguous fictive world, its narrative ordered around the experience of a female character who inflicts and dispassionately watches suffering, as well as enduring it. Like *The Color Purple,* but with greater historical specificity, *Sula* tells the story of a black community in white America.[12] This particular community is born in exploitation at the novel's beginning and dies at the end, drowned in the unfinished tunnel that symbolizes the failure of its hopes. Structurally, Sula represents that community in the novel, even as the community rejects her and transforms her ritually into its scapegoat.

Sula plays a variant on the dynamic of female oppression and resistance, transforming it into a narrative of social rigidity and female subversion. Sula's refusal (or inability) to behave decorously, fix on a mate, settle down, reproduce; her insistence on defying such fundamental codes of behavior as the taboo against sleeping with white men; even her indulgent affair with her best friend's husband constitute a form of resistance, not so much against male dominance as against the sex-gender system as it operates within her black community. Like many, perhaps all, feminist heroes, her presence in the text subverts and interrogates the gendered relations and behavior considered natural and normal by the dominant culture.[13]

Closely related to and often integrated within the narrative of oppression and resistance, or, in more ambiguous texts like *Sula,* of rigidity and subversion, is the narrative of female bonding, friendship, kinship, "reparenting."[14] Often in feminist novels—certainly in both *Woman on the Edge of Time* and *The Color Purple,* for example—the hero's mythic progress is guided and mediated by a mentor who also becomes friend and sometimes lover—Luciente in *Woman on the Edge of Time,* clearly Connie's alter ego, an embodiment of the potentials within her that a differently structured social world would allow to blossom; Shug in *The Color Purple,* whose acceptance of and love for Celie undoes the harms of years of oppression and nurtures her into love, laughter, and a healthy interdependence.

Sometimes the narrative of female bonding constitutes the central movement of feminist novels, as two women enact dramas of separation and individuation, rupture and reconciliation, renunciation and consummation. Indeed, the movement toward (or, in some instances, away from) the bonding of two female figures, whether friend and friend, aunt and niece, loved and lover, constitutes one of the most pervasive of feminist narrative strategies. Certainly *Sula* exemplifies this pattern. As Barbara Smith pointed out in her classic essay, "Toward a Black Feminist Criticism," the novel must be read not simply as the story of the rebellion and death of one subversive black woman, but as the story of a relationship between its two central female characters, Sula and Nel.[15] Nel's marriage to Jude marks the moment of separation between the childhood friends, and Nel's discovery of Jude's adultery with Sula widens their breach. Yet the novel moves irrevocably toward Nel's final recognition that all these years it is Sula, not Jude, she has been missing. And Sula's final thoughts evoke her oldest and only habit of intimacy: "Wait'll I tell Nel."[16] The novel belongs as much to Nel as to Sula; its narrative moves Nel toward an epiphany that represents a fundamental change of consciousness, one that enables Nel, unlike Sula, not only to mourn for what she has lost but also to regret what she has betrayed— her human commonality with the Sula fascinated by death as well as by life.

Marilynne Robinson's *Housekeeping*, like *Sula* a text that deploys a set of tensions characterized by alienation, deviance, subversion, marginality, on the one hand, and community, society, and heterocentrist rigidity on the other, provides another example of the plot of female bonding. In the female and elemental world of this novel, two bereft girls and their hobo aunt, even more than Sula a self-exiled outcast utterly indifferent to the mores of the local community, establish a tenuous household in which house is not kept, but rather allowed to decline gradually into earth and water, until the intercession of horrified townspeople and the defection of the more conventional of the two girls bring the housekeeping to its end. At the book's conclusion, the aunt and the older girl, the narrator, leave town together as wanderers, misfits by temperament, chance, and choice, whose bonds with one another help to redeem their losses and lighten the burden of their memories. In this novel of "reparenting," both aunt and niece save one another from the isolation of absolute uniqueness and eventually constitute a community of two that challenges from the margins the decorum and conventionality of middle American life.

The centrality of relations among women in feminist novels coincides with their tendency to demystify, reject, marginalize, or subvert the narratives of heterosexual love and passion that constitute so much pre-twentieth-century literature and so much popular literature today. As Rachel Blau DuPlessis has pointed out, this subversion of the romance, with its inevitable resolution in marriage or death, generally separates women's fictions of the nineteenth century from those of the twentieth.[17] Indeed, heterosexual romance plots in feminist novels are not simply subverted; they have become, in much of this literature, virtually irrelevant. In the mid-eighties, however, such narratives were re-admitted to women's fiction, constituting one of the hallmarks of postfeminist fiction.

Not that feminist fiction obliterated physical passion. Pop feminist novels like Erica Jong's *Fear of Flying* (1973), Rita Mae Brown's lesbian bildung *Rubyfruit Jungle* (1973), or Kate Millett's lesbian romance *Sita* (1976) moved the gratification of female desire, and the rewriting of taboos concerning its presence and expression, to their narrative centers. But in novels like these, women become the initiating agents of their own fulfillment and, more important, agents of their own discourses of eroticism, which they do not confuse with everlasting love. Many feminist novels problematize the sexual politics of heterosexuality, though usually only as one moment, one thread, in larger plots of personal and political awakening: much of Atwood's work, Piercy's *Small Changes* (1972), Walker's *Meridian* (1976), French's *The Women's Room* (1977). Some, like both *Sula* and *The Color Purple*, contain plots that feature triangular relations in which men are marginal, the female friendship primary.

In *The Color Purple*, Mr.——, whose brutally controlling presence dominates the first part of the book, recedes gradually into powerlessness as the two women, his wife and his lover, unite in a homoerotic bond of their own until, in the crucial Memphis sections of the book, he is exiled not only from Celie's life but from the text itself, reappearing finally as a rehabilitated male who sits on the porch helping Celie sew the androgynous pants that have won her her self-sufficiency. This process is not always so simple. Margaret Homans suggests that Nel's cry at the conclusion of *Sula*—"a fine cry—loud and long—but it had no bottom and it had no top, just circles and circles of sorrow" (p. 149)— expresses "her woman-identified self," "her allegiance to Sula and her protest against the violence of heterosexuality." Locating one source of *Sula*'s undeniable ambiguity, she points out that "the heterosexuality that the novel thematically devalues nonetheless evokes (its) most spectacular passage, Sula's prose poem about making love with Ajax, while Nel's woman-identified cry is, paradoxically, nonmetaphoric, referentless, non-representational"—a paradox, she suggests, with disturbing implications for female self-expression.[18]

Yet other feminist novels seem untroubled about virtually eliminating heterosexual passion, and sometimes men themselves. This is especially true of utopian or experimental fiction like Sally Miller Gearhart's *The*

Wanderground (1979), Toni Cade Bambara's *The Salt Eaters* (1980), or Bertha Harris's masterpiece of lesbian modernism, *Lover* (1976). It is also true of Robinson's *Housekeeping*, a novel written in a mode I can only call mythic realism. As Elizabeth Meese points out in an extended analysis of the novel, Robinson presents

> a world almost exclusively populated by women, where experience filters through female consciousness and reflects the actions of women. This is not a world of Amazons or utopian androgynes. . . . It is not the milieu of Ernest Hemingway, Jack Kerouac, or Norman Mailer in reverse. . . . she elects the "unnatural"—to characterize women's experience in its own right, thereby subverting the oppositional view of seeing and understanding women only or principally in relation to men. The politics of sexual relationship are for the most part enacted off-stage. . . . In this choice lies Robinson's single most significant strategy for the construction of a world endowed with striking originality and artistic force.[19]

Meese emphasizes the singularity of *Housekeeping;* while indebted to her fine analysis, I emphasize the novel's continuity with other texts of feminist fiction.

A related tendency in these novels, reflecting the theory and practice of the women's movement, questions the primacy of the nuclear family and the centrality for women of motherhood. In feminist novels, family life, when it is depicted at all, appears typically boring at best, oppressive and destructive at worst. Much feminist fiction poses possibilities for the dismantling of traditional familial structures and the establishment of other relations of support and nurturance. In Piercy's *Woman on the Edge of Time* families are replaced by other configurations—sweet friends, pillow friends, comothers—all relations of choice rather than of blood, all resolutely structured to eliminate the monogamous nuclear couple from the social fabric. This novel radically severs the connections between culture and biology, between reproduction, sexuality, and mothering—a rejection of biological determinism that lies at the heart of much feminist theory. *The Color Purple* is less resolutely antifamilial, since Celie's rupture from and longing for her sister Nettie permeate the text and since Nettie's own marriage and that of Adam and Tashi constitute an important part of the novel's utopian closure—a family reunion, in every sense of the word. Yet the novel's most evocatively familial scenes take place far from the site of blood kinship, in Shug's erotic but not exactly domestic digs in Memphis; and the novel's primary and most appealing relationship is the erotic—indeed, adulterous—relationship between Celie and Shug. *Housekeeping* fractures family life and familial bonds, not by eliminating them but by reducing them to the intense, isolated association of aunt and niece, whose unconventional "household" becomes a comment on and perceived threat to the conventional family life, the heterocentrist orthodoxy, of the rest of the town. Unlike many other feminist novels, *Housekeeping* resonates with loss, mourning the successive deaths and growing dearth of close kin, but ultimately it shares with other feminist novels a certain delight, albeit a tentative and ambivalent one, in the final freedom from familial, sexual, and geographic bonds and expectations.

Feminist novels, then, have interrogated two of the institutions essential to the maintenance of patriarchal power: heterosexuality and family life. They have frequently situated their critiques within a broader context of class and race relations. Their narratives have been bildungsromans in a particular sense—stories of political awakening and resistance, their tone most typically a compound of rage against injustice and hope for a better world. As such, they are an important site for the production and representation of feminist ideologies.

> I used to attend meetings. I used to have ambitions. I used to read books. I used to love women.
> —Josie in Jan Clausen, *Sinking, Stealing*, p. 249

The linear progress of feminist narratives, like their utopian vision, has been hard to sustain in the contemporary era. The discouraging victories of the neoconservatives have pushed much discourse rightward; the initial culture shock of women's mass entry into the labor force, a process feminism helped to mediate, has abated;[20] feminists have increasingly recognized, but have not always been able to work across, the vast differences among women in race, nationality, class; feminists may have made some mistakes in emphasis and strategy that cost us potential allies;[21] and finally, feminism has not been immune to the postmodern impulse to question all totalizing theories. So we see now the emergence of the feminist novels' progeny, the postfeminist novels, as linked to them as daughter to mother and sometimes as rebellious. In fact, several postfeminist novels feature daughters for whom their mothers' feminism is problematic. Anne Roiphe's *Lovingkindness* is prototypical, though its reaction against feminism is harsher and more explicit than most, and disturbingly homophobic. This novel, narrated by a feminist mother whose daughter rebels against too much freedom and too much pressure toward achievement, moves toward a resolution in which the mother finally colludes in her daughter's flight into the safety of the most rigid form of religious orthodoxy. *Lovingkindness*, like most postfeminist novels, contains competing voices—feminist voices and voices that question the verities, the consequences, the universal applicability of feminism.

The narrator, a feminist professor, concludes in one long passage explaining her decision not to attend a feminist symposium, "Strategies needed reshaping. It was not a time to be giving lectures" (p. 37). The passage is a strange admixture of feminist anger and anger at feminism.

Yet postfeminist fiction shares a good deal with its feminist predecessors. Most important, it has retained a vision of women's oppression. Margaret Atwood's *The Handmaid's Tale*, Sue Miller's *The Good Mother*, and Jan Clausen's *Sinking, Stealing* contain excoriating and frightening representations of patriarchal power. In *The Good Mother*, the protagonist, Anna, loses custody of her daughter, Molly, to her ex-husband and his new wife, both proper lawyers judged to offer a far more respectable home life than a single mother with small means and no profession. In *The Handmaid's Tale*, a dystopian fantasy, a fundamentalist regime overthrows the current U.S. government and transforms it into the fascist theocracy of Gilead. Through flashbacks we learn that the protagonist, Offred (of Fred, her master), has lost her husband and her daughter in a failed effort to escape to Canada. Her feminist mother has been shipped to the colonies to clean up toxic wastes and die. Her new role in life, after suitable indoctrination, consists entirely of mating with her master—in the company of his wife—until she bears them a child, since the gradual poisoning of the environment has rendered most women of childbearing age sterile. (Men too suffer from sterility—though the ideology of Gilead will not admit it.)

As in *The Color Purple* and *Woman on the Edge of Time*, women in these novels lose those most dear to them at the hands of powerful men or powerful male-dominated institutions. In *Woman on the Edge of Time*, *The Handmaid's Tale*, and *The Good Mother* the worst loss is that of a biological daughter. The loss of a child—the daughter of the protagonist's female lover, killed in an automobile accident—motivates the plot too of Jan Clausen's novel, *Sinking, Stealing*, postfeminist in its bleakness of mood and unraveling of the feminist myth of liberation, though it undertakes an analysis of marriage and heterosexuality that can only be considered feminist.[22] That women should suffer the threat or actuality of both physical violation and profound emotional loss constitutes a central dimension of almost all these novels, feminist and postfeminist alike. The deepest anxieties common to these books arise from women's loss of control over their bodies, their physical selves, and the disruption of the human relationships that mean most to them.

Both feminist and postfeminist novels also frequently define women's issues in economic terms. Celie belongs to a world of southern black farmers and sharecroppers; in her emergence from poverty and ignorance as she acquires knowledge and a measure of economic independence, Walker represents both the utopian aspirations of black women and the historical transformation of southern black culture imminent with the onset of World War II. Consuelo Ramos, with roots like Celie's in a rural childhood, grows up to experience the struggles and humiliations of the urban ghettoes; the Mattapoisett sections of the novel dwell extensively on Piercy's utopian socialist solutions to economic problems.

Anna in *The Good Mother* is downwardly mobile after her divorce—deliberately so, until she learns to her dismay that money and the things it can buy (like live-in nannies) matter the moment one's life comes under the scrutiny of social workers and courts, a revelation not unlike Consuelo Ramos's. Offred recalls in horror the moment in the right-wing revolution when she loses independent access to her own bank account and her job in one agonizing and banal afternoon: all women in the new society are now totally dependent economically on male partners. She wonders retrospectively if Luke, her deeply loved husband, has not on some level been pleased with this transaction. "He doesn't mind it at all," she thinks. "Maybe he even likes it. We are not each other's anymore. Instead, I am his" (p. 236).

Postfeminist texts, then, like postfeminist culture and ideology generally, do retain a pained sense of gender inequity. But they are less clear than feminist texts about how to fight it, or even about who the enemy is. They are less likely to locate the sources of inequity primarily in a masculine lust for power and control or a male ruling class's determination to maintain its privileged status; they are more likely to acknowledge a diversity of human conduct that includes mistakes and totalitarian inclinations among women, decencies and vulnerabilities even among men. As complexity of vision, this tendency can enrich postfeminist texts; as ambivalence, it can depoliticize the very issues they raise.

The Handmaid's Tale is the most explicitly political of these postfeminist novels. Indeed, one might well read it more as a socialist feminist critique of both the New Right and of radical feminism than as a postfeminist novel. But it shares with other postfeminist fiction a deep skepticism about myths of political progress, and a preference for ambiguity over certainty. In Piercy's utopia, patriarchal capitalism is clearly the enemy. Atwood's dystopia suggests that the advent of the totalitarian theocracy owes something to radical feminist collusion with the religious right, especially on silencing pornography. Its unforgettable rendition of the couvade, the attendance of the Handmaids at the birth of a new baby to one of their number, as her mistress sits above her on the birthing stool, culminates in an interrogation of the tendency of some feminists to build a politics on a romanticized association of women's biology and women's culture: "Mother, I think. Wherever you may be.

Can you hear me? You wanted a women's culture. Well, now there is one. It isn't what you meant, but it exists. Be thankful for small mercies" (p. 164). The irony of this passage is a characteristic postfeminist stance.

In such works, the narrative of oppression, growing consciousness, resistance, and victory is replaced by a multiplicity of plots, sometimes contained within the same text, or is called into question by other structural devices that insist on an ambiguity of interpretation. In *The Good Mother*, Anna, the narrator, gets an amicable divorce from her lawyer husband, Brian, primarily because both of them are bored with their unimpassioned marriage. Anna takes custody of their four-year-old daughter, Molly. Subsequently she becomes involved with the talented and vital artist Leo, with whom she feels herself to be, for the first time, "a passionate person" (p. 116). Fleetingly, the intensity of Anna's maternal involvement with her daughter decreases, but gradually she includes both Molly and Leo in a warm circle of love, a "new world . . . where I was beautiful, sex together was beautiful, and Molly was part of our love, our life" (p. 236). This idyllic fusion of the maternal and the erotic is disrupted when Brian accuses Leo of sexually abusing Molly. Half paralyzed with terror at the prospect of losing her daughter, Anna sacrifices her relationship with Leo. But Brian and his new wife, Brenda, win custody, and at the end of the book, bereft of both her lover and her daughter, Anna begins painfully to reorganize her life around the effort to maintain limited contact with Molly.

Some feminists have loved *The Good Mother*; others have been outraged by it.[23] They hate Anna's passivity in the face of danger, resent the implication that Anna is somehow to blame for what has happened to her, object to the valorization of traditional motherhood and family life implied by Anna's bereft longing at the conclusion, and resent what seems to them a cautionary tale warning women not to seek too much pleasure in life lest they be punished for it. What has perhaps most disturbed feminist readers, however, is this novel's narrative reversal of the progress of the feminist myth. *The Good Mother* begins at the moment when many feminist plots—starting perhaps with Ibsen's *Doll House*—end: with the departure of the wife from the stuffy husband, the final rejection of the domestic routine. It begins, that is, with an event that has marked, in many feminist texts, the moment of transcendence, the assertion of self over circumstance, the remaking of one's world. When Anna's happiness is shattered by Brian's phone call, she becomes more victim than agent, despairingly trying to outguess the social workers and courts in her effort to keep custody of Molly, masking the grounds and implications of her own rebellion against conformity, tradition, upward mobility, nuclear family life, in her vain effort to convince the

patriarchal bureaucracy that she is indeed a "good mother." At the conclusion, her only triumph is a will to resist despair, an ability to contemplate with a certain dignity the remaking of her life on new and
unsatisfactory terms.

Like *Housekeeping*, *The Good Mother* suggests the possibility for re-
configuring a household to magnify the enjoyment and minimize the
conventional obligations of its mother (or mother-surrogate)/daugh-
ter inhabitants. But whereas *Housekeeping* moves toward Sylvie's and
Ruthie's flight from the social order into a subversive transiency, *The
Good Mother* leads toward Anna's submission to that order. Like Consuelo Ramos, Anna has lost a child to the interventions of the state.
Unlike Piercy's novel, though, this one offers no suggestion of political
struggle or resolution, no real suggestion of the possibility for social
change. Anna's only hope seems to lie in cooperation with the courts,
the social workers, the psychiatrists, some of whom, unlike Piercy's
monolithic bureaucrats, are represented as both intelligent and decent
human beings. She loses Molly partly because her own guilt leads her to
make damaging disclosures that persuade the especially conservative
judge assigned her case of her dangerous lifestyle. Anna's isolation embodies the kind of individualism, her guilt the kind of self-hatred, and
her cooperation the kind of compliance with "the system" that feminist
texts challenged. Where feminist novels express hope, a kind of revolutionary optimism, this postfeminist novel expresses skepticism and
doubt; where feminist novels encode quests for identity and expression
and move their protagonists and readers toward a heightened social consciousness, this one asserts a recognition of limits, a sense of the hard
possibilities for individual failure. Like Roiphe's book, *The Good Mother*
encodes some of the deepest anxieties of feminist claims—demands, often, on ourselves. Anna resolutely refuses to be a superwoman; the plot
refuses her the role of warrior hero. Yet its critique of the patriarchal
social structures that ultimately judge her life as a single mother partakes
of, indeed is enabled by, feminist analysis. This ambiguity helps to explain the divided reaction among its feminist readers.

The Handmaid's Tale, even more than *The Good Mother*, rewrites the
feminist myth into a dystopian nightmare. It is almost as though Atwood, in her fantasy of the future, has deliberately reversed Piercy's
dreams in *Woman on the Edge of Time* of a socialist feminist victory. The
nightmare itself is still a feminist nightmare: a detailed delineation of
right-wing Christian fundamentalism extrapolated to its furthest patriarchal extreme. As in feminist narratives, *The Handmaid's Tale* depicts a
movement from the protagonist's passive submission—here, not out of
lack of knowledge but out of fear and hopelessness and numbed grief

over the loss of her husband and daughter—to her gradual resistance, and finally to her ultimate flight via underground railroad—a flight presumably successful, since her story has been transmitted to us, constituting the body of the novel. Yet Atwood adds a surprise twist to Offred's narrative. In a final section titled "Historical Notes on The Handmaid's Tale," we hear the manuscript discussed at an academic conference on Gileadean Studies convened in 2195. The keynote speaker intones pompously about the academic significance of the manuscript and makes sexist jokes about "tale" and "tail," and about "underground frailroads." The epilogue disrupts reader identification with Offred, distances the narrative, and reveals thereby a postfeminist sense of irony. Meaning lies in the interplay between Offred's narration, full of circularities and lacunae of its own, and its surprising frame. Is Atwood offering hope or despair? The possibility for liberation or the inevitability of sexual oppression? I see her text as writing against precisely such dualisms. Whatever else it does, the text opposes the dualistic mind-set of "either-or": the mind-set of Gilead, in which a woman under certain circumstances becomes an unwoman, in which a baby born deformed is an unbaby; but also the mind-set in which one who is not antiporn is proporn, in which matriarchy is the answer to patriarchy. Both in structure and in substance, the text warns that a democratic society must be content with imperfection, lest freedom falter in the process of embracing one side of a false antinomy.[24]

Louise Erdrich's successful recent novel *Love Medicine* weaves together stories of modern American Indian life, composing a fabric whose warp and woof are two entwined narratives: Nector Kashpaw's attempt to reconcile his divided love for Marie Lazarre, his wife, and for Lulu Lamartine, his mistress; and Lipsha Morrissey's quest for his identity, for knowledge of his parentage. The triangular relationship between Nector, Lulu, and Marie may be read in the light of feminist fiction as a narrative of female bonding.[25] As in many feminist novels, this plot works finally to eliminate the male, Nector, who dies before either of the women. In a richly comic finale set in an old age home, Marie and Lulu come at last to a mutual understanding and respect. Lulu, who narrates this episode, accepts help from Marie when she is temporarily blinded after a cataract operation, shortly after Nector's death. The two women mourn Nector together; Lulu recalls, "For the first time I saw exactly how another woman felt, and it gave me deep comfort, surprising" (p. 236). The final image of the chapter is one of female reparenting; Lulu, her bandages removed, sees Marie swaying down "like a dim mountain, huge and blurred, the way a mother must look to her just born child" (p. 236).

In this postfeminist novel, however, there is room for the traditional masculine quest for paternal identify, the yearning "to be a son of a father" (p. 271), in Lipsha Morrissey's words, as well as for the feminist valorization of bonding among women. Lipsha's quest for identity falls as much to the reader as to Lipsha; it is specifically a quest for the lost father. Erdrich lets the reader know early the identity of his mother, but withholds his father's identity till the conclusion, thus forcing the question of his paternity into the foreground and making its answer crucial to the textual structure of meaning. Lipsha is the son of Gerry Nanapush, "famous politicking hero, dangerous armed criminal, judo expert, escape artist, charismatic member of the American Indian Movement, and smoker of many pipes of kinnikinnick in the most radical groups. That was . . . Dad" (p. 248). He is also grandson of Old Man Pillager, a mysterious figure in whom ancient shamanic powers still reside. The Lipsha plot has feminist elements: he himself is an androgynous figure who seems unlikely to join the masculinist world of the other characters, even though his father (to a feminist) exemplifies that world. He must learn to acknowledge his matrilineage, including his biological mother, June Morrissey, the numinous female figure whose spirit broods over the text as a whole, and his grandmother, Lulu Lamartine, as well as Marie Lazarre, who has raised him. But this plot remains essentially a quest for identity and manhood—a quest predicated on the importance of knowing one's paternity.

It should be apparent from the discussion of narrative patterns in these works that many postfeminist novels restore heterosexual love and passion to a position of considerable importance. *The Good Mother*, in part a novel of a repressed woman's sexual awakening, positively throbs with Anna's and Leo's acrobatic passion, lingering on every detail of their sexual encounters. Lulu Lamartine's jubilant sexuality in *Love Medicine* produces a host of offspring; her lifelong affair with Nector provides a series of tragicomic episodes that cumulatively infuse the text with a rich eroticism. In the repressed and secretly perverse world of Gilead, Offred risks death to carry on a liaison with Nick, the chauffeur, who finally becomes her liberator. The patterns of relationship and desire between men and women thus figure in recent fiction by women as one of a number of possible "stories." I suspect, though, that feminism has changed the terms of discourse too profoundly for their restoration to the center of narrativity—or to the center of women's lives.

Certainly these novels, at least those written by heterosexual women, relax feminism's political critique of heterosexuality as institution. Yet they do not abandon it completely. Anna tells Leo, enraged at his judgment of her for her lack of commitment to her music: "It used to be that men would say, 'I want a woman who' and the list would be a little different. 'Who cooks, who sews, who can entertain my friends.' But it's the same impulse. The same impulse. It's still *your* judgment, *your* list, your game. Just all the rules have changed.... You're still saying I'm just an extension of you, that I'd better look good to the world so I make you look good. That's all it is" (p. 118). Ultimately, Anna cannot take Leo back, though he still loves her; it is she who rejects him. Yet Miller's portrayal of Leo and of his and Anna's passion and playfulness have been so positive that readers must feel her final rejection of Leo as her loss. Lulu Lamartine thinks about Nector, "He always did have to have his candy come what might and whether Lulu or Marie was damaged by his taking it. All that mattered was his greed." Yet she goes on to acknowledge some of the same greed in herself: "We took our pleasure without asking or thinking further than a touch" (p. 231). In these postfeminist novels, as in postfeminism generally, feminism's critique of heterosexuality as a social institution exists in uneasy tension with a tendency to redeem the more joyful aspects of heterosexual relations.

Postfeminist texts differ most from feminist ones in their pervasive nostalgia for family life, whatever its boredoms and betrayals. The feminist mother in *Lovingkindness,* who looks with real horror at the narrow religious profamilism of her indoctrinated daughter and her daughter's fiancé, both initiates into Jewish Chasidic orthodoxy, ultimately supports their choice because she cannot be sure she has anything better to offer. *Love Medicine, The Good Mother,* and *The Handmaid's Tale* have in common a valorization of the bonds and influences of family. *Love Medicine* is preeminently a family epic, composed of interlocking stories of three familial configurations: Kashpaws, Lazarre/Morrisseys, and Nanapushes, linked by the union of Gerry Nanapush and June Morrissey. One can barely read it without making a family tree. Self-knowledge in the novel means knowledge of one's parentage and, through parentage, one's heritage. "You never knew who you were," Lulu tells Lipsha, her newly acknowledged grandson. "That's one reason why I told you. I thought it was a knowledge that would make or break you" (p. 245). At the conclusion of *The Good Mother,* Anna reconciles herself to Molly's loss: "Brenda is pregnant again, and Molly is part of a family there. She loves being a big sister, she loves them—Brian and Brenda and Elizabeth, the baby. And sometimes when I imagine how it must be—the order, the deep pleasure in what happens predictably, each day, the healing beauty of everything that is commonplace—I yearn again myself to be in a family" (p. 308). Anna goes on to regret the "diminished and fragile connections" in her own maternal family, whose "affectionate and difficult hierarchy" has been so important in her own life. She broods over the loss of the "safe circle of family that closed the world out," for "No matter what the price, I think there was value in all that" (p. 309). Acknowledging that this is not what she can offer her daughter, she takes a certain grim pride in her ability to manage in her "different set of circumstances" (p. 309).

The tone of loss that pervades *The Good Mother* is if anything even more profound, more elegiac in *The Handmaid's Tale*. In this novel, the protagonist is haunted by memories of her husband, Luke, even while she acknowledges his potential for sexism, and of her daughter, whom she cannot bear to name, remembering her only as "she." The novel is infused with a painful and extraordinarily powerful yearning for a configuration of institution and emotion that feminism virtually abandoned: the nuclear family as a locus of both desire and reproduction, erotic and maternal love. Moira, the narrator's radical lesbian friend, emerges as a repository of courage, wit, and audacity, but she is marginalized in the narrative structure and defeated in the end.

In Clausen's *Sinking, Stealing*, the lesbian narrator, Josie, holds center stage. Having established a family unit with her lover, Rhea, and Rhea's daughter, Ericka, she finds after Rhea's death that she has no legal rights whatsoever even to visit the child she has come to love as her own, let alone to continue to act as "flommy." She kidnaps Ericka to try to force her priggish father to grant her more access to the child, but in the end, defeated by his intransigence and worn out by the difficulties of being on the run with a cooperative but anxious nine-year-old, she returns Ericka to her maternal grandparents in Florida, hoping that the girl's grandmother will be able to effect a compromise. This open-ended novel critiques compulsory heterosexuality and the legal institutions that maintain it. Josie turns, as she puts it, "a jaundiced feminist eye" on Daniel's conventional "domestic arrangements" (p. 11). The very suggestion that someone's lesbian lover might become, in effect, a non-biological parent whose rights deserve recognition threatens traditional understandings of family in a way that the heterosexual texts I discuss here do not. Yet Clausen's narrator wants less to disrupt family life than to participate in it on equal terms with heterosexuals. In her effort to do so she, like Anna, acts virtually alone, and, as in *The Good Mother*, the only reference to a feminist community—in this instance a group of lesbian feminists with whom Josie and Ericka take refuge—leaves a distinctly unpleasant impression. Her representation of the lesbian community of Systersea Sharespace, far from providing an attractive alternative, offers a soured caricature of lesbian feminist culture.

Cumulatively, these texts imply the elusiveness of acceptable substitutes for familial life—that is, forms of social relations that will provide some measure of stability, intimacy, and structure in our daily existence. Their renderings of both heterosexual relations and family life imply that postfeminist fiction is partly an effort to reconcile what some feminists have experienced as disparities between ideology and emotion. Although the restoration of scripts of heterosexual romance in some of these novels suggests a retreat from territories hard won for women alone and women together, although the profamilism in some of these novels strikes a disturbingly conservative note, in the long run a renewed feminism can only benefit from such a reconciliation.

Many of these postfeminist texts are infused with a sense of terrible loss. This mourning, unlike that in feminist novels, rarely turns into rage and hope. Stoicism in the face of despair is about the best most of them can manage. Though often they grieve explicitly for the loss of a child, I am convinced that the less tangible loss they mourn is the certainty of the feminist dream, the myth of a progress toward liberation surely attainable within the immediate future.

Yet we as readers need not despair. The interrogative mood of postfeminism is already bringing feminist thought into a potentially fruitful, though ambiguous, alliance with postmodernism.[26] The collapse of a unifying, totalizing analysis of gendered relations of power, inscribed in the dissolution of the feminist myth into multiple stories, multiple narrations, represents an inevitable skepticism about the adequacy of one feminist, even socialist feminist, interpretation of reality to account for the complexity of women's experience, gendered relations, and relations of dominance in general in the modern world. As political philosopher Jane Flax writes in a recent issue of *Signs:* "Any episteme requires the suppression of discourses that threaten to differ with or undermine the authority of the dominant one. Hence within feminist theory a search for a defining theme of the whole or a feminist viewpoint may require the suppression of the important and discomforting voices of persons with experiences unlike our own. The suppression of these voices seems to be a necessary condition of the (apparent) authority, coherence and universality of our own."[27]

Postfeminist literature is a reflux of "other" voices—including the other voices of feminists ourselves. The multivalent, contradictory, conflicting voices of postfeminist texts confirm the postmodern belief that no singular explanation for relations of power will suffice, that no monolithic interpretation or alteration of praxis will in itself effect sweeping social change. If things have indeed fallen apart and the center has not held, including the center of feminist analysis, perhaps we need to delight rather than despair in the loosing of mere anarchy upon the world, in the fluidity and multiplicity afforded us. Our acknowledgment of partiality, disunity, imperfection—an acknowledgment cumulatively rendered by postfeminist texts—can empower instead of paralyze, suggesting not that we cannot act at all but that we may act where we can, even from partial knowledge, with unpredictable success, certain only of our inconsistencies.

In spite of the difference between feminist and postfeminist texts, the interplay in all of them between the representation of women's concerns and the construction of women's consciousness makes them an important part of the tradition of socially engaged women's literature. This literature plays a vital role in articulating the hopes and the equally important disappointments of generations of American women. As Lucy Stone told us long ago, the deepening of disappointment may be the greatest catalyst for social change.

NOTES

1. Jan Clausen, *A Movement of Poets: Thoughts on Poetry and Feminism* (Brooklyn, N.Y.: Long Haul Press, 1982). Clausen is writing of poets rather than novelists, but her concern about "the blurring of distinctions between literary prominence and political leadership" (p. 25) is equally applicable to fiction.

2. In a paper I co-authored with sociologist Judith Stacey, we defined *postfeminism* as demarcating "an emerging culture and ideology that simultaneously incorporates, revises, and depoliticizes many of the fundamental issues advanced by second-wave feminism" ("Second Thoughts on the Second Wave," *Feminist Studies* 13 [Summer 1987], 341–62).

3. The editions I cite in this essay are as follows: *Sula* (New York: Bantam, 1975); *Woman on the Edge of Time* (New York: Fawcett, 1976); *Housekeeping* (New York: Bantam, 1982); *The Color Purple* (New York: Harcourt Brace Jovanovich, 1982); *Love Medicine* (New York: Bantam, 1984); *Sinking, Stealing* (Trumansburg, N.Y.: Crossing Press, 1985); *The Handmaid's Tale* (Boston: Houghton Mifflin, 1986); *The Good Mother* (New York: Harper and Row, 1986); *Lovingkindness* (New York: Summit, 1987).

4. Some examples are Sherley A. Williams's *Dessa Rose* (1986); Valerie Miner's *All Good Women* (1987); and Marge Piercy's *Gone to Soldiers* (1987).

5. Valerie Miner, a feminist novelist, has told me of several episodes in which publishers have rejected her own work and that of other writers because of its feminist content.

6. Richard Ohmann describes the process of canon formation in recent years as a "nearly closed circle of marketing and consumption, the simultaneous exploitation and creation of taste, familiar to anyone who has examined marketplace culture under monopoly capitalism," presided over by "gatekeeper intellectuals," among the most powerful of whom are reviewers for the *New York Times Book Review* ("The Shaping of a Canon: U.S. Fiction, 1960–1975," in *Canons,* ed. Robert von Hallberg [Chicago: University of Chicago Press, 1984], pp. 377–401; quotation on p. 380).

7. Chikwenye Okonjo Ogunyemi, "Womanism: The Dynamics of the Contemporary Black Female Novel in English," *Signs* 11 (Autumn 1985), 63–80; quotation on pp. 64–65.

8. Among those who have done so are Agnes Smedley, Tillie Olsen, Marge Piercy, Margaret Atwood, Valerie Miner, and Rosellen Brown.

9. This is so even though Walker herself, even before Ogunyemi, coined the term *womanist* to distinguish herself from white feminists.

10. Deborah Silverton Rosenfelt, "Getting into the Game: American Women Writers and the Radical Tradition," *Women's Studies International Forum* 9, no. 4 (1986), 363–72.

11. Catherine Belsey, *Critical Practice* (London: Methuen, 1980), p. 91.

12. For a materialist feminist analysis of the place of community in *Sula* and in the works of other black women writers, see Susan Willis, "Black Women Writers: Taking a Critical Perspective," in *Making a Difference: Feminist Literary Criticism,* ed. Gayle Green and Coppélia Kahn (London: Methuen, 1985), pp. 211–37.

13. Barbara Christian makes a similar point: "By the mid-1970's, the fiction makes a visionary leap. In novels like *Sula* and *Meridian,* the woman is not thrust outside her community. To one degree or another, she chooses to stand outside it, to define herself as in revolt against it. In some ways, Sula is the most radical of the characters of seventies fiction, for she overturns the conventional definition of good and evil in relation to women by insisting that she exists primarily as and for herself—not to be a mother or to be the lover of men" ("Trajectories of Self-Definition: Placing Contemporary Afro-American Women's Fiction," in *Conjuring: Black Women, Fiction, and Literary Tradition,* ed. Marjorie Pryse and Hortense J. Spillers [Bloomington: Indiana University Press, 1985], pp. 233–48; quotation on p. 241).

14. Rachel Blau DuPlessis's *Writing beyond the Ending: Narrative Strategies of Twentieth-Century Women Writers* (Bloomington: Indiana University Press, 1985) has profoundly influenced my thinking on this and other dimensions of contemporary women's fiction. For DuPlessis, reparenting "as a narrative strategy is the return by the female hero to parental figures in order to forge an alternative fictional resolution to the oedipal crisis . . . " (p. 83), with a reconstituted pre-Oedipal mother-child dyad offering the most powerful alternative. Another important essay on female bonding in recent women's fiction, even more grounded than DuPlessis in Nancy Chodorow's feminist adaptation of object relations theory, is Elizabeth Abel's "(E)Merging Identities: The Dynamics of Female Friendship in Contemporary Fiction by Women," *Signs* 6, no. 3 (1981), 413–35; see also Judith Kegan Gardiner's "The (US)es of (I)dentity: A Response to Abel on '(E)Merging Identities,'" *Signs* 6, no. 3 (1981), 436–42).

15. Smith argues that *Sula* contains a barely repressed lesbian subtext ("Toward a Black Feminist Criticism," *Conditions: Two* [Oct. 1977], 25–52; reprinted in *Feminist Criticism and Social Change,* ed. Judith Newton and Deborah Rosenfelt [New York: Methuen, 1985], pp. 3–18).

16. For a psychoanalytic interpretation of Nel's and Sula's friendship that develops ideas about complementarity and identity, see the exchange between Abel and Gardiner cited above, esp. Abel, "[E]Merging Identities," pp. 426–29, and

Gardiner, "The (US)es of (I)dentity," pp. 438–40, and Abel's "Response to Gardiner" (pp. 442–43) in the same issue.

17. DuPlessis, *Writing beyond the Ending,* esp. pp. 1–19. Judith Kegan Gardiner, who concurs that "the conventional old plots of heterosexual seduction and betrayal play a minimal role in contemporary women's fiction," attributes the "antiromantic treatment of heterosexuality in twentieth-century women's writing" to a "contrast between secure gender identity and a denial of cultural truisms for appropriate sexual emotions and behavior" ("On Female Identity and Writing by Women," in *Writing and Sexual Difference,* ed. Elizabeth Abel [Chicago: University of Chicago Press, 1982], pp. 177–91, quotation on p. 190).

18. Margaret Homans, "'Her Very Own Howl': The Ambiguities of Representation in Recent Women's Fiction," *Signs* 9, no. 2 (1983), 186–205, esp. 191–94. In Morrison's remarkable recent novel about slavery, *Beloved,* the heterosexual love that Sula represses wells up to take a central place in the narrative; in this regard, as in its implicit skepticism about the consequences of extending pre-Oedipal mother-daughter dyads into adult life, *Beloved* is affiliated with post-feminist fiction.

19. Elizabeth Meese, *Crossing the Double-Cross: The Practice of Feminist Criticism* (Chapel Hill: University of North Carolina Press, 1986), especially ch. 4, "A World of Women: Marilynne Robinson's *Housekeeping,*" pp. 55–68.

20. For an account of the relation between feminism and women's socioeconomic status in postindustrial capitalism, see Judith Stacey, "Sexism by a Subtler Name? Postindustrial Conditions and Postfeminist Consciousness in the Silicon Valley," *Socialist Review* 96 (Nov.-Dec. 1987), 7–28.

21. Judith Stacey and I consider this concession more fully in "Second Thoughts on the Second Wave," especially pp. 351–53.

22. The theoretical implications of these disrupted mother-daughter relationships—disruptions probably reaching a pinnacle of horror in Morrison's *Beloved*—cannot be considered here, but it seems clear that contemporary women's fiction cumulatively constructs the mother-daughter bond as both extraordinarily powerful and extraordinarily threatened, for a complicated nexus of literary, social, and psychological reasons.

23. *The Good Mother* provoked more heated discussion than any other text in my class on contemporary women's novels (Spring 1987); a reading group of feminist faculty from various Bay area institutions was similarly divided. Susan Barnard's indignant response to a favorable review in the *New York Times Book Review* (Letter to the Editor, 22 June 1986) sums up feminist objections to the novel, which Barnard labels "one of the most anti-woman to appear in a long time."

24. At the Modern Language Association Convention in December 1987, where I gave a version of this paper, Cora Kaplan, another panelist, argued during discussion that I was talking not about postfeminist texts but about post-modernist feminist texts. There is certainly some slippage between these terms, and one may choose to read these texts as a (postmodernist) feminist, liberating feminist meanings from them. Kaplan's category seems particularly applicable

to the textual politics of *The Handmaid's Tale*. The designation "postfeminist" signifies the particular historical relationship of these texts to second-wave feminism.

25. I am indebted to discussions with Jane Gurko and to an unpublished paper by Genny Lim for interpretations of *Love Medicine* that emphasize its continuities with feminism.

26. Some of the essays that influenced my understanding of the relations and potential meeting grounds between feminism and postmodernism are the following: Linda Alcoff, "Cultural Feminism versus Post-Structuralism: The Identity Crisis in Feminist Theory," *Signs* 13, no. 3 (1988), 405–36; Jane Flax, "Postmodernism and Gender Relations in Feminist Theory," *Signs* 12, no. 4 (1987), 621–43; a paper by Nancy Fraser and Linda Nicholson, "Social Criticism without Philosophy: An Encounter between Feminism and Postmodernism," subsequently published in *Theory, Culture, and Society* 5 (June 1988), 373–94; Sandra Harding, "The Instability of the Analytical Categories of Feminist Theory," *Signs* 11, no. 4 (Summer 1986), 645–64; Donna Haraway, "A Manifesto for Cyborgs: Science, Technology, and Socialist Feminism in the 1980's," *Socialist Review* 80 (1983), 65–107, and the draft of "Situated Knowledges: The Science Question in Feminism as a Site of Discourse on the Privilege of Partial Reserve," subsequently published in *Feminist Studies* 14, no. 3 (1988), 515–600.

27. Flax, "Postmodernism and Gender Relations in Feminist Theory," p. 633.

SONIA SALDÍVAR-HULL

Feminism on the Border:
From Gender Politics to Geopolitics

Is it possible for Chicanas to consider ourselves part of this sisterhood called feminism? Can we assume that our specific interests and problems will be taken care of by our marxist compañeros? In her essay "Feminism, Marxism, Method, and the State," Catharine MacKinnon decrees that "sexuality is to feminism what work is to marxism: that which is most one's own yet most taken away."[1] MacKinnon argues that while we can draw parallels between marxist and feminist methodologies, we must remember not to conflate these two "theories of power and its distribution"(p. 2), that one theory must not be subsumed into the other. She continues: "What if the claims of each theory are taken equally seriously, each on its own terms? Can two social processes be basic at once? Can two groups be subordinated in conflicting ways, or do they merely crosscut? Can two theories, each of which purports to account for the same thing—power as such—be reconciled? Or, is there a connection between the fact that the few have ruled the many and the fact that those few have been men?" (p. 3).

But to the Chicana, a woman with a specific history of sex- and class exploitation, it is essential that we further complicate the feminist/marxist discussion by adding the problems of race and ethnicity. Our feminist sisters and marxist compañeras urge us to take care of gender and class issues first and then race will naturally take care of itself. This, of course, is illusory, and even MacKinnon, as thorough as she is, constantly watching that she herself does not re-create a monolithic Woman, has to use footnotes to qualify the difference between the white woman's and the African American woman's situations. She claims to have checked her statements "to see if women's condition is shared, even when contexts or magnitudes differ" (p. 6). If her check system fails, then "the statement is simply wrong and will have to be qualified or the aspiration (or the theory) abandoned" (p. 6).

My project does not suggest that we abandon either the aspiration or the theory. It does, however, insist that our white feminist sisters recognize their own blind spots. When MacKinnon uses solely the African American woman as her sign for all dispossessed women, we see the extent to which Chicanas, Asian American, Native American, or Puerto Rican women, as examples, have been rendered invisible in a discourse whose explicit agenda is to expose ideological erasure. Chicana readings of color *blindness* instead of color consciousness in "politically correct" feminist essays, those blind spots that socialist feminists scorn as the discourse of liberal feminists, indicate the extent to which the issues of race and ethnicity continue to be ignored in feminist and marxist theories.[2] Theorists such as Rosaura Sánchez, Alma Gómez, Cherríe Moraga, Mariana Romo-Carmona, Gloria Anzaldúa, and Helena María Viramontes, working collectively as in *Cuentos* and individually as in *Borderlands,* insist on illuminating the complications and intersections of the multiple systems of exploitation: capitalism, patriarchy, and white supremacy.[3]

As Chicanas making our works public—publishing in marginalized journals and small, underfinanced presses, and taking part in conferences and workshops—we realize that the sisterhood called feminism professes an ideology that at times comes dangerously close to the phallocentric ideologies of the white male power structure against which all feminists must struggle.[4] In her essay "Ethnicity, Ideology, and Academia," Rosaura Sánchez reminds us of the ideological strategies that the dominant culture manipulates in order to mystify "the relation between minority cultures and the dominant culture" (p. 80). She accurately points out that U.S. cultural imperialism extends beyond the geopolitical borders of the country, "but being affected, influenced, and exploited by a culture is one thing and sharing fully in that culture is another" (p. 81). Thus, if we extend the analogy to feminism and to the totalizing concept of sisterhood, we begin to understand how the specific interests of Anglo-American and other European feminists tend to erase the existence of Chicana, Puerto Rican, Native American, Asian American, and other Third World feminisms.

In our search for a feminist critical discourse that adequately considers our position as women under multiple oppressions, we must turn to our own "organic intellectuals."[5] Unfortunately, because our work has been ignored by the women and men in charge of the modes of cultural production, we must be innovative in our search. Hegemony has so constructed the idea of method and theory that often we cannot recognize anything that is different from what the dominant discourse constructs.

As a consequence, we have to look in unsanctioned places for our theories: in the prefaces to anthologies, in the interstices of autobiographies, in our cultural artifacts, in our *cuentos,* and if we are fortunate to have access to a good library, in the essays published in marginalized journals not widely distributed by the dominant institutions. While Chicana academics do publish feminist essays in journals such as *Crítica, The Americas Review* (formerly *Revista Chicano-Riqueña*), and *Third Woman,* to name a few, I will focus on one specific type of Chicana feminism that deconstructs the borders erected by Eurocentric feminism.

The prefatory *testimonio* to *Cuentos: Stories by Latinas*—collectively written by Alma Gómez, Cherríe Moraga, and Mariana Romo-Carmona—offers such a site of radical Chicana and Latina theory. The editors identify themselves and with each other as "U.S. Third World women," writers who want to break the tradition of silence imposed upon them by the pressures of the dominant culture, which works against the viability of an oral tradition. The realities of women of color under capitalism in the United States urge the Latina woman to write. The material realities of life in the urban barrio or ghetto cannot sustain, in the authors' words, "a tradition which relies so heavily on close family networks and [is] dependent upon generations of people living in the same town or barrio" (p. vii).

The Gómez, Moraga, and Romo-Carmona project explodes previous Euro-American feminist assumptions about women's writing. As women whose daily existence confronts institutionalized racism, class exploitation, sexism, and homophobia, the U.S. Third World woman does not enjoy the luxury of privileging one oppression over another. While recognizing that Latinos are not a homogenous group, the editors acknowledge that "as Latinas in the U.S., our experience is different [from that of white people]. Because living here means throwing in our lot with other people of color" (p. x). Unlike Anglo-American and European feminists, Gómez, Moraga, and Romo-Carmona reject Eurocentrism and "claim 'la mezcla,' la mestiza, regardless of each author's degree of indio, africano, or european blood" (p. x).

While feminist models like Elaine Showalter's classic work, *A Literature of Their Own,* insist that the first stage of feminist criticism looks back to find a literary tradition,[6] the collaborators of *Cuentos* believe that, for writers who hope to forge a new affiliation among working-class people of color in the U.S. who share a kinship of exploitation, looking to a romanticized past is a luxury in which we cannot indulge. Instead, the stories they present are tied to the specific historical imperatives of the woman of color.

Expanding on her collaboration with the other U.S. Latinas in *Cuentos*, Cherríe Moraga writes a new foreword to the second edition of the breakthrough anthology, *This Bridge Called My Back*.[7] With this new foreword, her theoretical approach transforms her previous brand of radical feminism. Moraga also begins to bridge the chasm between radical women and oppressed men, acknowledging that if the first edition had been written in 1983 instead of in 1979, "it would speak much more directly now to the relations between women and men of color, both gay and heterosexual." In the four years between editions, she envisions a more internationalist *Bridge* that would affirm the connections between U.S. people of color and other "refugees of a world on fire."

As Moraga elaborates what is in fact a theoretical statement, she clarifies the many ways in which this feminist theory differs from what the elite call "theory" or from Euro-American versions of feminist theory. The Chicana feminist does not present Kristevan "signifying spaces," but rather material geopolitical issues that redirect feminist discourse.[8] Chicana feminism on the border is explicitly political, historical, and revolutionary. No longer limiting the feminist agenda to issues of race, class, ethnicity, and sexual orientation, Moraga expresses solidarity with the Third World people struggling against the hegemony of the United States. Many issues that Moraga presents in 1983 remain urgent:

> The U.S. is training troops in Honduras to overthrow the Nicaraguan people's government. Human rights violations... on a massive scale in Guatemala and El Salvador (and as in this country those most hard hit are often the indigenous peoples of those lands). Pinochet escalates political repression in Chile. The U.S. invades Grenada. Apartheid continues to bleed South Africa. Thousands of unarmed people are slaughtered in Beirut by Christian militiamen and Israeli soldiers. Aquino is assassinated by the Philippine government. And the U.S.? The Reagan administration daily drains us of nearly every political gain made by the feminist, Third World, and anti-war work of the late 60's and early 70's. (Moraga, Foreword)

Gloria Anzaldúa's *Borderlands/La Frontera*, an elaboration of her own feminist theory begun while she served as Moraga's co-editor of *Bridge*, examines the dynamics of race, class, gender, and sexual orientation. For Anzaldúa, feminism emerges as the force that gives voice to her origins as "the new mestiza." This "new mestiza" is a woman alienated from her own, often homophobic, culture as well as from the hegemonic culture. She envisions the new mestiza "caught between *los intersticios*, the spaces between the different worlds she inhabits" (p. 20). Anzaldúa's feminism exists in a borderland not limited to geographic space, resides in a space not acknowledged by hegemonic culture. Its inhabitants are what Anzaldúa calls "*los atravesados* ... : squint-eyed, the perverse, the queer, the troublesome, the mongrel, the mulatto, the half-breed, the half-dead ... " (p. 3). By invoking racist, homophobic epithets, Anzaldúa obliterates the power that the dominant culture holds over what is "normal" or acceptable.

Whereas the earlier works of women like Angela de Hoyos articulate Tejana feminist issues, Anzaldúa makes the leap from the history of colonization by the United States to the history of colonization as a *mestiza*, a Native American woman. And although some Chicana critics reject the internal colony model because, as Maria Linda Apodaca states, "when the land was conquered, the Mexican population in the Southwest was small given the total land mass," the specific history of the Tejano/Tejana urges us to remember that there is not one monolithic Chicano/Chicana experience in the United States.[9] Apodaca's assumptions neglect to acknowledge the historical specificity of the Tejanas/Tejanos who were forced to live under a reign of terror in post-1848 Texas.[10]

In the poem "Hermano," Angela de Hoyos taunts the Anglo usurper by reminding him of his own immigrant status. He is told to "scare up your little 'Flor de Mayo'—/so *we* can all sail back/to where we came from."[11] While de Hoyos identifies with her European heritage, the Pinta, the Niña, and the Santa María of the Spanish conquerors, Anzaldúa, in opposition, insists on identifying with the indigenous Indian tribes as well as with the African slaves who mixed with the conquerors, resulting in the mestizo. She bases her political, feminist position on the Chicana's history within multiple cultures, including indigenous Mexican and African, and always "grounded on the Indian woman's history of resistance" (p. 21).

Anzaldúa's text is itself a *mestizaje*: a postmodernist mixture of autobiography, historical document, and poetry collection. Like the people whose lives it chronicles, *Borderlands* resists genre boundaries as well as geopolitical borders. The text's opening epigraph is an excerpt from a song by the *norteño* conjunto band Los Tigres del Norte. But if Anzaldúa's historical ties are closer to the *corrido* tradition than to the historical imperatives of postmodern theory, hers is the new *corrido* of the mestiza with a political analysis of what it means to live as a woman in a literal and figurative Borderland. She tells us that "the U.S.-Mexican border *es una herida abierta* [is an open wound] where the Third World grates against the First and bleeds. And before a scab forms it hemorrhages again, the lifeblood of two worlds merging to form a third country—a border culture" (p. 3). Through issues of gender politics,

Anzaldúa locates personal history within a history of the border people. Legitimacy belongs to the Anglo hegemony; the indigenous population is nothing more than an aberrant species. To the white power structure, the *mojado* (wetback) is the same as the *mexicano de este lado* (Mexican from the U.S. side). As she chronicles the history of the new mestiza, Anzaldúa explores issues of gender and sexual orientation that Chicano historians like David Montejano, Arnoldo De León, and Rodolfo Acuña have not adequately addressed.[12]

Presenting this other history of Texas that Anglo-Texans, such as J. Frank Dobie and Walter Prescott Webb, never cite, Anzaldúa further merges autobiography with historical document.[13] Her family history becomes the history of the Chicana/o experience in South Texas after colonization and occupation by U.S. forces. Those who dared resist were lynched by the Texas Rangers. "My grandmother," Anzaldúa informs us, "lost all her cattle/they stole her land." The history of dispossession is transmitted orally from one generation to the next. Anzaldúa's mother tells the story of *her* widowed mother, who was cheated by the Anglo usurper: "A smart *gabacho* lawyer took the land away, *mamá* hadn't paid taxes. No *hablaba inglés*, she didn't know how to ask for time to raise the money" (p. 8).

Autobiography for the new mestiza *is* the history of the colonization of indigenous southwestern peoples by Anglo-American imperialists intent on their manifest destiny. Texas history, in Anzaldúa's revision, is incomplete without the presentation of the Mexican woman who dares to cross the border. She is the one who is the most easily exploited, physically as well as sexually. The *coyote* can enslave her after raping her. If she is lucky enough to make it to the U.S. side, she can look forward to laboring as a maid "for as little as $15 dollars a week" (p. 12).

Once she establishes a working definition of the mestizo border culture with which she identifies, Anzaldúa begins her internal critique of that world. Because she is so much a part of this world, she can penetrate its inner dynamics and understand the oppressions that it in turn uses to control women within the culture. When Anzaldúa tells us how she rebelled, we can see the intense power that the Chicano culture holds over women: "Repelé. Hablé pa' 'tras. Fuí muy hocicona. Era indiferente a muchos valores de mi cultura. No me dejé de los hombres. No fuí buena ni obediente." [I argued. I talked back. I was quite a big-mouth. I was indifferent to many of my culture's values. I did not let the men push me around. I was not good or obedient (p. 15, my translation).] The ideal woman for the people of the borderland is one who stands behind her man in silence and passivity. If she refuses her female role as housekeeper, she is considered lazy. To study, read, paint, write are not legitimate choices for the mestiza. Her testimony rings true for many Chicanas who struggle against their gender indoctrination. That her history exists for us to study is a testament to her resistance: "Every bit of self-faith I'd painstakingly gathered took a beating daily. Nothing in my culture approved of me. *Habia agarrado malos pasos.* [I had taken the wrong path.] Something was 'wrong' with me. *Estaba más allá de la tradición*" [I was beyond the tradition (p. 16, my translation)].

Cultural tyranny for the Chicana feminist imposes an additional hegemonic power against which she must struggle. She must not only contend with the racism of the dominant Anglo-American restraints, she must also resist the oppressive yoke of the sexist Chicano culture: "Culture is made by those in power—men. Males make the rules and laws; women transmit them. How many times have I heard mothers and mothers-in-law tell their sons to beat their wives for not obeying them, for being *hociconas* [big mouths], for being *callejeras* [going to visit and gossip with neighbors], for expecting their husbands to help with the rearing of children and the housework, for wanting to be something other than housewives?" (p. 16). Anzaldúa's gender politics are always aware of the women who are agents of the patriarchy.

Additionally, Anzaldúa understands that for the new mestiza an education is imperative for liberation. But the realities of living in a borderland, a muted culture in the midst of the hegemonic power of the United States, mean that the chances are slim that a Chicana will survive the battle against the combined forces of a sexist Chicano culture and the racist power of the dominant culture. Further, economic exploitation ensures that Chicanas stay in their place because "as working class people our chief activity is to put food in our mouths, a roof over our heads and clothes on our backs" (p. 17).

Anzaldúa's project threatens further still the traditions of Chicanismo, when, as a lesbian Chicana, she forces the homophobes of the Chicano community to see their prejudice. If the heterosexual Chicana is ostracized from her culture for transgressing its rules of behavior, for the Chicana lesbian, "the ultimate rebellion she can make against her native culture is through her sexual behavior" (p. 19). She makes the "choice to be queer" and as a result feels the ultimate exile, cultural as well as geographic, from her homeland. She transforms the bourgeois concepts of safety and home to concepts she can carry with her along with her political commitments. And, as a Chicana "totally immersed" in her culture, she can choose to reject the crippling aspects of traditions that oppress women and silence homosexual men and women. Her refusal to "glorify those aspects of my culture which have injured me and which have injured me in the name of protecting me" signals the agenda for the new mestiza, the border feminist (p. 22). The border feminist that Anzaldúa presents is a woman comfortable with new affiliations that subvert old ways of being, rejecting the homophobic, sexist, racist, imperialist, and nationalist.

In addition to gender transgressions that Anzaldúa's new mestiza introduces, new subject matter for poetry is another "aberration" that the Chicana feminist presents. Afro-Americanists from Ida B. Wells to Hazel Carby and Wahneema Lubiano have explored the terroristic method by which the dominant culture kept African American people under control: the law of the rope.[14] Likewise, Chicanos, particularly in Texas, have lived under the threat of lynching. But while historian Arnoldo De León investigates lynching as an institutionalized threat against Tejanos, it takes Anzaldúa's poem "We Call Them Greasers" to flesh out the ramifications of the lynch law to Chicanas. In the poem, whose title pays tribute to De León's history, *They Called Them Greasers,* the connection between the history of oppression of nineteenth-century African slaves and ex-slaves and that of nineteenth-century mestizos/Chicanos emerges. Narrated by the Anglo-American usurper, this example of what Barbara Harlow has called resistance poetry speaks of how Tejanos lost their lands and often their lives.[15] The Anglo narrator assumes the role of deity as he forces the Tejanos to place their hats "over their hearts" and lower their eyes in his presence. He rejects their collective farming techniques, cultural remnants of indigenous tribal traditions of the mestizo. He sneers, "they didn't even own the land but shared it." The Tejano "troublemakers" who actually have "land grants and appeal to the courts" are called laughingstocks, "them not even knowing English" (p. 134). For the Anglo-American imperialists, literacy in Spanish or any other nonstatus language is illiteracy. The women, in particular, suffer an additional violence before they are murdered by the gringo.

While Chicano (male) historians have done much to expose the realities of violent acts against the Tejanos, they have, to a great extent, been reluctant to voice the perhaps unspeakable violences against Tejanas. Even Américo Paredes in his breakthrough text, *With His Pistol in His Hand,* cannot articulate the violence that Gregorio Cortez's wife, Leonor Díaz Cortez, must have suffered in the four months that she spent in a Texas jail, incarcerated for her husband's alleged crime.[16] During the Rangers' manhunt for Cortez, a Mexican woman is alleged to have given information to the sheriff, leading to Cortez's capture. Paredes states: "The woman, whoever she was, at first refused to talk, but 'under pressure' told Glover where Cortez was going.... What sort of pressure Glover used, whether it was physical or psychological, there is no way of telling" (p. 68).

Precisely because "there is no way" for a male historian to tell the history of the Chicana, it takes Anzaldúa's voice to articulate the violence against nineteenth-century Tejanas. In "We Call Them Greasers," she finds the words that acknowledge the history of violence against the Tejana. This history includes rape as institutionalized strategy in the war to disempower Chicano men. While the Tejano is tied to a mesquite tree, the Chicano version of the African American hanging tree, the gringo rapes the Tejana.

> She lay under me whimpering.
> I plowed into her hard
> kept thrusting and thrusting
> felt him watching from the mesquite tree
> heard him keening like a wild animal
> in that instant I felt such contempt for her
> round face and beady black eyes like an Indian's.
> Afterwards I sat on her face until
> her arms stopped flailing,
> didn't want to waste a bullet on her.
> The boys wouldn't look me in the eyes.
> I walked up to where I had tied her man to the tree
> and spat in his face. Lynch him, I told the boys.
> (Pp. 134–35)

Once the rapist gains total control over the Tejano through the violation of his woman, the rapist can feel only contempt for her. Within the hierarchy of powerlessness, the woman occupies a position below the already inferior brown man. While De León chronicles how Anglo-American occupiers made their conquests and massacres more bearable by comparing their victims to animals, similarly, by emphasizing the mestiza's *Indian* features, the Anglo-American imperialist further relegates the Chicana to the savagery of the Indian.[17] Anzaldúa's reluctance to condemn the passive observers, "the boys," in the poem is due not to a misguided loyalty to the gringo, but to an implicit recognition of the power of the class structure even in nineteenth-century Texas, where the rich land barons controlled all of their workers, regardless of race or ethnicity.

In poems like "Sus plumas el viento," "Cultures," and "Sobre piedras con lagartijos," Anzaldúa reasserts her solidarity with the exploited men and women along the border. "El sonavabitche" protests the exploitation of undocumented farmworkers in places like Muncie, Indiana. Her poetry exposes the methods by which unscrupulous farmowners create a modern-day slave system. Hiring undocumented Mexican laborers to work their fields, they tip off the Immigration and Naturalization Service (INS) for a raid before payday. The Chicano narrator expresses solidarity with his undocumented *compañeros* when he refuses to work for the *sonavabitche* who has used the INS tactic "three times since we've been coming here/ *Sepa dios* [God knows] how many times in between./ Wets, free labor, *esclavos* [slaves]./ *Pobres jijos de la chingada* [Poor sons of bitches]./ This is the last time we work for him/ no matter how *fregados* [desperate] we are" (pp. 126–27, my translation).

Finally, in the poem "To Live in the Borderlands Means You" Anzaldúa sums up her definition of the new mestiza, the feminist on the border. She is one who "carries five races" on her back—not Hispanic, Native American, African American, Spanish, or Anglo, but the mixture of the five which results in the mestiza, mulata. She's also "a new gender," "both woman and man, neither" (p. 194). While not rejecting any part of herself, Anzaldúa's new mestiza becomes a survivor because of her ability to "live *sin fronteras* [without borders]/ be a crossroads" (p. 195).

While Anzaldúa transgresses aesthetic boundaries in her text, transgresses gender boundaries in what she names her "choice" to be a lesbian, transgresses ethnicity and race in her formulation of the new mestiza combining Indian, Spanish, African, and even Anglo blood to form a *mestizaje*, her project is nonetheless articulated within the vital history of the Texas Chicana. If history is what forces Anzaldúa's escape into what Jenny Bourne has called "identity politics" in her essay "Homelands of the Mind," it is because the only history for the Chicana is the history of the mestiza's colonization by both the Spanish conquerors and the Anglo-American imperialists in their conquest of South Texas.[18] Once Anzaldúa establishes a history of the border people who "were jerked out by the roots, truncated, disemboweled, dispossessed, and separated from [their] identity and [their] history" (p. 8), the Chicana feminist can turn to other concerns. Patricia Fernández-Kelly's *For We Are Sold, I and My People* presents a history of the mestiza laboring in the exploitative *maquiladora* (factory) system that Anzaldúa alludes to in her own work.[19] In addition, Anzaldúa calls attention to the unwritten history of the mestizas in the *colonias* of South Texas and the border cities such as El Paso and Ciudad Juárez, homelands of contemporary victims of U.S. multinational corporations. These people are being poisoned by the water they are forced to store in chemical drums that once held carcinogens.[20]

The Chicana feminist's methodology is ideological analysis and materialist, historical research, as well as race, class, and gender analysis. Her theory is never an ahistorical "politics of equal oppressions," because Chicana feminism develops from an awareness of specific material experience of the historical moment. Unlike the feminism of sisterhood, "feminism which is separatist, individualistic and inward-looking," Chicana feminists look inward in moments of self-exploration and see themselves as daughters of nonwestern indigenous tribes.[21] Anzaldúa's feminist discourse leads her to look inward for a deeper understanding of a larger, erased history.

Anzaldúa's text can be seen as a bridge that forms a continuum between her collaboration with Moraga in *This Bridge Called My Back* and Helena María Viramontes's "The Cariboo Café" in her collection, *The Moths and Other Stories*. One of the Chicana contributors to the *Cuentos* anthology, Viramontes continues the internationalist connection with women in Latin America and other Third World countries. If Anzaldúa's antihegemonic strategy is to re-create border history for the mestiza, in "The Cariboo Café" Viramontes's strategy is to expose the extent of the United States' political power. Viramontes presents the oppression of the reserve army of laborers that the U.S. creates and then designates as "other," the "illegal" immigrants. In this story, Viramontes shows us that we *can* combine feminism with race and class consciousness, even if we recognize the fallacies of an all-encompassing sisterhood. In this Chicana political discourse, Viramontes commits herself to a transnational solidarity with other working-class people who, like all nonindigenous tribes, are immigrants to the United States. In *The Political Unconscious*, Fredric Jameson has said that "history is what hurts."[22] For the most recent wave of brown immigrants who come to the United States in search of political freedom, the pain intensifies when they realize that for the brown, African American, and Asian races, the suppressed history of the U.S. is the history of exploitation as well as racism.

"They arrived in the secrecy of night, as displaced people often do, stopping over for a week, a month, eventually staying a lifetime" (p. 61). So Viramontes begins her history of the displaced immigrants of the 1980s. They are the "illegal aliens," the racist label by which the U.S. government designates an exploited subculture it has created. As James Cockcroft asks: "if so many employers and all consumers depend so heavily on these people, then why is it that they are viewed as a 'problem' or as 'illegals'? Human beings can *do* illegal things, but can a human being actually *be* illegal? Moreover, since when under capitalism is it an illegal act to sell one's labor power for a low wage to an employer engaged in a socially approved business?"[23]

In "The Cariboo Café," Viramontes interweaves narrative voices to tell the history of the undocumented worker in the U.S. She gives the story of the killing of an undocumented female worker wider political significance in the heteroglossic versions of life at the borders, at the periphery of North American society.

The Cariboo Café is the center around which Viramontes constructs her revision of history. The café, a sleazy diner on the wrong side of the tracks, attracts the outcasts of late capitalism. Burned-out drug addicts, prostitutes, and undocumented workers frequent the place run by a petit bourgeois man who becomes the mouthpiece of the dominant society. Although his speech places him in the working class, he spouts the ideology of the dominant class. What to him are unexamined platitudes—"family gotta be together" (p. 73)—are for the outsiders like the undocumented workers charged statements, expressing an ideology that Viramontes resists and unmasks in her tale. Viramontes transforms this cynical short-order cook with a grease-stained apron into a grotesque Uncle Sam, a living contradiction of core and periphery. The great irony here is that this man is almost as much a victim of the capitalist system as are the undocumented workers. If the new immigrants are exploited by capital as they labor in the sweatshops of the garment warehouses, this Anglo-American does not realize that he has been similarly victimized by the imperialistic urges of a U.S. government that led the country into a war in Southeast Asia. We learn that the man's only son is dead; it still haunts him that he will never know "what part of Vietnam JoJo is all crumbled up in" (p. 73).

The owner of what the workers call the "zero zero place" is able to voice the dominant ideology, not because of a class privilege but because of his privilege as a white man. It is here that Viramontes exposes how the hegemonic forces of race, class, and gender intersect and collide. When she gives equal weight to the voices of the young daughter of undocumented workers and to a Salvadoran political refugee, Viramontes gives voice to the counter-hegemonic.

The first voice we hear in the story is that of Sonya; we see the urban landscape through her eyes. Both her parents work so that the family may one day have a "toilet [of] one's own." For the feminist reader, this turn of phrase resonates of Virginia Woolf's desire for financial independence for the woman writer, but it also reminds us of the vast difference between the concerns of bourgeois feminists and border feminists. Sonya is a latchkey child whose duties as a female include caring for her younger brother, Macky. The children lose the key to their apartment and become lost trying to find their way to safety. A premise for survival in hostile territory for these children is never to trust the police; the "polie" is "La Migra in disguise and thus should always be avoided" (p. 61). Lost, the children see "a room with a yellow glow, like a beacon light at the end of a dark sea," which Sonya thinks will be a sanctuary from the alleys and the dead ends of the urban barrio. Ironically, the beacon is the "zero zero place" (p. 64).

In the "double zero café," we hear the story of the children's fate in flashback. The café owner tells his version as if he were on trial. Indeed, Viramontes *is* putting U.S. immigration policies and ideology on trial. The man constantly presents himself as honest, yet in the same breath he admits to lacing his hamburgers with something that is "not pure beef." He thinks that he redeems himself when he proclaims, at least "it ain't dogmeat" (p. 64). Then he remembers the basic contradiction of the "American" ideal: "It never pays to be honest." He continues his version of how it came to pass that a Salvadoran refugee was killed in his café. When he first saw "that woman," he immediately labeled her as Other: "Already I know that she's bad news because she looks street to me. Round face, burnt toast color, black hair.... Weirdo... " (p. 65). Through his voice, we hear the articulation of the dominant race's rationale for excluding brown races from integration into the U.S. society. Because immigrants of different skin color belie the melting-pot myth, it is harder for them to be accepted in the same way that European immigrants have been accepted in the history of U.S. colonization. When the woman speaks Spanish to the children with her, he states: "Right off I know she's illegal, which explains why she looks like a weirdo" (p. 66). Here Viramontes unmasks how the dominant marginalize on the basis of color and language.

Only when we get the third voice does Viramontes allow us to realize what has happened to the lost children of the first section. They have been taken by a Salvadoreña who mistakes Macky for her missing son. This woman is a modern day *llorona* (the wailing woman of mestizo folklore) who has fled her country after her own child was murdered by the right-wing, U.S.-backed government. The child is one of the countless *desaparecidos* in those countries whose dictators the U.S. government keeps in power.

The Salvadoreña tells her story and, indeed, becomes the modern-day wailing woman, representing in this version all women who are victimized by conquering races and classes, all women "who come up from the depths of sorrow to search for their children ... [she] hear[s] the wailing of the women and know[s] it to be [her] own" (pp. 68–69). In his essay "On Language as Such and on the Language of Man," Walter Benjamin argued that the lament "is the most undifferentiated, impotent expression of language; it contains scarcely more than the sensuous breath."[24] Viramontes uses the lament motif in this story not only to expose the socially sanctioned, passive roles for women within the patri-

archy, but to show the powerlessness of the victims of repressive govern-
ments. Thus the lament contains much more than Benjamin would have
it do.

In her abjection, the Salvadoreña believes Macky is her son. She cares
for him and cannot understand why the café owner would call her act a
kidnapping. For her, as for the children, the police here are no different
from the police in the country she has fled. They will take her son away
from her. She resists arrest and throws boiling coffee at the man pointing a gun at her forehead. With the Salvadoreña's final act of resistance,
Viramontes explodes the boundaries of family, of safety, and of home.

From Anzaldúa's important re-vision of Texas history, to the theoretical proclamations by collective voices of Moraga, Gómez, and Romo-
Carmona, to Viramontes's questioning the constitution of family,
Chicana feminism challenges boundaries defined by the hegemony.
When Eurocentric, liberal feminists define "theory" and "methodology,"
they become part of the hegemonic power that constructs the idea of
"method" and "theory" and therefore do not recognize racial or ethnic
difference. Chicana feminism, in both its theory and method, is tied to
the material world. When feminist anthologizers like Toril Moi fail to
recognize Chicana theory, it is because Chicanas ask different questions,
which in turn ask for a reconstruction of the very premises of
"theory."[25] Because the history of the Chicana experience in the United
States defines our particular *mestizaje* of feminism, our theory cannot be
a replicate of white feminism nor can it be only an academic abstraction.
The Chicana feminist looks to her history (to paraphrase Bourne's plea
for feminist praxis) to learn how to transform the present. For the Chicana feminist on the border, it is through our consciousness of history
and our affiliation with the struggles of other Third World people that
we find our theories and our methods.

NOTES

This essay had its origins in a 1987 MLA talk that was expanded for publication in *Chicano Literary Criticism: Studies in Culture and Ideology,* ed. Héctor
Calderón and José David Saldívar (Duke University Press, forthcoming). I
would like to thank Héctor Calderón for his careful reading of the original essay
and his suggestion that I look at the prefaces of Chicana and Latina anthologies
for an elaboration of this theory. In addition, José David Saldívar's essay "Texas
Border Narratives as Cultural Critique" spurred my reading of the border narratives written by men and led me to Anzaldúa's text as the necessary revision of
that narrative. None of my work in Third World and feminist theories would
have been possible without the encouragement of my mentors, Barbara Harlow
and Jane Marcus.

1. Catharine A. MacKinnon, "Feminism, Marxism, Method, and the State: An Agenda for Theory," in *Feminist Theory: A Critique of Ideology,* ed. N. O. Keohane, Michelle Z. Rosaldo, and Barbara C. Gelpi (Chicago: University of Chicago Press, 1981), pp. 1–30.

2. Because of space limitations and the general context of this collection, it was necessary to delete a critique of Euro-U.S. feminist critical practice. For an elaboration of my critique of feminist theorists such as Elaine Showalter, Toril Moi, and Julia Kristeva, see the original version of this essay in *Chicano Literary Criticism.*

3. Rosaura Sánchez, "Ethnicity, Ideology, and Academia," *The Americas Review* 15 (1987), 80–88; Alma Gómez, Cherríe Moraga, and Mariana Romo-Carmona, eds., *Cuentos: Stories by Latinas* (New York: Kitchen Table Women of Color Press, 1983); Gloria Anzaldúa, *Borderlands/La Frontera: The New Mestiza* (San Francisco: Spinsters/aunt lute, 1987); Helena María Viramontes, *The Moths and Other Stories* (Houston: Arte Publico Press, 1985). All quotations from these texts will be cited parenthetically within the essay.

4. See Hazel Carby's important discussion of the (mis)use of the term *sisterhood* in *Reconstructing Womanhood: The Emergence of the Afro-American Woman Novelist* (New York: Oxford University Press, 1987), pp. 3–19.

5. See Antonio Gramsci, *Selections from the Prison Notebooks of Antonio Gramsci,* ed. and trans. Quintin Horare and Geoffrey Nowell Smith (New York: International Publishers, 1971), pp. 3–43.

6. Elaine Showalter, *A Literature of Their Own: British Women Novelists from Brontë to Lessing* (Princeton: Princeton University Press, 1977), pp. 3–36.

7. Cherríe Moraga and Gloria Anzaldúa, eds., *This Bridge Called My Back: Writings by Radical Women of Color,* 2d ed. (New York: Kitchen Table Women of Color Press, 1983), n.p. for this foreword.

8. See the original version of this essay for an elaboration of Kristeva's "signifying spaces."

9. María Linda Apodaca, "A Double Edge Sword: Hispanas and Liberal Feminism," *Critica* 1 (1986), 96–114.

10. See Rodolfo Acuña's *Occupied America: A History of Chicanos* (New York: Harper and Row, 1981) for an overview of Texas history and how the Chicanos lived under a reign of terror after the 1848 Treaty of Guadalupe Hidalgo.

11. Angela de Hoyos, "Hermano," in *Chicano Poems for the Barrio* (San Antonio: M & A Editions, 1975), pp. 12–13. Emphasis added.

12. In addition to Acuña's text cited above, see David Montejano, *Anglos and Mexicans in the Making of Texas, 1836–1986* (Austin: University of Texas Press, 1987), and Arnoldo De León, *They Called Them Greasers: Anglo Attitudes towards Mexicans in Texas, 1821–1900* (Austin: University of Texas Press, 1983). While these history texts do not present adequate gender analyses, they are nonetheless important documents.

13. J. Frank Dobie, *The Flavor of Texas* (Dallas: Dealey and Lowe, 1936), and Walter Prescott Webb, *The Texas Rangers: A Frontier's Defense* (Cambridge: Houghton Mifflin, 1935).

14. See Ida B. Wells, *On Lynching* (New York: Arno, 1969); Hazel Carby, "'On the Threshold of Woman's Era': Lynching, Empire, and Sexuality in Black Feminist Theory," *Critical Inquiry* 12 (1985), 262–77; and Wahneema Lubiano, "Messing with the Machine: Four Afro-American Novels and the Nexus of Vernacular, Historical Constraint, and Narrative Strategy" (Ph.D. diss., Stanford University, 1987).

15. Barbara Harlow, "Resistance Poetry," in *Resistance Literature* (New York: Methuen, 1987), pp. 31–74.

16. Américo Paredes, *With His Pistol in His Hand: A Border Ballad and Its Hero* (Austin: University of Texas Press, 1958), p. 87.

17. De León, *They Called Them Greasers,* pp. 14–23.

18. Jenny Bourne, "Homelands of the Mind: Jewish Feminism and Identity Politics," *Race and Class* 29 (1987), 1–24.

19. Patricia Fernández-Kelly, *For We Are Sold, I and My People: Women and Industry in Mexico's Frontier* (Albany: State University of New York Press, 1983).

20. *Austin American Statesman,* 27 March 1988.

21. Quotes from Bourne, "Homelands of the Mind," pp. 16, 2.

22. Fredric Jameson, *The Political Unconscious: Narrative as a Socially Symbolic Act* (Ithaca, N.Y.: Cornell University Press, 1981), p. 102.

23. James D. Cockcroft, *Outlaws in the Promised Land: Mexican Immigrant Workers and America's Future* (New York: Grove, 1986), p. 64.

24. Walter Benjamin, "On Language as Such and on the Language of Man," in *Reflections: Essays, Aphorisms, Autobiographical Writings,* ed. Peter Demetz (New York: Harcourt Brace Jovanovich, 1978), pp. 314–32.

25. See the original version of this essay in *Chicano Literary Criticism* for a discussion of Toril Moi's *Sexual/Textual Politics: Feminist Literary Theory* (London: Methuen, 1985).

PART FIVE

Reprise:
The Tradition Re-Visioned

ELAINE SHOWALTER

Miranda and Cassandra: The Discourse of the Feminist Intellectual

Margaret Fuller and Florence Nightingale met only once, in November 1847, in Rome; and they disliked each other on the spot. Fuller, thirty-seven years old and at the height of her fame as the editor of the Transcendental journal *The Dial* and the author of *Woman in the Nineteenth Century*, was in exile from the puritanism of American culture, and had begun her clandestine affair with Angelo Ossoli, a young Catholic nobleman and supporter of the Italian revolution. Nightingale, twenty-seven, was traveling on the continent with friends in a manner befitting a cultivated English lady. In a letter to her mother in England, Nightingale lightly observed: "The Miss Fuller of Woman in the 19th Century has rather made up to us, but she does drawl out Transcendentalism in such a voice, that I do [not] feel myself equally drawn out towards her."[1] It is ironic that these two brilliant and troubled women, profoundly alike in their intelligence, aspirations, and psychological circumstances, did not recognize each other. Fuller desperately needed a confidante, Nightingale a role model. They might have found in each other the combination of mind and heart each sought fruitlessly from male mentors and companions.

The histories of Nightingale and Fuller are part of that secret archive of feminist intellectuals attempting to work within a discourse and an institution that has been shaped and controlled by men. What are some of the problems we face as women thinkers, speakers, and writers? Can they be resolved, or at least illuminated, by comparison with the narratives of feminist thinkers in the past? Fuller and Nightingale provide particularly useful narratives for such investigation, I think, because they were seeking answers through the revisionist exploration of myths of female knowledge. Choosing, in Fuller's case, the persona of "Miranda," and in Nightingale's case, "Cassandra," both developed analyses of the cultural dilemma of the feminist intellectual. In reviewing their experience, I want to ask whether these mythic personae still represent the major alternatives for feminist critics, or whether we now have new directions and solutions.

We need to ask first why Nightingale and Fuller did not get along. Nightingale may have been put off by Fuller's personality, which many of her contemporaries regarded as abrasive. Emerson, for example, recalled that "Margaret made a disagreeable first impression on most persons, including those who became afterwards her best friends.... This was partly the effect of her manners, which expressed an overweening sense of power, and slight esteem of others, and partly the prejudice of her fame."[2] James Russell Lowell caricatured Fuller as an egotistical bluestocking "with an I-turn-the-crank-of-the Universe air."[3] Even Perry Miller, taking his cue from these masculine accounts, notes in his discussion of Fuller's work that she was "phenomenally homely" and that her image cannot "be dissociated from the hyperbolically female intellectualism of the period, the slightest invocation of which invites our laughter."[4]

While Nightingale did not share Perry Miller's easy amusement at female intellectualism (a laughter that says as much about the Cambridge of the 1930s as about the Cambridge of the 1850s), she distrusted female peers. A lifelong contest with her mother and sister, conventional women who resisted her personal struggle for work and independence, had made her suspicious of women's friendship. She could not accept in other women the authority she admired in men. At the same time, Fuller was unwilling to go beyond the social facade to pursue more intimate contact with the women she was meeting in Rome. Caught up in a love affair and in the energy of the revolution, she was withdrawing from the English-speaking social world that seemed to represent conventional disapproval of her manner, her politics, and her feminism. "I suffer more than ever from that which is peculiarly American or English," she noted a few weeks before meeting Nightingale. "I should like to cease from hearing the language for a time ... at present I am in a state of unnatural divorce from what I was most allied to."[5]

Despite Nightingale's disclaimer, however, the meeting was not wholly lost on her. In 1851, a few months after Fuller's tragic death at the age of forty, in a shipwreck as she was returning with her lover and infant son to New York, Nightingale wrote her own three-volume feminist treatise, *Suggestions for Thought to Searchers after Religious Truth*. Strongly influenced by *Woman in the Nineteenth Century*, Nightingale's work has had a very different cultural history. Except for the brief section called "Cassandra," originally part of the second volume and first published in 1928, it has remained unknown.[6] And while *Cassandra* has since been reprinted and studied as a text by feminist scholars, it too has never been published in a complete and accurate form.[7]

Woman in the Nineteenth Century and *Cassandra* have many structural, thematic, and stylistic parallels. Both works have a peculiar history of composition and publishing that makes it difficult to assign them to a recognizable genre. We might call them feminist polemic; they might also be called feminist manifestos, or "womanifestos," in the tradition of Mary Wollstonecraft's *Vindication of the Rights of Woman*.[8] They bristle with erudite allusions, epigraphs, and marginal glosses, and they have odd narrative structures, punctuated by gaps, by mysterious argumentative leaps, by confessional moments and lyric asides. Partly argument, partly autobiography, partly analysis, both have been criticized as digressive and loose. Nightingale's first biographer, Edward Cook, found her book "as remarkable for literary felicities in detail as it is deficient in the art of literary arrangement." There have been similar complaints about *Woman in the Nineteenth Century*. Orestes Brownson complained that the work had "neither beginning, middle, nor end, and may be read backwards as well as forwards." And Perry Miller described the book as "full of wearisome digressions and excursions into fantasy and murky dreams."[9] Indeed, in modern terms, both texts could be seen as "hysterical narratives," incoherent stories like those told by Freud's hysterical women patients.

Thematically, both texts are studies of the dilemma of the feminist intellectual in the nineteenth century. Fuller's book, an expansion of an essay she had written in 1843 for *The Dial*, applies Transcendental principles of full individual development to the question of women's intellectual and moral growth. At the center of Fuller's discussion is the autobiographical portrait of the brilliant feminist intellectual whom she calls "Miranda," "a woman, who, if any in the world could, might speak without heat and bitterness of the position of her sex." Fuller's Miranda is the product of a demanding patriarchal education. "Her father was a man who cherished no sentimental reverence for Woman, but a firm belief in the equality of the sexes. . . . From the time she could speak and go alone, he addressed her not as a plaything, but as a living mind. . . . He called upon her for clear judgment, for courage, for honor and fidelity. . . . " Thus when Miranda grew up, "she took her place easily, not only in the world of organized being, but in the world of mind," where "her mind was often the leading one, always effective." Trained in self-respect, "fortunate," according to Fuller, in lacking the feminine charms that might attract "bewildering flatteries," Miranda seems to be the model of the successful woman. Yet even she is disappointed in her lot, because she sees that men, despite their rhetorical esteem for feminine virtue, "never in an extreme of despair, wished to be women," but rather taunted each other with "feminine" weakness, and regarded all her intellectual strengths as "masculine" traits. The woman of genius thus does not change attitudes toward women in general; she is simply perceived as a woman with a "masculine mind," as someone who has surpassed and even transcended her sex.[10]

By retelling the story of Miranda, Fuller inaugurates a central and influential tradition of the American feminist intellectual—as motherless and isolated from other women. Shakespeare's Miranda in *The Tempest* is a woman who has been entirely educated within the male world of Prospero's magic island. Indeed, it is one of the curiosities of the play that we do not even know what has happened to Miranda's mother. Shakespeare does not explain why Prospero abandoned her when he fled with his two-year-old daughter, and Miranda has no memory of her mother at all. Separated from her mother in the transition from the pre-Oedipal to the Oedipal phase, it is as if Miranda had been born only of man; Stephen Orgel suggests that psychologically it is as if she were "an adolescent boy."[11] As Caliban has become the model for Third World and black intellectuals, Miranda, the hyper-rationalist who falls in love with the language of the Other, suggests a metaphor for the feminist intellectual.[12] Caliban curses with his language, or deconstructs it; what should Miranda do with hers?

Fuller also invokes the figure of Cassandra, or the Muse, as another side of the woman of genius, the woman of inspiration, prophetic insight, and "impassioned sensibility." Unlike the male-identified Mirandas, modern-day Cassandras, she argues, "are very commonly unhappy at present," because their intellectual style does not fit the expectations of the masculine world. Yet with complete freedom and unimpeded growth, the side represented by Cassandra, the prophetic, radiant aspect of female intellect, ought to have equal importance with the rationality represented by Miranda.[13] If women are to have any hope of developing both sides of their nature, Fuller concludes, they must attempt to separate themselves from patriarchal influences, however seductive: "I would have Woman lay aside all thought, such as she habitually cherishes, of being taught and led by men."[14]

Nightingale may have taken the figure of Cassandra from Fuller, although in her journals and letters she had often cited the myth of Cassandra in describing her own sense of intellectual isolation and futility. Nightingale's Cassandra is a woman who in seeking independence has found only solitude and alienation; while her visions are unlike those of men, they are also too daring to find support from the female community. In Nightingale's narrative, Cassandra dies "withered, paralyzed, extinguished" at the age of thirty, asking why women have "passion, intellect, and moral activity," yet social lives in which "no one of the three can be exercised."[15] Bright women, she argues, live primarily in fantasy, trying to subdue the "perpetual daydreaming" which supplies all the interest in their lives. They fritter away their intellects in the mindless and maddening occupations dictated by society, or they are destroyed by the selfishness of the family, which uses them for its own interests: "A woman cannot live in the light of intellect. Society forbids it. Those conventional frivolities, which are called her 'duties,' forbid it." Woman in the nineteenth century, according to Nightingale, "has an immense provision of wings, which seem as if they would bear her over earth and heaven; but when she tries to use them, she is petrified into stone, her feet are grown into the earth, chained to the bronze pedestal."[16]

Yet Nightingale also refused to involve herself in the organized women's movement of her time. "I am brutally indifferent to the rights and wrongs of my sex," she wrote to Harriet Martineau.[17] Like Fuller, she placed her faith more in the example of great women leaders, and especially in the vision of a female savior who would appear to change women's lives. In their writings, both Fuller and Nightingale envision the coming of a feminist Messiah, who (in Nightingale's words) "will resume, in her own soul, all the sufferings of her race"; and (in Fuller's words) will "vindicate their birthright for all women," will "teach them what to claim and how to use what they obtain." Indeed both Fuller and Nightingale thought they might be the feminist Messiah themselves ("I feel chosen among women," Fuller wrote; and Nightingale recorded a series of mystical visions in which God spoke to her and called her to his service).[18] No doubt this is another reason they did not get along.

Understanding the circumstances in which the two works were written can explain much of their apparent incoherence, and help us understand some of the factors that shape feminist intellectual discourse. Like her heroine Miranda, Margaret Fuller's education reinforced her own distance and difference from women's culture or a female tradition; in Elizabeth Hardwick's words, "she sprang out of the heads of all the Zeuses about her."[19] Her father, Timothy Fuller, a lawyer and politician, instructed her in Latin and classical history starting at the age of six. Moreover, he kept her away from the novels, plays, poetry, and etiquette books deemed suitable for girls, and drilled her instead in an exact and rigorous use of language. As Fuller recalled, her father "demanded accuracy and clearness in everything: you must not speak, unless you can make your meaning perfectly intelligible to the person addressed; must not express a thought, unless you can give a reason for it, if required; must not make a statement unless sure of all particulars—such were his rules."[20] Held to this strict logical accountability, Fuller was also forbidden the linguistic markers of feminine euphemism, self-depreciation, and qualification: " 'But,' 'if,' 'unless,' 'I am mistaken,' and 'it may be so,' were words and phrases excluded from the province where he held sway."[21] This early discipline gave her speech a force and directness unusual in nineteenth-century women, an assertiveness some (without analyzing the cause) found impressive, others merely arrogant and odd.

Moreover, Fuller recalled, her father had no understanding or tolerance for other ways of knowing. Himself "accurate, ready, with entire command of his resources, he had no belief in minds that listen, wait, and receive. He had no conception of the subtle and indirect motions of imagination and feeling." She repressed her own imagination in the interests of the active intellect he desired: "My own world sank deep within, away from the surface of my life. . . . But my true life was only the dearer that it was secluded and veiled over by a thick curtain of available intellect."[22]

Fuller wrote about the split in her psyche in spatial terms, as her father's library and her mother's garden, the paradigmatic spaces that have become associated with the masculine and feminine traditions in American women's writing from the nineteenth century up to Alice Walker. For Fuller, her father's territory was the "proud world" of old books, draped with the thick curtains she internalized as smothering veils of intellect. Her mother's territory was the flower garden, which she recreated wherever the family moved, "the little garden, full of choice flowers and fruit-trees . . . here I felt at home." Her mother's garden was a place of free sensual pleasure: "There my thoughts could lie callow in the nest, and only be fed and kept warm. . . . I loved to gaze on the roses, the violets, the lilies, the pinks; my mother's hand had planted them and they bloomed for me. I culled the most beautiful. I looked at them on every side. I kissed them. I pressed them to my bosom with passionate emotions, such as I have never dared to express to any human being."[23] While the library was the austere space of the patriarchal intellect, the garden was a warm extension of the infant's bond with the mother's body, a space where thoughts did not have to be mustered, trained, and disciplined, but rather could be nurtured, where they could wait and receive.

Fuller also felt a split between the free flow of language in conversation, at which she excelled, and the labor and restraint of writing according to patriarchal laws of rhetoric and exposition. Many of Fuller's contemporaries also believed that her particular kind of female genius was most fully expressed in speech, especially through her role as the leader of a series of "Conversations" for women. These sessions had afforded Fuller much pleasure (a term she associated with the maternal), since the women had "time, patience, mutual reverence and fearlessness eno' to get at one another's thoughts."[24] But writing was always painful. Horace Greeley, Fuller's editor in New York, could not understand why she had so much trouble writing her columns for his paper: "While I never met another woman who conversed more freely or lucidly, the attempt to commit her thoughts to paper seemed to induce a singular embarrassment and hesitation."[25] James Freeman Clarke noted of Fuller that "it was only in conversation that she was perfectly at home"; and the Reverend Frederic Henry Hodge observed that "for some reason or other, she could never deliver herself in print as she did with her lips."[26]

Hodges's metaphor suggests an oral birth or self-delivery through the lips, which suggest female sexual difference. The woman is "at home" in conversation, which both echoes the domestic and private mode of feminine experience, and also suggests the Mother Tongue of gossip, of female chatter and babble. In his review of Fuller, Orestes Brownson noted that while it was "no book," "as talk it is very well and proves that the lady has great talkative powers, and that, in this respect at least, she is a genuine woman."[27]

Fuller's male mentor, Ralph Waldo Emerson, was often troubled by her brilliant conversation, in which he felt discomforted by her pleasure in the word. As he wrote in his memoir of Fuller, he "found something profane" in her "amusing gossip," and "fancied her too much interested in personal history." He remembered that "she made me laugh more than I liked."[28] The language that Emerson preferred was more public, aggressive, and phallic; as he wrote in his journal in 1841, "give me initiative, spermatic, prophesying, man-making words."[29] In his discussion of Fuller's literary style, Emerson deplored her lack of phallic power. "Her only adequate channel was in her conversation," he wrote. "Her pen was a non-conductor."[30] To Emerson, Fuller's conversation became her feminine "channel," associated with the vaginal canal, while the spermatic ejaculations of the pen were unavailable to her.

Perhaps it is this conflict or disparity Emerson had in mind when he wrote that he could not understand her: "There is a difference in our constitution," Emerson wrote to Fuller. "We use a different rhetoric. It seems as if we had been born and bred in different nations. You say you understand me wholly. But you cannot communicate yourself to me. I hear the words sometimes but remain a stranger to your state of mind."[31] Writing from the doubled world of women, Fuller was indeed "born and bred" in a nation, or at least a state of mind, very different from Emerson's, spoke another language. They remained strangers who could not be "at home" in each other's conversation. In Emerson's system, as David Leverenz has argued, "the women's world of relations and feelings becomes irrelevant.... Emerson's ideal of manly self-empowering reduces womanhood to spiritual nurturance while erasing female subjectivity."[32] As Louisa May Alcott ruefully noted, explaining why she had struggled to restrain her own natural ambition for "gorgeous fantasies," "To have had Mr. Emerson as an intellectual God all one's life is to be invested with a chain armor of propriety."[33]

Fuller struggled with the effort to combine patriarchal rhetoric and matriarchal rhetoric into a coherent literary style. In her journal she noted: "For all the tides of life that flow within me, I am dumb and ineffectual when it comes to casting my thought into a form. No old one suits me. If I could invent one, it seems to me the pleasure of creation would make it possible for me to write.... One should be either private or public. I love best to be a woman; but womanhood is at present too straitly-bound to give me scope. At hours, I live truly as a woman; at others, I should stifle; as, on the other hand, I should palsy when I would play the artist."[34]

Fuller might have resolved her conflict between the mother and father tongues by writing novels. In 1835, while reading George Sand, she briefly considered such a possibility. "These books," she wrote in her journal, "have made me for the first time think I might write into such shapes what I know of human nature." Yet fiction was too negatively associated with the emotional and the feminine, as Fuller finally concluded: "I have always thought... that I would keep all that behind the curtain, that I would not write, like a woman, of love and hope and disappointment, but like a man, of the world of intellect and action."[35] Once again the heavy curtain of intellect smothered what she felt to be her "true life" of feeling.

In *Woman in the Nineteenth Century,* according to research by Annette Kolodny, Fuller had attempted to develop a new feminist discourse closely modeled on Richard Whately's *Elements of Rhetoric* (1832). In borrowing from Whately, Fuller refused the coercive strategies of rhetoric he called "persuasion," including ridicule of the opponent, lurid examples, trickery, artifice, and heightened emotionalism. Rather than forcing her readers' consent, Fuller wanted them to engage in a dialogue with her, to be respected rather than manipulated.[36]

Florence Nightingale's case was similar in many respects. She too had been educated by her father, and thought of mathematics, law, and phi-

losophy as masculine discourses superior to the feminine world of gossip, conversation, and fiction. Like Fuller, she was suspicious of the
romantic mythologies of the novel form, and its views of female destiny:
"The novel—what a false idea it is—" she wrote, "brings two people
through 'no end' of troubles, to make them at last—what? exclusive for
one another, caring alone for one another—'wrapped up,' as it is called,
in each other—an abyss of binary selfishness."[37] The novel was the instrument of a destructive ideology that locked women into the home.
Furthermore, like Fuller, Nightingale despised the "feminine" passivity
of fiction. As she told a friend in 1844, "Writing is only a supplement
for living. . . . I think one's feelings waste themselves in words; they
ought all to be distilled into actions, and into actions which bring
results."[38]

Nightingale wrote *Suggestions for Thought* during a period of emotional despair after her thirtieth birthday, when it appeared that her family would never allow her to enter professional training as a nurse.
During this period, she experienced hysterical and depressive symptoms;
she fainted, fell into trances, and even thought of suicide. All of her
immense intellectual energy was channeled into her writing. Originally,
as manuscript drafts in the British Library show, she planned two
books.[39] The first book was a philosophical treatise on the oppressive
Victorian institutions of the family and the Church. Written from a
strong and original feminist perspective, it includes sections called "Theory of Daughters," and arguments for women's active role in religious
thought. At the same time, Nightingale was writing an autobiographical
novel called *Cassandra*. In letters to friends, Nightingale sometimes referred to herself as "poor Cassandra," feeling that, as the mythical Cassandra, having rejected the love of Apollo, was doomed to utter true
prophecies that would go unheeded, she, in rejecting marriage and
the common lot of woman, had doomed herself to silence, hysteria, and
futility.

The process of writing was therapeutic; Nightingale analyzed and released repressed emotions that had kept her paralyzed, and when the
books were complete, she found the courage to make the major break
with her family that took her to the Crimea. "I have come into possession of myself," she wrote to her father; and to her mother, "You must
now consider me married or a son."[40] Through writing, Nightingale
was able to find a voice and to release herself from self-destructive fantasies. As Diane Price Herndl has observed in her study of Bertha Pap-
penheim ("Anna O.") and Charlotte Perkins Gilman, writing could be a
cure for hysteria: "Hysteria can be understood as a woman's response to
a system in which she is expected to remain silent, a system in which her

subjectivity is continually denied, kept invisible. In becoming a writer, a woman becomes . . . a subject who produces that which is visible."[41] Writing was the bridge by which Nightingale made her escape from hysteria into feminism.

When she returned from the war as a national heroine in the late 1850s, she set about revising her books for publication. But rather than sending the manuscripts to any of the literary women she knew well, such as Harriet Martineau, Elizabeth Gaskell, or George Eliot, Nightingale sought the advice of the reigning male intellectuals of her day— John Stuart Mill and Benjamin Jowett, Master of Balliol College and Regius Professor of Greek at Oxford. Mill recommended publication, but Jowett suggested extensive revisions, including a more orderly arrangement of the text, cutting, and reorganization. He was particularly bothered by expressions of Nightingale's anger. A well-known opponent of the higher education of women at Oxford, Jowett had such confidence in his intellectual superiority and infallibility that he was the subject of satire even by his male contemporaries:

> First come I, Benjamin Jowett.
> If it's knowable, I know it.
> I am Master of this college.
> What I don't know isn't knowledge.[42]

Under Jowett's tutelage, Nightingale made extensive changes in her text. "Cassandra" became a section of the second volume of the treatise. Evidence that it had been a novel, such as descriptions of characters, dialogue, and dramatic scenes, were dropped. Nightingale then eliminated the first-person narrative and all personal allusions. In short, the "feminine" aspects of the text were subjected to rigorous discipline. Finally she abandoned the project altogether. A few copies of the gutted book were privately printed for friends. Like the "eloquent omission" of Cassandra's utterances in the *Oresteia*, the text of Nightingale's "Cassandra" is full of gaps and holes, although they are the product of censorship rather than intention.[43] Ironically, "Cassandra" *became* a hysterical narrative as Nightingale attempted to make it fit patriarchal epistemology.

I would like to suggest that the gaps in the texts of Fuller and Nightingale are sites of contradiction. They are the places where the writer's conflict between her internalization of patriarchal rhetorical forms and her need to articulate a feminine subjectivity reveals itself. Margaret Walters has suggested that the contradictory impulses of feminist writing can be conceptualized as the split between women's rights and women's wrongs. The language of women's rights is rhetorical, legalistic, logical, and objective; the language of women's wrongs is literary, personal, discursive, and emotional.[44] The feminist polemic oscillates between these two kinds of discourse, leaving many gaps, spaces, and disjunctions in the text where the transition is repressed. Such ruptures and intervals in the linearity of the feminist text are what the French feminist critic Xavière Gauthier describes as "holes in discourse," the places where women's writing becomes "compromised, rationalized, masculinized as it explains itself."[45] From Wollstonecraft's *Vindication of the Rights of Woman* to such twentieth-century texts as Olive Schreiner's *Woman and Labor* or Dorothy Dinnerstein's *The Mermaid and the Minotaur,* the seemingly random structure of the feminist polemic is the outcropping of a suppressed or submerged scheme.

One particularly interesting recent example of this phenomenon is the East German novelist Christa Wolf's *Cassandra* (1984). About half of the book is a novella retelling the story of the fall of Troy from Cassandra's point of view. The rest of the book is made up of four essays in different modes—the lecture, the travelogue, the diary, and the letter. Wolf uses the figure of Cassandra in these essays to represent several of her concerns: her fears about nuclear war, her thoughts about the role of women, her views on prophecy and spirituality, and especially her ideas about women's writing, feminist discourse, and the woman intellectual.

In many respects, Wolf's *Cassandra* resembles the feminist polemics of Fuller and Nightingale. Critics complained that the book did not belong to any recognizable genre, but seemed to be a peculiar hybrid with no clear relation between its various parts. Like her precursors, Wolf used feminist terms in defending the apparent formlessness of her text: "this fabric . . . did not turn out completely tidy, is not surveyable at one glance. Many of its motifs are not followed up, many of its threads are tangled. There are wefts which stand out like foreign bodies, repetitions, material that has not been worked out to its conclusions. . . . I feel keenly the tension between the artistic forms within which we have agreed to abide, and the living material, borne in on me by my senses, my psychic approaches, and my thought, which has resisted these forms." She argues that intellectual forms are patriarchal, that "thought has had no mothers, only fathers," and protests against the social obstacles facing the female intellectual: "Any woman in this century . . . who has ventured into male-dominated institutions—literature and aesthetics are such institutions—must have experienced the desire for self-destruction."[46]

What happens if we apply some of the questions raised by these texts to the discourse of feminist criticism? Are Miranda and Cassandra still the only models available to the feminist intellectual: to be either the motherless daughter of the fathers, the stranger in the father's library; or the "hysterical" woman who has rejected the protection of the male gods? Writing within a discourse that has been more of a male preserve than any literary mode except the epic and the pastoral elegy, feminist critics have tried both to identify with the father, to reproduce the forms of persuasion within which we have all agreed to abide, and to identify with the mother by accommodating a different kind of literary experience that resists these forms. Our sense of the tensions between the critical forms and the living material, and our struggle to find a language that can express these contradictions has many correspondences to the experience of Nightingale and Fuller.

One of the most important categories of critical rhetoric is that of "polemic," part of the agonistic tradition of male intellectual and academic discourse explored by Walter Ong in *Fighting for Life: Contest, Sexuality, and Consciousness*. The word *polemic* comes from the Greek word for war, and in modern life, according to Father Ong, polemic is one of the rituals by which a traditional or even biological male combativeness has expressed itself. Originally an oral rhetorical mode, polemic follows certain clear-cut rules of argument, challenge, and attack that men, in Ong's essentialist view, find natural and that women find unnatural: "Men characteristically (not always) develop a rhetorical argument by beginning with something like their final conclusion, while women characteristically (not always) begin with the expectation that they must pull their audiences around to their point of view by indirection.... The indirection of feminine persuasive discourse fits private conversational exchange."[47] Ong, too, sees female discourse as private, more suited to conversation than criticism, unaggressive if not passive.

Within literary criticism, Ong's polemical model has been extended by the agonistic theory and practice of Harold Bloom. In "The Breaking of Form," Bloom describes the task and stance of the critical theorist as "strong reading," a form of verbalized aggression. "Reading well," he argues, "is ... not a polite process and may not meet the academy's social standards of civility." Bloom's psychological formula for the strong poet applies to the strong critic as well: a "triadic sequence of narcissism, wounded self-regard, and aggression.... Change in poetry and criticism as in human endeavor comes about only through aggression."[48] Bloom contrasts the aggression of the strong reader to the polite civility of "the academy," a term which in this context carries echoes of the ladies' academy, the world of decorum and "sivilization" from which the virile American hero has traditionally fled.

Recently the Bloomian metaphor of "strong reading" has been literalized into something closer to aerobic reading. One might have thought that reading was one of the few remaining activities outside of such masculine virility contests; but instead it appears that with the threatened feminization of the profession of English, competitive reading has replaced jogging as the academic macho sport. The ironies of strong reading are multiplied as it is picked up by the mass media, ever eager to promote new champions in any field. While the *New York Times Sunday Magazine* pictured Bloom reclining on a sofa, supine amidst his piles of books like a New Haven odalisque, he has also told a reporter from *Newsweek* that he reads 1,000 pages an hour, that he remembers everything he reads, and that in editing 800 volumes of literary criticism, he has taken on all of literature.[49]

It is surely not coincidental that Emerson has become the patron saint, the Transcendental signifier, of Bloom and of other strong readers. As David Leverenz reminds us, outside of academia, Bloom's enthusiasm for Emerson was shared by Woody Hayes: "Both men are strenuously embattled champions of combat." Bloom and Hayes, according to Leverenz, "love Emerson because Emerson inspires feelings of access to manly power." On the playing fields of contemporary American criticism, quoting "Emerson," praising the genius of "Emerson," exchanging tributes to "Emerson" operates as a rich intertextuality of male academic bonding, promising access to a specifically male critical authority. To have this power shared by women would undermine its integrity and strength, and thus in the midst of an essay significantly entitled "Where Is Emerson Now That We Need Him?" Richard Poirier finds it necessary to announce his conviction that "the practice, as against the theory, of feminist criticism, has in many cases weakened the critical enterprise."[50]

Feminist critics must reject this dualistic vocabulary of aggression and weakness, and change the definitions of strong reading that implicitly exclude women's texts. In the introduction to *Provisions,* her anthology of nineteenth-century American women's writing, Judith Fetterley offers some stimulating notes toward a theory of feminist reading / writing. In her first book, *The Resisting Reader,* Fetterley explains, she had written polemically about classic American male literature. Although she had expected the book "to generate criticism, even hostility," in its style, she felt safe: "It was familiar, authoritative, even self-assured." But a book on women writers required a different style and technique. There was no established body of criticism to resist. "Now I wanted a voice that would facilitate receptivity, rather than resistance. I wanted my prose to impede as little as possible the reader's own relation to what I saw as the primary text. I wanted my words to serve as medium and instrument, not interference and armament." Fetterley believes that the process of

working on women writers who were marginal, uncanonical, and un-
nourished by the "placentas" of criticism—biography, bibliography, or
scholarly editions—changed her "critical persona, style, function, and
stance from 'masculine' to 'feminine.'" Yet for some this lack of polemical aggression made the book unacceptable. A reviewer of the book for
a university press found her argument "unfocused" and her style "im-
pressionistic." To a reader accustomed to the trappings of "strong reading," the absence of aggression could only signal weakness.[51]

Similar objections were raised to a feminist book very different from
Fetterley's—Jane Gallop's *Reading Lacan*. Gallop too tells the story of a
review of her manuscript for a university press by a reader who protested
that her text "demonstrated inadequate command of the subject matter"—a lack compounded by her own admission that she sometimes
found Lacan confusing. Gallop should wait to write about Lacan, the
reader's report concluded, until she is "no longer confused." Moreover,
the reader objected to Gallop's use of the pronoun *she* as generic, calling
it "an act of aggression." Thus the passive uncommanding female text is
mingled with the aggressive feminist rejection of the generic *he*.

Gallop persuasively sees these two objections as related. Her reader
assumed that the only correct reading was a strong reading "that speaks
from a position of mastery over a text." But Gallop was trying to write
from a more vulnerable and unsettling confrontation with the Lacanian
text, one which required an acknowledgment of "everyone's inevitable
'castration' [and powerlessness] in language." To challenge the "phallic
illusions of authority" by refusing to pretend an impossible mastery of
the contradictory Lacanian text, to "cover one's inadequacy in order to
have the right to speak," is a project Gallop calls both feminist and Lacanian. Her alternation of *he* and *she* insists that we remain aware of the
suppression of sexual difference in the discourse of male universals. Thus
Gallop presents us with a feminist literary practice "that neither reads
women's texts nor reads for the representation of women."[52]

At its best, the discourse of the feminist critic, like that of Fuller and
Nightingale, achieves its authority through both the demonstration of
mastery and the admission of uncertainty. Feminist reading insists both
on the right of the woman to speak as knower and on the need to expose the gaps in knowledge conventionally covered over. Although
women often feel guilty about their own competitive feelings, challenge,
polemic, and conflict are part of the feminist critical repertoire.[53] We
must speak from a position of strength and power, yet at the same time
put that power into question through self-criticism and humor, and
through criticism of the institutions that confer critical power. As Jane
Gallop has argued, the feminist reading, or the antiphallocentric read-

ing, attempts to "undo authority . . . from the position of authority, in a way that exposes the illusions of that position without renouncing it, so as to permeate the position itself with the connotations of its illusoriness."[54]

If feminist critics are now in a position to survive hostile or uncomprehending readings and to pursue a variety of innovative projects, it is in large part because we have recovered a history in which thought has mothers as well as fathers, a history that gives us confidence in the legitimacy of our own ideas. The experiences of Fuller and Nightingale are central to that history of feminist discourse, helping us to understand the contradictions mirrored in their texts, and the social and material contexts that produced those conflicts. For women writing criticism in the fin de siècle, the dilemmas of Miranda and Cassandra need not lead to silence, weakness, or self-destruction, but to new forms of discourse and strength.

NOTES

1. Letter, 29 November 1847, in *Florence Nightingale in Rome*, ed. Mary Keele (Philadelphia: American Philosophical Association, 1981), p. 78.

2. R. W. Emerson, quoted in Bell Gale Chevigny, *The Woman and the Myth: Margaret Fuller's Life and Writings* (New York: Feminist Press, 1976), p. 9.

3. James Russell Lowell, "A Fable for Critics," in *Poetical Works* (Boston: Houghton Mifflin, 1904), 4:62–64.

4. Perry Miller, *Margaret Fuller: American Romantic*, 1936; quoted in Marie Urbanski, *Margaret Fuller's "Woman in the Nineteenth Century,"* (Westport, Conn.: Greenwood Press, 1980), p. 38.

5. Letter, 17 November 1847, in *The Letters of Margaret Fuller*, ed. Robert N. Hudspeth (Ithaca: Cornell University Press, 1987), 4:310–11.

6. For a fuller discussion of the publishing history of *Cassandra*, see Elaine Showalter, "Florence Nightingale's Feminist Complaint," *Signs* 6 (Spring 1981), 395–412.

7. The best available text of *Cassandra* is Myra Stark's pamphlet for The Feminist Press in 1979; but neither this edition, nor the excerpt from it in Sandra Gilbert and Susan Gubar's *Norton Anthology of Literature by Women* (New York: W. W. Norton, 1985), pp. 804–13, includes the running titles and marginal glosses of the original. Katherine Snyder of Yale is currently editing a scholarly edition of *Cassandra*.

8. The term *womanifesto* is from Sandra Gilbert, Introduction to Hélène Cixous and Catherine Clément, *The Newly-Born Woman* (Minneapolis: University of Minnesota Press, 1986), p. x.

9. See Edward T. Cook, *The Life of Florence Nightingale* (London: Macmillan, 1913), 1:473; Orestes Brownson, *Boston Quarterly Review*, April 1845,

quoted in Urbanski, *Margaret Fuller's "Woman in the Nineteenth Century,"* p. 128; and Miller, *Margaret Fuller,* quoted in Urbanski, p. 38.

10. Margaret Fuller, *Woman in the Nineteenth Century* (New York: W. W. Norton, 1971), pp. 38–43.

11. Stephen Orgel, "Prospero's Wife," *Representations* 8 (Fall 1984), 1–13.

12. On Caliban, see Rob Nixon, "Caribbean and African Appropriations of *The Tempest,*" *Critical Inquiry* 13 (Spring 1987), 557–78. I have discussed the Miranda metaphor at length in *The Tenth Muse: Traditions and Contradictions in American Women's Writing* (New York: Oxford University Press, forthcoming).

13. Fuller also uses the image of Minerva to describe female intellectual rationality.

14. Fuller, *Woman in the Nineteenth Century,* pp. 116–20.

15. Nightingale, *Cassandra,* p. 25.

16. Ibid., pp. 37, 50.

17. Cook, *The Life of Florence Nightingale,* 1:385.

18. Chevigny, *The Woman and the Myth,* p. 136; Cook, *The Life of Florence Nightingale,* 1:43.

19. Elizabeth Hardwick, "The Genius of Margaret Fuller," *New York Review of Books,* April 10, 1986, p. 14.

20. Chevigny, *The Woman and the Myth,* p. 39.

21. Ibid.

22. Ibid., p. 42.

23. Ibid.

24. Margaret Fuller, quoted in Annette Kolodny, "The Problem of Persuasion in a Culture of Coercion: Margaret Fuller's *Woman in the Nineteenth Century,*" (Paper presented at MLA, December 1986, New York), p. 13. Thanks to Annette Kolodny for sharing this paper with me.

25. Horace Greeley quoted in Chevigny, *The Woman and the Myth,* p. 305.

26. James Freeman Clarke and Frederic Henry Hodge, quoted in Urbanski, *Margaret Fuller's "Woman of the Nineteenth Century,"* p. 7.

27. Orestes Brownson, quoted in Kolodny, "The Problem of Persuasion," p. 3.

28. Ralph Waldo Emerson, quoted in Chevigny, *The Woman and the Myth,* p. 91.

29. Emerson, quoted in David Leverenz, "The Politics of Emerson's Man-Making Words," *PMLA* 101 (Jan. 1986), p. 39.

30. Emerson, quoted in Urbanski, *Margaret Fuller's "Woman of the Nineteenth Century,"* p. 7.

31. Emerson to Fuller, 24 October 1840, in *The Letters of Ralph Waldo Emerson,* ed. Ralph L. Rusk, 6 vols. (New York: Columbia University Press, 1939), 2:353.

32. Leverenz, "The Politics of Emerson's Man-Making Words," p. 39.

33. Louisa May Alcott, quoted by LaSalle Corbett Pickett, *Across My Path: Memories of People I Have Known* (New York: Brentano, 1916), pp. 107–8.

34. Fuller, quoted in Chevigny, *The Woman and the Myth,* p. 63.

35. Ibid., p. 57.

36. See Kolodny, "The Problem of Persuasion in a Culture of Coercion."

37. Florence Nightingale, quoted in C. Woodham Smith, *Florence Nightingale 1820–1910* (New York: McGraw-Hill, 1951).

38. Nightingale, quoted in Cook, *The Life of Florence Nightingale*, 1:93.

39. The manuscript drafts of *Suggestions for Thought* are part of the Nightingale Papers in the British Library, Add. Mss. 45837, 45838, and 45839.

40. Margaret Goldsmith, *Florence Nightingale* (London, 1937), p. 99.

41. Diane Price Herndl, "The Writing Cure: Charlotte Perkins Gilman, Anna O., and 'Hysterical Writing,'" *NWSA Journal* 1 (1988), 53.

42. *Oxford Anthology of Humorous and Light Verse*. Thanks to Grant Webster of SUNY-Binghamton for this reference.

43. See Robert Fagles, Introduction, *Oresteia* (Harmondsworth: Penguin, 1984).

44. Margaret Walters, "The Rights and Wrongs of Women," in *The Rights and Wrongs of Women*, ed. Juliet Mitchell and Ann Oakley (Harmondsworth: Penguin, 1976), pp. 304–78.

45. Xavière Gauthier, "Is There Such a Thing as Women's Writing?" in *New French Feminisms*, ed. Elaine Marks and Isabelle de Courtivron (Amherst: University of Massachusetts Press, 1980), p. 164.

46. Christa Wolf, *Cassandra: A Novel and Four Essays*, trans. Jan van Heurck (New York: Farrar Straus Giroux, 1984).

47. Walter J. Ong, *Fighting for Life: Contest, Sexuality, and Consciousness* (Ithaca: Cornell University Press, 1981).

48. Harold Bloom, "The Breaking of Form," in *Deconstruction and Criticism*, ed. Bloom et al. (New York: Continuum, 1985), pp. 6, 7, 16.

49. David Lehman, "Yale's Insomniac Genius," *Newsweek*, 18 August 1986, pp. 56–57.

50. Leverenz, "Politics," p. 39; Poirier, "Where Is Emerson Now That We Need Him?" *New York Times Book Review*, 8 February 1987, p. 3.

51. Judith Fetterley, *Provisions* (Bloomington: Indiana University Press, 1985), pp. 36, 37.

52. Jane Gallop, *Reading Lacan* (Ithaca: Cornell University Press, 1985), pp. 18–20.

53. See the ground-breaking essay by Evelyn Fox Keller and Helene Moglen, "Competition and Feminism: Conflicts for Academic Women," *Signs* 12 (Spring 1987), 493–511, reprinted in *Competition: A Feminist Taboo*, ed. Valerie Miner and Helen Longino (New York: Feminist Press, 1987).

54. Jane Gallop, *The Daughter's Seduction* (Ithaca: Cornell University Press, 1982), p. 121.

CHARLOTTE GOODMAN

From Uncle Tom's Cabin *to Vyry's Kitchen: The Black Female Folk Tradition in Margaret Walker's* Jubilee

My grandmothers were strong.
They followed the plows and bent to toil.
They moved through fields sowing seed.
They touched the earth and grain grew.
They were full of sturdiness and singing.
—Margaret Walker, "Lineage"

Thanks to the recent efforts of feminist critics, one of America's most important nineteenth-century American novels, Harriet Beecher Stowe's neglected and often denigrated *Uncle Tom's Cabin,* has begun to receive the serious critical attention it so richly deserves. Although F. O. Matthiessen devoted only one sentence to *Uncle Tom's Cabin* in his monumental and very influential study of nineteenth-century American literature, *The American Renaissance,* new perspectives on Stowe's novel afforded by such critics as Nina Baym, Elizabeth Ammons, and Jane P. Tompkins have enabled us to appreciate the rhetorical brilliance of this work, which aimed to engage the sympathies of its readers so profoundly that they would be moved to abolish slavery.

A white woman addressing her jeremiad principally to other white women, Stowe beseeched the "mothers of America" to "pity those mothers that are constantly made childless by the American slave trade."[1] Appealing to her readers' maternal sentiments, she effectively dramatized the way in which the patriarchal institution of slavery threatened the Christian values of nurturing mothers like Mrs. Shelby, Mrs. Byrd, and Rachel Halliday—the true heroines of her narrative. As Elizabeth Ammons has pointed out, through these maternal figures Stowe postulates an alternative system of values to challenge the patriarchal status quo.[2]

Yet, brilliant though it is, *Uncle Tom's Cabin* is nevertheless a novel written by a privileged nineteenth-century white woman to an audience of privileged white women like herself. Although Stowe herself emphasized the historical accuracy of *Uncle Tom's Cabin* both in the novel itself and in the *Key to Uncle Tom's Cabin* that she published subsequently, a twentieth-century reader cannot help but be aware of the significant omissions in Stowe's portrait of the lives of slave women. What is lacking in Stowe's novel is a picture of the black women's own community, of their daily interactions with one another, and of the rich cultural life that flourished in the slave quarters. In part, no doubt, Stowe's failure to depict the life of characters like Eliza and Aunt Chloe in all their particularity and complexity was deliberate, for what Stowe wished to emphasize was the common humanity of all women rather than the cultural differences that distinguished black women from white ones. However, as a white woman living in the nineteenth century, Stowe also was not privy to the culture of black women, nor did she have access to the historical documents about the lives of black women that are available to us today. Consequently, if we wish to read a novel that will afford us a perspective on the actual day-to-day experiences of black women under slavery, we must turn to a work other than *Uncle Tom's Cabin*.

One twentieth-century novel that provides a compelling, detailed portrait of the daily lives of black women during the Civil War period is Margaret Walker's *Jubilee*, published by Houghton Mifflin in 1966. The impetus for this historical novel, which took Margaret Walker thirty-two years to complete, was her conviction that other fictional narratives about life in the South in the nineteenth century were lacking in verisimilitude because they failed to depict accurately the experience of black women. Believing that "the black woman's story has not been told, has not been dealt with adequately," Margaret Walker set out to depict the lives of black women from a black woman's perspective.[3] Defining *Jubilee* as a "folk novel based on folk material: folk sayings, folk beliefs, folkways," she said that she sought to give her own chronicle "the feel of a fabric of life."[4] Just as Zora Neale Hurston incorporated into her fiction the material she had culled from her anthropological investigations of black culture, so Walker included in *Jubilee* the rich material she had gathered painstakingly during the many years she spent investigating the black oral tradition, historical accounts of slavery, primary documents, and newspapers from the Civil War era. When Walker was a child, her grandmother Minna had told her stories about her great-grandmother, Elvira Ware Dozier, insisting that these tales about slave life in Georgia were "the naked truth."[5] Explaining the motivation for her own extensive research on life in the South in the nineteenth century, Walker wrote: "What was I trying to prove through this search among the old documents? I was simply determined to substantiate my material, to authenticate the story I had heard from my grandmother's lips. I was using literary documents to undergird the oral tradition."[6]

In a recent interview, Walker observed that she had deliberately set out to revise the stereotypical portraits of "the mammy, the faithful retainer, the picaninny, little Eva and Topsy, the tragic mulatto, the conjure-woman or witch, the sex object, the bitch goddess, the harlot ... and last but not least, the matriarch" that had appeared in the fiction of other writers.[7] While Walker does not specifically mention *Uncle Tom's Cabin*, the fact that she includes the names of Stowe's little Eva and Topsy among the stereotypes she had set out to revise suggests that one of the important texts that helped to shape her own countertext in *Jubilee* was Stowe's novel. By depicting the history of black women, including their healing arts, their recipes, their crafts, and their oral tradition, Margaret Walker fills in some of the lacunae in Stowe's novel, presenting a comprehensive account of the rich cultural heritage black women have passed down from one generation to the next.

Topsy illustrates what has been omitted in Stowe's novel. When queried about her origins, Topsy replies, "Never was born ... never had no father nor mother, nor nothin'" (p. 85). With no mother or father, without any ties to a black community of her own, Topsy is adopted by a white family, as are several other black characters in the novel. In contrast to Topsy, however, Walker's protagonist, Vyry, is vitally connected to her own black community, though she too has no parents to protect her. When Vyry is two years old, her mother dies while bearing a child fathered by the owner of the plantation, who is Vyry's father as well. Never acknowledged as kin by her biological father, Vyry is raised by other black women in the slave community.

Stowe's Eliza is also more closely connected to white women like Mrs. Shelby, Mrs. Byrd, and Mrs. Halliday than to black women like herself. Rarely depicting Eliza interacting with the black community, Stowe describes how she is nurtured by Mrs. Shelby and is even married in Mrs. Shelby's parlor rather than in the slave quarters. Instead of having Eliza speak in black dialect, as do other black characters in *Uncle Tom's Cabin*, Stowe assigns to Eliza speech identical to that of her white owners, emphasizing Eliza's essential similarity to the white women who comprised the intended audience for the novel. Dressed in clothing given to her by her exemplary mistress and carrying with her no language or other signifiers of her black cultural heritage, Eliza does not appear to possess any emblems of her past to transmit to the next generation. In contrast to Eliza, however, Margaret Walker's Vyry speaks the same black dialect as the other slaves, and when she departs from the

Duttons's plantation, she carries with her the story of her own past and the artifacts signifying her own black female cultural heritage. Walker depicts Vyry's life not only in the plantation house but in the slave quarters, where Vyry is nurtured by other black women and learns about the traditions of her own people. One of these traditions is the making of cloth. In her introduction to *Jubilee* Walker writes: "I have a true photograph of my own great-grandmother, who is the Vyry of this story. The picture was made approximately one hundred years ago. In it she is wearing a dress of black maline and her shawl is of yellow and red challis. From spinning the thread to weaving the cloth, the garments are entirely her handiwork."[8]

The clothes each character wears symbolize the difference between Stowe's conception of Eliza and Walker's of Vyry. While Eliza is dressed in the "spotted muslin gown" of her benevolent mistress (p. 77), Vyry, demonstrating the skills she has learned from other black women, wears the products of her own handiwork. In addition to wearing the clothes she herself has made, Vyry also carries with her the inscription of her own tragic history: the scars on her back record a brutal whipping she once received when she tried to run away.

A central determiner of Vyry's history is the fact that she is a product of miscegenation. While Stowe makes Eliza a mulatto to emphasize the similarity between her black protagonist and the white Mrs. Shelby, as well as between Eliza and the mothers Stowe addresses in the novel's final chapter, Walker chooses to emphasize instead the negative impact miscegenation had on the relationship between black and white women. Rather than conferring on Vyry special privileges, her light skin and blonde hair cause her to be singled out for special abuse by her mistress, who cannot bear to acknowledge the uncanny resemblance between Vyry and her own daughter. Stowe mentions the issue of miscegenation "en passant" (p. 182), while Walker shows miscegenation to be one of the most central issues in the history of both black and white women in the South.

Jubilee includes numerous signifiers of the black woman's history and culture, linking Vyry to past and future generations of black women. The novel incorporates the tales Vyry recites again and again about her journey from slavery to freedom as well as explicit descriptions of her herbal medicines, her cooking, her needlework, her songs and sayings—all the folk traditions her black female ancestors have passed on to her. As she departs from the plantation, she carries in her wagon

> iron pots and kettles, a wash pot, skillets, smoothing irons, candle molds and tallow candles, tin plates and cups and dippers of gourd and tin, a china wash bowl and pitcher and a slop jar. She had quilts and croker sacks of cotton and feathers for beds and pillows, a precious spinning

wheel, lots of potash soap, and most important of all, she had sacks of cracked corn meal, and sacks of seed. She filled the chest with the most valuable keepsakes from the plantation and Big House and tied it on the wagon. (P. 316)

Walker enumerates these items in such detail not only to lend verisimilitude to her novel but also to demonstrate how these material signifiers are passed on from slaves to free black women.

Two items in this list are especially significant: a china wash bowl and pitcher. In an earlier scene, which depicts the death of Vyry's mother in childbirth, Walker mentions a china wash bowl that the black midwife, Granny Ticey, uses to wash the dying woman; subsequently, other black women wash Vyry's bleeding back to remove the salt her cruel captors had poured on it after beating her for trying to run away; later, Vyry herself becomes a nurse to her ailing mistress and her mistress's daughter. As the list of items in Vyry's wagon reveals, the china wash bowl and pitcher are two treasured possessions Vyry brings with her to her new community. There she takes on the role of midwife that Granny Ticey had formerly assumed for the slaves on the plantation. By tracing the history of the china wash bowl and pitcher, Margaret Walker symbolically portrays how the healing arts are transmitted from black woman to black woman.

Another aspect of a vanishing culture that Walker preserves in her text is the tradition of black folk medicine. She describes, for example, how Vyry learns the lore of herbs and roots from other black women, and later depicts her gathering herbs and roots on her own. When Vyry is accosted by the white foreman, she explains that the mullein she has picked is "for the feets and legs to stop swelling and heart dropsy"; barefoot root is one of the ingredients in a salve for rheumatism; mayapple is good for the bowels; cherry roots strengthen the appetite; pulsey and pomegranate hulls cure diarrhea; and tansy tea, red shank, and hazel roots are effective remedies for "womanhood troubles" (p. 100). Vyry's recitation of this herbal lore enriches the texture of the novel and also records for posterity a part of the black female folk tradition Walker feared was in danger of disappearing.

In addition to revealing how the healing arts are transmitted from one generation to the next, Walker also describes the transmission of other traditional black female arts such as cooking and needlework. In the novel, the older black women on the Dutton plantation instruct the younger ones in the art of food preparation. Showing how Vyry is initiated by another woman into the rites of the kitchen, Walker writes: "Under the watchful eye of Aunt Sally, Vyry learned to churn. The child would watch eagerly and delightedly to see the first pat of butter form around the paddle. Aunt Sally showed her how to put milk in crocks, how to separate the heavy cream from the milk, make cottage cheese and clabber, and how to add warm water when you were in a hurry to make butter come fast" (p. 41). Just as Faulkner's Sam Fathers initiates the young Ike McCaslin into the rites of the hunt, which will signify Ike's entry in adulthood, so Aunt Sally teaches Vyry those skills that will prepare her to assume her role as a black woman.

In *Uncle Tom's Cabin* Stowe depicts the way in which black women feed white people, describing, for example, how Aunt Chloe feeds griddle cakes to Mrs. Shelby's son George when he pays a visit to the slave quarters. "Now Mas'r George, you jest... set down now with my old man, and I'll take up de sausages and have de first griddle full of cakes on your plate in no time," Aunt Chloe says, and she proceeds to feed the white boy before she feeds her own sons (pp. 69–70). In addition to depicting how black women feed white people, however, Walker also focuses on the way black women feed their own families. Thus Vyry not only learns from Aunt Sally the art of preparing food for the Big House but also the art of stealing food from her mistress's kitchen to supplement her own meager rations. "I ain't cooking nothing I can't eat myself," Aunt Sally proclaims defiantly to Vyry (p. 42). From Aunt Sally and other black women Vyry learns how to prepare the game and edible greens the slaves manage to obtain from the woods and fields. In the text of the novel Walker actually includes descriptions of dishes Vyry learns to cook, such as greens, parboiled and cooked with wild onions and salt meat, and a savory chicken stew. To emphasize the difference between the food black women prepared for their masters and the food they prepared for themselves, Walker mentions that one Christmas during the war Vyry cooked a ham for the Duttons but prepared possum and collard greens for her own family's Christmas dinner. One of the traditions black women have passed on from generation to generation, the culinary arts serve as important signifiers of the black female folk culture in *Jubilee*.

Although both Stowe and Margaret Walker celebrate the culinary skills of black women, Walker additionally emphasizes how much arduous labor is involved in the preparation of food. She mentions that house servants like Aunt Sally and Vyry take pride in their skills as cooks and bakers, but she also reveals how bitterly they resent the hard work they must do to prepare elaborate meals for their master's table. Confined in the sweltering kitchen of the plantation house, they perform their endless tasks because they know they will be beaten unless they do so.

Rather than using the preparation of food only to signify female nurturance, as Harriet Beecher Stowe had done, Walker also notes the way in which slavery had corrupted this activity. Associating food with acts of cruelty, Walker mentions, for example, that Salina Dutton regularly makes the slaves who work in her house ingest ipecac in order to determine whether they have been stealing food from her kitchen. One of the most cruel acts in *Jubilee* takes place in the kitchen: when Vyry accidentally breaks one of her mistress's dishes, Salina Dutton hangs her from a strap in a closet, leaving the terrified child suspended by her hands until she loses consciousness. To signify the devastation members of the Ku Klux Klan cause when they burn down Vyry's new house, Walker also mentions food, observing that all of Vyry's "rows of preserves and canned and pickled goods, jellies and jams" are lost in the fire (p. 386). Black women in *Jubilee* also perform destructive acts connected with the preparation of food. Walker mentions, for example, that two black women poison the food of their master and are later hanged at a public gathering on the Fourth of July. Thus Walker focuses on the culinary arts in *Jubilee* not only to celebrate the nurturing acts of black women but also to dramatize the way in which slavery corrupts basic human values.

Yet another signifier of the black female culture in *Jubilee* is needlework. Associating all of her major black female characters with sewing, Walker mentions a quilt in the cabin of Vyry's dying mother that is used to separate the bed from the rest of the room, quilts Aunt Sally hangs over the windows and door to keep out the cold, and quilts that Vyry packs in her wagon when she leaves the plantation. In one of the most joyous scenes in the novel, Vyry and her husband invite their white neighbors to a house-raising and a quilting bee during which Vyry herself works on a pieced quilt ornamented with pomegranates. Perhaps Walker found the pomegranate to be an appropriate design for Vyry's quilt because the pomegranate originated in Africa and was a fruit whose hull black women used to prepare one of their remedies.

To demonstrate how the art of sewing is passed from mother to daughter, Margaret Walker shows Vyry instructing her daughter Minna in the art of piecing quilts, and Minna gives her brother a gift of a handkerchief that she herself has hemmed. In the beginning of the novel Walker had described how Vyry, as a child, had observed with awe the "high mountain of feather mattresses always . . . covered with a snow-white counterpane" in her mistress's bedroom; by the novel's end, Vyry has triumphantly succeeded in replicating these furnishings in the bedroom of her own house. Minna admires the "high mounds of feather mattresses with the snowy counterpane, crocheted, tasseled, and fringed with white matching shams that Vyry had made for herself" (p. 496). Like the quilts a black mother passes on to her daughter in Alice Walker's widely anthologized short story, "Everyday Use," Vyry's needlework is one of the legacies she bequeaths to her daughter Minna.

More important, perhaps, than any other signifier in *Jubilee* are the verbal texts incorporated into the novel. These include female lore about menstruation, cautionary tales about sexual matters, information about pregnancy and childbirth, folk sayings, songs, and passages from the Old Testament. The novel is dedicated to the memory of Walker's grandmothers—her maternal great-grandmother, who is the Vyry of her novel, and her maternal grandmother, who told her the tales upon which the novel is based. Each chapter begins with a folk saying or lines from a song or spiritual, and Walker traces the way in which the oral tradition is passed on from one generation to the next. She depicts, for example, the two-year-old Vyry listening to a tune the black preacher is humming as he carries her to her dying mother's bedside, shows her listening raptly to the animal fables another preacher recites, and describes her as she hears his soulful rendition of "I Am a Poor Wayfaring Stranger." The young girl loves Aunt Sally's stories about "who she was and where she came from and what life was like" (p. 43) and is moved by the "mad-mood" songs the sorrowful Aunt Sally sings as she stirs the pot in her mistress's kitchen (p. 71). Walker also shows how the adult Vyry, in turn, tells stories about her past and sings the songs she learned in her youth to her own children.

In one of the scenes that Stowe introduces for comic relief in *Uncle Tom's Cabin*, Aunt Chloe confuses the words *poultry* and *poetry*, using the latter word to refer to the chickens she is about to cut up for chicken pie. As the final paragraphs of *Jubilee* suggest, for Margaret Walker "poultry" *is* "poetry," the daily domestic activities black women perform expressing their creativity. Walker concludes her novel with a description of Minna listening as her mother croons to a huge flock of laying-hens:

> Come biddy, biddy, biddy, biddy,
> Come chick, chick, chick, chick! (P. 497)

Vyry is surrounded by her "poultry," a symbol of fertility, and Walker reveals that Vyry herself is expecting another child. "I hopes this next child will be a gal. Gal babies don't never want to leave their maw easy," Vyry says (p. 496). Her words reflect Margaret Walker's own vision of an ongoing women's community—one that will guarantee the survival of the black folk tradition.

It is unfortunate that Margaret Walker's *Jubilee* has received relatively little attention from the critics. As Minrose Gwinn has pointed out in her recent discussion of the novel, *Jubilee* is not even mentioned by the male authors of several influential studies of Afro-American literature.[9] Moreover, despite the current interest in fiction by black women, *Jubilee* has been far less frequently discussed even by feminist critics than, for example, the novels of Toni Morrison, Alice Walker, and a number of other contemporary black women writers.[10] Since Walker imitates the conventional linear structure of the traditional slave narrative, perhaps one reason *Jubilee* has received so little critical attention is that it appears to be less innovative than novels like Morrison's *The Bluest Eye* and *Sula* or Alice Walker's *The Color Purple*. In addition, *Jubilee* does not focus on sexism within the black community as the novels of other contemporary black women writers frequently do.[11] Furthermore, Margaret Walker's espousal of the doctrine of Christian humanism in *Jubilee*, her endorsement of the principles of nonviolence, and her affirmation of the bonds between black women and white ones may have antagonized the more militant black writers of the seventies and eighties. Nevertheless, I would argue that *Jubilee* deserves to be much better known than it is at present, for in it Margaret Walker has succeeded in representing what no other American writer has represented with so much skill or authority: a compelling picture of the community of black women during the Civil War period.

If a case can be made for including Harriet Beecher Stowe's *Uncle Tom's Cabin* in the canon of American literature—as indeed it should be—then perhaps Margaret Walker's *Jubilee* should be included in the canon as well. A fine historical novel in its own right, *Jubilee* can also serve as an important countertext to Stowe's *Uncle Tom's Cabin*. Walker's richly imagined and carefully documented representation of the community of black women re-creates a world that is virtually invisible in Stowe's novel, in nineteenth-century male slave narratives, and in betterknown twentieth-century historical novels about the experiences of black people in the South during the Civil War period, such as Alex Haley's *Roots* and Ernest Gaines's *The Diary of Miss Jane Pittman*. Both Harriet Beecher Stowe and Margaret Walker emphasize the bonds between black and white women,[12] but in addition Walker also dramatizes the ways in which women within the black community were vitally connected to one another. Far from crowding too much into *Jubilee*, as one critic has accused her of doing, Walker scrupulously delineates the culture of black women that has been omitted in other works of fiction.[13] Like the preserves and the unfinished quilt in Susan Glaspell's play *Trifles*, the many objects Walker incorporates into her novel and the various aspects of black female culture she depicts are not mere "trifles" but important signifiers of the black female folk tradition. *Jubilee* documents what Alice Walker has called the "creative spark" of those black mothers and grandmothers who might have been poets, novelists, essayists, or short story writers, but who expressed their creativity instead in their gardens, in their quilts, and in the stories they told their children.[14] As critics have argued, Stowe's Uncle Tom becomes a black Christ figure; in *Jubilee*, whose typology is based on the Old, rather than the New, Testament, Uncle Tom's female counterpart, Vyry, functions as a black Moses leading her people from bondage to freedom. Like Toni Morrison's *Song of Solomon,* Alice Walker's *The Color Purple,* and Gloria Naylor's *The Women of Brewster Place,* Margaret Walker's *Jubilee* is both a portrait of a memorable black female folk heroine and a celebration of the black female community.

NOTES

1. Harriet Beecher Stowe, *Uncle Tom's Cabin* (New York: Penguin American Library, 1983), pp. 623–24. Further references to this novel appear in parentheses in the text.

2. Elizabeth Ammons, "Heroines in *Uncle Tom's Cabin,*" in *Critical Essays on Harriet Beecher Stowe,* ed. Elizabeth Ammons (Boston: G. K. Hall, 1980), p. 153.

3. Nikki Giovanni and Margaret Walker, *A Poetic Equation: Conversations between Nikki Giovanni and Margaret Walker* (Washington: Howard University Press, 1974), p. 91.

4. Margaret Walker, *How I Wrote "Jubilee"* (Chicago: Third World Press, 1977), pp. 25, 20, now available in *"How I Wrote Jubilee" and Other Essays on Literature and Life* (New York: Feminist Press, 1990).

5. Ibid., p. 12.

6. Ibid., p. 18.

7. Claudia Tate, "Conversation with Margaret Walker," in *Black Women Writers at Work* (New York: Continuum, 1983), p. 203.

8. Margaret Walker, *Jubilee* (Boston: Houghton Mifflin, 1966), p. x. Further references to this novel appear in parentheses in the text.

9. See Minrose Gwinn, *"Jubilee:* The Black Woman's Celebration of Human Community," in *Conjuring: Black Women, Fiction, and Literary Theory,* ed. Marjorie Pryse and Hortense J. Spillers (Bloomington: Indiana University Press, 1985), p. 149, note 9.

10. For a discussion of other novels by black women that also focus on the history and community of black women, see Hortense J. Spillers, Afterword, in *Conjuring.*

11. See Barbara J. Christian, "Trajectories of Self-Definition: Placing Contemporary Afro-American Women's Fiction," in *Conjuring,* pp. 233–48.

12. For a discussion of the bonding between black and white women in *Jubilee,* see Gwinn, *Jubilee,* pp. 131–50.

13. Arthur P. Davis, *From the Dark Tower* (Washington, D.C.: Howard University Press, 1974), p. 184.

14. Alice Walker, *In Search of Our Mothers' Gardens* (New York: Harcourt Brace Jovanovich, 1983), p. 234.

The Needle or the Pen:
The Literary Rediscovery of
Women's Textile Work

The rediscovery and celebration of women's traditional textile work—the domestic arts of spinning and weaving, sewing and quilting—constitutes by now a widespread and peculiarly interesting development in contemporary feminist thinking. In the past two decades visual artists and art historians, social historians, folklorists, poets and novelists, and most recently literary critics and theorists have discovered in the processes and products of the spindle, shuttle, and needle a major source for understanding women of the past, and, as well, a source of subject matter and of images and metaphors for new creative work. The rediscovery began in the early 1970s, when visual artists like Judy Chicago and Miriam Schapiro found new artistic inspiration and self-validation in women's needlework. Chicago's collaborative art projects—most notably *The Dinner Party* (1974–79) and most recently *The Birth Project* (1980–85)—resurrected an array of traditional needlework techniques, from weaving and quilting to lace making, stump work, and embroidery. And Schapiro, in canvases that combined paint with the fabrics of women's domestic lives—aprons, handkerchiefs, curtains, and patchwork—invented her female version of collage, which she called "femmage," to celebrate women's traditional craft activity, connect herself to earlier unknown artists, and embrace the domestic world of women that she had previously dismissed.[1] The extent of feminist artists' interest in women's textile work was clearly evident by 1978, when *Heresies* devoted an entire issue to "Women's Traditional Arts," with articles, in addition to Schapiro's on femmage, on weaving, knitting, quilting, lace making, embroidery, and plain sewing. And by that time the mainstream, or "high," art world had also acknowledged women's needlework. A widespread revival of interest in quilt making, beginning in the 1960s and paralleling, although not emerging out of, the new feminism, had been officially sanctioned, as it were, by the 1971 Whitney Museum exhibition of American quilts.

Meanwhile, as feminist historians moved from charting women's subordination under patriarchy to investigating positive sources of women's strength and survival, social historians like Nancy Cott and Carroll Smith-Rosenberg were finding in nineteenth-century women's domestic world important qualities of cooperation and friendship, of "love and ritual"—qualities often seen as engendered and nourished by such shared work as sewing and quilting. Thus for Pat Mainardi the quilting bee became an early form of consciousness-raising; for Dolores Hayden, a model for cooperative cooking and cleaning arrangements, through which women reformers tried to take charge of, and change, their domestic lives.[2] In the early 1970s, also, Alice Walker in her landmark essay "In Search of Our Mothers' Gardens" revealed the importance, for artistic and spiritual survival, of such domestic activities as gardening and quilting for generations of slave and free black women.[3]

By the mid-1970s also religious scholars were extending their scope, from documenting the damaging effects on women of male-defined religions to exploring women's own spirituality, and they found in women's textile work a vocabulary through which to formulate, in Mary Daly's words, "new ways of thinking, feeling, Be-ing." Daly's etymological researches uncovered the root, and radical, meanings of terms like "spinster," "weaver," and "spider." The controlling metaphor in *Gyn/Ecology: The Metaethics of Radical Feminism* (1978) was that of spinning, defined as a "creative enterprise of mind and imagination," of "connectedness within the cosmos."[4] In her chapter on "Spinning: Cosmic Tapestries" Daly quoted from poems published just a year or two earlier by Adrienne Rich and Robin Morgan, for by the mid-1970s poets were also finding in women's textile work a major source of what Rich had called for in 1971: new "language and images for a consciousness we are just coming into."[5] Both Rich's *The Dream of a Common Language* (1977) and Morgan's *Lady of the Beasts* (1976) employed tropes taken from quilt and tapestry work, as well as imagery of spiders and webs and the Spider-Goddess. In the early 1980s Judy Grahn (with acknowledgment to Rich, among other writers) published *The Queen of Wands,* a reading of Helen of Troy as one incarnation of an "astonishingly worldwide myth" of a female god of "beauty, fire, love, light, thought, and weaving"; and American Indian poets like Paula Gunn Allen (whom Grahn also acknowledged) were incorporating into their work their cultures' stories and legends of Grandmother Spider, weaver and controller of natural forces.[6]

Most recently, feminist literary theorists and critics have also been finding in the tropology of women's textile work a useful language of critical discourse. Reviving ancient connections between textiles and texts, they are rereading the legends of Arachne and her web, Ariadne and her thread, Penelope and her loom, Philomel and her embroidery in order to discover metaphors of female creativity. Thus, Susan Gubar has explored the connections between spinning, weaving, and writing in Isak Dinesen's "The Blank Page"; Nancy Miller has described her critical approach to women's writing as an "arachnology"; Jane Marcus has urged critics to become "readers of the peplos"; and Elaine Showalter argues for a point of entry into the "structures, genres, themes and meanings" of American women's writings through the "American woman's tradition of piecing, patchwork, and quilting."[7]

This widespread reappropriation of women's textile work, which finds in it such a range of empowering creative possibilities, might well have astonished earlier generations of American feminists and writers, for whom liberation was more often from, than by, the needle. For large numbers of women entering authorship in the nineteenth century, sewing—as material reality and also as powerful symbolic marker of their cultural condition, their restricted domestic role—functioned as both literal and psychological deterrent to ambition and achievement. This inverse association of sewing and literary creativity indeed persisted for well over one hundred and fifty years, from nineteenth-century writers through the women poets of the 1920s into the work of Sylvia Plath in the early 1960s. As such it represents a most important, but until now ignored, chapter in the story of the relation of women's textiles to their texts. While our contemporary interest in grounding both critical and imaginative writing in the tropes of women's textile work has helped us reclaim a rich and long-neglected tradition of women's creative expression, in doing the work of restoration, we must not overlook the efforts of generations of earlier women to achieve creative autonomy precisely by dissociating themselves from the self-same domestic work we now privilege. Especially if we want to reconstruct the literary traditions of nineteenth-century women in something approaching their true complexity, we cannot afford to ignore this adversarial relationship.[8]

This essay will, therefore, trace the negative relationship between women's textile and text making that had emerged by the early decades of the nineteenth century and that persisted well into the middle of the twentieth, culminating in the work of Sylvia Plath. It will then look at contemporary women writers, especially Adrienne Rich and Alice Walker, as paramount examples of the current literary rediscovery and celebration of women's textile culture.

American women's writing might be said officially to have begun with a protest against the needle—Anne Bradstreet's defense of her poems, in the Prologue to *The Tenth Muse* (1650), against anticipated detractors who would say "my hand a needle better fits."[9] And by the late eighteenth century, when women were beginning to enter authorship in small but significant numbers, the needle was already established as symbol of woman's proper, and confined, sphere. To write was to move out of that sphere, to transgress into male territory. As Cathy Davidson has observed, "In the division of labor of the time, the pen almost as much as the sword, was deemed an implement of a man's trade." Aspiring women writers might court public acceptance by camouflaging literary production as textile work. Davidson cites the case of Sukey Vickery, whose novel, *Edith Hamilton,* was fictively presented by its printer as the work of a "country girl... residing in an obscure town, and by her needle maintaining her aged parents." Vickery thus became "an innocent, self-sacrificing daughter whose pen is barely distinguishable from her needle."[10]

This defensive strategy continued to be resorted to by nineteenth-century women. In 1801 Eliza Southgate, hungry for the mental stimulation that corresponding with her cousin Moses offered, but wary of antagonizing him (he had threatened to stop writing if she showed too much intellectual ambition), disparagingly compared her intellectual interests to quilting. Having "pieced [my ideas] ingeniously... into a few patchwork opinions," she wrote, "they are now almost threadbare, and as I am about quilting a few more, I beg you will send me any spare ideas you may chance to have...."[11] Half a century later, in 1859, Harriet Beecher Stowe, despite her by then recognized professional status, was using the same self-deprecating strategy to introduce her novel, *The Minister's Wooing.* Presenting herself as unskilled at composition, she explained that "you have a whole corps of people to introduce that you know and your reader doesn't; and one thing so presupposes another, that whichever way you turn your patchwork, the figures still seem ill-arranged."[12] Nineteenth-century authors like Stowe who used sewing to excuse their writing or explain it away would have been aware that while they were thus ostensibly reassuring male critics of their amateur status they were also sending a coded message to women readers, who would have understood the very real skills involved in the patchwork and quilting they presumably belittled. But the need to apologize, to allay male fears of female ambition by assurance that one's work was merely an innocuous extension of domesticity, like the other excuses nineteenth-century women offered for their work—that it was somehow helplessly produced, or written only out of dire financial need—could not but contribute to that sense of self-division, ambivalence, and even guilt about one's literary work that, as Mary Kelley has demonstrated, colored the thinking of many women writers.[13] Indeed, Stowe herself seems to have used sewing not only publicly to excuse her writing but literally to camouflage it in private. According to Gerda Lerner, Stowe "hid her 'scribblings' in her sewing basket, working on them secretly when the room was empty, and resuming her 'proper occupation' of darning and mending when anyone was present."[14]

Such ambivalence about being a writer was promoted, and exacerbated, by the increasing preeminence given to sewing within the ideology of the cult of true womanhood as that ideology came to be more rigidly articulated in the course of the nineteenth century. From the 1820s and 1830s through the 1860s, as Barbara Welter has shown, a vast body of prescriptive literature appeared—advice books, sermons, essays, articles and stories in women's magazines—that instructed women in the duties and deportment appropriate to their newly redefined domestic role.[15] And whether the literature was advising women on their daughterly, wifely, and maternal duties, their religious and charitable responsibilities, or their etiquette and proper manners, sewing was introduced as a crucial subject of discussion. A survey of this advice literature shows that sewing came to represent such an array of both essential and desirable skills, habits, attitudes, and virtues as eventually to be defined as the quintessentially feminine activity—the one through which a woman most closely identified herself with and accepted her "sphere" role. Throughout the century home sewing—of clothing and bed and table linens—continued to be essential work for the vast majority of women. Factory-made clothing, especially women's clothing, was not widely available until the 1890s. The advice literature encouraged such sewing, not least for the moral qualities it fostered—of thrift and industry, patience, and the acceptance of repetition and routine. Sewing for the poor, long recognized as one of women's responsibilities, fostered a desirable selflessness. And ornamental needlework—embroidery, lace making, crochet—was widely encouraged as a paramount means through which women could fulfill their role as tastemakers and custodians of culture, transforming their homes into decorative and soothing retreats from the harsh public world. Overall, sewing, it was argued, would help a woman cultivate the "modesty" and "retiring manners" that were seen as her ideal demeanor.[16] From the 1830s through the 1860s a chorus of encomiums for sewing issued from writers of advice literature. Sewing was the "truly feminine employment" (1836), "ever ... the appropriate occupation of woman" (1858), and "essential to a woman's happiness, no less than her usefulness in accomplishing [the] mission of her life" (1859).[17] By 1868, when Sarah Josepha Hale, editor of *Godey's Lady's Book,* announced that not to sew was to be "un-feminine," the meaning of sewing had profoundly shifted from being practical, necessary work (in which young boys had sometimes been trained) to being a symbolic marker of a new, arbitrarily gendered definition of femininity.[18]

What this new definition did was to increase society's suspicion of the intellectual woman, by making womanliness and intellect seem incompatible. As early as 1837 Eliza Farrar, one of the more popular cult arbiters, warned that "a woman who does not know how to sew is as deficient in her education as a man who cannot write," and this gender dichotomy was still being insisted upon as late as 1879 by the popular and widely read needlework author, Mrs. Pullan.[19] In England, where the cult of true womanhood had earlier established itself, Mary Lamb had proclaimed in 1815 that "needlework and intellectual improvement are naturally in a state of warfare," and the sentiment was reiterated later in this country by the novelist Catherine Sedgwick, in her comment on the efforts of Lucretia Davidson's mother to discourage her daughter's interest in reading and writing poetry by diverting her to needlework, "that legitimate sedative," as Sedgwick caustically termed it, "to female genius."[20]

As more and more women like Davidson and Sedgwick nonetheless persisted in embarking on professional careers, the advice literature, forced to recognize the conflict, tried to argue it away. "Because a woman knows how to sew," Sarah Hale stated in 1868, it does not "follow that she must give up literary pursuits, if time and circumstances permit her to follow them."[21] And Eliza Leslie, warning her readers not to be "astonished" if they "chance to find an authoress occupied with her needle," insisted that "a large number of literary females are excellent needlewomen, and good housewives." In the same passage, however, she felt it necessary to encourage any "authoress" who might be reading her and who did *not* know how to sew that "with a little time and a little perseverance" she might become as "notable" at sewing "as if she had never read a book, or written a page."[22] At the height of the cult ideology Nathaniel Hawthorne interjected into *The Marble Faun* (1860) a description of the professional woman that also kept her well within the cult's boundaries. She would be one who could turn easily from "discovering a star" to "darn[ing] a casual fray in her dress." Needlework, with its "sweet, soft, and winning effect" would show that, their "high thoughts and accomplishments" notwithstanding, professional women were "at home with their own hearts."[23]

What all such advice sedulously ignored was the invasive reality of sewing as it actually functioned in women's lives. "If I should sew every day for a month to come I should not be able to accomplish a half of what is to be done," Harriet Beecher Stowe wrote to her husband in 1844.[24] In their diaries and autobiographies nineteenth-century women reveal a significant degree of resentment at the demands that sewing imposed on their time, beginning with its preemption of place in their formal education. Woman's rights activist Mary Livermore, for example, never forgot her sense of being cheated as a child, when two hours a day of prescribed needlework instruction left less time for academic subjects.[25] The diaries of young unmarried and of married women reveal similar frustration. In the 1860s in Milledgeville, Georgia, twenty-year-old Anna Green Cook complained "of how many women, sewing, sewing, stitching and mending from morning till night is a duty and how often they turn longingly to a book upon the table."[26] Letitia Miller, describing her mother's life in Mississippi in the same period, noted that "she sewed steadily, about twelve hours a day.... She loved reading but read only on Sunday, considering it a sinful waste of time. When I was the mother of several children ... she often reproached me for reading."[27] So central was sewing in women's lives that it was widely understood, in the nineteenth century, that when women referred simply to their "work" they meant their sewing.

For those women who had to earn money, sewing was one of the few available options (the others being primarily teaching and domestic work) and one to which many women who eventually became professional writers resorted, but only reluctantly. It was in fact the desire to avoid sewing as paid work that propelled some women into becoming writers. Already by the 1840s the conditions of seamstresses, especially of the piece-workers who sewed garments for long hours and low pay, often in badly lit and badly ventilated rooms, were a matter of public concern. In 1854 Sara Payson Willis Parton, alias Fanny Fern, pleaded with male critics to temper their condescending treatment of women's literary works, urging them "in God's name" not to "drive ... by this tone of patronizing tolerance, one literary female aspirant ... back to 'The Song of the Shirt.' "[28] And Frances Rollin, a black woman attempting shortly after the Civil War to earn her living as a writer, recorded her disappointment in her diary: "Went out to sew today. I thought when I began literature that ended, but find it otherwise."[29] The diaries of Louisa May Alcott, who had to support herself and contribute to the support of her parents and sisters, show her carefully recording the monies she made by doing piece work—sewing pillowcases, neckties, handkerchiefs, and shirts—and by writing, until she was able to state that "at twenty-five I supported myself by pen and needle; at thirty-five I supported myself and family by pen alone."[30] In Alcott's semi-autobiographical novel, *Work,* the efforts of her heroine, Christie

Devon, to become self-supporting include working as a domestic, an actress, a governess, a lady's companion, and a seamstress. It is the economic precariousness, the physical and mental exhaustion of the seamstress work, which she had "resolved not to try till every thing else failed," that leads her to consider suicide.[31] Similarly, the millinery work to which Edith Wharton's Lily Bart resorts in *The House of Mirth* is a dead end, weakening her will to live and contributing to the hopelessness that leads her to take her life.

It is within this double set of pressures—the pervasive ideological context of the cult of true womanhood and the actual material conditions of women's lives—that one must see the increasingly negative treatment of sewing in the late nineteenth and early twentieth centuries. By the second half of the nineteenth century the defensive apologias of a Southgate or a Stowe were being replaced by more open protest. An expressed distaste for, or an explicit rejection of, sewing became a hallmark in writing by or about the "new woman." Not to want to sew was a sign of intellectual seriousness, of literary or professional ambition. In the 1850s Fanny Fern had described her independent heroine, Ruth Hall, as having an "unqualified disgust" for such "common female employments and recreations" as "[s]atin patchwork... bead-netting, crochet-stitching."[32] By the 1870s such protests were mounting. Throughout her career Elizabeth Stuart Phelps waged a sustained attack on the needle. "Don't teach. Don't sew. Don't," one woman warns another in one of Phelps's short stories, and elsewhere Phelps insisted that "the feather which breaks the camel's back" is "the number of *stitches* which life requires [of a woman] in a year." In Phelps's *The Story of Avis* the heroine's commitment to her career as a painter is signaled by her husband's observation that she avoids all the "usual little feminine bustle of sewing," the "eternal nervous stitch, stitching." And Avis's daughter, who inherits her talent and at the end of the novel is her mother's hope for the future, is described as "hating her patchwork, always down by the sea, as full of dreams as a dark night."[33]

So too in Sarah Orne Jewett's *A Country Doctor* Nan Prince, who will choose a career in medicine over marriage, is described as "not a child who took kindly to needlework." By contrast, Jewett's women of an older generation, exemplars of women's culture at its best, are closely identified with sewing and textile work. In *The Country of the Pointed Firs* Mrs. Blackett's bedroom, "the heart of the house," is furnished with a quilted rocker and a "pink-and-white patchwork quilt," and her thimble is as ritualistically positioned, in the narrator's description of the room, as her Bible; and Mrs. Todd, looking like a "huge Sibyl" as she stands encircled by the black and grey rings of her braided rug, seems to inhabit an almost sacred space.[34] The deterioration of that women's culture, in turn, is suggested in *The Awakening*, when Edna Pontellier watches with bemused puzzlement as Adele Ratignolle, the "mother woman," busily sews winter garments for her children in the middle of summer.

By the 1920s the "new woman" was defining herself even more explicitly in terms of rejecting Victorian values, and sewing continued to serve as ready signifier of a set of repressive cultural attitudes. Writer and activist Inez Haynes Irwin early determined "not to let myself get caught in any of those pretty meshes which threaten young womanhood. I made a vow that I would never sew, embroider, crochet, knit."[35] And Genevieve Taggard, anxious to dissociate herself from the genteel tradition of late Victorian women's poetry, identified that tradition with Victorian fancy work. She would avoid, she said, the "decorative impulse" that was "the dead end of much feminine talent. A kind of literary needlework."[36] In the poetry of the twenties sewing came to symbolize domestic confinement, a circumscribed life, tethered ambition, and betrayed hopes. The marginality to "real" life of the speaker in Alice Dunbar Nelson's "I Sit and Sew" (1920) is imaged in "the little useless seam, the idle patch" she works on while men fight and die in World War I.[37] In Edna St. Vincent Millay's "Departure," staying indoors, making tea, and working with thread represent the repression of a young girl's secret dreams.[38] In Dorothy Parker's "To a Much Too Unfortunate Lady" a woman has woven her dreams into patterns to please her lover, to whom, however, they are as insubstantial as the thread of which they are made, a thread he will "pluck... from his sleeve."[39] In women's poetry of the twenties, clothing, as an extension of sewing, also functions to convey a sense of victimization, or confinement. The cry of the woman in Amy Lowell's "Patterns" for freedom from a world of whalebone and brocade echoes emptily, heard only by herself. And when women sew and don freer garments, in poems by Millay and Parker, their "bold" and "proud" satin fabrics and defiant red colors become their shrouds—the needle inscribing, as it were, their sense of the limits of their rebelliousness, or their own ambivalence about it.[40]

Only occasionally in the poetry of the twenties does a different tradition surface, an older set of associations to women's textile work that would reappear in the 1970s—that of the wild, magical, or witch-like weaver of spells. Millay's "The Ballad of the Harp-Weaver" draws on this tradition, but in a revealingly inverted way. Rather than weaving incantations from a loom, the woman uses her magic harp in desperation to weave clothing for her cold and hungry son. But as the harp strings speak textiles rather than songs or lyric poems, the woman's creative power (the harp has a woman's head), diverted into domesticity, is exhausted. Having worked all night to produce breeches and boots, a hat, mittens, and a "regal" red cloak, she is found dead in the morning.[41] Where not destructive to the self, woman's sewing or weaving is destructive to others, as in Anna Hempstead Branch's "Sonnets from a Lock Box" (1929). The garment woven by means of a "witchlike spell" is like Medea's weaving, one of "treacherous splendor" that will be fatal to its buyer.[42]

The anger that is only slightly concealed in Branch's poem would erupt in women's poetry in the 1960s, and, in what is a seeming reversal of earlier attitudes, the needle would be the instrument of this anger. But the reversal is only seeming, rage being the hidden underside of the victimization the needle had long inscribed. So, at the very beginning of her important poem, "Pro Femina" in 1963, her inventory, at a crucial transitional moment in the development of women's poetry, of women's and the woman writer's embattled past and present situation, Carolyn Kizer acknowledged all the women who, down through the centuries, had "sat quietly in the corner with their embroidery... stabbing the wool with the names of their ancient / Oppressors."[43] In the same year that Kizer wrote her poem, Sylvia Plath died, leaving behind a body of work in which the needle most angrily stabbed, becoming not only an adversarial, but at times a lethal, weapon. As such, however, it also ultimately became a weapon turned against its wielder, an instrument of self-destruction that exposed the terrible blockage and frustration of the rage it inscribed. For all its anger, Plath's world remains one in which the needle victimizes, and the malevolence of that world, as her needle and associated web imagery create it, is finally so encompassing that the destructive possibilities of the needle are, as it were, exhausted. In the writings of women who follow Plath, a reengagement with women's textile work on new, more positive terms would become both possible and desirable, and, one might say, inevitable.

Writing at the time of the "feminine mystique" and confronting in that new cultural context the same pressures that weighed on earlier writers—the conflicting demands of art on the one hand and marriage and domesticity on the other—Plath continued the tradition of using sewing as symbol of a repressive domestic world. In *The Bell Jar* Esther's worst fears that her art and she herself will be sacrificial victims to marriage are vividly realized in the fate of Mrs. Willard's handmade rug. An appealing piece of art in its own right, as Esther recognizes, woven out of handsome browns, blues, and greens, it has been placed on the kitchen floor where it has become "soiled and dull and indistinguishable from any mat you could buy for under a dollar in the five and ten"— flattened out and walked over, like Mrs. Willard herself.[44] In Plath's poetry, sewing imagery is used to judge and expose a domestic world that is at best ineffectual, at worst maddening and even death-dealing. If the mother in "Nick and the Candlestick" yearns to protect her child by hanging their "cave" with "roses" reminiscent of the crewel-worked flowers that nineteenth-century women wrought into wall decorations, the yearning is futile, "the last of Victoriana," helpless against the po-em's nightmare vision of icy or fiery death.[45] Equally ineffectual is the sewing of the woman in "Three Women" who has lost her child. The "isolate buttons, / Holes in the heels of socks" that she sews in an at-tempt to resume ordinary life will mark her as merely a "heroine of the peripheral," and her sewing stitches, subliminally associated with the surgical stitches of her hospital experience, cruelly parody true health: "I think I have been healing. . . . My hands / Can stitch lace neatly."[46] Else-where, knitting is a "bad smell" that "hooks itself to itself," and the fin-gers that knit (in "Old Ladies Home") or embroider (in "Finisterre") are "close to death." In "Wintering," one of the bee cycle poems, knit-ting is darkly ambiguous, the woman in the cellar, poised in uneasy stasis between winter's death and the uncertainty of spring's renewal, "still at her knitting, . . . Her body a bulb in the cold and too dumb to think."[47]

In "An Appearance" the precarious mental balance of the woman in "Three Women" tips toward madness, as the "red material" that should make "little dresses and coats" becomes the speaker's lifeblood and rage, "Issuing from the steel needle that flies so blindingly." And in "The Courage of Shutting Up" the domestic needle becomes an instrument of torture as, through Plath's typical associative rush of imagery, it is trans-formed into surgical and phonograph needles, digging into the grooves of the brain to stitch a record of grievance and outrage. The domestic world is a surreal, nightmare world, and its needlework a set of duplic-itous surfaces, false signs. Over such a nightmare world, inhabited also by sterile "spinsters" and spider-like widows sitting bitterly "in the cen-ter of [their] loveless spokes," there inevitably reigns a malevolent power, a male god-Death, who is imaged, in both early and late Plath poems, as a cosmic spider, who snares us like ants or flies in his destruc-tive web.[48]

In 1963, the year Plath died, Adrienne Rich published *Snapshots of a Daughter-in-Law*, poems in which, as she later said, she began "to write, for the first time, directly about experiencing myself as a woman."[49] Anger was a part of that experience, some of it directed, like much of

Plath's, at the crippling constrictions of domestic life, and some of it, again like Plath's, directed against the self. It was not, however, the needle that scarred, but, in the title poem—Rich's version of Plath's "viciousness in the kitchen"—the tapstream that scalded the arm, the match burning down to the thumbnail. These seared the speaker as she inventoried the sources in her own life and in cultural attitudes toward women of the same self-division that Plath had suicidally engaged. For Rich, however, the engagement would not be self-destructive, and the fire's heat would become the source of new creative energy. At the same time, though, the question for Rich (and, she urged, for all women writers) was how to use this fiery "energy of creation"—the artist's uninhibited freedom of imagination and self-expression—without denying the "energy of relation"—woman's traditional work of nurturing, conserving, and caring for others.[50] The answer began to emerge in "Incipience" (1971), where fire imagery is joined to imagery of "the composing ... thread," as the poet "feel[s] the fiery future / of every matchstick in the kitchen" and also "know[s] the composing of the thread / inside the spider's body / first atoms of the web / visible tomorrow."[51] No longer in conflict, the energy of creation and the energy of relation here found a home in the domestic world that in "Snapshots" had been antagonistic to the artist. By the time of *The Dream of a Common Language* (1977) imagery of webs and looms, and of knitting and sewing, mosaic and quilt work, traceable from some of Rich's earliest poems, had emerged to comprise a central body of imagery, providing a new language of access and insight into women's lives.

Rich's earliest uses of textile imagery are to be found in her very first volume, *A Change of World* (1951), where tapestry work introduced what would become central concerns: women denied full expression of their own creative power and women cut off from their own history. In "Aunt Jennifer's Tigers" (a key poem for Rich, as she indicated in her essay "When We Dead Awaken"), the exotic green world inhabited by "proud" and "prancing" tigers that Aunt Jennifer has woven provides essential release for the creative imagination from the self-denials of marriage. But Aunt Jennifer's life and imagination remain divided, and the creative energy, confined inside the tapestry panel and inside the poem's strictly controlled form, cannot free her from "the massive weight of Uncle's wedding band." The hands that can weave defiance are "terrified" in death, and there is no one, except the poem's carefully distanced speaker, to read her textile text.[52] In "Mathilde in Normandy" the Queen and her ladies weave into their tapestry not their own history but a male one of violence and war—the Norman invasion and conquest of England—a history to which they are marginal. Their needlework is "patient handiwork," considered merely a "pleasing pastime," "proper" to their station, and only the knots in their cloth are witness to their concealed anxiety.[53]

As Rich moved out of the drawing-room world of her first two volumes, where tapestry work comfortably comported with imagery of diamonds and crystal, into the disorderly kitchen of "Snapshots" with its banging pots and pans, her textile imagery began to change. The tapestry's "expensive threads," fit material for leisured women, were replaced by the more pliant, and ordinary, strands of women's knitting. In "Necessities of Life," written while she was working on "Snapshots," she peeled away the false layers of her life to find, in the poem's concluding image, "invitations" to new self-definition "waiting / like old women knitting, breathless / to tell their tales."[54] By 1971 this simile had been transformed into one of her most compelling metaphors, as not only the urgency but the arduousness and pain of undoing the damage of a lifetime and remaking the self became clear. The opening section of "When We Dead Awaken," in which she painfully exposed the "scars" that were at once her own and those of the world's war-ravaged landscapes, concluded with the poet speaking to her "sister"

> sitting across from me, dark with love
> working like me to pick apart
> working with me to remake
> this trailing knitted thing, this cloth of darkness
> this woman's garment, trying to save the skein.[55]

From a canvas on which women inscribed a male history separate from their own, or onto which they displaced their anger, dividing themselves from themselves, the textile artifact had become woman's own self-habitation, dark with both her suffering and her hidden potential, the skein her very skin.

In the poetry that followed, women's suffering is never overlooked, and often it is imaged through the language of domestic needlework. Male-imposed thought patterns are the "set-piece[s] I'd learned to embroider / in my woman's education / while the needle scarred my hand"; and the sufficient signifier of an immigrant woman's harsh life is her "down quilt sewn through iron nights."[56] But as Rich's vision of renewal, of "remaking," continued to unfold, textile imagery increasingly provided a way of communicating a sense of women's power and potential. In *The Dream of a Common Language* this imagery—especially imagery associated with quilts, the piecing together of salvaged remnants to create a new pattern of connections, an integrated whole—eventually provides the elements, in two of the volume's concluding poems, for a new transformative vision.

The vision in "Natural Resources" and "Transcendental Etude" emerges out of and is communicated through the quotidian details of women's domestic lives. Underlying both poems is the idea of salvage, the need to rescue or retrieve the "treasures that prevail" amidst the loss, the damage and waste, of women's past lives. Like Rich's earlier "Diving into the Wreck," "Natural Resources" is a quest poem, describing the ordeal of the journey. It begins with a descent into the darkness—into the "mine" of women's past suffering and survival—and from this darkness the speaker emerges into the daylight clarity of a cold barn, where, spread out on tables, are the journey's reward and goal: china saucers and picture frames, ribboned letters and snapshots, scrapbooks and "scraps, turned into patchwork." "These things by women saved" are "humble things" that yet comprise a "universe," and at the poem's conclusion Rich has "cast [her] lot" with these women, who "age after age"

> with no extraordinary power,
> reconstitute the world.[57]

In "Transcendental Etude" we watch this process of reconstitution, as the disassembled fragments of women's lives, "the truths we are salvaging," begin to be joined into a new composition. "Transcendental Etude" has been called "a meditation on the web of interrelated life," and the interrelationships extend to include the natural world—those ravaged landscapes of earlier poems—which women inhabit and which must also be reclaimed.[58] Aunt Jennifer's tapestry had created an exotic but alien "world of green" that provided temporary release, and in another poem in *A Change of World*, "Design in Living Colors," the poet had imagined herself inside a stylized landscape, an "embroidered . . . tapestry of green."[59] Now the world she lives in, and inside which her culminating vision will occur, is the actual world of Vermont, one of poverty, disease, and sickness, but one that is also "green . . . with life." Inside this world vision emerges slowly, out of the poet's brooding on a set of interrelated concerns, chief among them women's loss of their birthright attachment to the mother and to other women, a loss repeatedly enforced by language, the male "oratory [and] formulas" that separate us from ourselves and keep us, in one of the poem's key words, "dismembered." The striving now is to "re-member," and like Mary Daly, Rich breaks open the word to suggest both the physical pain of separation and loss, and the nature of the reconstitutive process. The vision with which the poem ends images this reconstitution and introduces "a whole new poetry beginning here":

> as if a woman quietly walked away
> from the argument and jargon in a room

and sitting down in the kitchen, began turning in her lap
bits of yarn, calico and velvet scraps,
laying them out absently on the scrubbed boards

The composition the woman begins to create contains further elements, lovingly and meticulously enumerated in the lines that follow, including shells, feathers, and a wasp-nest curling, "skeins of milkweed . . . original domestic silk," and "the lace of seaweed." And as she forms her pattern, joining the fabrics and fibers of her human and natural worlds, the natural world itself is reclaimed for women through domestic textile metaphors. The woman in "Transcendental Etude" is "pulling the tenets of a life together" through a compositional process that is the result of "the musing of a mind / [at] one with her body."[60] It is this vision of wholeness, of separations overcome, that finally fulfills the need that was given such urgent expression at the end of "Planetarium" (1968), for "images   for the relief of the body / and the reconstruction of the mind."[61]

Such a transcendent vision, however, does not mean closure. "Natural Resources" had cautioned that it is "the fibers of actual life / as we live it now" to which the poet must constantly attend, and in the poetry since *The Dream of a Common Language* life's dailiness, and the world's political realities, continue to press on the poet. The process of re-membering is "daily, prose-bound, routine." Vision continues to inform the search for meaning, vision described, in a submerged quilt metaphor, as that of "Putting together, inch by inch / the starry worlds. From all the lost collections."[62] And textile imagery also continues to provide a way of sustaining the important connection, as in "Transcendental Etude," between the natural and the human worlds: mountain laurel like needlework, snow like a quilt of crystals; or, in an extended metaphor in "For Julia in Nebraska" (1978, 1981), the man-made landscape reclaimed, as the railroad stretching across the plains where Willa Cather lived is reenvisioned as "a braid of hair / a grandmother's strong hands plaited / straight down a grand-daughter's back."[63] From such reclaimed landscapes flow new perceptions. But visions of healing and wholeness must also continue to take into account both women's past suffering—imaged in "Natural Resources" as a "fraying blanket with its ancient stains"—and the incompleteness of our knowledge, the difficulties of making connections—women's story as a "weaving, ragged because incomplete." The poet therefore is like the spider, the strands of meaning, understanding, and connecting constantly spun from her own body, her own perceptions, and with the spider's "passion" always to "rebuild . . . to make and make again."[64]

Rich's poetry after *The Dream of a Common Language,* as well as her
prose essays, show this need constantly to remake, and to do so with
"never-ending care." The enterprise is described as one of "trying to
clarify and connect," but the "threads of connectedness" are "hard-
won."[65] Especially is this so in poems in which Rich pays scrupulous
regard to the differences among women—black, white, Asian, African,
lesbian, heterosexual, Jewish, Gentile. Fiber artifacts representing
women are often real, resistant objects introduced into the poems: "the
Alabama quilt / the Botswana basket" are what specifically need to be
"clarified and connected" in "The Spirit of Place" (1980).[66] Dense with
their own particularity and history, they are often presented as a way of
resisting the danger of easy generalization, of too-easy composition or
patterning. The poems themselves often proceed by way of an enumera-
tion of disparate particularities, revealing in their movement the very
process of trying to understand, to make connections. In "Culture and
Anarchy," a long poem written the year after "Transcendental Etude,"
Rich is once again, in the words of the poem, "beginning to stitch together" the pieces of women's lives, in this case those of actual
nineteenth-century American women, including Susan B. Anthony. It is
the quotidian details that must tell the story, presented like unassembled
pieces of a quilt: Anthony staining and varnishing the library bookcase,
fitting out a fugitive slave for Canada, reading Mrs. Browning's sonnets,
putting a quilted petticoat in the frame. But the poem also offers its
vision. Near its beginning, in a muted parallel to the woman in "Transcendental Etude," the poet sits "at the kitchen table typing." Spread out
before her are

> heaped up letters, a dry moth's
> perfectly mosaiced wings, pamphlets on rape,
> forced sterilization, snapshots in color
> of an Alabama woman still quilting in her nineties.[67]

These are the disparate elements of a world, threatening in its violence
yet containing the promise of the moth's mosaic and the strength of the
unnamed woman still making her own connections. In "Poetry: II, Chicago" (1984) Rich in effect passes on this vision to the unknown poet,
"of whatever color, sex," whom she imagines emerging from the "wasted
tracts" of a Chicago housing project, bearing the precious salvage of a
cultural heritage and finding in it the visionary source of poetry

> the twist
> of old strands   raffia, hemp or silk
> the beaded threads   the fiery lines[68]

In *Writing Beyond the Ending* Rachel Blau DuPlessis argues that twentieth-century women writers have been replacing the "patriarchal script," in which the heroine's eventual marriage or death was "a trope for the sex gender system," with new narrative strategies and new narrative modes. And as sibling ties and bonds between women replace the heterosexual love plot, she sees a new esthetic emerging, a "poetics of domestic value—nurturance, community building, inclusiveness, empathetic care"—in which women's "artisanal" creations, hitherto marginal to high art, move toward the center. As an example of this new poetics DuPlessis cites Alice Walker's short story, "Everyday Use," in which the bonds between a mother and daughter are reaffirmed through their family and cultural heritage of quilts.[69] Following upon "Everyday Use," Walker's *The Color Purple*, which appeared in 1982, may well be the most ambitious literary effort to date to give women's artisanal creations pride of place, in both the esthetic and the ethic of the prose narrative.

Walker's account of her preparations for writing *The Color Purple* is interestingly reminiscent of Rich's description of the compositional process in "Transcendental Etude." Just as the woman in Rich's poem abandoned the world of argument, entering into silence and her own creative space in order to begin her mosaic, so, Walker has told us, composing *The Color Purple* meant accepting silence (she gave up all public lecturing), moving from urban New York to the quiet of a small town in northern California, and making a quilt.[70] The quilting and sewing that are essential to the plot and themes, the moral and esthetic schema, of *Purple* emerge, as actual work, out of the realities of the lives of southern, and particularly rural, black women, for whom such sewing activity has existed in an unbroken continuum since the time of slavery. And from this perspective Walker's novel is her fullest artistic acknowledgment of her creative connection to earlier black women, first expressed in her now classic essay, "In Search of Our Mothers' Gardens," in 1974. Celie in *Purple* is the direct descendant of those earlier generations of women, for whom sewing and quilting meant psychic survival. But she also moves radically beyond them. The quilts Celie makes and the pants she sews provide the occasions for, and themselves become the agents of, her physical, emotional, spiritual, and economic liberation— her total transformation, indeed, from silenced victim, complicit in her own oppression, to a woman who comes fully into her own voice and her own distinct sense of self.

Nor is Celie the only beneficiary of the empowering potential, the healing and transformative possibilities that Walker attributes to sewing and quilting. These activities are responsible for a remarkable series of reconciliations, in a novel in which reconciliation is an overarching theme. Quilts and quilt making forge bonds of understanding between and among Celie, Sophia, and Shug, and between Nettie and Corinne; sewing is what ultimately unites Celie and Albert; and quilt making, as a shared cultural activity, also joins the Olinkas and the Mississippi blacks. All of these bondings are essential to the fulfillment of Walker's "womanist" vision of community and wholeness. Throughout the novel it is the needle, as agentic instrument, that joins and heals.

Quilting ritualistically marks Celie's first step out of victimization when, admitting her wrong in urging Harpo to beat his wife (as she had been beaten), she is reconciled with Sophia. As the two women begin to make a quilt out of the "messed up" curtains, Celie's gift to her, that Sofia had been ready angrily to return, it is Celie's "messed up" mind that begins to recover and heal. Because she knew that she had committed a "sin against Sofia spirit," Celie tells us that "for over a month I have trouble sleeping." Having begun the quilt, "I sleeps like a baby now."[71] When Celie's network of female enablers expands to include Shug Avery, the occasion is also marked by the ceremony of quilt making. Appearing on the porch one morning shortly after her arrival at Celie's and Mr. ——'s home, Shug is still perceived by Celie as "halfway between good and evil," and her smile is threatening, "like a razor opening." Whether she will become Celie's ally or enemy is moot. When she agrees to sew a square for another quilt that Celie and Sophia are making, she symbolically aligns herself with the women. Shug's long crooked stitches remind Celie of the "little crooked tune" Shug sings, and as Shug thus incorporates her voice into the quilt, that voice becomes available to Celie, who through it will find her own. Once again, Walker has Celie underscore the occasion's importance by a concluding comment: "Then I see myself sitting there quilting tween Shug Avery and Mr. ——. . . . For the first time in my life, I feel just right."[72] Later, after pieces of Shug's yellow dress, cut into stars, are included in the quilt (which is being made in the pattern called "Sister's Choice"), the quilt functions to signal a further step in Celie's development. When Sophia decides to leave Harpo, Celie, in the tradition of women's friendship quilts, chooses to give her the quilt—a gesture of support for Sophia's assertion of independence, which Celie herself will later emulate.

As with Celie / Sophia, and Celie / Shug, it is a quilt that unites Nettie and Corinne, effecting a major reconciliation. Tormented on her deathbed by the thought that Nettie is the real mother of her adopted children, Corinne is freed from suspicion and enmity when Nettie, using the fabric scraps in one of Corinne's quilts, helps her recall a repressed piece of her past—her meeting with Celie in the dry goods store where she bought the fabric for the quilt and her realization then that Celie was the children's real mother. Encouraging Corinne to read her textile as a text, Nettie is able to repair their damaged relationship and create new understanding, necessary precursor to her marriage to Samuel and the continued cohesion of the missionary family group.

It is of course Celie's remarkably successful business venture of designing and sewing pants that eventually brings her economic independence and power over her own life (a major reversal of the situation of nineteenth-century seamstresses) and that channels her rage against Mr. —— into constructive work. And not just work, but art, for Celie's pants are the product of her creative imagination, crafted out of love and caring: "soft, flowing [and] rich," they "catch the light." "A needle not a razor in my hand, I think" is Celie's version of Adrienne Rich's belief that women's anger can be "converted into creation." Celie's needle does not stab; rather, as she writes to Nettie, "every stitch I sew will be a kiss."[73]

And just as the needle thus releases Celie into the fullness of her own power, so it is instrumental in both her reconciliation with Mr. —— (whom she is finally able to name, as Albert), and in Albert's own self-redemption. Ridiculed in boyhood, we are told, for liking to sew, Albert at the end of the novel is contentedly sewing shirts to complement Celie's pants. He has returned to the purity of a pregendered time, before the imposition of sex roles and the emergence of sexual conflict, and it is in this context that he and Celie can meet as friends, the needle joining them to each other. No longer the marker of woman's separate and unequal sphere, the needle has abolished gender role differences. As Celie tells Albert, Olinka men also make quilts, and African men wear "dresses."

When toward the novel's close Celie describes her new relation to Albert—"Now us sit sewing and talking and smoking our pipes"—one is reminded of the reconciliation scene at the end of Walker's "Everyday Use," where Mama's gift of the family quilts to Maggie empowers the previously silenced and victimized daughter. For the first time Maggie smiles "a real smile, not scared." And at the story's end mother and daughter, joined through the quilts, sit in their yard, with a dip of snuff, "just enjoying, until it was time to go in the house and go to bed."[74] In "Everyday Use," published in the short story collection *In Love and Trouble* in 1973, Walker had described the changed attitude toward black women's textile work that had occurred between the 1950s and the 1960s. For Dee, Mama's other daughter in the story, quilts had been an embarrassment during her college years, and it is the civil rights movement and the development of black pride that have led her (if too possessively) to learn to admire them. By 1976 in *Meridian* a quilt was being used to bridge the alienation that had developed between Lynne, the northern civil rights worker, and Meridian. In a reunion scene, where they are drawn together by their suffering and their concern over Truman, whom they both love, they "rummage around the apartment, looking for some traces of their former Southern home." What Lynne finds, and what consoles, is a "Turkey Walk" quilt that she spreads over her knees.[75]

Joining mothers to daughters, blacks to whites, women to women, females to males, Americans to Africans, textiles cover Alice Walker's fictional landscapes with a repeated pattern of reconciliations: misunderstandings overcome, new ties of affiliation formed. It is a pattern also evident in the work of other contemporary women writers, in which, especially, the bonds between mothers, grandmothers, and daughters are reaffirmed. Karen Swenson's "The Quilt" (1971), in which the wife who makes a quilt from pieces of her dresses is "fettering the failures together," strikes a discordant note in what has been since the late 1960s a growing chorus of affirmation for rediscovered generational ties.[76] In Nancy Willard's "Crewel" (1967) a grandmother's embroidered bed hangings are her celebration of life, of sexual and marital fulfillment, and, composed as they are of exotic flora and fauna—leopards and parrots, peacocks and panthers—they become the obverse of Aunt Jennifer's tapestry, since now the life and the art are fused, as the needlework, "praising in lovestitch with thread," holds out a "promise of lion and lamb and herself wed."[77] Other poets, in the manner of Walker's "Our Mothers' Gardens," pay tribute to their mother's or grandmother's textile work as anticipatory of and analogous to their own texts. Sandra Hochman's typewriter on which she "stitches up [her] dreams" is her version of her grandmother's sewing machine, and in Erica Jong's "Dear Marys, Dear Mother, Dear Daughter," reconciliation with the mother occurs when "this twisted skein / of multi-colored wool, this dappled canvas / or this page of print / joins us."[78] In Joan Chase's *During the Reign of the Queen of Persia* (1983) a star quilt begun by a grandmother is resumed by her daughters when the impending death of one of them prompts a ritual of "piecing" that brings "peace" by filling the final hours and dignifying the dying.[79]

The quilt in Chase's novel is in the tradition of nineteenth-century mourning quilts, made by family members, often including the dying person, to help bridge the abyss between life and death. A related nineteenth-century tradition, that of reading quilts as allegories of life, finding in them philosophical and religious meanings, lies behind other recent literary works, such as Robin Morgan's poem, "Piecing," in which the fabric pieces she is given and what she chooses to "make" of them represent the mix in life of fate and free will, and the finished quilt is read as the record of a life honorably "worn," like the fabric pieces themselves, "into translucency / held up toward the light."[80] The quilt offers "lessons for living," in the words of the poem, and for critic Gayle Graham Yates these are spiritual lessons. Yates cited "Piecing" as one of several important contemporary women's "texts for spiritual guidance" in a 1981 review essay on women's spirituality.[81] And such a reading of women's traditional textile work—of its processes as well as its finished products—has led Mary Daly to offer Dorothy Canfield Fisher's 1915 story "The Bedquilt" as a paradigm of the "Musing," which she urges is women's religio-epistemological mode. Musing, as both ruminating and engaging in ecstatic contemplation, wonderment, or marvel, is Daly's description of the work process of the "spinster" in Fisher's story, who approaches the task of making her magnificent and original quilt, in Fisher's words, "with the solemnity of a priestess performing a rite."[82] In Judy Grahn's *The Queen of Wands* the textile is a sacred script, its thread "the one true cord, / the umbilical line" from which the cloth of life is woven. Grahn's volume of poems is her reclamation of the original spinning and weaving goddess, imaged in cultures throughout the world as the source of "life and time and understanding."[83] The power of that goddess, historically embodied in the Mediterranean cloth trade and the skilled women weavers whom the Greek soldiers kidnapped from Troy, is, in the figure of Helen of Troy, reclaimed from male ab- duction and rape. Urban factories are imaged as gigantic looms, the mu- sician's strings as originating in the shuttle's threads. Both science and art, technology and song or voice, are thus reclaimed for women.

As contemporary women have thus been placing at the centers of their texts the very textiles and textile processes that previous genera- tions of women writers often found it necessary to distance themselves from, or reject, we are indeed witnessing a widespread and most signif- icant reclamation of an earlier female world of domestic work and cul- ture. The tropes of that world have provided writers, in Adrienne Rich's phrase, with a new "common language" through which to communicate their affirming visions of women's individual and collective experience and, as well, with a way of bridging the gulf between domestic and artistic life that until recently women writers have found such difficulty in negotiating. In the poetry of a Rich or a Grahn, in the etymological discoveries of a Daly, this new common language can function meta- phorically to enhance vision, enlarge our sense of possibility, and imag- inatively connect us to some of the physical and spiritual energy that for so long women have channeled into their textile work.

So, too, such language and imagery can function in *The Color Purple*, read as fable or romance. But insofar as that book, despite its romantic or fabulous elements, is still rooted in the realism of the genre of the novel, there may be a question whether the needle doesn't at times move too magically to dispel conflict, to solve complex issues of gender and male power. At the end of *The Color Purple* Celie has become her own entrepreneur, and we can trust her to do well by Sofia, whom she has hired as a clerk. But the conditions of women's lives that in the nineteenth century forced them into exploitation as piece-workers and seamstresses are with us still, as women throughout the world provide the low-paid labor for handicraft and industrial textile work. In the midst of our long-overdue celebration of women's textile traditions, a knowledge of the often embattled relationship of nineteenth-century women to their needles can, at the least, act as a check on any temptation to romanticize or sentimentalize women's domestic culture and particularly their textile work; and it may serve also to help us keep the continued oppressive reality of that work, for large numbers of women, steadily in mind.

NOTES

1. See Judy Chicago, *The Dinner Party: A Symbol of Our Heritage* (New York: Doubleday, 1979); Chicago, *The Birth Project* (New York: Doubleday, 1985); Miriam Schapiro, "Notes from a Conversation on Art, Feminism, and Work," in *Working It Out: 23 Women Writers, Artists, Scientists, and Scholars Talk about Their Lives and Work,* ed. Sara Ruddick and Pamela Daniels (New York: Pantheon, 1977), pp. 283–305.

2. Patricia Mainardi, "Quilts: The Great American Art," *Feminist Art Journal* (Winter 1973), 20; Dolores Hayden, *The Grand Domestic Revolution: A History of Feminist Designs for American Homes, Neighborhoods and Cities* (Cambridge, Mass.: MIT Press, 1981), p. 79.

3. Alice Walker, "In Search of Our Mothers' Gardens," *Radcliffe Quarterly* (June 1974), 2–6.

4. Mary Daly, *Gyn/Ecology: The Metaethics of Radical Feminism* (Boston: Beacon Press, 1978), pp. 389, 390.

5. Adrienne Rich, "When We Dead Awaken: Writing as Re-Vision," in *Adrienne Rich's Poetry,* ed. Barbara Charlesworth Gelpi and Albert Gelpi (New York: W. W. Norton, 1975), p. 91.

6. Judy Grahn, *The Queen of Wands* (Trumansburg, N.Y.: Crossing Press, 1982), p. xii; on Paula Gunn Allen and others, see for example Rayna Green, ed., *Contemporary Poetry and Fiction by Native American Women* (Bloomington: Indiana University Press, 1984).

7. Susan Gubar, " 'The Blank Page' and the Issue of Female Creativity," *Critical Inquiry* (Winter, 1981), 243–64; Nancy K. Miller, "Arachnologies: The Woman, the Text, and the Critic," in *The Poetics of Gender,* ed. Nancy K. Miller (New York: Columbia University Press, 1986), pp. 270–95; Jane Marcus, "Still

Practice, A/Wrested Alphabet: Towards a Feminist Esthetic," *Tulsa Studies in Women's Literature* 3, nos. 1/2 (Spring/Fall 1984), 79–97; Elaine Showalter, "Piecing and Writing," in *The Poetics of Gender,* p. 223.

8. As the following pages will show, my study of nineteenth- and twentieth-century women's writings leads me to significantly different—indeed, often diametrically opposite—conclusions from those of Elaine Showalter in her essay, "Piecing and Writing." Not just toward its close, as Showalter says, but throughout the nineteenth century there is an ambivalent and troubled relationship between women's texts and their textile work. Furthermore, the widespread use of textile work and imagery in contemporary women's writing that I document contradicts Showalter's conclusion that women's textile (especially quilt) culture may by now have become a "burden" for the woman writer.

9. Jeannine Hensley, ed., *The Works of Anne Bradstreet* (Cambridge, Mass.; Harvard University Press, 1967), p. 16.

10. Cathy N. Davidson, "Female Authorship and Authority: The Case of Sukey Vickery," *Early American Literature* 21, no. 1 (Spring 1986), 20.

11. Eliza Southgate Bowne, *A Girl's Life Eighty Years Ago* (New York: Scribner's, 1888), pp. 56–57.

12. Harriet Beecher Stowe, *The Minister's Wooing* (Ridgewood, N.J.: Gregg Press, 1968), p. 1.

13. Mary Kelley, *Private Women, Public Stage* (New York: Oxford University Press, 1984).

14. Gerda Lerner, *The Female Experience: An American Documentary* (Indianapolis: Bobbs-Merrill, 1977), p. 58.

15. Barbara Welter, "The Cult of True Womanhood: 1820–1860," *American Quarterly* 18, no. 2, pt. 1 (1966), 151–74.

16. Sarah Josepha Hale, *Manners; or, Happy Homes and Good Society All the Year Round* (Boston: J. E. Tilton, 1868), p. 78.

17. Eliza Farrar, *The Young Lady's Friend* (Boston: American Stationer's Co., 1836), p. 122; Lydia Sigourney, *Letters to Young Ladies* [1858], in Welter, "The Cult of True Womanhood," p. 33; Florence Hartley, *The Ladies' Handbook of Fancy and Ornamental Work* [1859], quoted in Thomas K. Woodward and Blanche Greenstein, *Crib Quilts and Other Small Wonders* (New York: Dutton, 1981), p. 10.

18. Hale, *Manners,* p. 192.

19. Farrar, *The Young Lady's Friend,* p. 122; Mrs. Pullan, *The Mothers' Home Book* (1879), quoted in Deborah Graham, *The Victorian Girl and the Feminine Ideal* (Bloomington: Indiana University Press, 1982), p. 74.

20. Mary Lamb, "On Needle-Work" (1815), in *The Works of Charles and Mary Lamb,* ed. E. V. Lucas (New York: Putnam, 1903; AMS Press, 1968), 1:176; Cheryl Walker, *The Nightingale's Burden: Women Poets and American Culture before 1900* (Bloomington: Indiana University Press, 1982), p. 73.

21. Hale, *Manners,* p. 191.

22. Eliza Leslie, *Miss Leslie's Behaviour Book: A Guide and Manual for Ladies* (Philadelphia: 1859), pp. 262–63.

23. Nathaniel Hawthorne, *The Marble Faun,* in *The Complete Novels and Selected Tales of Nathaniel Hawthorne* (New York: Random House, 1937), p. 612. Hawthorne, of course, with his peculiar ambivalence, both supported cult ideals and recognized the imperative of their subversion. In *The Blithedale Romance* the demure Priscilla, foil to the feminist Zenobia, is a seamstress. Yet in emblazoning her scarlet letter with embroidery Hester Prynne uses her needle to turn penance into defiance.

24. Annie Fields, ed., *Life and Letters of Harriet Beecher Stowe* (Boston: Houghton Mifflin, 1898), p. 109.

25. Mary A. Livermore, *The Story of My Life; or, The Sunshine and Shadow of Seventy Years* (Hartford, Conn.: A. D. Worthington, 1897), p. 87.

26. Anna Green Cook, *Journal of a Milledgeville Girl, 1861–1867,* ed. James C. Bonner (Athens: University of Georgia Press, 1964), p. 91.

27. Letitia D. Miller, "Some Recollections of Letitia D. Miller," 1926 MS., Chapel Hill, University of North Carolina, Southern Historical Collection, p. 15.

28. Fanny Fern, "Letter," *The Una,* August 1854, p. 320. The "Song of the Shirt," by British poet Thomas Hood (1799–1845), a protest poem describing the degraded conditions of sweatshop sewing workers in England, was widely reprinted and cited in both England and the United States.

29. Frances Rollin, "Diary" [1 July 1868], in *We Are Your Sisters: Black Women in the Nineteenth Century,* ed. Dorothy Sterling (New York: W. W. Norton, 1984), p. 460.

30. Louisa May Alcott, quoted in the Introduction to *Work,* ed. Sarah Elbert (New York: Schocken Books, 1977), p. xvi. Although humorously presented, a friend's account of her advice to Harriet Beecher Stowe in 1838 suggests how widespread was the recognition of the desirability of substituting writing for sewing—in this case, the unpaid sewing of the homemaker. Anxious to get Stowe to finish a story she'd begun but put aside because of household chores, the friend urged that "three hours' labor of your brains will earn enough to pay for all the sewing your fingers could do for a year to come" (Fields, *Life and Letters,* p. 98).

31. Alcott, *Work,* p. 16.

32. Fanny Fern, *Ruth Hall and Other Writings* (New Brunswick: Rutgers University Press, 1986), p. 51.

33. Elizabeth Stuart Phelps, "Hannah Colby's Chance," *Our Young Folks* 9 (Oct. 1873), 603; "The Song of the Shirt," *The Independent* 23 (10 Aug. 1871), 1; *The Story of Avis* (Boston: James R. Osgood, 1877), pp. 271, 330.

34. Sarah Orne Jewett, *The Country Doctor* (Boston, 1884; rpt. Upper Saddle River, N.J.: Gregg Press, 1970), p. 45; *The Country of the Pointed Firs* (New York: Doubleday, 1955), pp. 52, 17.

35. Inez Haynes Irwin, quoted in *The American Woman: Who Was She?* ed. Anne Firor Scott (Englewood Cliffs, N.J.: Prentice-Hall, 1971), pp. 52–53.

36. Genevieve Taggard, quoted in *These Modern Women: Autobiographical Essays from the Twenties,* ed. Elaine Showalter (New York: Feminist Press, 1978), p.

63. The nineteenth-century tradition of disparaging one's literary work by comparing it to patchwork also continued into the 1920s. See Amy Lowell, "To a Gentleman Who Wanted to See the First Draft of My Poems," *The Complete Poetical Works of Amy Lowell* (New York: Houghton Mifflin, 1955), pp. 535–36.

37. Alice Dunbar Nelson, "I Sit and Sew," in *The World Split Open: Four Centuries of Women Poets in England and America, 1552–1950,* ed. Louise Bernikow (New York: Random House, 1974), p. 260.

38. Norma Millay, ed., *Collected Poems: Edna St. Vincent Millay* (New York: Harper, 1956), pp. 163–64.

39. Dorothy Parker, *Enough Rope* (New York: Horace Liveright, 1926), p. 28.

40. See, for example, Millay, *Collected Poems,* p. 43; Parker, *Enough Rope,* p. 23.

41. Millay, *Collected Poems,* pp. 177–83.

42. Anna Hempstead Branch, "Sonnets from a Lock Box" (1929), in *The World Split Open,* ed. Bernikow, p. 245.

43. Carolyn Kizer, "Pro Femina," in *Knock upon Silence* (New York: Doubleday, 1965), p. 42.

44. Sylvia Plath, *The Bell Jar* (New York: Harper and Row, 1971), p. 93.

45. Sylvia Plath, *The Collected Poems* (New York: Harper and Row, 1981), p. 241.

46. Ibid., p. 182.

47. Ibid., pp. 201, 120, 169, 219.

48. Ibid., pp. 189, 210, 49, 48, 265.

49. Adrienne Rich, "When We Dead Awaken," in *Adrienne Rich's Poetry,* p. 97.

50. Ibid., p. 96.

51. Rich, "Incipience," in ibid., p. 64.

52. Ibid., p. 2. "Aunt Jennifer's Tigers" is reprinted in *Adrienne Rich's Poetry.*

53. Adrienne Rich, "Mathilde in Normandy," in *A Change of World* (New Haven: Yale University Press, 1951), pp. 52–53.

54. Rich, "Necessities of Life," in *Adrienne Rich's Poetry,* p. 23.

55. Rich, "When We Dead Awaken," in ibid., p. 60.

56. Rich, "For L. G.: Unseen for Twenty Years," "From an Old House in America," in *The Fact of a Doorframe: Poems Selected and New 1950–1984* (New York: W. W. Norton, 1984), pp. 210, 217.

57. Adrienne Rich, "Natural Resources," in *The Dream of a Common Language* (New York: W. W. Norton, 1977), pp. 66, 67.

58. Wendy Martin, "A Nurturing Ethos in the Poetry of Adrienne Rich," in *Reading Adrienne Rich: Reviews and Re-Visions, 1951–81,* ed. Jane Roberta Cooper (Ann Arbor: University of Michigan Press, 1984), p. 165.

59. Rich, "Design in Living Colors," in *A Change of World,* p. 67.

60. Rich, "Transcendental Etude," in *Common Language,* pp. 72–77.

61. Rich, "Planetarium," in *Adrienne Rich's Poetry,* p. 46.

62. Rich, "For Memory," in *A Wild Patience Has Taken Me This Far: Poems 1978–1981* (New York: W. W. Norton, 1981), p. 22.

63. Rich, "The Spirit of Place," in *A Wild Patience*, p. 41; "Toward the Solstice," in *Common Language*, p. 68; "For Julia in Nebraska," in *A Wild Patience*, p. 16.

64. Rich, "Natural Resources," pp. 66, 67, 64.

65. Rich, "Disobedience and Women's Studies," in *Blood, Bread, and Poetry: Selected Prose 1979–1985* (New York: W. W. Norton, 1986), pp. 77–78.

66. Rich, "The Spirit of Place," in *A Wild Patience*, p. 41.

67. Rich, "Culture and Anarchy," in ibid., pp. 10, 11.

68. Rich, "Poetry: II, Chicago," in *Your Native Land, Your Life: Poems* (New York: W. W. Norton, 1986), p. 67.

69. Rachel Blau DuPlessis, *Writing beyond the Ending: Narrative Strategies of Twentieth-Century Women Writers* (Bloomington: Indiana University Press, 1985), pp. ix, 103, 94.

70. Alice Walker, "Writing *The Color Purple*," in *In Search of Our Mothers' Gardens* (San Diego: Harcourt Brace Jovanovich, 1983), pp. 355–60.

71. Alice Walker, *The Color Purple* (New York: Washington Square Press, 1983), pp. 45, 47.

72. Ibid., pp. 60, 61.

73. Adrienne Rich, "Three Conversations," in *The Poetry of Adrienne Rich*, p. 111; Walker, *The Color Purple*, pp. 191, 192.

74. Walker, *The Color Purple*, p. 238; "Everyday Use," in *In Love and Trouble: Stories of Black Women* (New York: Harcourt Brace Jovanovich, 1973), p. 59.

75. Alice Walker, *Meridian* (New York: Harcourt Brace Jovanovich, 1976), p. 177.

76. Karen Swenson, "The Quilt," in *We Become New: Poems by Contemporary American Women*, ed. Lucile Iverson and Kathryn Ruby (New York: Bantam Books, 1973), p. 91.

77. Nancy Willard, "Crewel," in *Skin of Grace* (Columbia: University of Missouri Press, 1967), p. 13.

78. Sandra Hochman, "What the Old Man Left Me," in *Earthworks: Poems 1960–1970* (New York: Viking, 1971), p. 42; Erica Jong, "Dear Marys, Dear Mother, Dear Daughter," in *Loveroot* (New York: Holt, Rinehart and Winston, 1975), p. 16.

79. Joan Chase, *During the Reign of the Queen of Persia* (New York: Harper and Row, 1983), pp. 157, 169.

80. Robin Morgan, "Piecing," *Feminist Studies* 4, no. 3 (Oct. 1978), 87–89.

81. Gayle Graham Yates, "Spirituality and the American Feminist Experience," *Signs* (Autumn, 1983), 71.

82. Mary Daly, *Pure Lust: Elemental Feminist Philosophy* (Boston: Beacon Press, 1984), p. 305; for a reprint of "The Bedquilt" see *Women Working: An Anthology of Stories and Poems*, ed. Nancy Hoffman and Florence Howe (New York: Feminist Press, 1979), pp. 203–13.

83. Grahn, *The Queen of Wands*, pp. 81, xiii. For other contemporary writers who use patchwork as an analogy to the female creative process, see Marge Piercy, *Parti-Colored Blocks for a Quilt* (Ann Arbor: University of Michigan Press, 1982), pp. 3–4; Linda Pastan, "Off-Islander," in *Ariadne's Thread: A Collection*

of Contemporary Women's Journals, ed. Lyn Lifshin (New York: Harper and Row, 1982), pp. 312–13. Morgan's poem "Piecing" is also her metaphor for writing: "the pleasure of rescuing some particle into meaning." And several critics have interpreted Walker's use of the quilt in *The Color Purple* as a metaphor for the female aesthetic. See, for example, Mae Henderson, "*The Color Purple*: Revisions and Redefinitions," *Sage* 2, no. 1 (Spring 1985), 17; Chikwenye Okonjo Ogunyemi, "Womanism: The Dynamics of the Contemporary Black Female Novel in English," *Signs* 11, no. 1 (Autumn 1985), 78. For yet other examples of contemporary artists who have found creative sources in traditional textile work, see Vera L. Norwood, " 'Thank You for My Bones': Connections between Contemporary Women Artists and the Traditional Arts of Their Foremothers," *New Mexico Historical Review* 58, no. 1 (1983), 57–78, and Diane P. Freedman, "Living on the Borderland: The Poetic Prose of Gloria Anzaldúa and Susan Griffin," *Women and Language* 12, no. 1 (1990), 1–4.

NOTES ON CONTRIBUTORS

JEAN FERGUSON CARR is an assistant professor at the University of Pittsburgh and co-editor of a book series at the University of Pittsburgh Press on composition, literacy, and culture. She was textual co-editor of two volumes of *The Collected Works of R. W. Emerson* (Harvard University Press, 1979, 1983) and has published essays on Dickens, Elizabeth Stuart Phelps, autobiography, McGuffey's Readers, and pedagogy. She is currently working on a book about nineteenth-century American literacy and letters and the contested emergence of women readers and writers.

MARGARET W. FERGUSON, professor of English at the University of Colorado/ Boulder, has written *Trials of Desire: Renaissance Defenses of Poetry* (1983) and numerous articles on Renaissance authors, both male and female. She has co-edited, with Maureen Quilligan and Nancy Vickers, *Rewriting the Renaissance: The Discourses of Sexual Difference in Early Modern Europe* (Chicago: University of Chicago Press, 1986) and, with Mary Nyquist, *Re-membering Milton: The Texts and the Traditions* (New York: Methuen, 1987). Her current project, which she will be working on with the aid of a Guggenheim Fellowship, is entitled "Limited Access: Female Literacy and Literary Production in the Renaissance."

BLANCHE H. GELFANT teaches American literature at Dartmouth College, where she holds an endowed chair as the Robert E. Maxwell Professor in the Arts and Sciences. She has published widely on a variety of twentieth-century American writers and themes, and written a pioneer study of urban literature. Her recent book, *Women Writing in America: Voices in Collage* (Hanover, N.H.: University Press of New England, 1985), deals with diverse figures, all of whom in some way dramatize the possibilities of women's survival.

CHARLOTTE GOODMAN is professor of English at Skidmore College. Her publications include an edition of Edith Summers Kelley's *Weeds* (Feminist Press, 1982), as well as essays about Harriette Arnow, Joyce Carol Oates, and Tillie Olsen. Her literary biography of Jean Stafford will be published in 1990 by the University of Texas Press.

ELAINE HEDGES is professor of English and coordinator of Women's Studies at Towson State University, Baltimore, Maryland. She chaired the Modern Language Association's Commission on the Status of Women from 1972 to 1973, and served on the Reprints Advisory Committee of The Feminist Press from 1973 to 1983. Her books include an edition of Charlotte Perkins Gilman's *The Yellow Wallpaper* (Feminist Press, 1973); *In Her Own Image: Women Working in the Arts* (Feminist Press, 1980), with Ingrid Wendt; and *Ripening: Selected Work of Meridel Le Sueur* (Feminist Press, 1981). She is coauthor of *Hearts and Hands: The Influence of Women and Quilts on American Society* (Quilt Digest Press, 1987), and an editor of *The Heath Anthology of American Literature* (1989). She is currently completing a full-length study of the quilt culture of nineteenth-century women. In 1988, she was one of five authors honored by The Feminist Press for her contributions to reconstructing the literary canon.

NANCY HOFFMAN, currently on leave from the University of Massachusetts at Boston, is Academic Services Dean at the Harvard Graduate School of Education. She served on the Modern Language Association's Commission on the Status of Women from 1969 to 1974, and co-edited for the commission *Female Studies VI: Closer to the Ground, Women's Classes, Criticism, Programs* (Feminist Press, 1972). Her books include *Spenser's Pastorals* (Johns Hopkins, 1978); *Women Working: An Anthology of Stories and Poems* (Feminist Press, 1979), with Florence Howe; *Woman's 'True' Profession: Voices from the History of Teaching* (Feminist Press, 1981). She has also edited a special volume of *Women's Studies Quarterly* on Teaching about Women, Race, and Culture. She is working on an essay for a new edition of a Pulitzer-prizewinning novel of 1934, *Now in November* by Josephine Johnson (Feminist Press, 1990).

FLORENCE HOWE is director of The Feminist Press at The City University of New York and professor of English at the City University of New York. She was the first chair of the Modern Language Associations' Commission on the Status of Women (1969–71) and one of the founders of The Feminist Press. She was president of the MLA in 1973. Her books include *No More Masks! An Anthology of American Women Poets* (Doubleday, 1973), with Ellen Bass; *With Wings: An Anthology of Literature by and about Women with Disabilities* (Feminist Press, 1987), with Marsha Saxton; *Myths of Coeducation: Selected Essays, 1964–1983* (Indiana University Press, 1984). She is currently writing autobiography; preparing her uncollected essays on teaching for publication; and editing a new edition of *No More Masks* to be published by Harper and Row in 1992.

JEAN M. HUMEZ is associate professor in the Women's Studies Program at the University of Massachusetts at Boston. She has published *Gifts of Power: The Writings of Rebecca Jackson, Black Visionary and Shaker Eldress* (University of Massachusetts, 1981). She is presently completing *Mother's First-Born Daughters: Selected Writings of Shaker Women,* to be included in the Religion in North America series of the Indiana University Press.

KAREN LAWRENCE is professor of English and department chair at the University of Utah. She is the author of *The Odyssey of Style in "Ulysses"* (Princeton University Press, 1986) and the editor of a forthcoming collection of essays on the twentieth-century British literary canon. She currently has a Guggenheim Fellowship to write a book on representations of women's travel in the British literary tradition.

JANE MARCUS, on leave from The City University Graduate Center and the City College of New York, is Iris Howard Regents Professor of English at the University of Texas, Austin. She is the author of *Virginia Woolf and the Languages of Patriarchy* (Indiana University Press, 1987) and *Art and Anger: Reading Like A Woman* (Ohio State University Press, 1988). She has edited three volumes of feminist Woolf criticism and *The Young Rebecca West* (Viking, 1982; paperback, Indiana University Press, 1989). Her other publications include an edition of *The Convert* by Elizabeth Robins (Feminist Press, 1980) and three recent Feminist Press editions: *Not So Quiet . . .* by Helen Zenna Smith (1989); *We That Were Young* by Irene Rathbone (1989) and *Sister Gin* by June Arnold (1989). She is a member of the Publications and Policies Committee of The Feminist Press at CUNY. She is currently working on *One's Own Trumpet: Ethel Smyth and Virginia Woolf, A Portrait in Letters*.

NELLIE Y. MCKAY is professor of Afro-American Studies and American literature at the University of Wisconsin / Madison. She was a member of the MLA's Commission on the Status of Women from 1985 to 1987. She has also held positions in the American Studies Association, on the advisory and editorial boards of several journals, and on the Publications and Policies Committee of The Feminist Press. Her publications include *Jean Toomer, Artist: A Study of His Literary Life and Work* (University of North Carolina Press, 1984); an edited volume, *Critical Essays on Toni Morrison* (1988), essays written for two Feminist Press editions: *The Changelings* by Jo Sinclair (1985) and *Daddy Was a Number Runner* by Louise Meriwether (1986). She is co-editor of *Twentieth Century Afro-American Autobiography* (forthcoming).

NANCY PORTER is an associate professor of English at Portland State University where she co-founded the Women's Studies Program in 1971. She was associate editor of the *Women's Studies Quarterly* from 1978 to 1982, and since that date has been its editor. She has published essays on women, education, and literature, including one for The Feminist Press edition of *A Woman of Genius* by Mary Austin.

DEBORAH SILVERTON ROSENFELT is professor of Women's Studies and English at the University of Maryland / College Park, following a decade of directing the Women's Studies Program at San Francisco State University. She was a member of the Modern Language Association's Commission on the Status of Women from 1974 to 1977. She has published essays on women's literature, women's studies, and women's status. She is an editor in American literature and culture for *Feminist Studies*. She edited and wrote an extensive commentary for the screen play *Salt of the Earth* (Feminist Press, 1978), and with Judith Newton, co-edited *Feminist Criticism and Social Change* (Methuen, 1986). She is working on a volume of fiction from the thirties.

LOIS RUDNICK is associate professor of English and director of the American Studies Program at the University of Massachusetts at Boston. She has published a biography, *Mabel Dodge Luhan: New Woman, New Worlds* (University of New Mexico Press, 1984). She is working on *Utopian Vistas: A Cultural History of the Mabel Dodge Luhan House* and is co-editing a book of essays on *The Cultural Moment: 1915*.

SONIA SALDÍVAR-HULL, a graduate student in English at the University of Texas at Austin, will be assistant professor at the University of California/Los Angeles in fall 1990. She served as chair of the Women's Caucus of South Central Modern Language Association, 1987–88. She was a Dorothy Danforth Compton Fellow from 1985 to 1989. Her publications include essays on Gertrude Stein, Angela de Hoyos, and Franca de Armino.

ELAINE SHOWALTER is the Avalon Foundation Professor of the Humanities at Princeton University. She was a member of the Modern Language Association's Commission on the Status of Women from 1971 to 1972. She served on the Reprints Advisory Committee of The Feminist Press from 1973 to 1979. Her books include *A Literature of Their Own* (Princeton University Press, 1977); *The Female Malady* (Pantheon, 1985); and *Sexual Anarchy* (Viking, forthcoming). She has edited *These Modern Women: Autobiographical Essays from the Twenties* (Feminist Press, 1979; second edition, 1989); *The New Feminist Criticism: Essays on Women, Literature, and Theory* (Pantheon, 1985); and *Speaking of Gender* (Routledge, 1989).

INDEX

DATE DUE

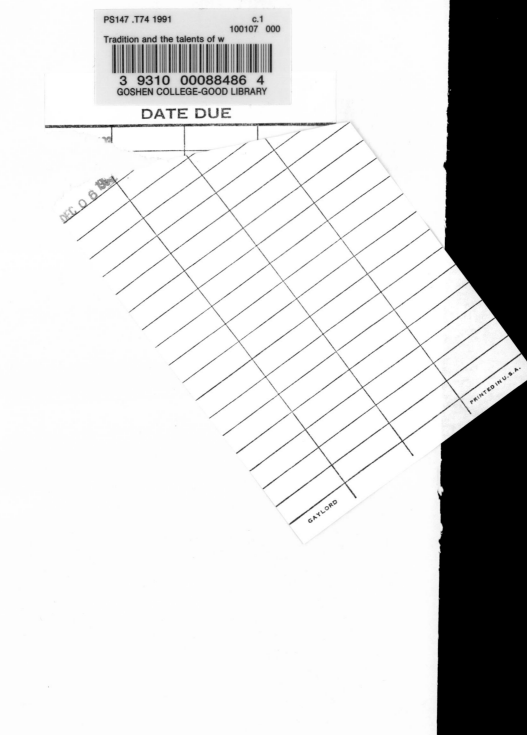

DEC 0 6 1991

GAYLORD   PRINTED IN U.S.A.